W9-DER-213

H 62.5 .U5 G85 1986

Guide to federal funding for social
scientists

GUIDE TO FEDERAL FUNDING
FOR SOCIAL SCIENTISTS

GUIDE TO FEDERAL FUNDING FOR SOCIAL SCIENTISTS

Prepared by the
Consortium of Social Science Associations

Susan D. Quarles,
Editor

RUSSELL SAGE FOUNDATION   NEW YORK

The Russell Sage Foundation

The Russell Sage Foundation, one of the oldest of America's general purpose foundations, was established in 1907 by Mrs. Margaret Olivia Sage for "the improvement of social and living conditions in the United States." The Foundation seeks to fulfill this mandate by fostering the development and dissemination of knowledge about the political, social, and economic problems of America. It conducts research in the social sciences and public policy, and publishes books and pamphlets that derive from this research.

The Board of Trustees is responsible for oversight and the general policies of the Foundation, while administrative direction of the program and staff is vested in the President, assisted by the officers and staff. The President bears final responsibility for the decision to publish a manuscript as a Russell Sage Foundation book. In reaching a judgment on the competence, accuracy, and objectivity of each study, the President is advised by the staff and selected expert readers. The conclusions and interpretations in Russell Sage Foundation publications are those of the authors and not of the Foundation, its Trustees, or its staff. Publication by the Foundation, therefore, does not imply endorsement of the contents of the study.

Library of Congress Cataloging-in-Publication Data
Consortium of Social Science Associations
Guide to federal funding for social scientists.
    Includes indexes.
    1. Social sciences—Research grants—United States—
Directories. 2. Federal aid to research—United States—
Directories. I. Quarles, Susan.
H62.5.U5G85 1986   300'.72   86-10014
ISBN 0-87154-699-X

Cover and text design: Huguette Franco

10 9 8 7 6 5 4 3 2 1

The Consortium of Social Science Associations

The Consortium of Social Science Associations (COSSA) represents more than 185,000 American scientists across the full range of the social and behavioral science disciplines. It functions as a bridge between the research world and the Washington community. COSSA was initially established as an informal coalition of the major disciplinary associations in the social sciences. The founding Member associations, which govern the Consortium, are:

American Anthropological Association American Sociological Association
American Economic Association American Statistical Association
American Historical Association Association of American Geographers
American Political Science Association Association of American Law Schools
American Psychological Association Linguistic Society of America

At the present time, 45 universities or independent research institutes are also contributing to COSSA. Some 29 scholarly associations are COSSA Affiliates.

COSSA monitors research and research funding in most federal agencies where externally granted, competitively awarded research and research-related funds form a significant portion of the portfolio. It also concerns itself widely with research management and policies affecting good practice in the conduct of federally funded research. Increasingly, COSSA also serves as a source of information and guidance for social science groups—professional, interdisciplinary, subdisciplinary—that do not have a ready understanding of or a "presence" on the Washington scene. With them, COSSA identifies and monitors issues of long-range importance.

One of the primary missions of COSSA is to inform and educate members of Congress, congressional staff, and officials in the administration and in federal agencies about recent research in the social and behavioral sciences, its importance, and the need to maintain adequate financial support for it. To this end, COSSA conducts congressional seminars and briefings on important current and emerging research in the social and behavioral sciences, particularly in areas of congressional interest and responsibility.

In order to keep social and behavioral scientists informed about legislative actions and federal policies that bear directly on the conduct of social and behavioral science research, COSSA issues a biweekly newsletter, the COSSA Washington Update, which is sent to over 1,000 social scientists, research managers, and policy-makers and is circulated indirectly to many more. COSSA also stays closely in touch with the science and general press.

Advisory Committee

The following persons acted as an Advisory Committee to the COSSA staff in the preparation of this *Guide.*

STEPHEN G. BRUSH
Professor, Institute for Physical Science and Technology
University of Maryland

SAMUEL R. GAMMON
Executive Director
American Historical Association

FRANCES DEGEN HOROWITZ
Vice Chancellor for Research
University of Kansas

THOMAS E. MANN
Executive Director
American Political Science Association

ROBERTA BALSTAD MILLER
Director, Division of Social and Economic Science
National Science Foundation

DAVID L. SILLS
Executive Associate
Social Science Research Council

LAWRENCE J. RHOADES
Assistant Chief, Research Planning and Evaluation
National Institute of Mental Health

HOWARD SCHUMAN
Director, Survey Research Center
Ann Arbor, Michigan

DAVID JENNESS (ex officio)
Executive Director
Consortium of Social Science Associations

Contents

Preface

The Consortium of Social Science Associations was formally organized in 1981 to represent the interests of the social and behavioral science community, especially the research community, in Washington. Stated more dramatically, the Consortium came into being when it appeared that most federal funding for research in those fields might cease.

The appearance of the *Guide* in 1986 shows that danger is now remote. What would have been a devastating blow to a large research community and a crippling injury to American universities, where the social and behavioral sciences hold a valued position, has been averted. However, the situation today is not one to cause complacency. Federal investment in these research fields stands at about 4 percent of the total federal research budget; in 1971 it was 8 percent. In constant dollars, federal research funding for social and behavioral science was 33 percent greater in 1971 and 25 percent greater in 1980 than it is today.

The federal government remains the largest funder of that research. Most of the research is performed in academic institutions. The response to the threats of 1981–82 was successful largely because the social science community rallied together to protest. They had forceful public backing from university leaders who recognized that entire research fields, largely university-based, were in danger. (To their credit, universities themselves continue to provide substantial amounts of funding for social and behavioral science research, at a level perhaps half that of government when all research-related expenses are taken into account.)

In recent years, federal intramural research in these fields has been diminishing, with dollars and research positions coming under severe pressure. In addition, theoretically based policy research related to the specific missions and programs of federal departments and agencies, customarily conducted by social scientists not employed by government, has been sharply reduced. The scientific cost of this reduction in social and behavioral research conducted within, or commissioned directly by, government is hard to calculate. In terms of opportunities for researchers, however, the trend is disturbing.

For many years, proportionately more social scientists have been employed by the academy, and proportionately fewer by business and industry, than is the case with other science Ph.D.s. (The pattern is somewhat different for psychologists, whose employment in business has been substantial.) In the 1960s and 1970s social scientists were employed in large numbers in government. In the 1980s that proportion is dropping. Moreover, many or most trained scientists employed by government do not actually do research. Especially in the social sciences, "research" in the sense of disciplined inquiry is thus becoming an enterprise largely restricted to university and university-related settings and to a few for-profit firms that hire university-trained scientists. There is a degree of localization, perhaps isolation, here that may be a cause for concern.

In the mid-1980s research dollars will be stretched further and further, as well-qualified new researchers are trained and as the knowledge base, which partly determines how much new research is feasible, expands. In all fields of science, research will be highly valued—and difficult to fund. If that seems paradoxical, so does the prevailing rationale for federal support of research at present. On the one hand, government is increasing its support of "basic" in preference to "applied" research. On the other hand, federally funded research is held to be justified insofar as it contributes to national productivity and competitiveness. The argument, as put forward by federal science leaders, is that basic research gives rise to whole new technologies. That is not the rationale for basic research that comes most readily to the minds of academic researchers. Nevertheless, basic social science does in fact generate "technologies" that are of great consequence to society. There is ample room within these parameters for social and behavioral scientists to propose research that they themselves regard as significant and that will be so regarded by the larger society. To do so, experienced researchers need to be venturesome in seeking new funding sources, ingenious in explaining clearly why what they propose is important. Younger researchers need to be reassured that talent and perseverance will be rewarded. The *Guide* is intended not only to provide information but to re-orient older researchers and stimulate younger ones to compete.

We are grateful to the Consortium's first executive director, Roberta Balstad Miller, for seeing the need and initiating plans for the *Guide,* and to a distinguished advisory committee, listed on page vi, for overseeing its progress. We thank the Russell Sage Foundation, historically the most prominent foundation concentrating in the social sciences, for granting funds essential for the *Guide*'s preparation. In one sense, the *Guide* is an amplification of the Consortium's regular activity of monitoring federal research support. For example, each issue of its biweekly publication, the *COSSA Washington Update,* covers one federal research program in detail. Those who find this *Guide* helpful should regard the *Update* as a useful supplement.

The entire professional staff of the Consortium has cooperated in interviewing agency personnel; poring over program announcements, scientific reports, and grants and contracts lists; and discussing with those inside and outside the process, those who fund and those who are funded, their observations of the federal research-support system. COSSA staff members who have worked intensively on the *Guide* include:

JOHN H. HAMMER   JANET RASMUSSEN

DAVID JENNESS   HOWARD J. SILVER

KATRINA R. STYLES

All have worked diligently and with a growing sense of gratification at the knowledge being assembled at COSSA.

By far the single most important person in the entire process, however, has been the editor of the volume, Susan D. Quarles. Her efforts have been untiring, selfless, and splendidly productive. All those connected professionally with COSSA and all those who benefit from this *Guide* owe Susan Quarles more than they can possibly realize.

David Jenness

Executive Director
Consortium of Social Science Associations

Chapter 1

Understanding and Using the Guide

The *Guide to Federal Funding for Social Scientists* has two purposes: to introduce new scholars to the variety of federal agencies that provide funding for research and research training and to inform established scholars of alternative funding opportunities in federal agencies, a need that has become more acute in this era of scarce resources. The *Guide* is intended to serve not only individual academic researchers, but also administrators and researchers working outside the academy, student advisors, officers of professional groups, and others. To use the *Guide* effectively, one must first understand the process by which it was prepared. Quite different in style and content from traditional information sources and commercial grants directories, the *Guide* is based largely on personal, in-depth interviews with over 70 program directors and agency staff; their current funding practices and likely research agendas over the next several years were discussed in detail.

Perhaps the most heartening experience encountered in producing this first edition was discovering the enthusiasm of federal research program managers for the project. The recurrent reaction was that a guide written specifically for social and behavioral scientists should be encouraged as a means of involving that portion of the scientific community more extensively in federal research. Despite the sometimes drastic budget cuts in federal support of social and behavioral science research in many agencies over the past several years, those scientists and professional staff actually involved in administering extramural research programs consistently voiced their support and their own continuing need for input from and involvement with that scientific community. It was also reassuring to discover how many persons involved in the grant-making process are themselves social and behavioral scientists.

Almost uniformly, staff at those agencies that currently rely heavily on certain disciplines in the social and behavioral sciences expressed a desire that other such disciplines participate more; and staff at agencies that have been only marginally supportive of these fields felt that there could be more support if these scientists would apply in greater numbers. Thus, the rather bleak outlook implied by current budget levels does not imply that the funding programs themselves discourage proposals by social and behavioral scientists. In fact, it is true, even in the federal funding arena, that supply is a factor of demand. If a field of science becomes discouraged from submitting proposals, it may be interpreted as a lack of need.

Understanding Program Descriptions

The *Guide* contains nearly 200 separate entries describing over 300 federal programs. Most entries contain the appropriate contact person for substantive inquiries, relevant budget information, application and review procedures, funding mechanisms, and, where appropriate and available, examples of funded projects. The major portion of each entry, however, is a detailed, substantive discussion of the program's areas of interest, priorities, and future directions.

One of the difficulties in preparing descriptions of each program in a uniform format is that the programs themselves are not uniform either within agencies, within departments, or across departments. Each department, and in most cases, each agency within a department has different structures, funding processes, and reporting systems. Thus, one of the hazards in using a uniform format in a guide such as this is that it may give readers an oversimplified or incorrect view of the structure of federal funding. To avoid this, the individual components of each entry are described below.

Agency or Program Title. Readers will find that in most cases, descriptions are given for individual programs, not for departments or agencies within departments; e.g., a description is provided for the University Research and Training Program, not the Urban Mass Transportation Administration in which it is located. There are many exceptions to this practice, particularly in cases where an agency has several programs, but we have included detailed descriptions only of one or more individual programs that are relevant to the readership of the *Guide.* In those cases a brief overview of the agency is still provided.

Contact Persons. Immediately after the title of the program, the name of the appropriate contact person and his/her title is provided. These are people to contact for substantive inquiries—i.e., for questions about particular research ideas or proposals one is contemplating submitting to a program. In cases where no one individual is designated to field such inquiries, the primary director of the program is listed. The director or his/her office staff will generally direct phone or mail inquiries to the appropriate person.

It is important to note that there is a fair amount of turnover among federal staff. If the listed contact person is no longer with the program, simply ask for the person now in that position. Most offices do try to be helpful in determining who best can answer your specific questions.

Addresses. In most cases, addresses include specific room numbers and building names. Again, these tend to change frequently. For mail delivery, the important parts of the address are the department, specific division or agency, locality, and zip code. Since official program titles may change from time to time, and since some departments have more than one program or branch with the same name, it is important to include in an address the administrative entity. For example, in the Alcohol, Drug Abuse, and Mental Health Administration of the Department of Health and Human Services, both the National Institute on Drug Abuse and the National Institute of Mental Health have a "Prevention Research Branch." Thus, it is important to include the name of the Institute in the address. Most departments have unique zip codes reserved for them, and all mail to that zip code goes to a central office for processing and distribution.

Telephone Numbers. Although all phone numbers were verified and accurate as of February 1, 1986, inevitably many will have changed by the time this guide is in print. When numbers are changed, a recording with the new number or the number of an information operator is generally provided. The only advice is to be persistent.

Program. Program descriptions are based on printed agency materials, research announcements, annual reports, and, most important, personal interviews with program staff. For most major programs, interviews of an hour to an hour and a half were used to obtain a thorough understanding of program missions, priorities, and future research agenda. All interviews were tailored specifically to the social and behavioral sciences. Staff were questioned about the role of these sciences in their programs and what specific problems or advice could be shared with the research community. When the phrase "future research priorities" is used, keep in mind that most interviews took place in mid to late 1985 and that the "future" is probably now.

Program descriptions are *interpretative.* Many express the opinion of the COSSA staff (based on interviews and the review of program award lists) and are not officially sanctioned by the agency. Although in nearly all cases program staff were given the opportunity to review their program's description and make comments, the content of all descriptions are the responsibility of the editor of the *Guide.*

There were two major exceptions to this procedure. Both the National Institute of Mental Health and the Office of Research in the Office of Educational Research and Improvement (formerly the National Institute of Education) underwent major reorganizations in 1985. Because final program plans and staff appointments were not completed before the end of 1985, it was not possible to conduct comprehensive interviews. Thus, the descriptions of these programs are based primarily on printed materials provided by the agencies and supplemented by telephone contact.

Budget. Budget figures are provided only to give readers an idea of how large a program is. Figures should be taken with a grain of salt, since they are constantly changing and since most program managers do not truly know what their exact budget is until it has been spent (i.e., at the end of the fiscal year). Budget figures can sometimes be misleading in that they often include monies that are earmarked for mandated projects, include funds for both new and continuation awards, or may be substantially supplemented or reduced by inter- or intra-agency transfers of funds.

In most cases, the budget figures given are for extramural research funds. We have tried to distinguish between funds available for new awards and total budget amounts, and also how much of a program's budget goes to the social and behavioral sciences. Figures given are based on the most current information available at the time of an interview. Thus, for most interviews that took place in early to mid 1985, the FY 1985 figure is given.

Affecting the status of all agency budgets is the potential impact of the Gramm-Rudman-Hollings legislation. Whether the automatic across-the-board budget reductions mandated by the legislation go into effect in 1986, or whether agencies reduce their research budgets themselves in anticipation of the automatic cuts, it is almost a certainty that all the budget figures projected for FY 1986 in the *Guide* will be affected.

Application/Review Process. A fair amount of space is given to the procedures by which applicants submit proposals and the way agencies review them and make funding decisions. An important factor in submitting a successful proposal is understanding the review process and designing a proposal based on that knowledge. (Chapter 4 discusses this aspect of grantsmanship.) Applicants should understand who is going to review their proposal and play as active a role as possible in ensuring that the review is fair and proper. This is not to imply that applicants have any legal authority in the review process; however, particularly when programs use ad hoc peer review panels, applicants can question or suggest the membership of peer review groups.

Deadlines for proposals/applications vary widely among agencies. While some programs have one or more standard deadlines each year, others are established primarily as a function of when announcements and requests for proposals are ready and printed as public notice. We have tried to indicate the normal cycle for programs rather than list the particular deadline established for 1986.

Funding Mechanisms. Federal programs use many types of funding mechanisms, including grants, contracts, cooperative agreements, and matching funds. The mechanisms listed for each program are those most typically used for that program, but it should not imply that other funding arrangements are not, at least on occasion, possible. Whenever possible, the average or typical dollar range and project period are given.

Examples of Funded Research. Examples are provided to give readers an idea of the range of topics supported by a program. Examples were chosen that would be of interest to social and behavioral scientists in general, and readers should not infer that these fields are the primary focus of the program. (The proportion of a program's support for these fields should be determined by carefully reading the program description.)

Agencies do not have uniform reporting systems for their awards. Whenever possible we have included the title of a project, the project period, and the award amount. However, this information is not readily available for many programs. In most cases there is, at least, a list of titles of funded projects. No examples are given for programs where no information could be obtained, for new programs that had not yet completed a first competition, or in the case of some fellowship or career training awards, where there was not a specific project to identify.

Incomplete Entries. There are some entries in the *Guide* that do not have all of the components listed above—e.g., the Central Intelligence Agency, the Defense Advanced Research Projects Agency, and the Economic Research Service in the Department of Agriculture. There are several reasons for this. For some programs these details are not available; for others, only a general description is given if the program does not have a traditional research support mechanism.

Using the Indexes

Topical Index. In establishing the guidelines for indexing this volume, it was decided that no entries would be included in the index for the major disciplinary fields (e.g, "political science," "psychology"). Because federal programs do not support disciplines per se, the National Science Foundation being a major exception, and because numerous programs will fund proposals from any disciplinary source, the sheer number of references that would appear with an index entry such as "psychology" would render it useless. Therefore, the primary index contains only research topics or topic areas. Readers will find entries for recognized subfields, such as "health economics" and "cultural anthropology," but, in the context of this index, these are defined as topic areas and should not be taken to be of interest only to the discipline or disciplines normally associated with that subfield.

Research opportunities in the various programs have been topically indexed based on knowledge gained from staff interviews and "key terms"used by the agencies themselves in their materials. In cases where an agency's term for a topic or research area might not be generally familiar to researchers, we have used the more common equivalent term. In cases where an agency's key word was recognizable by a narrow set of specialists, but where the agency in fact welcomes or accepts proposals with a broader focus, we have retained the specialized term, but have also included broader terms more familiar to the various researchers who may be eligible for funding. In general, we have erred on the side of inclusion, so that recoding is less common than supplementary or redundant coding.

In cases where a particular topic is not mentioned specifically in a program description, yet appears in the index, readers can assume that the topic is generally of interest to the program. In most cases, program staff were given the opportunity to review and comment on the key words used to index the program.

Readers should not rely solely on the topical index for locating programs that may support their research. Because some agencies' missions are quite broad and research interests are loosely defined, it is impossible to list every possible research topic for some programs. Readers are encouraged, therefore, to consider the substantive descriptions of programs to locate non-obvious sources of funding.

Index to Fellowships. A separate index is included for fellowship and dissertation support. This was done primarily because most fellowship programs are open to individuals in many disciplinary fields; therefore, it was not feasible to index them by research topic. It will also serve as a quick reference to young scholars and student advisors seeking such support.

Although every attempt was made to make the *Guide* as complete and comprehensive as possible, the list of programs covered is not exhaustive. Undoubtedly, there are other programs that may offer funding for social and behavioral scientists that have been inadvertently omitted. We have tried to include those programs that are the *most likely* (or potential) sources of support. Some programs that in reality have very little in the way of discretionary research funds are included, primarily because of their past history and because their stated scope is appropriate.

Chapter 2

Structure and Organization of the Social Sciences in the Federal Funding Arena

David Jenness, Executive Director,
Consortium of Social Science Associations

Federal funding for research is not directed at the support of disciplines, or even at the growth or sustenance of disciplinary-based fields, but rather at the support of research judged on a topical basis—by criteria such as substantive scientific interest, pathbreaking methodology, or potential relevance to the mission of the funding agencies.

Some qualifications are immediately necessary. Certain agencies—such as the National Endowment for the Humanities (NEH), the National Science Foundation (NSF), or some programs of the National Institutes of Health (NIH)—occasionally give conference grants or commission state-of-the-art studies that assess a scientific field with regard to recent progress or future directions. In addition, federally funded fellowships (less common today than in years past) support the intellectual and technical development of individuals at various stages and thus help to sustain and stimulate fields.

The most important qualification is that while the intrinsic merits of individual proposals, judged competitively, are the essential basis for funding, these judgments are made by working scientists from within the frame of reference of fields, theoretical priorities (i.e., where a field is or should be going), and methodological rigor as understood within fields. Thus, especially in agencies that encourage field-initiated proposals and that depend heavily on peer review for the judgment of relative merit, one effect is in fact to support fields—and, less directly, disciplines, departments, and universities. In part, it reflects federal policy toward the historic partnership between government science funding and the nearly unique pattern of American research universities, where most non-problem-oriented research (and some problem-oriented research) is conducted. The grants mechanism itself makes the university the responsible legal agent; the scientific capability of a department or an institute within the university may be a decision factor in awarding some grants; the mechanism of institutional overhead awards keeps the university science system working; etc. Federal research grants have indirect impacts: they are never simply a means for procuring "data" from individual scholars or payment for services rendered.

However, to repeat, the principal intention is not to support categories of research but, rather, instances. It is the science system, largely in universities, that relates categories to instances, "fields" to projects, training to research, in particular ways. Universities are comfortable with a disciplinary organization. They choose to base their research capacity on departments (for the most part), and departments are of course loosely tied to professional disciplines. But not all who work in, for example, a department of economics have degrees in economics; and not all economists belong to the American Economic Association. Furthermore, most "disciplines" are pluralistic and comprise individuals using very diverse approaches or methods. In some broad fields of scientific knowledge—e.g., biomedical science—the disciplines of training do not coincide with major fields of research. To federal granting agencies, "discipline" means "field" rather than "guild": the research proposer asserts that his or her subject matter is economics, not that he or she has a degree in economics or works in a department of economics.

As the essay by Levine in chapter 4 makes clear, the NSF is the research funding agency that expresses the most conscious commitment to the dynamic importance of "fields" of science. The guiding philosophy is that fields generate proposals that are salient to themselves, and then that the most persuasive proposals are funded. The NSF does not intentionally guide or shape fields. Grants are not made to adjust or redress balances within a field—so much for regulatory as against household economics, for example; and even a high field-determined priority may be outweighed by the Foundation's decision (taken also on the advice of researchers) to devote some of its budget to special areas—for example, management science or social indicators. By contrast, at the NIH any funded proposal can be said to have high peer-reviewed status vis-à-vis its scientific field; but at a given moment some fields are of higher stated priority to an Institute than others, and that affects the ultimate funding pattern.

There are also "local traditions" within government funding agencies which need to be taken into account. The Economic Research Service of the U.S. Department of Agriculture supports economic research—but not all economic research, and not exclusively economics. The Department of Defense research offices support much psychology, but not all psychology—and not psychology exclusively. The Center for Population Research of the National Institute of Child Health and Human Development has a particular distinctive portfolio. It is the purpose of the *Guide* to describe these local traditions, emphases, and programmatic priorities of agencies—and to relate them, more precisely than government program announcements can do, to opportunities for "fields."

It is an appropriate approach for a guide prepared by the Consortium of Social Science Associations, an organization created by the major American disciplinary associations in the social and behavioral sciences. It is, however, an organization that serves not only the disciplines per se but, in principle, the entire research community: those outside university departments or, indeed, universities; those who work between disciplines; those whose main identification is with a field that is defined by nondisciplinary considerations. For example, the Consortium has as Affiliates the American Association for Public Opinion Research, the Society for the History of Technology, the Gerontological Society of America, the Regional Science Association, and many other scholarly, field-defined and field-defining groups. (For a list of these scientific and scholarly societies affiliated with the Consortium, see the last page of this chapter. There are, of course, many other such societies in the United States to which a researcher may feel a primary, or a lesser, allegiance.)

In the pages following, we outline the organization and structure of disciplines, with descriptions that have been prepared in cooperation with the disciplinary associations. It is worthwhile for members of one discipline to learn more about the fine-structure of adjacent ones—and for those in special research fields to be reminded of that structure. More important, by showing the fine-structure, as it were, of today's disciplines, lines of connection and correspondence can be traced between topical areas of research that cross—sometimes jump—disciplinary lines. Each discipline, when looked at in detail at the componential level, proves to shade into or find resemblances in other disciplines. Thus, "disciplines," being boundary-permeable, are like species; the concept is a necessary and meaningful one, but is logically imperfect.

Following the presentation of disciplines, here identified with their primary associations, we return to the more general topic of fields and their relevance to federal funding.

American Anthropological Association

Edward J. Lehman, Executive Director
1703 New Hampshire Avenue, NW
Washington, DC 20009
(202/232–8800)

Since its founding in 1902 the purposes of the American Anthropological Association have been to "advance anthropology as the science that studies humankind in all its aspects . . . and to further the interests of anthropologists, including the dissemination of anthropological knowledge and its use to solve human problems."

The Association was organized on the initiative of representatives from Section H of the American Association for the Advancement of Science, the American Ethnological Society, and the Anthropological Society of Washington.

The Association is now the world's largest organization of anthropologists. Its individual membership is almost 9,000, of whom one third are students and the remainder are professionals in anthropology or related fields. Approximately three quarters of the professional members are engaged in teaching and research in academia; others are consultants or employed in government and the private sector.

In 1985 the Association comprised 16 constituent units, 9 of which were created through the merger of formerly independent societies with the Association:

American Ethnological Society
Archaeology Section
Biological Anthropology Section
Central States Anthropological Society
Council on Anthropology and Education
General Anthropology Division
National Association for the Practice of Anthropology
Northeastern Anthropological Association
Society for Cultural Anthropology
Society for Humanistic Anthropology
Society for Latin American Anthropology
Society for Linguistic Anthropology
Society for Medical Anthropology
Society for Psychological Anthropology
Society for Urban Anthropology
Society for Visual Anthropology

The *American Anthropologist,* whose centennial will be observed in 1987, remains the general journal of the Association. The Association also publishes the *Anthropology Newsletter,* and special publications. Publications of the constituent units include six quarterly journals—*American Ethnologist, Anthropology and Education Quarterly, Anthropology and Humanism Quarterly, Cultural Anthropology, Ethos,* and *Medical Anthropology Quarterly*—and a number of newsletters and annuals.

The Association conducts a Congressional Fellowship Program in Washington.

The science of anthropology seeks to explain human physical and cultural variation at different times and in different locales, as well as to understand how physical and cultural factors influence each other. Its methodology emphasizes a holistic view that discourages too-narrow definitions of problems in the early stages of research and emphasizes participant observation, the systematic collection of case studies and artifacts, and cross-cultural comparisons. Once hypotheses have been constructed, anthropologists may use surveys or other quantifiable methods to test them. Its several subfields—ethnology, archaeology, anthropological linguistics, and biological or physical anthropology—all contribute to a core body of data which is likely to be drawn upon by any or all of the subfields to advance knowledge about the human species. Anthropologists may focus on social or cultural phenomena found in industrial or ancient civilizations, as well as among preliterate peoples who either lived long ago or live today as isolates or enclaves in the contemporary global community.

Ethnology is the comparative study of human culture—of the norms, values, folklore, world view, and traditional ways of life which are passed from one generation to the next. Ethnologists or cultural anthropologists do research by means of firsthand observation, i.e., by interviewing in the native tongue and participating in the ordinary as well as ritual life of a community. Observations are interpreted comparatively, vis-à-vis results of similar studies done in other cultural groups. Ethnologists focus on such areas as kinship, religion, art, ritual, politics, law, and economics, or try to characterize a way of life as a whole. They aim to understand the internal logic of their societies and to avoid "ethnocentrism," the tendency to judge strange or exotic customs on the basis of preconceptions derived from one's own cultural background.

Archaeologists study the material remains of extinct or past cultures in an effort to understand prehistory. By retrieving and interpreting what people leave behind —tools, artifacts, and any detectable shreds and patches—archaeologists piece together stories from the past.

Excavation is the archaeologist's tool for exploring the long ago. Scientific excavation is more than recovering buried artifacts, which themselves can tell relatively little about an extinct culture. More important is the artifact's "context," its location relative to the placement of other cultural remains. To date a find, archaeologists must be familiar with techniques such as stratigraphy, radiocarbon dating, and tree-ring analysis. Salvage archaeology is increasingly important in construction areas; cultural remains must be recovered and preserved before they are destroyed.

Linguistic anthropologists study the historical development of human languages and the ways in which it can be used to unravel relationships between different societies. Linguistic anthropologists are interested in the nature of language itself, as well as in relationships between language, thought, and behavior. Language is unique to the human species, and anthropologists recognize speech as perhaps the most important avenue through which culture is transmitted across generations. They are especially concerned with non-Indo-European languages, whose structure and sound systems may never have been studied. Many anthropologists record languages on the verge of extinction.

Biological or *physical anthropologists* study the evolution of the human body. Paleoanthropologists study fossil hominid and hominoid (human-like) ancestors. Genetic anthropologists study the micro-evolution of living human populations and trace the genetic closeness of the human species to our nearest relatives, the monkeys and apes. Osteologists study the dynamics of the skeletal system. Epidemiologists examine patterns of disease in past and present populations, and demographic anthropologists examine vital statistics in modern and ancient societies. Forensic anthropologists apply their knowledge of the human skeletal system to aid medical examiners; anthropometrists, who study physical measurements of humankind, are active in human factors engineering.

In the last 25 years anthropology has evolved specific interdisciplinary and applied foci. *Development anthropologists* have turned their attention to improving the lives of people whose traditional ways of life have been disturbed by warfare, drought, migration, urbanism, or the spread of the world technology and economy. These anthropologists devise ways to lessen the shock of sudden culture change and advise in matters of health care, resettlement, and agricultural development. *Medical anthropologists* study indigenous health beliefs and curing adaptations, the dynamics of "sick role" behavior, and the legitimization of curing practices in public health and clinical-care delivery systems. Medical anthropologists draw upon cultural and biological anthropology as well as related social science disciplines to understand native concepts of disease and health.

Psychological anthropologists study the perceptions, mental illnesses, and psychic development of Western and non-Western peoples. Cross-cultural parenting, child-rearing, socialization, emotional communication, dream expression, and cognitive functioning are among the topics examined by psychological anthropologists from a comparative perspective.

Today's anthropologists may specialize further in areas such as visual anthropology and examine the role of photography, moving pictures, and videotape as tools in the study of dance, ritual, hunting activities, or economic exchange. Legal anthropologists may analyze the role of oral or written law in settling disputes over territorial boundaries. Urban anthropologists may focus on the role of graffiti-style artwork and competitive dancing in relations between rival inner-city teenage gangs. Nursing anthropologists may specialize in the rituals of physician-patient communication in modern health care facilities in the United States.

Despite ever-branching, ever-more-diverse research topics, anthropology still strongly emphasizes the value of fieldwork—firsthand observation in the society or geographical area under investigation—for all practitioners. Most anthropologists have stable areal specialties within North or South America, Africa, Asia, the Pacific Islands, Eurasia, or the circumpolar regions of the earth.

American Economic Association

C. Elton Hinshaw, Executive Secretary
1313 21st Street, South
Nashville, TN 37212
(615/322–2595)

The American Economic Association was organized in 1885 and incorporated in 1923. The purposes of the Association are (1) the encouragement of economic research, especially the historical and statistical study of the actual conditions of industrial life; (2) the issue of publications on economic subjects; and (3) the encouragement of perfect freedom of economic discussion. As stated in the charter, "The Association as such will take no partisan attitude, nor will it commit its members to any position on practical economic questions." The spirit of these objectives has been maintained throughout its history.

From 1885 to about 1910 the membership of the AEA consisted mainly of college and university teachers of economics. With the growing general interest in the subject of economics after the turn of the century, the Association attracted an increasing number of members from business and professional groups. Today the membership is approximately 20,000. Over 50% of the membership is associated with academic institutions, 35% with business and industry, and the remainder largely with federal, state, and local government agencies.

There are two journals of the Association, each appearing quarterly. The *American Economic Review* contains articles and shorter papers on economic subjects. The *Journal of Economic Literature* contains abstracts of articles from foreign and domestic periodicals, lists of new books classified according to subject matter, book reviews, and survey or review articles on topics of interest to the profession. These two journals are distributed to all members and subscribers of the Association, which also publishes a *Survey of Members* (approximately every three years), *Job Openings for Economists* (bimonthly), a cumulative *Index of Economic Articles,* and a *Guide to Graduate Studies in Economics and Agricultural Economics in the United States and Canada.*

The central subject matter of economics is the choices people make concerning the allocation of scarce resources, especially with regard to the production, distribution, and consumption of commodities. Traditional economic analysis has centered on supply and demand in the market (monitored, for example, by quantities and prices) as the essential mechanism. Rudimentary abstract models may deal with the economic conduct of an individual under fixed general conditions, or with the behavior of an economic system—e.g., a national economy—under conditions of mutual freedom of exchange of goods and services. Realistic technical analysis of actual economic systems must, however, take account of special factors or constraints—social institutions, legal decisions, technological developments, etc.—and various inherent dynamic aspects of the system leading to profit, surplus, capital accumulation, investment, business cycles, fiscal policies, labor and wage agreements, etc.

In microeconomics, individuals, businesses, or groups are assumed to make judgments about what to produce and when to buy, with wages and prices bringing demand into line with supply and vice versa. Macroeconomics, by contrast, involves aggregating analyses of economic activity in particular sectors or from different levels into models of national income, investment levels, growth, and the like, in whole economies—extending even to comparisons across different economic systems or types of systems.

The modern technique of econometrics cuts across the various levels and sectors, applying statistical methods to the analysis of economic activity. Currently, considerable theoretical attention is being given to decision-making by participants in economic systems, and the role of expectations in altering or driving those systems at any level. Such interests and concepts may lend themselves to an experimental approach to economic analysis, as contrasted with (or supplementing) the analysis of records or data obtained from ongoing data series.

There are, of course, many subfields of economics: labor economics, welfare economics, development economics, money and banking, human capital theory (e.g., investment and return in education and training), agricultural economics, economic history, etc. A fuller taxonomy of the field is shown below.

General Economics
General Economic Theory
History of Thought; Methodology
Economic History
Economic Systems
Economic Growth; Development; Planning Theory and Policy
Country Studies
Economic Fluctuations; Forecasting; Stabilization; Inflation
Econometric, Statistical, and Mathematical Methods and Models
Economic and Social Statistical Data and Analysis
Domestic Monetary and Financial Theory and Institutions
Fiscal Theory and Policy; Public Finance
International Trade Theory
Trade Relations; Commercial Policy; International Economic Integration
Balance of Payments; International Finance
International Investment and Foreign Aid
Administration
Business Finance and Investment
Marketing
Industrial Organization and Public Policy
Economics of Technological Change
Industry Studies
Economic Capacity
Agriculture
Natural Resources
Economic Geography
Manpower Training and Allocation; Labor Force and Supply
Labor Markets; Public Policy
Trade Unions; Collective Bargaining; Labor-Management Relations
Demographic Economics
Human Capital
Welfare, Health, and Education
Urban Economics
Regional Economics

American Historical Association

Samuel R. Gammon, Executive Director
400 A Street, SE
Washington, DC 20003
(202/544-2422)

The American Historical Association is the oldest and largest of the many historical organizations in the United States. It was founded in 1884 and chartered by act of Congress in 1889 "for the promotion of historical studies, the collection and preservation of historical manuscripts, and for kindred purposes in the interest of American history and history of America."

Over the years the AHA's activities have emphasized the advancement of research and teaching. It produces the major scholarly journal in worldwide history, the *American Historical Review,* published five times a year, which contains reviews of scholarly books in all fields of history and offers a forum for the debate of scholarly issues. The AHA publishes a number of bibliographic aids of use to students, teachers, and researchers: *Recently Published Articles* (in journal format, three times a year), *Writings on American History: A Subject Bibliography of Articles* (in hardcover, annually), and *Doctoral Dissertations in History* (listing the titles of dissertations in progress and completed, semi-annually). Most recently the AHA has sponsored publication of the *Guide to the Study of U.S. History Outside the United States, 1945–1980* (5 vols., 1985).

Through its newsletter, *Perspectives* (published monthly during the academic year), the Association distributes news of general educational interest, employment information, election announcements, awards, and news of the Association. Almost 80 specialized historical organizations are affiliated with the AHA.

The AHA actively lobbies government through its major advocacy arm, the National Coordinating Committee for the Promotion of History. Supported by numerous history organizations and departments, the NCC's achievements include successful lobbying for passage of federal legislation creating an independent National Archives and Records Administration and a historian's office in the U.S. House of Representatives. An important aspect of the AHA's relations with government includes its official services on national advisory committees, such as those of the State Department Advisory Committee on Historical/Diplomatic Documentation and of the National Historical Publications and Records Commission.

The discipline of history is both a social science and one of the humanities. Its academic practitioners in fact split about five to one in thinking of themselves as "humanists," but it is more accurate to say that history is both. Recorded history is in essence one historian's (or a group of historians') construction of the collective memory. Just as for an individual, for a society everything that has happened "to it" or "around it" is potentially part of history. Since the total volume of such happenings is impossible for either a society or an individual to organize or recall, the memory of history consists only of those events or happenings considered in retrospect to be meaningful. It is the judgment of the historian that establishes what is meaningful.

Just as for an individual, what is worth remembering from one's past depends on where one is at present. Both an individual's memories and a society's memories are thus constantly changing, constantly being revised as time passes, as circumstances, attitudes, or values evolve and change.

The great nineteenth-century German historian Leopold von Ranke undertook a history of the world when he was in his early 80s. Since few contemporary historians are that optimistic, most of them work with smaller and more manageable segments of history. These are usually described as "fields" of history. Fields are capable of infinite subdivision down to the most detailed microcosm of history, but all depend for their validity on the existence of a larger fraction of the macrocosm of history.

Fields may be identified either geographically, chronologically, functionally, or all three. On the geographic grid a historian may be described as an African historian, or a Latin American historian, or perhaps by a country or regional label—American, English, Brazilian, or Southern (U.S.) for example. The historian may also use a chronological tag—medieval, ancient, Renaissance and Reformation, early modern, or perhaps even a briefer time period such as the Jacksonian Era. (Chronological notations often carry an implied geographic label—in the above examples they would include European, the Mediterranean or the Near Eastern World, and the United States.)

Functional classification of fields of history can be one of general types—such as political, economic, or intellectual (the history of ideas). They may also refer to a certain methodology, such as quantitative history or social history, or to other types of historical subjects, as in military history, the history of women, the history of science, and historiography (the history of historical study).

The learned disciplines over the last two thousand years have evolved in our civilization by a process of continuous subdivision. Philosophy (including theology) was the earliest discipline. Just as human development replicates earlier evolutionary forms, so the learned disciplines all carry the genetic code of their philosophical origins. If one pursues any of the natural sciences, social sciences, or humanities to their earliest known origins or indeed to their most advanced and esoteric theory, they will intersect in philosophy.

History was one of the first humanist daughters of philosophy to differentiate itself, and it, too, carries with it the marks of the many disciplines which have evolved in turn from it, such as political science, economics, and sociology, among others. History still has a place for these disciplines, at least in their historical approaches to their fields. It is this umbrella aspect of history that particularly distinguishes it from the other disciplines. All of the disciplines have a somewhat uneasy relationship with the predictive aspect of their utilization: to what extent do history, economics, political science, and sociology enable us to foretell what *will* happen hereafter? Historians are frank to confess that history never repeats itself *exactly* (making historians skeptical about using theories as modes of historical analysis), but at the same time they believe that an informed knowledge of the past conduct of the human species, both individually and collectively, helps to understand and to inform choices that confront us in the present and future.

American Political Science Association

Thomas E. Mann, Executive Director
1527 New Hampshire Avenue, NW
Washington, DC 20036
(202/483-2512)

The American Political Science Association is the major professional organization in the United States whose members are engaged in the study of politics. Founded in 1903, the Association provides members with services to facilitate research, teaching, and professional development. Association membership is composed primarily of political scientists doing research and teaching in U.S. colleges and universities, although one tenth of its 9,000 individual members reside in 70 other countries around the world and one fourth pursue careers outside academia—in government, research and consulting firms, and private enterprise.

APSA members receive three quarterly publications: *The American Political Science Review,* a scholarly journal of research reports and book reviews; *PS,* a magazine of political ideas and news of the profession; and *News for Teachers of Political Science,* a newspaper on teaching and learning materials. The Association conducts a Congressional Fellowship Program and other continuing professional educational programs and undertakes special activities such as Project '87, to commemorate the Bicentennial of the United States Constitution.

Political science is, in one sense, an ancient discipline and, in another sense, one of the most recently developed social sciences. In Western civilization, the Sophists began the systematic study of politics. With Socrates and Plato, that study became the heart of philosophy. In these respects political science, with history, can claim to be the earliest and most lasting of the humanities. Modern political scientists still address the issues with which these early philosophers dealt: those of community, justice, law, legitimacy, freedom, equality, and persuasion.

It is also true, however, that political science as it is practiced today is a very new discipline, one that has been developed primarily in the United States in the past 50 years. Borrowing and modifying models and techniques from the other social sciences, the discipline has sought to make objective, systematic, and quantifiable observations of human behavior and to formulate rigorous explanations of such behavior.

Political science in the broadest sense is the study of governments and governing procedures—whether these "governments" are sovereign states, international entities, or subunits of political systems (all elements of the public arena); or private associations, business firms, labor unions, churches, or universities. Political scientists are concerned with decisions by which a society distributes its resources and regulates its collective life. These broad concerns are addressed in each of the discipline's major subfields:

Political Thought and Philosophy
Formal and Positive Theory

Methodology
Public Administration and Organization Behavior
International Relations and World Politics
International Organizations and Law
Comparative Politics
Comparative Politics: Area Concentration
Asia
Africa
Latin America
Western Europe
USSR/Eastern Europe
Middle East
Public Policy
American Government and Politics
Federalism, State Politics and Intergovernmental Relations
Urban Politics
Politics of Race, Gender, Ethnicity
Public Law and Judicial Politics
Legislative Politics
Presidential or Executive Politics
Political Parties and Interest Groups
Voting Behavior and Public Opinion
Political Psychology and Socialization
Political Economy

The research interests of political scientists are also expressed by topical or substantive terms such as:

culture	regulation
development	ideology
modernization	generations
leadership	biopolitics
arms control	corporatism
public choice	constitution
mass communications	risk
religion	authority

In addition, many political scientists are interested in substantive policy areas such as agriculture, education, energy, environment, health, national security, science and technology, trade, transportation, and welfare.

American Psychological Association

Leonard D. Goodstein, Executive Officer
1200 17th Street, NW
Washington, DC 20036
(202/955-7600)

Founded 93 years ago, the American Psychological Association is the major organization representing psychology in the United States and is the world's largest association of psychologists. APA's membership includes more than 61,000 educators, clinicians, researchers, and consultants, as well as an additional 20,000 teacher, student, and foreign affiliates. APA works to advance psychology as a science, a profession, and as a means of promoting human welfare.

APA programs include disseminating psychological knowledge, promoting research, improving research methods and conditions, and developing the qualifications and competence of psychologists through standards of education, ethical conduct, and professional practice. The Association publishes books, 18 professional journals, the consumer magazine *Psychology Today,* the monthly *APA Monitor* newspaper, and pamphlets on a variety of psychological issues. APA also operates PsycINFO (Psychological Abstracts Information Service), a family of bibliographic and abstracting services covering the research literature of psychology.

Psychology is the scientific study of behavior. Its aim is to understand why we behave in the ways we do and what factors influence our behavior. It is a many-faceted discipline, combining social, biological, and health sciences. About one third of the Association's members perform research. Others apply the knowledge gained through research to help improve the quality of people's lives and to address society's problems. Many of these professional or practicing psychologists also have academic roles and conduct their own research.

Psychologists perform research on a broad array of subjects including learning; memory; perception; physiology; emotional, cognitive, and social development; personality; adjustment; achievement; attitudes; abilities; motivation; and the diagnosis and treatment of mental and emotional disorders. Psychologists seek answers to myriad questions about human behavior, from how the brain responds to stimuli to how individuals learn, form opinions, make decisions, and behave in social situations.

Research methods are various, ranging from highly controlled laboratory experiments to naturalistic investigations, which make use of information gleaned from individuals during their normal course of living. Naturalistic studies, for example, assess racial attitudes in college students by noting the seating patterns of black and white students in lecture halls.

Psychological research encompasses an enormous range of subjects simply because human beings themselves are so complex. Here is a samplingof some research specialties and work that psychologists are carrying out:

Biological and physiological psychologists study questions such as the changes in the brain that accompany schizophrenia and other severe mental disorders. These researchers are concerned with problems of physical and biological mechanisms and how they operate to influence behavior. Much of the recent research on endorphins, the body's natural opiates, was conducted by psychologists.

Developmental psychologists study the ways infants grow physically and psychologically into adults. They investigate the effects on behavior of aging, peer and family relations, and child-rearing environments. Developmental psychologists also conduct research on socialization and the development of sex differences.

Social psychologists explore the ways in which behavior is influenced by relationships with others. They are particularly interested in attitude formation and change. For example, some social psychologists are examining how proximity to cancer-causing substances affects attitudes and behaviors in the workplace. Social psychologists also conduct applied research in such areas as education, jury decision-making, the design of social environments, and the resolution of marital conflict.

A fuller description of psychological specialties is shown below.

Systems, Methodologies and Issues

History and Systems of Psychology
Experimentation and Observation, Experimental Design
Psychometrics
Statistics
Models and Mathematical Models

Factor Analysis and Related Techniques
Computer Applications and Programming
Apparatus/Equipment
Operations Research
Professional Issues in Psychology
Program Evaluation

Experimental Psychology (Human and Animal)

Learning/Learning Theory
Sensory and Perceptual Process
Experimental Analysis of Behavior
Behavior Modification
Operant Behavior/Conditioning
Motivation and Emotion
Memory
Thinking Processes
Decision and Choice Behavior
Attention, Expectancy, and Set

Motor Performance
Reaction Time
Comparative Psychology
Natural Observation
Instincts
Early Experience
Social and Sexual Behavior
Environmental Effects
Hypnosis and Suggestibility
Sleep, Fatigue, and Dreams

Physiological Psychology

Neurology
Sensory Physiology
Brain Lesions
Brain Stimulation, Chemical
Brain Stimulation, Electrical

Gastrointestinal Processes and Nutrition
Behavior Genetics
Motivation and Emotion
Personality Correlates

Electrical Activity
Biochemistry
Cardiovascular Processes
Environment and Stress

Sexual Physiology
Electrophysical Psychology
Psychophysiology

Developmental Psychology (Life Span)

Infancy
Childhood
Adolescence
Adulthood
Aging
Developmental Theory and
  Methodology

Development of the Mentally
  Retarded
Development of the Physically
  Handicapped
Thanatology
Cognition

Personality Psychology

Personality Theory
Personality Traits and Processes
Creativity
Intelligence and Measurement of
  Intelligence

Individual Differences
Personality Measurement
Personality Assessment
Social Learning and Personality

Social Psychology

Interpersonal Processes
Intragroup and Intergroup
  Processes
Communication
Attitudes and Opinions
Values and Moral Behavior
Alcohol Use
Drug Use
Smoking

Sexual Behavior
Human Ecology
Psychology and the Arts
Culture and Social Processes
Psychology of Ethnic Groups
Social Psychology of Education
Social Psychology of Science
Deviant Behavior

Clinical Psychology

Psychotherapy
Clinical Child Psychology
Psychoanalysis
Psychodiagnosis
Psychopathology
Behavior and Mental Disorders
Neurological Disorder
Mentally Retarded
Speech Disorder
Psychosomatic Disorder

Medical Psychology
Gerontology
Clinical Community Services
Hospital Care and
  Institutionalization
Applied Clinical Research
Reading Disorders
Physically Handicapped
Death and Dying
Program Evaluation

Community Psychology

Community Mental Health	Community Development
Research and Training in	Counselor Education
Community Psychology	Rehabilitation Administration

American Sociological Association

William V. D'Antonio, Executive Officer
1722 N Street, NW
Washington, DC 20036
(202/833–3410)

The American Sociological Association, founded in 1905, is the major organization in this country of persons interested in the research, teaching, and application of sociology. It seeks to stimulate and improve research, instruction, and discussion, as well as to encourage cooperative relations among individuals and associations engaged in the scientific study of society. Members number more than 12,000; about 1,000 are "international members" in various countries around the world. While the membership is composed largely of sociologists conducting research and teaching in colleges and universities, growing numbers of the membership pursue careers in government, research, consulting firms, and private industry. The official journal of the ASA is the *American Sociological Review,* published bimonthly and devoted to research papers and analyses. *Contemporary Sociology,* also bimonthly, carries extensive book reviews, review symposia, and occasional reviews of the literature. *Sociological Theory,* published semi-annually, is devoted to new substantive theories, history of theory, theory construction, and syntheses of existing bodies of theory.

The ASA also publishes four quarterly journals and an annual volume. *Social Psychology Quarterly* is devoted to research in social psychology, *Sociology of Education* publishes studies of education as a social institution, and the *Journal of Health and Social Behavior* is concerned with analyses of the problems of, and institutions in, human health and welfare. The newest quarterly is *Teaching Sociology,* which is devoted to articles on effective uses of sociology research and concepts in the classroom, strategies that enhance teaching, and book reviews on trends and findings in teaching. Also in this area, the ASA sponsors a Teaching Resources Center that distributes information and materials related to teaching. *Sociological Methodology* is published annually and is devoted to methodological issues, trends, and innovations in the discipline.

The ASA conducts research on the profession and operates a small-grants program to facilitate intellectual exchange on Problems of the Discipline. It also has a Minority Fellowship Program that provides funds for training of minority students in graduate schools across the nation.

Members with interests in special fields of sociology may join sections of ASA. Currently, there are 23 sections:

Medical Sociology	Family
Criminology	Sociological Practice
Sociology of Education	Sociology of Population

Theoretical Sociology
Sociology of Sex and Gender
Undergraduate Education
Community
Social Psychology
Environmental Sociology
Marxist Sociology
Methodology
Sociology of Aging
World Conflicts

Political Economy of the
  World-System
Collective Behavior/Social
  Movements
Racial and Ethnic Minorities
Comparative Historical Sociology
Political Sociology
Asia/Asian Americans
Sociology of Organizations and
  Occupations

Sociological Abstracts publishes synopses of articles and papers. It uses the following topical classification.

Methodology and Research
  Technology
Methodology (Social Science and
  Behavioral)
Research Technology
Statistical Methods
Models: Mathematical and Other
Sociology: History and Theory
Of Professional Interest
History and Present State of
  Sociology
Theories, Ideas, and Systems
Social Psychology
Interaction within (Small) Groups
Personality and Culture
Leadership
Group Interactions
Interaction between (Large)
  Groups (Race Relations, Group
  Relations, etc.)
Culture and Social Structure
Social Organization
Culture (Evolution)
Social Anthropology (and
  Ethnology)
Complex Organizations
  (Management)
Industrial Sociology (Labor)
Military Sociology
Social Change and Economic
  Development

Bureaucratic Structures
Political Interactions
Interactions between Societies,
  Nations, and States
Political Sociology
Social Differentiation
Social Stratification
Sociology of Occupations and
  Professions
Rural Sociology and Agricultural
  Economics
Rural Sociology (Village,
  Agriculture)
Urban Structures and Ecology
Sociology of the Arts
Sociology of Language and
  Literature
Sociology of Art (Creative and
  Performing)
Sociology of Education
Sociology of Religion
Social Control
Sociology of Law
Penology and Correctional
  Problems
Sociology of Science
Sociology of Science and
  Technology
Demography and Human Biology
Demography (Population Study)
Human Biology

Market Structures and Consumer
  Behavior
Mass Phenomena
Social Movements
Public Opinion
Communication
Collective Behavior
Sociology of Leisure
Mass Culture
The Family and Socialization
Sociology of the Child and
  Socialization
Adolescence and Youth
Sociology of Sexual Behavior
Sociology of Family
Sociology of Health and
  Medicine
Sociology of Medicine (Public
  Health)
Social Problems and Social
  Welfare

Social Psychiatry (Mental Health)
Social Gerontology
Social Disorganization (Crime)
Applied Sociology (Social Work)
Delinquency
Sociology of Knowledge
History of Ideas
Community Development
Sociology of Communities and
  Regions
Policy, Planning, Forecasting and
  Speculation
Planning and Forecasting
Social Indicators
Policy Sciences
Radical Sociology
Environmental Interactions
Studies in Poverty
Studies in Violence
Feminist Studies
Marxist Sociology

American Statistical Association

Fred C. Leone, Executive Director
806 15th Street, NW, Suite 640
Washington, DC 20005
(202/393–3253)

The American Statistical Association was founded in 1839. Currently it has over 15,000 members, as well as about 100 institutional members (universities) and 70 corporate members (industry, business, and government agencies); 10% to 15% of its membership is made up of foreign nationals outside the United States and Canada.

ASA has membership in educational institutions, in business and industry, and in government. The membership is composed of statisticians and quantitative scientists in many fields (e.g., the social, biological, physical, and health sciences), as well as users of statistics. The areas of application range from theoretical or mathematical statistics and probability to a wide range of substantive areas. Although approximately 50% of the membership hold Ph.D.s in statistics or other areas of science, there are no formal requirements for educational background.

ASA journals include the *Journal of the American Statistical Association* (the flagship journal), established in 1888. Other journals are the *American Statistician, Technometrics* (with the American Society for Quality Control), the *Journal of Educational Statis-*

tics (with the American Educational Research Association), the *Journal of Business and Economic Statistics, AMSTAT News,* and *Current Index to Statistics* (with the Institute of Mathematical Statistics).

The 11 sections and subsections of the Association indicate the different areas of application. They are Biometrics, Biopharmaceutical, Business and Economic Statistics, Statistical Graphics, Physical and Engineering Sciences, Social Statistics, Statistical Computing, Statistical Education, Survey Research Methods, and the two subsections—Statistics in Marketing and Statistics in the Health Sciences. These sections are an intersection of subject matter and areas of application. The Association maintains close ties with other professional associations such as the American Association for Advancement of Science, Biometric Society, Institute of Mathematical Statistics, Operations Research Society of America, The Institute of Management Sciences, Society of Industrial and Applied Mathematics, and Population Association of America.

The science of statistics per se is most aptly stated in the publication entitled *Statistics: A Guide to the Unknown* (available from ASA). Descriptively speaking, perhaps the distinctive character of the discipline is its interdisciplinary nature. Statistics pervades not only all the social sciences but most applied sciences and engineering in order that the work of the researcher may lead to conclusions based on information and evidence. Many local, national, and international programs tend to be meaningless without the support of the information provided by carefully selected, unbiased statistical evidence.

It is also engaged in several consortia such as Consortium of Social Science Associations, American Federation of Information Processing Societies, Council of Professional Associations on Federal Statistics, and the Conference Board of the Mathematical Sciences. The nature of these consortia indicates the interdisciplinary character of the Association.

Over the past 20 years the Association has been involved in national programs ranging from fellowship programs to review projects and research projects. Presently there are fellowship programs at the Bureau of the Census, Department of Agriculture, National Center for Education Statistics, and the Bureau of Labor Statistics. Advisory committees are maintained for the Bureau of the Census and the Energy Information Administration. Peer reviews, educational programs, and conferences have been held in conjunction with and supported by such agencies as the National Institute of Occupational Safety and Health, Environmental Protection Agency, Occupational Safety and Health Administration, Nuclear Regulatory Commission, and National Cancer Institute. The Association has been involved in international programs in several countries in Latin America, in India, and in the People's Republic of China.

Association of American Geographers

Robert T. Aangeenbrug, Executive Director
1710 16th Street, NW
Washington, DC 20009
(202/234–1450)

The Association of American Geographers was founded in 1904. It currently has a membership of 5,500 persons, the majority from academic institutions but a number from industry, government, and private institutions. Today over 1,300 colleges and universities in the United States offer programs in geography and over 150 institutions award graduate degrees.

Geography can be classified as both a natural science and a social science as it examines people and their environment and serves as a bridge between the physical and cultural worlds. To be sure, individual geographers tend to emphasize differing aspects of the spatial continuum—some specializing in physical geography by devoting their study to patterns such as climate, vegetation, soils, and landforms, others concentrating on patterns resulting from human activities and characteristics. Among the latter, economic, social, and political geographers investigate problems of agricultural land use, settlement patterns, boundary disputes, the trade areas of cities, cultural diffusion, the incidence of pollution, and the perception of environment. Although most geographic studies address contemporary patterns, an important branch of the discipline—historical geography—looks backward into time to reconstruct the geographies of the past. Likewise, a growing number of geographers use techniques of spatial analysis to assist in planning cities and regions that will constitute the geography and geographic problems of the future.

Traditionally, geographers relied on field observation as the principal means of gathering data. Such observations have, in turn, been combined and generalized to form the scaled-down spatial graphics we know as "maps." Yet, were our observations of the world around us limited to what we perceive through our own eyes—from an elevation of about five feet—our understanding of spatial relationships would be poor indeed. So geographers have sought to expand their perceptions by using data gathered from balloons, aircraft, and orbiting satellites. At the same time they have added to the narrow observational capabilities of films and more recently have exploited the more remote wave lengths of thermal images, radar, and even ultraviolet radiation. Thus geography is currently experiencing an explosion in data collection, and in its wake has come a growing reliance on such data-processing techniques as statistical analysis and computer mapping.

In American universities geography developed within other departments—especially geology, and in some instances history, economics, or anthropology—followed by the establishment of separate geography departments. In the middle 1930s the crisis of the Depression increased the involvement of geographers in national planning and research, especially in research development. In the later 1930s and during and after World War II a further surge of public interest in geography was related, in part, to the nation's increased international commitments. Entering graduate students during this period had a stronger systematic social science background than the prewar group, with its emphasis on geologic process and historic interpretation.

Closer relations with the social sciences developed in some universities when area-study programs were initiated and when interest heightened in urban and resource development study. The growth of mathematical and theoretical work in the 1950s added impetus to these trends, and linkages with economics and sociology began to grow rapidly. Involvement of geographers in policy-oriented research on highway development, urban renewal, resource management, and questions of environmental control provided additional stimulation. Quantitative studies and locational analysis, initially stressed at only a few U.S. universities, have expanded dramatically with major contributions coming from Scandinavia and the United Kingdom. American geographers today use highly sophisticated remote sensing, simulation, and statistical analysis techniques in their research. These methodological trends emphasize geography as a research discipline. A practical concern with problem-solving and more conscious attempts to develop theoretical structures have characterized this research, which has developed concurrently with geography's long-standing value as a part of liberal education.

Association of American Law Schools

Millard H. Ruud, Executive Director
1 Dupont Circle, Suite 370
Washington, DC 20036
(202/296-8851)

The Association of American Law Schools has as its purpose "the improvement of the legal profession through legal education." It is literally an association of law schools. It serves as the law teachers' learned society and as legal education's principal representative to the federal government and to other national higher education organizations and learned societies.

Founded in 1900, with 32 law schools as charter members, the Association was incorporated as a nonprofit educational organization. AALS is recognized as one of the two national accrediting agencies for law by the Council on Postsecondary Accreditation; the other is the Section of Legal Education and Admissions to the Bar of the American Bar Association.

There are Association interest groups, called sections, to which members of the faculty and professional staff of a member school and of those nonmember schools that pay an annual service fee may belong. Other interested persons may belong to sections upon paying annual dues. These interest groups concern substantive areas of the law, such as Contracts, Criminal Law, Maritime Law, and Property; relate to group interests such as Minority, Women, and Native Americans; and concern the interests of administrators, such as the sections on Administration of Law Schools and Institutional Advancement. A significant number of Canadian and foreign law teachers attend and participate in the Association's annual meeting.

The Association's *Journal of Legal Education* publishes, as its name suggests, articles concerning legal education but not concerning law and its development. Unusual, if not unique, is the custom of journals published by schools and edited by law students. Some schools now publish as many as five student-edited periodicals; a few are publishing journals edited by legal educators. A consequence is that a legal scholar finds it relatively easy to have her/his article published.

Historically, law teachers have emphasized library research to discover what the courts have said about a matter and then to subject this to analysis and speculation. In the 1920s this process was enriched by looking to other disciplines for understanding the facts that one must have to understand the problem. In the years since, law teachers and scholars have begun to involve colleagues from other disciplines in their teaching and research. Some law teachers, alone or with colleagues from the behavioral and social sciences, engage in empirical research concerning how the law functions and how the institutions that the law concerns may function.

Law may or may not be considered as a unitary discipline. The divisions that exist are probably not as marked as those in other disciplines. There are the teachers and scholars whose materials are largely legal authority—cases, statutes, constitutions, regulations, and the like. There are those who supplement this to a greater or lesser extent. A significant group employs the perspectives of economics; others use the social and behavioral sciences. Some, especially the environmentalists and law-and-medicine teachers, use the physical and life sciences. Clinical teachers are a relatively new phenomenon; their teaching method is different and their research interests tend to be empirical.

Linguistic Society of America

Margaret W. Reynolds, Associate Secretary-Treasurer
1325 18th Street, NW, Suite 211
Washington, DC 20036
(202/835–1714)

The Linguistic Society of America was founded in 1924 for the advancement of the scientific study of language. The Society serves its nearly 7,000 personal and institutional members through scholarly meetings, publications, and special activities designed to advance the discipline. An interest in linguistics is the only requirement for membership.

Members receive the quarterly journal *Language* and the *LSA Bulletin* (issued a minimum of four times per year, including a membership directory).

Among its special educational activities are the Linguistic Institutes, held in the summer and co-sponsored by a host institution. Inaugurated in 1928, these Institutes provide intensive training in applied and theoretical linguistics on the graduate and undergraduate level. Fellowships for students are available; visiting scholars are welcome.

The Society is an affiliate of the Permanent International Committee of Linguistics (CIPL) and is a constituent society of the American Council of Learned Societies (ACLS). The membership office for the American Association for Applied Linguistics is also housed at the LSA Secretariat.

Linguistics encompasses the study of language in all its aspects. At the heart of linguistic theory is the study of what sort of thing a language is and how people come to know and be able to use a language. A language, viewed in isolation, is a collection of forms which express particular meanings. Linguists generally hold that such collections can be described by systems of rules called *grammar*. Traditionally, "grammar" has meant the system of rules mediating between sounds and meanings in a given language. A number of broader theories of grammar are currently being developed, in an attempt to specify exactly these collections of forms which can properly be thought of as constituting a language. Some linguists also maintain that theories of grammar should be judged not only by their success in specifying what languages are, but also by how well they account for the ability of people to acquire knowledge of individual languages. The speed and accuracy with which children normally acquire knowledge of a language suggests that they know a great deal about what language is, even when they appear to manifest relatively minimal understanding of the particular languages they encounter. The codification of the knowledge about language that a child brings to bear on the task of language acquisition may itself constitute a significant part of grammatical theory.

The study of grammar can be further broken down into components, corresponding to different aspects of language. The forms of a language can be expressed and understood in a variety of ways: for spoken languages, speaking and listening; for written languages, writing and reading; and for sign languages, signing and watching. Linguistics has traditionally focused on spoken language. *Phonology* concerns the ways in which speech sounds are classified in the sound systems of particular languages and combined to form meaningful units. The study of the sounds themselves is known as *phonetics*. However, linguistics also encompasses the study of written and signed forms of language.

Morphology is the study of word formation; *syntax* is concerned with how words are combined in phrase and sentence formation. The study of higher-level formal structures is currently not as well developed as the fields of morphology and syntax, but is carried out by linguists under a variety of names, such as discourse analysis, narrative, stylistics, and poetics. The study of the meaning of linguistic forms, regardless of type, is called *semantics*.

Psycholinguistics includes both the study of how people actually produce and comprehend linguistic expressions and the study of how knowledge of a language (primarily, but not exclusively, one's native language) is acquired. *Neurolinguistics* is the study of the brain structures involved with the comprehension and production of languages.

Linguistics is also concerned with the comparison of languages with one another.

The comparison of different languages with respect to their grammatical characteristics is called *typology;* the comparison of different varieties of the same language is called *dialectology. Historical linguistics* includes the comparison of different historical stages of a language or group of languages and the reconstruction of earlier stages of a language or language group using available evidence from later stages.

Computational linguistics includes the formal design of programs or systems that simulate aspects of what people are able to do with language. It also includes the study of how to design programs or systems that can manipulate large bodies of text for editing and critiquing, retrieving information, abstracting, and translating from one language to another.

Linguistics also encompasses the study of language in a variety of contexts. *Pragmatics* is the study of how expressions are used and understood in different situations. *Anthropological linguistics* and *sociolinguistics* study the relation between languages and the culture and social institutions of their users, and ways in which speech communities are constituted and interact. *Applied linguistics* is concerned generally with the application of the results of linguistic analysis to practical problems such as language teaching, the design of orthographies for unwritten languages, literacy, and language planning.

For many of the human sciences, linguistics has been a model for development of new methods and theoretical approaches. For example, the family of theoretical approaches known as "structuralism," which has influenced such fields as literary theory, anthropology, and psychology, arose out of developments in linguistic theory.

Recently, linguistics has emerged from the academy to play an increasingly prominent role in addressing social and technological problems. Linguistic expertise has been applied to problems ranging from literacy to the improvement of document preparation, from the treatment of language disorders, including hearing and speech defects, schizophrenia, and aphasia, to learning disabilities. It is the technical and computational applications, however, that may have the most far-reaching consequences for the discipline. Computational techniques are being used in a wide range of traditional research areas in both theoretical and applied linguistics—from the analysis of speech signals to the development of systems that "understand" natural languages. The growth of computer science, data processing and retrieval, speech engineering, and technology have affected and will continue to affect the discipline by providing new outlets for linguistic knowledge, developing new sources of support for linguistic research and creating employment opportunities for linguists in the private sector, corporations, and public agencies.

Beyond Disciplines: Inter-, Multi-, and Cross-disciplinary Projects

In the preceding pages, the descriptions of some disciplines that were presented in an expository, nonschematic way—statistics, law, history—all contain statements attesting to their inherent interdisciplinary aspects. Others of the descriptions show in their taxonomies the effect of transdisciplinary influences and correspondences. To some extent that is due to a kind of historical succession effect of "master ideas" spanning all or most of the social sciences: early twentieth century *empiricism,* with its profound effects on, say, both Chicago-school sociology and, in a very different way, the "social realism" trend in law; *structural-functionalism,* an axiomatizing tendency in (at least) sociology, anthropology, psychology, and political science; *behaviorism,* evident not only in psychology but in political science, geography, economics, and other fields; *cognitivism,* with its two streams flowing from linguistic structuralism and computer science, which has profoundly altered psychology, anthropology, and sociology. It is significant that transdisciplinary counterparts (or, as an anthropologist might say, "affines") show up at the *sub*disciplinary levels of the various taxonomies. While it is meaningless to say that an entire discipline like anthropology is more "like" sociology than history is "like" political science, it is, by contrast, meaningful to observe that psycholinguistics, for example, is not some blend of all of psychology and all of linguistics, but rather a connection between a recent experimental trend in linguistic research; cognitive and/or developmental psychology; certain intersections of biophysics, computer science, and sensory psychology; perhaps together with some special areas of education research or anthropology.

Looking across the entire range of these disciplinary associations' taxonomies, one can see that "environmental science" can be viewed, in terms of its research procedures, as a combination of fields in virtually all the disciplines discussed in this chapter (with the possible exception of linguistics)—plus closely related work in the natural sciences, engineering, and public policy. Other relationships are more limited in scope. Health economics is done by those trained in economics and by those who have had to learn economics to do it. Social history is written by sociologists and anthropologists as well as historians. Psychological anthropology is not quite an anagram for anthropological psychology: there is a fundamental difference in assumptions. Social psychology is an important part of both psychology and sociology, the words being much the same with the tune somewhat different, depending on whether the group or the individual is taken as the fundamental unit. Human ecology, an active research field today, is studied by geographers, psychologists, anthropologists, economists, sociologists, and historians—together with those in the biological, environmental, and physical sciences. These examples, and many others, reflect the influence of "master ideas" on disciplines, on the one hand, and the emergence of particular empirical topic-fields, on the other. They are also interesting in their contrast with subdisciplinary entities that are *not* transdisciplinary in origin: econometrics, for one example; phonology, for another.

As is well known, some disciplines not only touch on and merge into adjacent social science disciplines, but span traditional divisions between entire branches of knowledge. Indeed, once one apportions parts of psychology into biology and biophysics; geography into the natural sciences; history and linguistics into the humanities; anthropology into the biological and evolutionary sciences; history and linguistics and political science into philosophy; statistics into mathematics—one can be led to the position that there is no such thing as a pure social science. Who cares? In practice, fields are defined by their styles and methodologies, not by their formal range of reference or their position on some vast tree of knowledge. For every assimilation of portions of social science into some broader, more abstract schema, there are new points of contact—between colonial historians and historical archaeologists, between plant physiologists and ethnographers—that extend and deepen the research enterprise. That is simply to assert, once again, that research generally proceeds at the topical level.

In proposing research for federal funding, investigators should not first ask, where can I get support? But, what specific topic (substantive or methodological) do I want to address? Having answered that question, they may then ask, is my project likely to be perceived as lying at the moving edge of a mainstream current? If so, it is reasonable to submit it to programs that emphasize a breadth or balance of field-initiated, peer-reviewed projects. But they should also ask, is there an obvious generic application of such research to the priorities of a mission-oriented agency?—i.e., not to a problem per se but to some problem *area* of stated concern to that agency. This is not the same as calculating whether "relevance" will "sell" a proposal. For one thing, two sets of criteria, the investigator's and the agency's, may operate simultaneously. The Social Security Administration, for example, may support research on what it deems a purely technical issue in health or welfare costs, which is also, from the research point of view, a major development in statistical or econometric or survey-research methodology. For another, with regard to grants from mission-oriented agencies, the decision to fund or reject a proposal will be made on *both* scientific and policy-relevance grounds. (With regard to contracts, see Morrill and Duby, chapter 3.)

In general, much federally funded research, being topically formulated, is inevitably co- or interdisciplinary in nature. If a single investigator proposes truly interdisciplinary research—addressing a problem associated with one field, for example, by using a method associated with another—that proposal may be reviewed, at the NSF, by two panels and co-funded from two program budgets. In the NIH, many projects involving the social-behavioral sciences have two "co-principal" investigators—e.g., one from a medical specialty and one from a social science. This requires no special procedures: a proposal will still be sent to the appropriate study section, selected solely in terms of the recognizable topical focus. (See Cuca, chapter 4.)

There is, nevertheless, the widespread impression in the research community that federal funding sources do not handle interdisciplinary proposals (to use the general, though sometimes misleading, term) well. This is probably not a just assessment. First, those who propose such research tend to have in mind a small sample of instances, or use an inappropriate baseline; they forget, or do not know, that most conventional single-disciplinary proposals fail. (And we have pointed out that many seemingly mainline "disciplinary" proposals are really multi- or interdisciplinary in heritage, but have been incorporated within a particular discipline.)

Second, as Kenneth Prewitt points out (Social Science Research Council *Annual Report,* 1984–1985): "Too few social scientists know the history of their own disciplines. Research on voting behavior is now regarded as mainstream political science, which it is; but it was pioneered by sociologists, social psychologists, psychometricians, and statisticians, not political scientists." Many other examples—e.g., decision theory or systems theory—can be cited where the various practitioners perceive the field to belong to one discipline, but disagree as to which one.

Third, available scholarship on the recent history of the social sciences, skimpy as it is, suggests that since 1940 or so many or most of the major advances have been interdisciplinary in nature. (As one example, Deutsch, Platt, and Senghaas, *Science,* 1971, vol. 171, pp. 450–59.) Most of these advances were at least partially funded with federal money.

Fourth, the NSF's Division of Science Resources Studies, which analyzes categories and patterns of federal science support, reports "NEC"—not elsewhere classified —as the largest single category of funding in the social sciences. The NSF's system is very unsatisfactory. For one thing, it lumps together funds for projects in disciplines that enjoy relatively small levels of research support from government, and thus are not broken out separately in the reporting scheme. It also includes in "NEC" much applied, technical research that is essentially atheoretical or that uses a nondistinctive methodology. But there is no question that "NEC" also includes an impressive number of clearly interdisciplinary, fundamental research projects.

The widely perceived difficulty in funding interdisciplinary research probably pertains to large-scale, coordinated, *multi*disciplinary research—that is, research which, from planning through dissemination, requires unusual working arrangements, institutional cooperation, etc. This is a problem of social and scientific organization: of scale, high risk, good intentions but imperfect execution. Even so, in the past funding agencies have made admirable efforts to facilitate such efforts, even though they have sometimes been prisoners of their own administrative rigidities or have failed to seize a unique opportunity.

In the present era of severely limited funding for social science, it seems certain that, for all the reasons discussed above, powerful topically focused research—which is often inter- or co-disciplinary in nature—will continue to be funded. What will happen to ambitious *multi*disciplinary projects is less clear. A proposal to describe three tenths rather than two tenths of the elephant (species: vulgaris) by elaborate multidisciplinary means may not be attractive to funding agencies, given the additional costs and organizational problems. (Presumably, proposing to describe three tenths of a rare species, or the very quiddity, of *elephant* might be more appealing.) On the other hand, carefully planned multidisciplinary cooperation in large-scale research projects may enjoy an advantage in the competition for funding, either at the stage of conceptualization, in breaking down a scientific topic into manageable parts, or at the stage of the analysis and further use of data—as fields share in the findings and implications of research and, as has always been the case, as science builds itself.

COSSA Affiliates

The following are scientific and scholarly societies affiliated with the Consortium of Social Science Associations at the time of publication of this guide.

Three of these organizations—the Association for Asian Studies, the History of Science Society, and the Society for the History of Technology—together with a number of other associations at the disciplinary, subdisciplinary, and interdisciplinary level are described in detail, as to their history and subject matter, in a 1986 publication, *The State of the Humanities,* by the American Council of Learned Societies.

Further information about the societies affiliated with the Consortium can be obtained from the COSSA office.

American Association for Public Opinion Research
American Educational Research Association
American Evaluation Association
American Society of Criminology
Association for Asian Studies
Eastern Sociological Society
Economic History Association
Gerontological Society of America
History of Science Society
International Studies Association
Law and Society Association
Midwest Sociological Society
National Council on Family Relations
National Council for the Social Studies
North Central Sociological Association
Northeastern Anthropological Association
Operations Research Society of America
Population Association of America
Regional Science Association
Rural Sociological Society
Social Science History Association
Society for American Archaeology
Society for the History of Technology
Society for Research in Child Development
Society for the Scientific Study of Religion
Southern Sociological Society
Southwestern Social Science Association
Speech Communication Association
The Institute of Management Sciences

Chapter 3

Academics and Contract Research

*William Morrill, Mathematica Policy Research, Inc.,
and Martin Duby, National Academy of Sciences*

Grants represent the primary mechanisms through which academically based social scientists obtain federal support for their research, and appropriately so. There does exist, however, a variety of opportunities for participating in important research, particularly policy-relevant research and larger projects, through the contract mechanism. This chapter seeks to characterize those opportunities and identify some important things to know and do, if one wishes to pursue them successfully.

Operational practice makes fuzzy any easy, sharp distinctions between the kinds of research undertaken by grants and by contracts; however, federal agencies tend to use the contract device when the topics to be researched and questions to be answered are specific, time-sensitive, and related to agency programs, processes, and decisions. Contracts are also more likely to be used when the research involves large, complex, and time-consuming projects.

A rough estimate of total federal expenditures for applied social science research, much of it through contracts, is that (in 1972 dollars) over $300 million was spent in 1979 and about $225 million in 1985. It is tempting to say that "basic" research is more likely to be done by grants and applied work by contract, but the exceptions are so numerous in both directions and misleading in other ways that it is not a very useful guide. Different agencies have adopted different practices, and it is more important to discover what they are than to rely on generalities. For example, the Department of Transportation University Research Program supports "basic" research via the contract mechanism. However, research performed under contract generally involves needs and requirements directly benefiting and for use by the sponsoring agencies rather than those of external institutions or individuals. Legally a federal grant is a grant-in-aid—i.e., in support of an institution conducting research —while a contract involves the procurement of services.

While research may, technically, be acquired through contract on either a sole source or competitive basis, the amount of sole source work available has dwindled to very little over the past decade. Exceptions are so specialized that we will devote little attention to them in this short piece other than to note that one may be successful with careful preparatory work. Some university sole-source contracts support important, large-budget research. An agency may award noncompetitive contracts based on unsolicited proposals where the research is unique, the product of "original thinking," and otherwise conforms to its agenda. One should not develop such a proposal, however, without careful informal determination that such a proposal would be welcome and acted upon. Our main focus here will be on the competitive research contract—how to get in the game, the proposal process, and what's important after you win.

The kind of work encompassed in our discussion of competitive contract research in the social sciences is broad. The research may involve primary data collection (or indeed be restricted to data gathering) or may be confined to analysis of secondary data. Primary data collection may range from a few case studies to rigorous and extensive sampling of households or businesses. The research may range from quick literature reviews through think pieces, rigorous designs, and quick evaluations to model building, simulations, and large-scale demonstrations and experiments. All of these examples and more are satisfied through the contracting process. We turn now to how this is done.

Preparing for the Game

The notice of availability of requests for proposals (RFPs) from federal agencies, advertised in the *Commerce Business Daily,* represents the starting gun for the beginning of the procurement process for specific competitive research contracts. Waiting to get organized until the date when notice does appear is usually too late for all but the most experienced and established research organizations which routinely submit proposals to such solicitations. Rather, planning and preparation is required before the *CBD* announcement sets off the specific proposal process.

Institutional Readiness. Award of a contract for research work involves a relationship that establishes organizational accountability for the completion of work (small, short contracts or consultantships are an occasional exception). The government also expects the organization to have the financial resources, internal processes (e.g., acceptable accounting systems), approved or verifiable overhead rates, etc., needed both to complete the work and to satisfy the numerous socioeconomic objectives (e.g., minority employment fairness) contained in the contract "boilerplate." While occasional holes in the panoply of financial requirements and standard representations and certifications are tolerable, it is virtually impossible to complete all the institutional readiness aspects in the time allowed for the solicitation process, generally 30 to 60 days. Most institutions—academic or otherwise—who do much grant or contract work with government sponsorship have the infrastructure in place; one just needs to find out where and what it is in your institution. In the event it is not in place, one should either agitate for its existence and/or explore teaming arrangements where another organization is the prime contractor.

Agenda Setting: Yours and Theirs. The federal agencies are usually quite open about their broad research agenda. Some of them publish annually in the *Federal Register* a statement of their major research questions and issues plus some information on the character of the projects they intend to sponsor. Their agency budget is a good source of intelligence. Other agencies are willing to discuss their opportunities with interested researchers. Contact should be made with federal agency program staff (usually to be found in research, evaluation, and/or planning offices) and their publications to match personal and institutional research objectives. In this process, good ideas from external researchers may well find their way into the agendas and solicitations of the federal agencies when they relate closely to important agency objectives and agendas.

The form of the contract will vary with the agency and substantive work of interest, but a few suggestions are generally applicable. Federal project staff will usually be available in their offices to talk briefly with researchers about the agency's agenda. Professional meetings are another good locale for getting acquainted. Do not, however, expect agency staff to visit you; their travel budgets and time are often too limited for such trips, though they may be enticed to a campus that has a particularly interesting program.

One note of caution is in order. Federal agency staff will, appropriately, not be forthcoming in advance about the precise specifications or content of a specific RFP, since such advance information confers competitive advantage over other offerors. Also, agencies occasionally use external researchers in the preparation of RFPs. Should you serve in such a role, you should expect to be excluded from further involvement either as an offeror or participant in the proposals of others on that RFP.

Teaming: How to Play Rewarding Supporting Roles. There are two kinds of teaming arrangements (not necessarily but sometimes mutually exclusive), which can be satisfying to individual researchers who have interests in federal contract research. For those with applied research interests who are not in major academic research institutions where such interests can be realized, it is possible to establish an ongoing relationship with a public or private research organization whose agenda and contracts complement individual interests and expertise. In such relationships, the researcher usually assists the organization during the summer months in preparing one or more proposals in which the individual will participate later if the contract is won. These relationships are more common when the researcher has an established reputation, thus imparting added value to the organization's proposals.

A second kind of teaming occurs when a research organization needs special expertise or additional staffing for a particular bid that it does not possess in its internal staff. This kind of teaming may be tentatively arranged in advance of an expected RFP, but is not usually consummated until the RFP's work statement is made public. This kind of arrangement can also be quite satisfying to individual researchers with applied interests. The mutual satisfaction is most often achieved when the external researcher can be assigned a quite specific task component of the project's research specifications.

Teaming on specific projects may also occur after a prime contractor has already been selected for a broadly based contract effort. The process is similar, though a specific proposal may be much more informal. This kind of opportunity may be available from contractors who are not themselves wholly social science research firms, but who may be identified through experienced colleagues working in areas of mutual interest.

Specific Proposal Preparation: The Running Start and the Decision to "Scratch." With very large contract proposals, even the normal 30-to-60-day period for proposal preparation may not be adequate to win the contract, particularly if it is in a relatively new area for the researcher or proposing organization. If such a large RFP is relatively certain from the agency's agenda, you can count on the fact that skilled, interested researchers will start literature reviews and other proposal-relevant work in advance of the issuance of the RFP.

The decision to submit a proposal commits the researcher to a significant expenditure of resources, very large indeed if it is a complex, multiyear project. Given the finite nature of energy and resources, it is always wise to assess the character of the likely competition and one's position in it before making the commitment. The government will assess past institutional and individual experience with the work to be undertaken in making its award. Thus, for example, a new university-based team of researchers is likely to be at a competitive disadvantage in a procurement context for a complex project with a large, well-known research organization with a successful track record in similar projects for the soliciting agency. In such a case, the new team may be better served by teaming with a large experienced organization or deciding to sit that proposal out. Informal conversations with other organizations and colleagues will often provide clues about the nature of the competition and help avoid mismatched competition.

The Proposal Process—Some Practical Hints

The RFP normally specifies in excruciating detail what the agency desires in the proposal—both technical and business sections, usually submitted separately bound. Without question, there is much in a standard RFP to put one to sleep, but virtually nothing that can be ignored, including the precise time and date when the proposal is due. To ignore the instructions risks summary rejection of the proposal as nonresponsive (which will certainly happen if you deliver it even a few minutes late). We will not seek to cover here all that will be learned by reading a sample RFP, but we will try to highlight some important aspects of the proposal and the process of selecting the winner.

The Technical Proposal. Above all other rules, it is important to be responsive to the agency's requirements as stated in the RFP's work statement rather than your own. Even if you believe the agency's approach is asinine, you should submit a plan to follow it and then propose a better alternative or a formal option (or not propose at all) rather than ignore the approach and risk summary rejection. If you are going to make the effort to win, it is foolish to give the agency easy grounds to dismiss your efforts. Beyond responsiveness, there are several aspects of a technical proposal that contribute to a successful submission. It is important to convey your knowledge of the subject and the research literature concerning it. On the other hand, you will not be paid by the pound, and the recitation of everything you know about the subject regardless of its relevance to the work statement is as likely to turn off a reviewer as inspire him or her. Some agencies deal with this problem via page limitations, but it is always useful to make some judgment about length and technical detail in terms of what the RFP says and what you know about the interests and skills of agency reviewers.

The best sponsoring agencies will welcome innovation in your proposal (use a formal option where such innovation departs from specific RFP requirements). They will also welcome discussion of the choices to be made in the research (whether tentative decisions are described in the proposal or held for later in the project if won). Above all, they will admire clarity in the technical approach. In writing a good technical proposal, it is also important to describe clearly what the project team will do and how its work will be scheduled and managed as well as to describe the technical approach. Keep in mind also that your proposal will become part of any final contract, and you will have to deliver what you promise.

The Business Proposal. For most researchers, the business proposal is the hair shirt part of the process. One is apt to discover that the agency wants task-level budgets through time in detail with respect to personnel and other direct costs, which take considerable time to prepare. One cannot wait to turn to the business section requirements until the last hours before a proposal is due. Such delay risks getting the proposal in on time. Worse yet, it risks the all too late discovery that the cost of performing the marvelous technical approach you have concocted exceeds by a factor of two the amount of resources the agency has available for the work. At this point most agencies and RFPs (unfortunately not all) send out some signal, usually in the form of expected professional person-years, as to how much they expect the award to be. While it is not uniform within or between agencies, one can estimate a roughly accurate range of dollars which the agency has set aside for the project. In any event, last-minute and unwelcome budget surprises can and should be avoided by preparing rough-cut budgets early in the process and refining them in tandem with the technical proposal.

As noted earlier, technical alternatives to RFP specifications are appropriate and sometimes desirable. If, however, your baseline proposal assumes such an alternative, you are customarily expected to budget it together with the RFP-specified approach in the same level of detail—an active discouragement to excessive use of alternatives. It is usually possible, however, to treat alternative budgets initially in more summary form when your baseline proposal conforms to RFP specifications and the alternative is merely suggested for the agency's consideration.

The business section of the proposal will also include the varying representations and certifications required by the agency. For the institutionally ready as earlier described, these "reps and certs" are simple boilerplate. For the institutionally unprepared, they can constitute last-minute disasters.

Other Important Matters. In addition to the primary features of the business and technical sections of a proposal described above, there are critical and sometimes sensitive matters that need to be considered affecting one or both of these sections. These matters include key personnel and staffing pattern commitments and requirements, confidentiality, and publication clauses.

The government has had experience with being promised nationally recognized talent, but receiving instead much more junior researchers and also getting more or less than promised of varying skill levels on cost reimbursement contracts. It has responded in two ways that require serious attention. The first is key personnel clauses regarding principal investigators, project directors, and other senior staff who are identified by name (usually starting in the proposal and later in the contract) and who may not be substituted for without agency approval. While most agencies react responsibly to the exigencies of personnel changes, it is unwise to treat the requirement in a cavalier fashion, and it is further useful to minimize the number of key personnel so identified to the extent possible. The second and potentially more troublesome approach is the establishment of time commitment ceilings and floors for individuals or categories of individuals. Given the norm of changed circumstances in all but the briefest of projects, these provisions should be treated as the plague and avoided or minimized where possible.

Confidentiality is another important matter whenever primary data collection is involved, though the government's interests should be identical to those of the researcher. The crucial rule for the long-run credibility of the researcher is that the respondent knows whether his or her responses are confidential and that confidentiality commitments, if made, are kept. The RFP may well specify the agency's intent, but may also be silent on the matter. The proposal, however, should always be clear on the bidder's intent. Agencies are usually interested in protecting respondents from external exposure and are often glad to leave the protection to the contractor. Agencies are, however, sometimes interested in possessing respondent identity information rather than being content with sanitized records which remove such identities, even when their capacity to protect identities from Freedom of Information Act inquiries or other governmental use may be shaky. Misunderstandings about this issue are avoided if the proposal is explicit on proposed procedures.

Publication clauses are a matter of greater concern since the government's interest may diverge from the researchers'. Most agencies indicate their policy in the RFP boilerplate, or it can be otherwise obtained from the contracting office. It is standard for the federal agencies to insist on some period of time after submission of the final report (say three months) before independent publication is allowed. It is understandable that the federal agency wishes to present the case first on the work it contracted for, particularly where important policy reports to the Congress and the like are involved. There is, of course, the danger that waiting periods can be abused by federal agencies to suppress "bad news." If the RFP contains publication clauses of excessive or non-time- limited duration, they should be taken exception to in the proposal and thrashed out with the agency early on. There is one comfort, however, for researchers regardless of the terms of publication clauses. Even onerous provisions or dilatory tactics in accepting final reports can be countered over time with appropriately arranged and timed Freedom of Information requests or other external pressures, unless the research is classified on national security grounds. Moreover, a contract binds both parties, and contractors should realize that contractual vagueness can work to their advantage in achieving professionally valid ends.

After the Proposal is Submitted: Questions, Orals, Best and Finals. After receipt, proposals are typically evaluated by a panel composed of agency or agency and external technical personnel. The process weeds out nonresponsive and weak proposals which show little promise of meeting agency needs. What is left are a number of proposals which do show promise and with whose authors the agency is obligated to negotiate. Negotiation involves written or oral discussions (sometimes both) of the technical and business aspects of proposals. A careful assessment of the questions can provide exceedingly useful clues as to the strengths and weaknesses of your proposal and permit some improvement in your score or competitive position.

Proposals will also be eliminated until several, or perhaps one, will be asked to submit a "best and final offer." That occasion is obviously welcome, but it is also anxiety-producing because you must decide what further changes, if any, to make in your technical proposal or price. There is neither advice nor a pill to alleviate fully the stress, but the better you have read the competitive situation and the intermediate colloquy, the more likely you are to obtain a satisfactory outcome.

Doing the Work and Taking the Bows—Details Matter

Once the contract is won and the work begins, there are other important considerations in undertaking contract research involving deliverables, cost accounting, relationships with the sponsoring agency, and dissemination of results. Not troublesome if properly handled, they can create real issues if not.

Deliverables. Unlike the grant structure, the research contract is likely to be full of explicit deliverables and schedules. The deliverables will include not only ultimate research reports, but also intermediate products of both a technical and administrative nature. The government put those requirements in for a reason and usually cares whether they are met. Some deliverables are more important than others, but even the less important ones may be indirectly important. For example, contracts normally call for a monthly or quarterly progress report, whether very much is happening or not. Project officers may not get too excited with non-delivery of one or two; however, routine delivery on schedule of such reports may store up some "credit" for a real schedule problem somewhere during the course of the project.

There is always a crisis of sorts if real problems are encountered in meeting the deliverable schedule. They are common enough in large projects and may arise out of issues on either the sponsor or contractor side (e.g., OMB questionnaire clearance is delayed, government data arrives late, a tape is unreadable, data takes longer to collect). If the issue is with the contractor, there is sometimes a temptation not to share the problem with the sponsor in hopes that the problem can be made to go away quickly. That is human enough, and not troublesome if a solution can be quickly implemented—but hiding a substantial problem can get a contractor into real trouble with the government. It is better to acknowledge the problem and resolve it openly with the government.

Cost Accounting. Unlike the case with grants, project officers and contract administrators require precise and detailed documentation for reimbursement of services. For example, the government wants to know what hours on what days were worked on the contract, with some auditable record to prove it. Assertions that some fraction of total time was spent on the contract won't do. What's at risk is reimbursement for the work done; thus, a system needs to be in place that will pass muster.

Relationships with the Sponsor. Beyond the formal relationships specified in the contract, there is always a question about how close a relationship to maintain with the project officer in the sponsoring agency. To the extent that the relationship is friendly, professional, and mutually respectful, the answer is easy. The relationship should be open and forthcoming. The problems arise when the situation is not an easy one, though our advice remains to err on the side of openness. There are circumstances, however, where intrusions by the project officer need be met with tactful—but firm—rebuff. Constant involvement with project staff below the senior level, efforts to skew or mischaracterize results, or inappropriate efforts to seek joint authorship of journal articles are illustrations of situations necessitating such firmness. As we commented above, a contract cuts two ways; blatant interference can, if necessary, be challenged. Such disputes should be handled with discretion. One would not take a fight with a project officer to one's Congressman except on the most severe provocation—and then with the expectation of receiving little work in the future from that project officer or office.

Another dimension of sponsor relationships deserving some comment is the important differences in roles between the project office and the contracting office in performance of the contract. The judgment about the quality of the work is within the purview of the project office, but business matters and interpretation of contract provisions are the domain of the contracting office. It is crucial to understand this difference, since it is a common source of tension. Project officers typically are interested in expanding the scope of the effort; but until such new scope is incorporated in a contract modification issued by the contract officer, the contractor is at risk for all out-of-scope work or, at a minimum, must suffer the embarrassment of "cost overruns." While occasionally done to meet schedules, it should not be undertaken without a thorough understanding of the probable behavior of the contract officer.

Dissemination of Results. We earlier addressed the important issue of publication clauses. Beyond those clauses, there may be special requirements concerning public use, if any, of collected data sets or of special clearing houses where the agency may desire the reports to be filed or abstracts prepared. More generally, it is not uncommon for a calendar race to occur between agency clearance of a final report and the occurrence of a long-planned presentation at a professional conference. Such timing issues need to be worked out with the agency, and usually (but not always) can be. Since it is generally to the sponsoring agency's benefit for final results to gain the widest dissemination, copyright and credit issues in subsequent books and other publications can usually be satisfactorily arranged and are covered by standard clauses, but they also need to be explicitly dealt with in the event such clauses are not automatically included in the contract.

While we have described and alluded to quite a bit of detail associated with undertaking research by contract, we do not wish to leave the impression that the experience is a prolonged bureaucratic nightmare. Perhaps difficult and confusing the first time or two, the process can be mastered, and the emphasis shifted to the substance of the proposal and the subsequent research. At its best, the preparation of a good proposal is an intellectually creative and challenging process; and a well-executed research plan can produce meaningful additions to the knowledge base, some of which may have tangible consequences for policy or other action.

Note: With reference to surveys, especially those conducted for federal statistical agencies, a useful technical discussion is *Contracting for Surveys,* Statistical Policy Working Paper 9, Federal Committee on Statistical Methodology, Office of Management and Budget (Washington, DC: U.S. Government Printing Office, 1983).

Chapter 4

Research Funding Agencies: Some Inside Views

Even the most scientifically exciting, skillfully crafted research proposal may not be funded if the investigator does not understand the ins and outs of federal research agencies, their review processes, and management. Most agencies use peer review to evaluate applications, but peer review procedures may vary. Agencies also vary in the extent to which program staff participate in the review process, what criteria are used to evaluate proposals, and how factors such as scientific creativity, methodological excellence, budget restrictions, and program relevance are weighted. A detailed understanding of these factors can help the investigator in preparing a successful proposal.

In this chapter we present three essays written by agency staff to provide some inside views. The entities discussed are the National Science Foundation, the National Institutes of Health, and the Alcohol, Drug Abuse, and Mental Health Administration. Together, these agencies represent the largest block of federal funding available for social and behavioral scientists.

The essay on the National Science Foundation, written by Felice Levine, program director for the Law and Social Sciences Program, takes a holistic approach to the Foundation its commitment to basic science, its relationship to the academic community, and the procedures by which proposals are reviewed and funded.

Janet Cuca, a Health Scientist Administrator and Executive Secretary of the Behavioral and Neurosciences Study Section in the Division of Research Grants, provides a broad overview of the review process of the National Institutes of Health. Proposals to the institutes that constitute the Alcohol, Drug Abuse, and Mental Health Administration are also directed to the NIH Division of Research Grants, but some procedures differ slightly. Thus, a second piece, prepared with the assistance of Salvatore Cianci, Grants Referral and Review Officer for ADAMHA, discusses the review process from that perspective. Although the two essays overlap on some points, both contain important advice and information. Investigators contemplating submitting proposals to any of the Public Health Service agencies should consider both pieces.

Social and Behavioral Science Support at NSF: An Insider's View

Felice J. Levine, Program Director, Law and Social Sciences Program, National Science Foundation

The National Science Foundation (NSF) is the most comprehensive source of federal support for research in the social and behavioral sciences in the United States.[1] Whether based in universities, colleges, or research institutes, scholars pursuing the scientific study of social phenomena are encouraged to seek funding from NSF.[2] No doubt, in an inherently competitive situation, applying for a grant can be quite a formidable task. The difficulty can be compounded, however, if there is an informational vacuum regarding how the system works, what is expected, what actually happens along the way, and why. The purpose of the essay is to minimize this source of difficulty by providing an insider's view of the social and behavioral sciences at the Foundation and thus making more understandable what is inside the "black box."

---

[1] This essay focuses on research support for the social and behavioral sciences in the Directorate for Biological, Behavioral, and Social Sciences (BBS) at the National Science Foundation. BBS has the primary responsibility for the support of research in these fields. Chapter 5 of this volume outlines funding activity in the social sciences in the other directorates at NSF. The ideas and opinions expressed in this essay are those of the author and do not necessarily reflect the views of the National Science Foundation.

This essay is the product of many exchanges of ideas over the years on important questions of science policy. I wish especially to thank Bonney Sheahan, Associate in Division of Social and Economic Science, for her substantive reactions and careful reading while the ink on the dot matrix was still wet. Also, Bertha Rubinstein, former Acting Division Director of Social and Economic Science, provided her usual thoughtful guidance, constructive suggestions, and critical eye. Professor Richard Lempert of the University of Michigan, former panelist in Law and Social Sciences, offered helpful comments and detailed critique as well. In addition, Professor June Louin Tapp of the University of Minnesota added counsel and support. Finally, Susan Quarles, Executive Associate of COSSA and general editor of this volume, was a valuable source of guidance from the initial idea through the very last draft. I also appreciate the many suggestions of my NSF colleagues and former panelists: Ronald Abler, Murray Aborn, Mark Abrahamson, James Blackman, Charles Brownstein, Paul Chapin, Mary Greene, Jean Intermaggio, Robert Kagan, Alan Leshner, Richard Louttit, Stewart Macaulay, Roberta Miller, Daniel Newlon, Ronald Overmann, Stuart Plattner, Stanley Presser, Lee Sigelman, Sonja Sperlich, Fred Stollnitz, Robert Thrall, and Joseph Young.

[2] While the vast majority of applicants have affiliations or affiliate with institutions for purposes of submitting a proposal, unaffiliated scholars may also submit applications to the National Science Foundation.

The Role of NSF in Federal Research and Development

Mandated Purpose. The National Science Foundation is unique among federal agencies in its singular commitment to the advancement of science. Established in 1950 as an independent agency in the Executive branch of the federal government, its primary mission is to encourage and preserve the health of all fields of science, including the social and behavioral sciences. Despite limited resources (commanding less than 5% of the total NSF budget), the social and behavioral sciences play a significant and vital role within the NSF family of science. With all programs having an "open window" for investigator-initiated research and with decisions based on full peer review, in large measure the strength of the social and behavioral science programs at NSF depends heavily on the richness of the ideas that are proposed for funding and the commitment of intellect and time exhibited by the scholarly community. In essence, while NSF is an agency of the federal government, its mandated purpose places it *in* and *of* the science community.

Structure of Funding. The social and behavioral sciences are funded primarily through programs in the Divisions of Social and Economic Science, Behavioral and Neural Sciences, and Information Science and Technology—all in the Directorate for Biological, Behavioral, and Social Sciences. (For details on each program, see chapter 5.) All programs are directed by program officers who are scholars in their respective fields. At NSF programs are the central vehicle for recommendations on the support of research. This substantial delegation of responsibility to programs (to be considered further in the proposal processing section of this essay) embodies NSF's philosophy that the agenda of funding in science can best be set by active scientists in an area (i.e., by program officers' making funding recommendations based on the expert counsel of peer reviewers). Each fiscal year, once an appropriations bill or continuing resolution for NSF has been passed by Congress and signed by the President, programs are allocated operating budgets and each program director knows approximately what resources are available. Other, generally modest, opportunities for expansion of a program's resources include special initiatives, joint funding with other programs, other agency support via inter-agency transfers, and funds held in reserve at the division director level. Once program budgets are set by the division director, however, program directors generally know the parameters within which they can navigate for their fields.

Role of Program Officers. While program officers vary in how they conceive of their roles, they share the view that their goal is to advance science through presiding over the funding of research in their fields and educating and advocating (within their disciplines, within NSF, to other fields of science, and to lay audiences and policymakers) about scientific accomplishments, possibilities, and resource needs in their areas. As do editors of scientific journals publishing the end-products of research, program officers base their funding recommendations on expert counsel and critique. Although the outcome is often straightforward, the real test of a program officer is in the complex case—when there is genuine diversity of view or when the well-reasoned use of discretion can enhance science in significant, though sometimes subtle, ways. Also, a program officer's judgment is especially important in determining how best to balance the allocation of resources among subfields, large and small projects, and even high risk/high gain research.

At NSF there is strong encouragement for program officers to remain professionally active in and knowledgeable about their fields. Some program officers continue active participation in research, serve on editorial boards, or are officers in scientific societies. NSF's commitment to maintaining a dynamic environment is affirmed by the "rotator" system. Under this system, many program officers are visitors from academic or research institutions, typically for two or three years. The synergism created by the interaction of career scientists and "rotators" is a special feature of NSF's science policy. Currently a third of the program officers in the social and behavioral sciences are rotators.

Why Submit a Proposal?

Research costs money, and sometimes it is quite expensive. Therefore, scientists typically require additional resources to pursue their theoretical and empirical strands of research. In large measure, this is the fundamental reason for applying to NSF. Beyond this material "why,"however, there are more subtle "whys" that deserve consideration. Drafting a proposal is itself part of the research process, for most people explicate their concepts, questions, and plans more fully when they are presenting them for others to examine. Also, the peer review system is an institutionalized vehicle for providing expert opinion on the strengths and weaknesses of a line of work before its initiation. The comments and critiques received by the applicant are usually informative and are important indicators of how the work may be received. Even reviews that seem unhelpful may reveal areas in the proposed work that are prone to confusion or open to misinterpretation. Thus, while from one vantage the peer review process seems to be a hurdle (i.e., something to be transcended as a predicate to funding), from another it is an important opportunity for the investigator to gain genuine feedback from other scholars.

Common Myths[3]

To the extent that institutional processes are unknown or unclear, myths may readily evolve to explain how a system works. When the competition for funds is severe, as is the case in the social and behavioral sciences, the need to find causes and meaning is especially compelling. The technical elements and language that shroud the applica-

---

[3] The importance of "debunking" myths was first called to my attention by William Mishler when he and I conducted a workshop on research support in the social and behavioral sciences at the State University of New York at Buffalo in April 1983. In particular, he engaged the audience with his discussion of the myth of *Non-Sufficient Funds.* See also *PS* 17 (Fall 1984):849. Professor Mishler, a former rotator at NSF, served as Associate Program Director for Political Science from 1982 to 1984.

tion process (e.g., target dates, ad hoc reviewers, addendum, revise-and-resubmit, OPAS) can further mystify researchers even though NSF is self-consciously trying to reduce the barriers to the funding and doing of science. Especially since the dramatic budget reduction in 1981, myths abound; several illustrate the point.

One of the most frequently expressed myths among social and behavioral scientists is that NSF means *not sufficient funds.* One of the adverse consequences of this myth for the health and growth of science is that truly exciting work may never be developed into a proposal or may be so altered in structure and scope (prior to submission) as to limit its scientific significance. There is no doubt that money is scarce (in constant dollars, substantially reduced from a decade ago), and success rates, while varying by program, in no instance cover all meritorious research. Nevertheless, budgets have rebounded somewhat since 1981; most high priority projects (as judged by peer review) are funded, albeit at reduced levels; and programs try to ensure that significant research receives sufficient resources. Indeed, program officers seek to avoid stretching dollars in ways that could compromise the viability of funded proposals.

A second myth, which could have a chilling effect on the preparation of proposals, is that *only quantitative studies receive support.* While much of the work of science is grounded in quantification, statistical analyses, or mathematical expressions, there is no automatic bias in favor of quantitative research. There *is* a definite preference for systematic, rigorous strategies and for the use of methods that are appropriate to the scientific issues motivating the research, but research need not be quantitative to meet this test. Although fields of science vary among themselves and over time in the prevalence and popularity of certain research methods, the full spectrum of methodologies (including case studies, ethnography, and observational techniques) and modes of analysis *can* and *do* receive support.

Another myth is that *only established scholars at leading research institutions receive support.* Across programs, periodic program reviews and studies of relative success rates show broad-based support of new as well as established scholars and awards to a range of institutions, from major research universities to small colleges.[4] While valuing stable funding for productive scientists, panels and program officers are conscious of and attentive to the needs of young and new scientists, scientists resuming research activity after a hiatus for personal and professional reasons, and scientists in diverse situations of employment (e.g., on "soft money" appointments, at primarily teaching institutions, at research institutes and laboratories). There is also a commitment to encouraging the active participation of women, minorities, and the physically handicapped.

A final myth is that *programs really have a research agenda* and that only certain sub-areas within a field or discipline receive research support. This myth is perhaps the hardest to dispel. As noted earlier, peer reviewers have ideas about what consti-

---

[4] Although funding patterns and submissions concentrate some at the major research institutions, this is often less than one might expect and does not account for the funding picture. See Mishler, p. 851.

tutes truly important work, and these perceptions come into play in the evaluation of proposals. As also pointed out, it is the job of the program officer to select reviewers and weigh feedback attentive to the fact that the "community" interest may be either too uncritical or too critical from time to time. These processes, however, are distinct from a priori agenda setting. NSF programs do not themselves fix subfield priorities or predetermine the areas of science that are eligible or ineligible for support. Even when special initiatives are pursued, to the extent possible, recommendations are made on the merits of individual proposals.

The view that scientific progress is more likely through a structure that is scientist-driven has led to the "open window" and to a reluctance, without substantial encouragement from the research community, to target particular areas for the infusion or reduction of support. Agendas may evolve over time, but they reflect the quality of individual proposals and research activity within a field. Thus, strong theoretical ideas can be examined on basic or applied problems; research can proceed in the laboratory, in the field, or working with extant data; studies can be grounded over time or across contexts; designs can be longitudinal, cross-sectional, or experimental. Later in this essay specific consideration is given to the preparation and review of proposals. The best advice about a program's priorities is for scholars not to second guess agendas but to propose the scientific work that they consider most promising.

Frequent Questions[5]

Beyond some misconceptions, there are also questions regarding the proposal preparation process that are frequently on the minds of applicants, especially those submitting for the first time. A technical or procedural question can divert energy from the substantive task of proposal development. The following address some of the most common questions asked in symposia and workshops, by mail, and by phone. While certainly not exhaustive, they suggest the range of concerns that arise and the general orientation of program officers.

How's the program budget? This is perhaps the threshold question for those seeking support. As is commonly known, the social and behavioral sciences operate under tight budgets, and not much relief is expected during the next few fiscal years. While there is some variation across programs (with different views and explanations as to where funding is least adequate), even the most affluent programs operate under extreme constraints. Although one should not be an ostrich on budget issues, resources *are sufficient* so that individual decisions to apply should not rest on the size or relative size of the pie. Both individually and collectively, it is in the best interest of the social and behavioral sciences to bring quality proposals to NSF for support.[6]

---

[5] I wish to thank my colleague Lee Sigelman, a rotator serving as Program Director for Political Science, for generating a list of his "favorite" questions to complement mine.
[6] Program officers do try to provide a current picture of the budgetary situation to prospective applicants, individual investigators, advisory panels, and other constituents in their fields. Also, the Consortium of Social Science Associations, the Federation of Behavioral, Psychological,

Does mainstream science have a better shot than an offbeat idea? Conversely, does a normal science increment to knowledge have any chance given scarce resources? Such questions reflect the ambiguities regarding funding under limited budgets. Those who may be undertaking high-risk work at the frontiers worry about whether their peers will be more inclined to go with proven frameworks; those working within established paradigms and adding bits of knowledge wonder whether the additional steps will appear important enough to command continued funds. There are no easy answers, but programs are keenly aware of and struggle with these important issues of science policy. As important, there are no fixed perspectives. Programs are dynamic entities that introduce change and re-evaluate their approaches over time. Ultimately the empirical realities suggest a mix of new directions and mainstream strategies. As might be expected with a modest investment portfolio (and in reality programs are investing in scientific advancements), the situation is more "both-and" than "either-or."

Is it worth proposing a major new project that requires substantial resources and a multiyear commitment? The answer is yes. Significant pieces of work are welcomed by programs. To the extent that NSF is the central vehicle for the support of fundamental research in the social and behavioral sciences, programs cannot fulfill their functions if they limit funding to small-scale soundings or the major large-scale databases (e.g., the National Election Study or the General Social Survey). For example, field experiments, panel studies, multi-site or comparative projects, and national or cross-national research are all labor intensive, typically long term, and necessarily expensive, but with considerable potential for testing explanatory models across time and space. While the importance of the scientific advance must be commensurate with the size of the initiative, programs are interested in valuable work—whether large or small. Investigators anticipating major projects may want to talk with relevant program officers both to receive guidance (e.g., other recently funded related work, budget rules of thumb) and to alert the program that a substantial proposal is in the offing.

Can I or should I submit a preproposal or prospectus? In the social and behavioral science programs, there is no formal requirement that a preliminary proposal or prospectus be submitted. Although all program officers make themselves available to talk with prospective applicants, they vary as to whether they encourage written material.[7] For many applicants (especially those who have not done much peer reviewing), some form of communication with a program officer—whether in writing, in person, or by phone—can be very helpful. Such contact, however, should not be viewed as a substitute for the substantive comments of colleagues, who are most often the best source of guidance.

---

and Cognitive Sciences, and the scholarly associations themselves are valuable sources of information, education, and advocacy.

[7] This difference in view is reflected by the comments of NSF colleagues to a preliminary draft of this essay. One program director urged "more stress on the desirability and *necessity* of preproposal contact with Program Directors." Another wrote, "we tell people that we are reluctant to substantively evaluate a preproposal because we are often not specialists and might mislead the investigator." Both are highly committed program directors who will read what they receive *and* are readily available for discussion and exchange with prospective applicants.

If a preproposal is submitted, it should be an abbreviated statement of the investigator's central analytic ideas, research objectives, and research plans, including an explanation of why the project is scientifically important and the anticipated costs. Preproposals should not be long and detailed, and they generally should be sent well in advance of the next target date for a full proposal. An investigator submitting a preproposal can expect feedback about the components of a competitive scientific proposal and about the appropriateness of the proposal given the scope of a particular program or field or science. A program officer may offer suggestions about what needs to be addressed in a proposal to improve the prospects of eventual funding (e.g., elaboration of hypotheses, access to or quality of data, data analysis plans). Also, if a proposal does not seem appropriate for a particular program or for NSF, the program officer may suggest other programs or other federal agencies to which an applicant might apply.

If I've never submitted a proposal before, what are my chances? This is one of the most frequently asked questions from young investigators, those who have pursued atypical career paths, and those not at major research universities. The myth that only established scholars receive support was considered earlier. Because of the saliency of these concerns, it is worth reiterating that proposals from new investigators have a very good shot and that every effort is made to try to identify new targets of opportunity. While a researcher's track record is taken into consideration by peer reviewers, it is a judgment that is made relative to one's age and stage. No doubt some learning occurs during the first several experiences with writing proposals. Most program officers appreciate this and, all other things being equal, try to make some allowance for a strong idea and a doable project framed in somewhat rough terms. If, however, an investigator does not succeed the first time, receiving a declination should not discourage future submissions on the same issue (depending on the reviews) or on other scientific problems.

What if I am unsure to which program I should submit? The best approach is for an applicant to talk with the relevant program officers and gain their views. It can be helpful if program officers understand why the investigator is uncertain about the best programmatic fit given the scientific thrust of the work. Based on this discussion, the proposal should then be submitted to the program that seems to be the most comfortable "home." An investigator may request joint review by more than one program by specifying such on the cover page of the proposal or by writing to the relevant program officers.[8] Ultimately, with all proposals, the decision as to which program or programs should review a proposal rests with the program officers. Every effort is made to undertake the review that seems to be in the best interest of the applicant and to ensure that proposals do not fall between two stools.

Does joint review help or hurt my chances? This is a difficult question to answer. Joint review does not and should not put an applicant in double jeopardy, meaning that it should enhance one's opportunities for support and not impose multiple approvals

---

[8] It can be helpful for investigators who are requesting joint review to send personal copies to all programs which are being asked to participate.

in order to obtain funding. The review procedures are designed to accomplish this goal. Although the relevant program officers together select a single set of ad hoc reviewers, the advisory panel for each program evaluates the proposal independent of the other panel(s). In making funding recommendations, program officers may proceed alone when proposed work holds promise for one scientific field but appears to contribute less significantly to another. Also, joint review can expand program resources by encouraging contributions, even modest ones, from programs that otherwise would not alone have a strong enough interest in the work. Although in the overwhelming majority of cases joint review can help or at least have no negative impact, occasionally it can hurt. While judgments regarding the scientific contribution to one field are not affected by judgments regarding the contribution to another, a program officer must consider significant criticisms about the research plan wherever they were raised. Thus, in that sense, review by one program can sometimes adversely affect the recommendation of another. All of these considerations are weighed by program officers in deciding whether or not to participate in joint review.

Can I simultaneously pursue other sources of federal support? In contrast to the submission of an article to a refereed journal, it is acceptable, appropriate, and even encouraged to explore various sources of support for research proposals. Investigators do have the obligation to list such submissions and anticipated submissions on the cover page of the proposal and on the "current and pending support" statement and to keep the cognizant program officer informed about any changes in the status of pending proposals. Review at each agency proceeds independently until a program is ready to recommend funding. Then communication between NSF and the investigator (regarding all outstanding pending support) and between the agencies is initiated. Duplicate funding is, of course, not possible. If the work is funded elsewhere, the investigator can withdraw the proposal from consideration at NSF. This is most frequently the case when major funding is forthcoming from a mission-oriented agency (e.g., Department of Health and Human Services, Department of Justice). Assuming favorable review in an NSF program, joint funding across agencies is also possible either through simultaneous, complementary awards or through a single award with an interagency transfer of funds.

How do I construct a budget? What can I ask for? What can't I ask for? The best advice is for an investigator to ask for what is needed to accomplish the research. It makes sense to be conservative, but also realistic. Peer reviewers can be put off by extravagant budgets; therefore, "wish lists" should be avoided. It is unnecessary (and not especially helpful) to ask for more than one needs under the assumption that negotiation will occur. Conversely, if the budget is too low, it might suggest that the investigator is unaware of what the research will take.

Assuming that there is a favorable recommendation, program officers review each budget individually in light of the objectives of the research, the financial demands of the research plan, and the resources available in the program. Budget cutting is not automatic. Indeed, some investigators receive exactly what they request, and at times budget requests may be modestly increased (for example, in response to reviewer concerns that the sample size or equipment is not adequate). Frequently, under current circumstances, the budgets must be reduced, but the extent of such reductions is largely dependent on the justification in scientific terms of the various categories of support. Although a program officer may recommend a reduced level of funding and can explain to the investigator how that level was established, there is no micro-management of a budget by a program. Also, while rules of thumb may vary some by program, all programs focus on essential research costs. Related categories like secretarial support, travel to scholarly meetings, and publication costs may not survive or may be substantially reduced in the program officer's arriving at a "bottom line" recommendation. Ultimately an investigator can structure a revised budget in whatever way seems optimal for accomplishing the research. (See the proposal processing section of this essay.)

Can I ask for academic released time? What if I really need it to do the study? While there is some variation again by program, and all programs do try to cover summer salary for those with regular academic appointments, resources are scarce for salary support for the academic year. Projects vary, however, in terms of their time demands, and, especially for some forms of empirical study (e.g., non-U.S. projects, multi-site, multi-method inquiries), the data could not be collected without labor-intensive and continuous work in the field. Investigators also vary in terms of the teaching demands on their time. Therefore, requests for released time may be included. The applicant should, however, indicate (as a budget note) why released time is being requested, for which phase(s) of the research, and what she or he is being released from (i.e., the normal teaching load and the amount of the reduction). Investigators who are on "soft money" appointments or at research institutes usually need to ask for large blocks of salary support. Program officers make every effort to allocate dollars in ways that are sensitive to individual needs. Under such circumstances, cost-sharing from institutions (e.g., salary matching) can often be helpful.

What is the success rate in your program? Success rates vary across programs and from year to year, but in general they range from about 20% to above 40%. Even at the bottom end, this rate is more favorable than the probabilities of publication in most quality journals, although, to a prospective applicant, such knowledge may provide little solace. Like statistics on the average size of awards, success rates may be more misleading than informative.[9] In any year, the success rate for new submissions is affected by such factors as the amount of continuing commitments and the size and scope of the most competitive work considered (e.g., one or two major initiatives may lower an annual rate). Also, programs with a larger proportion of proposals that are withdrawn because of funding elsewhere (e.g., the National Institutes of Health) may appear to have a lower success rate because a withdrawal is part of the base rate.

---

[9] These aggregate statistics do not address the potential variation in success rates within subfields, which is most crucial for applicants working in a particular field or discipline. Nor does this statistic, even if reliably measured, reflect the quality of proposals in different programs. Assuming constant quality, differential success rates (whatever their history) are troublesome, but success rates alone cannot be taken as an indicator of quality. Also, self-selection may affect either the mix or quality of proposals and may operate differently in different circumstances.

Concerned applicants can get bogged down in these data. While the process is competitive, no fixed success rates are used, and every effort is made to support as many of the favorably reviewed proposals as possible.

Do I have a better chance if I submit a proposal in the fall or spring cycle? In both cycles the review process is much the same. The best advice to an investigator is to submit when he or she is ready. Historically, many programs receive more proposals in the spring than fall, but program officers use their budgets mindful of patterns in their field and the two cycles each year. In some programs, a few fundable, but not high-priority projects submitted in the fall are held over until the spring to see how they fare relative to others *or* to be considered in a reserve fund competition. This is done as an alternative to an early declination when keeping a proposal pending may help its chances. Also, programs vary as to their rate of spending over a fiscal year, with some spending early and then committing a larger proportion of funds from the next fiscal year during the spring cycle. Whatever a program's funding strategy, if there is an exceptionally strong spring cycle (with more competitive proposals than usual), a program officer can hold a proposal over for funding from the next fiscal year budget and also can appeal to the division director for reserve funds. As with success rates, there is no fixed number of awards or budget allocation for any one cycle, and every effort is made to accommodate competitively reviewed research.

Assuming that an investigator seeks summer funding and is ready to submit a proposal for review in the fall cycle, there is some virtue to submitting then. As emphasized above, there is no real advantage in terms of the probable success of a particular submission. An applicant whose proposal is declined in the fall, however, has a second opportunity to submit in the spring without altering the anticipated start date of the work. Also, if the project is funded, the investigator has more lead time to plan the research. Thus, while the chances of success do not systematically vary by cycle, early submission may have other strengths.

Preparation of a Research Proposal[10]

Of all of the questions asked about the application process, perhaps the most salient, particularly for first-time investigators, concerns what needs to be done to prepare a competitive proposal. There are no simple cookbook answers. Just as with the writing of a scientific paper, scholars vary as to how they present their conceptual ideas, research, and findings. Peer reviewers and program officers appreciate this diversity, and NSF accordingly imposes no set structure or format for crafting the substance of

---

[10] This essay focuses on investigator-initiated research proposals directed to methodological or substantive advancements. Proposals may also be submitted to support such science-related activities as conferences, the development or improvement of data resources, group international travel, and the acquisition of specialized research and computing equipment. Also, programs in the social and behavioral sciences consider proposals for doctoral dissertation support. While many of the issues discussed here can be adapted to these other requests, investigators seeking other forms of support should contact the program director of the relevant program for specific guidelines.

a proposal. There are, however, some key issues that should be addressed in a submission and some common problems that surface across proposals.[11]

The booklet *Grants for Scientific and Engineering Research* (NSF 83–57) provides technical guidance on the who, when, where, and what of a submission and is essential for applicants. In preparing a proposal, investigators should keep in mind that it will be evaluated primarily in terms of the quality of its potential scientific contribution; i.e., the probability of an important discovery or theoretical generalization over time, across contexts, or even extending to other fields of inquiry *or* the probability of a significant methodological improvement or innovation. Therefore, the heart of the narrative should focus on the theoretical or analytic foundation of the anticipated research, links to related literature, and a clear and detailed presentation of the research design and methodology.

Sometimes investigators are initially drawn to a particular problem, topic, or context rather than to a theoretical question. Because personal interests often lead in that direction, this is natural. Once a researcher has identified the problem, however, it is necessary to specify the theoretical ideas to be illuminated by this exploration. Why is the work interesting? What analytically important problems will be addressed? What hypotheses or fundamental questions guide the research? For pure theory, one, too, should strive to describe what is interesting, important, or novel about the inquiry. While exploratory as well as explanatory work can receive support, it is essential to convey what is scientifically engaging about the project.

Consideration of related literature should also be analytic. This is an opportunity for the investigator to show the potential contribution of the proposed work to the extant research. Perfunctory comments on a list of undifferentiated references should be avoided. Instead, an investigator should focus specifically on how prior research, including her or his own, relates to this submission. A strong discussion of the literature should assess the strengths and weaknesses of other studies in relation to the theoretical formulation and methods used in the proposed research.

When empirical research is proposed, the section on design and methods should be a fully elaborated, prominent portion of the proposal that sets forth the operational research activities. It should include details on the selection of contexts or sites and on the unit(s) of analysis for the study—the population, cases, subjects, or data. If a sample is to be used, attention should be paid to how it will be drawn or specified. If experiments are to be conducted, consideration should be given to critical manipulations and control groups. If extant data are to be examined, their adequacy should be discussed in terms of quality, completeness, and appropriateness. Although appendices can be used for research-related materials (e.g., interview schedules, survey or other instruments, observational inventories, codebooks, content analysis schemes), the text of the proposal should include a freestanding treatment of data collection, data reduction, and data analysis plans. Key variables and measures should be spe-

---

[11] In thinking about these issues, I benefited from many of the ideas presented in "Guide for Writing Research Proposals for Program in Law and Social Sciences," prepared by H. Laurence Ross, a rotator and one of my predecessors (1976–78).

cified, and, when appropriate, procedures for coding the data and ensuring their reliability should be discussed. Plans for data analysis, whether grounded in quantitative or qualitative methods, should be provided, with care being taken to avoid "boilerplate" language like "appropriate measures will be devised" or "multivariate statistical techniques will be used."

With purely theoretical work, the design and methodology issues described above are not germane, but investigators will still want to present their research plan. There are problems with providing only a list of disparate topics that are unconnected to the theoretical ideas. In describing the theoretical model and anticipated work, investigators should seek to engender confidence that the assumptions in the model are realistic and to describe the solution methods to be employed. To dispel concerns about empty formalism, it is worthwhile to show that the work can yield meaningful, testable hypotheses. This is analogous to the concern in empirical inquiry that data collection not proceed without adequate conceptual grounding.

With either theoretical or theory-based empirical research, the proposal represents an opportunity to inform reviewers about the scientific importance of what needs to be done, the feasibility of the research plans, and the capacity of the investigator to accomplish the goals. For example, any pretesting, pilot study, or preliminary work should be noted, and assurances of cooperation or access to data should, when necessary, be obtained. Also, when necessary, human subjects approval by an institutional review board should be included, and, even when such review may not be required, a proposal should show sensitivity to issues of informed consent, confidentiality, and anonymity. In addition, if the study requires special skills (e.g., language competence, experience with certain data analytic techniques), the applicant should indicate relevant experience or background; this is especially important for young investigators who may not yet have a track record. Further, investigators with prior or current NSF support should specifically address progress and accomplishments. Finally, investigators should aim to be concise and direct in setting forth their scientific ambitions. They should view the guideline of 15 single-spaced pages or the double-spaced equivalent for the proposal narrative (i.e., exclusive of references, budget, vita, appendices, etc.) to be very important.[12]

Proposal Processing: Inside the Black Box

Almost all proposals submitted in the social and behavioral sciences are designated by principal investigators for particular programs. Those that arrive without designation are sent to the most likely program or division to make the assignment. Applicants should allow six months for the review and processing of proposals. While proposals may be submitted at any time, target dates provide the applicant with

---

[12] The guideline for proposal length does not preclude appendices or, if necessary, larger proposals. If an investigator believes that adhering to the guideline (plus or minus a page or two) will jeopardize the submission, he or she is urged to contact the relevant program to ascertain what latitude there is.

guideposts to ensure consideration in a particular review cycle. The time span from submission through program recommendation is largely consumed by selecting, obtaining, and evaluating peer reviews. In the Divisions of Social and Economic Science and Behavioral and Neural Sciences, this includes consultation with advisory panels.

The Structure of Peer Review. With the exception of programs in the Division of Information Science and Technology, which use ad hoc mail review only, all programs in the social and behavioral sciences use a two-pronged process for the review of standard proposals: ad hoc reviewers and advisory panel(s) of experts.[13] Ad hoc reviewers are selected because of their special expertise relating to conceptual or methodological elements of a particular proposal. Advisory panels also comprise active scientists from a field or discipline. They consider all proposals submitted in a cycle and bring broad expertise across an entire area of science. Both sets of input are invaluable to program officers in making recommendations.

The Construction of an Advisory Panel. Program officers recommend panel members to the division director who provides counsel and formal approval of membership. Panels range in size from 5 to 14 members, with a regular rotation of membership and typical terms of two or three years. In considering panel appointments, program officers aim to create an advisory group that in the aggregate reflects the major subfields of inquiry within a field or discipline, has complementary methodological skills and competencies, and brings diverse sets of research experience. Attention is given to both specialty skill and breadth of interest. Also, a history of service to the field and evidence of effectiveness in working with and advising colleagues are especially valued traits. (One important indicator of this is the quality of the peer reviews provided in the past.) In addition, attention is paid to balance within the panel in terms of age, stage of career, institutional affiliation, and geographical location. Program officers also take into consideration the importance of appointing women and minorities to the panel. All in all, panel appointments are taken very seriously, and program officers reach out to the scientific community for recommendations and evaluations. The names and institutional affiliations of panel members are public information.

The Process of Ad Hoc Review. A program officer generally selects six or more ad hoc reviewers for each proposal. The choice of reviewers reflects the program officer's reading of a proposal and his or her assessment of the kinds of expertise necessary to make an informed judgment about its merits. In selecting reviewers, program officers attempt to bring to bear a number of perspectives, including, when appropriate, the views of individuals with divergent theoretical or methodological frames of reference. Program officers identify potential reviewers through relevant work cited in the proposal, their substantive knowledge of the field, their awareness of active

[13] This is the usual mode of review for investigator-initiated research proposals. (See note 10 above.) Other submissions may be similarly reviewed, may receive only ad hoc or panel review, or could be the subject of a site visit with either ad hoc or panel review. For example, in many programs doctoral dissertation proposals are evaluated only through ad hoc mail review. Similarly, conference proposals may be taken only to the advisory panel.

researchers and those who have previously provided helpful reviews, and their consideration of articles and conference papers. Also, NSF maintains a computerized reviewer file with some attribute information on reviewers. The value of this database as a tool varies considerably depending on whether programs have had the time and resources to develop the attribute listing to the point where it adds significantly to the program officer's store of information. Beyond these mechanisms for reviewer selection, applicants may also suggest reviewers. While these suggestions are advisory, program officers usually include one or two such persons. Finally, every effort is made to select new reviewers, young reviewers, reviewers located outside of major research universities, and reviewers from groups who have thus far been underrepresented in science.

Response rates from ad hoc reviewers vary considerably by program ranging from about 50% to 80%. Reviewers are asked to provide a narrative evaluation of the scientific merits of the proposal; the ability of the investigator(s) to accomplish the work; if applicable, the results of prior NSF support; and related technical issues. Also, reviewers are asked to provide a rating on a 5-point scale ranging from "excellent" to "poor." Instructions to reviewers and guidelines for the selection of research projects are available from NSF. Reviewers are also informed of the rules pertaining to conflicts of interest in case they have a connection with the institution or person(s) submitting. In selecting reviewers, program officers screen for obvious conflicts (e.g., persons who are from the same institution as the investigator or are currently collaborating on other work with him or her) but occasionally reviewers themselves declare a conflict and will not review a proposal.

The Process of Advisory Panel Review. [14] Advisory panels generally meet twice each year—once in the fall and once in the spring—typically for two days. In most of the programs, panelists receive all proposals to be considered by the panel well in advance of the meeting. Based on their area of expertise and backgrounds, panelists are asked by the program officer to be primary reviewers for approximately the same number of proposals. Usually two panelists serve as primary reviewers for each proposal; i.e., prior to the meeting they provide independent written reviews (in the same fashion as do the ad hoc reviewers), and during the meeting they take the lead in discussion. While programs vary in the extent to which panelists read beyond their primary assignments, they may elect to read (and write reviews on) any proposal being considered, and usually they are familiar with many more than assigned.

Discussions of proposals can vary considerably, from little or virtually no time (indicating a clear case of strong agreement among panelists and ad hoc reviewers) to extensive considerations of half an hour or more. Deliberations are usually very stimulating and engaging, and many panelists report that it is the meetings themselves that are sustaining despite the magnitude of work. Panel discussion includes attention to the ad hoc reviews received by the time of the meeting. In some programs, these

---

[14] An interesting glimpse of the operations of a highly structured panel appears in David Klahr's "Insiders, Outsiders, and Efficiency in a National Science Foundation Panel," *American Psychologist* 40 (February 1985).

are circulated in advance of the panel meeting (to all panelists or to primary panel reviewers); in other programs, they are distributed at the panel meeting; and in still others, the program officers present them for consideration. While the specific techniques vary (and program officers do try different methods), the basic goal—having panel discussion informed by subfield expertise—remains the same.

Following the discussion, the advisory panel makes a recommendation to the program. Although a consensus usually evolves, panelists are not pushed to agreement, and the written summary of the deliberations may reflect a significant diversity of views (without revealing the identities of who took which positions), including divergent recommendations. Typically there is no formal vote. The advisory panel reaches an agreement on a recommendation and may provide a rating (often on a 5-point scale like that used in the written evaluation) or a categorical assessment (e.g., "priority fund" or "fundable"). In terms of guidance to programs, these quantitative and qualitative judgments are functionally equivalent. It should be noted that the same conflict of interest rules apply to panelists and to program officers as to ad hoc reviewers. Panelists or program officers with a conflict leave the meeting during the discussion of a proposal and do not participate in any way. Panelists' proposals are not considered by their program's panel.

Peer Review and Program Recommendations. In arriving at a program recommendation to fund or decline a proposal, both ad hoc and panel reviews are extremely important. Without an overall favorable appraisal from ad hoc experts, a proposal is likely to have tough going. A generally positive assessment from ad hoc reviewers of the quality of the anticipated work, its likely scientific contribution, and the capacity of the investigator is typically a necessary, though not sufficient, condition for funding. Bringing the broader perspective of the field or discipline and having the advantage of seeing all proposals, panels weigh their own judgments and the ad hoc reviews in making a recommendation. Here the substantive content of ad hoc reviews is particularly important (e.g., to illuminate opportunities despite problems or, conversely, to raise questions that might be unknown without substantive or technical expertise). Thus, ad hoc reviews are used by program officers in identifying issues for panel discussion *and* by panels in their deliberations. Irrespective of the amount of attention they receive from the panel, however, ad hoc reviews (including those that arrive subsequent to the panel meeting) are still considered by the program officer in making a recommendation.

In considering ad hoc and panel reviews, program officers focus primarily on the substantive appraisal, although the 5-point rating scale accompanying the written review is used as a shorthand way of getting a grasp on the overall evaluation of a proposal and how it compares with other proposals. Despite NSF guidelines for the use of summary ratings, ad hoc reviewers and panelists vary on how they rate proposals and on the meaning that can be attributed to different scores. Therefore, even in instances of disparate ratings, reviewers may share a rather similar appraisal of proposed work. Also, program officers typically do not average individual ratings as a method of decision-making. A mean rating with a large standard deviation may generate more "noise" than "signal." For example, with a proposal that has been quite favorably reviewed, one or two negative outliers (e.g., those who raise peripheral points) could adversely affect the recommendation of meritorious work if such a metric were used.

Although panel recommendations are extremely influential, program officers are charged with the responsibility of making the program recommendation on funding and the allocation of resources. Proposals that are considered very competitive by panels ("high priority," "must fund") are only rarely recommended by a program officer for a declination assuming that sufficient resources are available. Similarly, it is rare that a program officer would reverse a strong and clear recommendation by a panel to decline a proposal. Program officers are, however, often called on to use their scientific knowledge and judgment in deciding among fundable proposals ("could fund," "should fund," "fund if sufficient resources are available"). Here they must weight the panel's recommendation, its assessment across a range of fundable proposals, and the counsel of ad hoc specialists. Also, program officers are not infrequently faced with ambiguous cases when there are strong differences among panelists, between panelists and ad hoc reviewers, or when panelists may have reconciled ad hoc reviews in a way that may miss an important scientific opportunity. For example, a program officer may recommend funding in instances where the panel was not persuaded that the payoffs cited by ad hoc reviewers outweighed the risks. That program officers make the program recommendations does not undercut or diminish the importance of the panel. It does, however, make meaningful the two-pronged structure (panel *and* ad hoc) of the peer review process.

Based on peer review, program officers are usually in a position to make a recommendation to fund or decline a proposal without seeking further information. At times, particularly with proposals considered "fundable, but not of high priority," program officers may request additional information or clarification on substantive or technical points (e.g., guarantees of access to field sites, more detailed specification of data analysis plans). Such requests are more typical in some programs than others; usually, however, they reflect either explicit urging from the panel or an issue of general concern to ad hoc and panel reviewers. Whether additional information is sought or not, under current budgetary circumstances, program officers must often request a revised budget and an impact statement outlining changes, if any, in scope or plan.

Delegation of Authority. Predicated on the full use of peer review, program officers are responsible for funding recommendations. Indeed, a central part of the documentation for either an award or declination is a confidential analysis prepared by the program officer of the results of peer review and the basis for the program's recommendation. While in the social and behavioral sciences the program officer is the key recommending official, the division director is the NSF official delegated the authority for final programmatic approval. The division director has the responsibility for ensuring that the case presented for the recommendation is scientifically sound and that the peer review process has been adequate, sufficient, and properly considered in arriving at a recommendation. This programmatic review and approval help to ensure the integrity of the selection process.

Outcomes and Actions. Assuming concurrence by the division director with the program's recommendation, declinations are officially transmitted from the division director; award recommendations are forwarded to the Division of Grants and Contracts for the official commitment of NSF funds. Before that time, there is frequently informal communication between a program officer and principal investigator. Program officers may need to obtain more information from the investigator, even if only a revised budget and statement of how the work can be accomplished with reduced funds. While no news should not be interpreted as bad news, applicants can contact the relevant program (the primary program in the case of joint review) about the status of a pending proposal. Given the scheduling of panel meetings for most programs, informal word is generally not available before December in the fall cycle or June in the spring cycle. Informal discussion with a program officer, whether encouraging or discouraging, can not be considered an official action. When a favorable recommendation has been made, applicants have reason to feel confident, but they should appreciate that recommendations are reviewed and approved by the division director and that a grant is not assured until the official letter is signed by the Division of Grants and Contracts.

When the official decision is made, investigators and their institutions are notified by mail. Whether or not the recommendation is favorable, the applicant receives all reviews of the proposal in anonymous form. Also, the applicant receives a written summary of the panel discussion. In most instances, the summary is prepared by program staff based on notes taken during the panel meeting; in some cases, a panelist (one of the primary reviewers) drafts an initial summary during the meeting, which is later edited by program staff. Panel summaries vary considerably by program in the amount of feedback, although even the briefest statement should provide a sense of the issues underlying the panel recommendation. Therefore, investigators, in either launching the research or considering its further development (in the case of a declination), should find the full packet of materials to be very instructive and helpful.

Is There Life After a Declination? In a competitive situation where resources are scarce, even proposals that are fundable or have potential for funding are declined. As the declination letter *says and means,* not all work of merit can be funded. In most instances, a declination is not a statement about scientific competence or capacity, but a judgment based on guidance from the peer review community about the value or relative value of allocating resources to support the work. Applicants—especially those who receive a declination before they have had a successful submission—should realized that they are in distinguished company and that there is no "black mark" in being rejected. Notice of a declination is given only to the investigator and the submitting institution. Neither the proposal nor reviews are released to others in the scientific community. Reviewers are requested to honor this confidentiality. Only funded proposals, but not reviews, are matters of public information as required by law.

Depending on the feedback from peer reviewers, a decline can be as much a beginning as an ending. As difficult as it may be, applicants who have been declined should study the reviews in terms of what can be learned about the limitations of a proposal. Do reviewers see the scientific potential of this work? On balance do they see the central issues as worth pursuing? Were the theoretical ideas sufficiently well articulated? Were problems identified with the research plan and methodology? Are the links between concepts and research operations adequately drawn? Based on an assessment of such questions, an applicant should be able to determine whether or how to proceed. Program officers are also available to discuss the basis of a declination. Sometimes an advisory panel will encourage continued development of a proposal. The tone and content of the panel summary provide an indicator. The panel may explicitly recommend a resubmission (i.e., "revise-and-resubmit"), although this is infrequent. In most cases, the panel does not offer an opinion about resubmission but leaves the decision up to the investigator. Whether encouraged by the panel or not, a revised proposal goes through the same review process, using some repeat reviewers who can assess the adequacy of growth and changes and some new reviewers to provide a fresh assessment of its merits.

Ideally, questions about the review process and the basis for a decision can be satisfactorily handled by the program officer. If, after communication with the program officer, a principal investigator is still not satisfied that the proposal was fairly handled and reasonably evaluated, he or she can formally request reconsideration of the decision. A reconsideration is handled by the Assistant Director for Biological, Behavioral, and Social Sciences and is primarily a procedural review to determine whether the program recommendation and decision were arrived at properly and in accordance with Foundation policies. The reconsideration procedure is described in an NSF circular and can be obtained from the program or division. If the appeal for reconsideration is not granted, the investigator retains the option of submitting a revised proposal for fresh review.

Conclusion

This excursion inside social and behavioral science at NSF has sought to explore and explain how the process of seeking support works and what investigators should expect in submitting a proposal. Undoubtedly, lingering questions may remain where further clarification would enhance one's understanding. It *is* appropriate to continue to ask questions and to seek answers. Program officers are available to help. Informed assistance may also be obtained from colleagues and institutional administrators. The important message is to begin the process. The preparation of a research proposal and the review of an application are not adversarial procedures. Both the research community and NSF staff are dedicated to the same goal—the progress of science, and thus, ultimately, both are dependent on the submission of strong and engaging proposals.

The National Institutes of Health: Extramural Funding and the Peer Review Process

Janet M. Cuca, Health Sciences Administrator and Executive Secretary, Behavioral and Neurosciences Study Section, Division of Research Grants

The primary mission of the National Institutes of Health (NIH) is to support and conduct research "to improve the health of the people of the United States." This broad mandate, which includes basic and clinical, biomedical and behavioral science research, is carried out for the most part through the funding of research conducted in extramural settings throughout the nation, though it is also accomplished in NIH's intramural laboratories in Bethesda, Maryland. In FY 1984 over $3.6 billion of NIH's total obligations of nearly $4.5 billion were devoted to the extramural activities of its Institutes (excluding the National Library of Medicine).

The funds to underwrite Institute extramural activities are awarded through three generic types of mechanisms—grants, contracts, and a new hybrid of grants and contracts called the cooperative agreement. In FY 1984, $3.1 billion was obligated through the grant mechanism. Research grants are classified as research projects, research centers, or other research, and in FY 1984, $2.4 billion, $0.4 billion, and $0.2 billion was expended on each kind, respectively. Of the $2.4 billion expended on research projects, $1.9 billion was expended on the traditional research project or, according to its computer code, R01 grant. Viewed in terms of number of awards, the R01 still looms large in the NIH picture—15,757 of the 21,487 competing and noncompeting grants awarded in FY 1984 were R01s. Of the 15,757 R01 grants funded in FY 1984, 2,527 were new, another 2,111 were projects that competed for continuation funding, and 10,692 were noncompeting continuations. The 4,638 new and competing awards had competed successfully against 12,154 other research project applications (including 9,844 RO1 applications) that failed to receive funding. Let us consider, now, sources of funding in the Institutes.

The NIH comprises 13 Institutes and Divisions plus several central administrative units; 11 of the Institutes award R01 grants. Each Institute was established by legislation that, to a greater or lesser degree, specifies the areas of research toward which it should direct its activities. The budget of each Institute is separately authorized and appropriated by the Congress: in FY 1985 the Institute budgets ranged from $1,182 million for the National Cancer Institute (NCI) to $101 million for the National Institute of Dental Research (NIDR). Certain of the Institutes, in response to their legislative mandates, devote a not inconsiderable percentage of their total budget to behavioral and social science research; others devote little, if any. However, some of the Institutes with larger budgets, though they give less emphasis in their overall program to behavioral and social science research, spend more on it than Institutes with smaller budgets that give to it greater attention. Thus, in identifying potential sources of funding for social and behavioral science research, one should not overlook the more biomedically oriented, but larger-budgeted Institutes. In two

Institutes, behavioral and social science research is specifically mandated in their enabling legislation, and ongoing programs respond to those mandates in their support of research. In the National Institute on Aging (NIA), it is the Behavioral Sciences Research Program; in the National Institute of Child Health and Human Development (NICHD), it is the Demographic and Behavioral Sciences Branch. A detailed description of most NIH programs is provided in chapter 5. In addition, there are several other resources, both published and human, for obtaining details on program research areas.

The biennially published *NIH Extramural Programs* provides general information about the areas of research being supported by the different programs of the Institutes and the types of mechanisms used to fund each. The "NIH Guide for Grants and Contracts," which appears monthly, publishes Program Announcements that publicize more detailed background information about new and ongoing research programs, Requests for Applications (RFAs) that solicit grant applications on specific research topics, and other items regarding policies and procedures relevant to extramural activities. Subscriptions to the "Guide" are available without charge by sending a self-addressed mailing label and a request for the subscription form to the Office of Grants Inquiries of the Division of Research Grants (DRG). This office is another important resource; its staff are generally familiar with the research programs of the various Institutes and can refer callers to the appropriate persons for specialized information. It is also the resource for information about application procedures, forms, and receipt dates. However, most universities have an office of sponsored research that can provide general information about NIH programs and that usually keeps supplies of the application kits on hand.

The acknowledgments footnotes of research articles published in journals can also give an idea of the types of research funded by the Institutes (though one has to know the two-letter codes used to designate the Institutes and their grants). Let us consider now what happens to a research grant application sent to NIH.

All applications submitted to the NIH, and certain other agencies of the Public Health Service, including those for the National Institute of Mental Health (NIMH), the National Institute of Drug Abuse (NIDA), and the National Institute of Alcohol Abuse and Alcoholism (NIAAA) (these three Institutes are components of the Alcohol, Drug Abuse, and Mental Health Administration, not NIH), as well as those for the Office of Population Affairs in the Office of the DHHS Assistant Secretary for Health are directed to and received by the Division of Research Grants (DRG). In fact, the same forms are used for applying to NIH and to these other Institutes and Office. There are three receipt dates per year for most grant applications, though the dates differ depending on the type of proposal; thus, there are three review cycles per year. (Note: See the chart at the end of this chapter.)

The DRG is one of the central administrative units of NIH and, as such, has no research program; its major role is to receive, assign, and provide for the scientific review of grant applications. In the DRG Referral Office, professionals who also serve as Executive Secretaries of DRG Study Sections/Initial Review Groups (IRGs) decide to which Institute and study section to assign applications for review on the basis of the scientific content of the application, their knowledge of Institute research programs, and their knowledge of the assignment guidelines of the study sections. Detailed referral guidelines are followed in making these assignments, though cover letters accompanying applications that suggest or request assignment to a particular Institute or study section are given due consideration. At this point a postcard submitted with the application is returned to the applicant informing him or her of the Institute and study section assignments and of the assignment number given to the application. An applicant may appeal these assignments by contacting the Referral Office. The assignment and referral process is preliminary to the actual review process.

The NIH peer review process separates review into two stages. The initial stage is concerned primarily with an application's scientific merit. The second stage is concerned with its relevance to the scientific programs and mission of the Institute to which it has been assigned for possible funding. While applications for certain grant mechanisms such as program projects are reviewed in the initial stage by Institute IRG's, almost all R01s are initially reviewed by DRG study sections. The recommendation resulting from the initial DRG review is sent to the Institute in the form of a Summary Statement and used in the second or "Council" stage of review when the Institutes' national advisory councils make a final recommendation to NIH program staff to fund an application or not.

There are 66 DRG study sections chartered by the DHHS Secretary; however, because some consist of two or more subcommittees, the number of standing review panels totals almost 100. Each is administered by a doctoral-level Executive Secretary who is assisted by a Grants Technical Assistant. Organized around a scientific area, each study section is composed of up to 15 to 20 members. Members are nominated by the Executive Secretary and formally appointed by the NIH Director for rotating 4-year terms; they are selected foremost for their scientific expertise.Geographic, sex, and minority representation on the study section are additional considerations. One of the members is designated by the Executive Secretary to chair the study section. The membership (and the authority, structure, and function) of each study section as well as the Institute national advisory councils and all other NIH advisory groups is listed in the annual publication *NIH Public Advisory Groups.*

Most of the DRG study sections review research grant applications, while 3 sections composed of 13 subcommittees review postdoctoral and senior fellowship applications. Meetings of the study sections are convened three times a year for 1-to-3-day sessions to discuss the applications that were submitted for review in that cycle. The meetings are closed to the public but are observed by Institute staff of the particular programs for which applications are being reviewed. In addition to the standing study sections, there are "special study sections" that are organized on a one-time basis to review research grant applications that, for a variety of reasons, cannot by reviewed by one of the standing study sections.

Once assigned to a study section, an application is further assigned by the Executive Secretary to two or more members who will serve as principal reviewers for the application, write detailed evaluations of it, and lead the discussion at the meeting; however, all members receive a copy of the entire application prior to the meeting and are expected to be knowledgeable about it and to participate in the discussion and evaluation. In certain cases, the Executive Secretary may also send the application to an expert who is not a study section member for a written "outside opinion" that will provide additional information for the study section's consideration.

The criteria for reviewing research grant applications are set forth in the Public Health Service (PHS) Scientific Peer Review Regulations. They concern: (1) significance of the research problem; (2) experimental approach and methods; (3) the investigators' qualifications; (4) institutional and other resources available to support the research project; (5) budget; and (6) protection of subjects, human and/or animal, from research risks.

Once discussion of each of these areas has been completed, a formal vote is taken to recommend to the relevant Institute's national advisory council either approval or disapproval. In cases where two or more members vote against the majority, the number of votes for and against and a written minority opinion are included in the summary statement or written report of the review. In votes to approve, each member also privately rates the application on a scale from 1 (highest priority should be placed on funding the project) to 5 (lowest priority). After the meeting, the ratings are averaged and multiplied by 100 to eliminate decimals; the resultant priority scores range from 100 to 500. The recommendation may also be deferred by the study section in order to obtain additional information either by mail or a site visit.

As the last step in the initial review stage, a summary statement, or "pink sheet," is written by the Executive Secretary containing the major points of the discussion and action, including the assigned priority score. At this point, initial review is complete, DRG responsibility for the application is ended, and the summary statement is forwarded to the Institute for release to the applicant prior to council review and for council review.

Initial review results are presented to the Council by the Institute extramural program staff. The Council reviews applications in light of two basic considerations: the contribution that the proposed research would make to the advancement of the Institute's mission if it were performed, and the availability of Institute funds for extramural research. With respect to the former, program staff may indicate to the Council certain applications with "high program relevance" or "low program relevance," in both cases giving greater weight to program relevance in the decision to fund. In no case can applications that were disapproved in the initial review be approved for funding by the Council, though they may be returned for re-review if the review process had, in any way, been deficient. In FY 1984 less than 13% of reviewed applications were not approved.

The particular manner in which the two considerations are balanced—i.e., budget and program relevance—depends on the particular Institute. Generally, the Institutes rely heavily on the results of the initial review, ranking applications by priority score and awarding grants to those applications with the best priority scores, i.e., the ones closest to 100, down to the last one for which funds are available. The priority score that separates funded from unfunded applications has come to be known informally as the "payline." In recent years, a few Institutes have begun to percentile the priority scores of all applications assigned to their Institute during a 1-year period in order to standardize priority scores across review cycles and study sections. In FY 1984 approximately 37% of approved competing research project grant applications were awarded. Once the Council action has been taken, the review process is complete, and, for a successful application, the award process begins.

The ADAMHA Grant Review Process

[This essay was prepared with the assistance of Salvatore N. Cianci, Ph.D., Grants Referral and Review Officer for the Alcohol, Drug Abuse, and Mental Health Administration.]

Applications for extramural research grants and cooperative agreements submitted to programs in the Alcohol, Drug Abuse, and Mental Health Administration (ADAMHA) are mailed to the Division of Research Grants of the National Institutes of Health. Referral officers, representing components of the Public Health Service, assign applications to the appropriate program unit and Initial Review Group on the basis of the substantive area of the proposal and in accordance with clearly defined referral guidelines describing the parameters of research in each program unit. The referral officer for ADAMHA is responsible for assigning those proposals deemed appropriate for either the National Institute on Drug Abuse (NIDA), National Institute on Alcohol Abuse and Alcoholism (NIAAA), or National Institute of Mental Health (NIMH).

Initial Review Groups (IRGs) review and evaluate grant applications. IRGs are pre-selected panels of highly qualified scientists chosen for their expertise in a given field. Panel members are generally nonfederal employees. Within ADAMHA, each Institute has a designated component which is responsible for managing the review of grant applications. There are 17 Initial Review Groups assigned to the three ADAMHA institutes: the NIMH manages 12 IRGs, NIDA manages 3 IRGs, and NIAAA manages 2 IRGs.

IRGs range from 12 to 35 members; names and institutional affiliations may be found in the publication entitled *ADAMHA Public Advisory Committees: Roster of Members,* issued annually. The publication may be requested from the ADAMHA Committee Management Office (Room 13–103, Parklawn Building, 5600 Fishers Lane, Rockville, MD 20857). The standing committees are based on fairly broad areas of scientific endeavor.

Each grant application submitted is sent to all members of the committee and is assigned for intensive reading and critical review to two or three members whose expertise is most relevant to the proposal. One of the panel members is designated as the primary reviewer. Written opinions from highly specialized experts in a particular field are sometimes obtained for consideration in the review of an application. A project site visit may be arranged when information is needed which can only be gained firsthand during extended discussions with the investigator at the proposed site. Large, complex, high-budget projects are more likely to be visited. Site visits may occur for competing renewal applications as well as new ones.

The Initial Review Group provides an evaluation of the scientific merit of each application using the following general criteria: scientific, technical, or health significance and originality of the proposed research; appropriateness and adequacy of the experimental approach and methodology to be used; qualifications and experience of the principal investigator and staff in the area of the research; reasonable availability of resources; reasonableness of the proposed budget and duration; and in cases where an application involves activities which could have an adverse effect on humans, animals, or the environment, the adequacy of the proposed means for protecting against or minimizing such effects. In cases of applications submitted in response to a specialized program announcement, there may be additional criteria specified along with the general ones.

A review committee can make three types of recommendations: to approve (sometimes with modifications in the requested time or budget), to disapprove, or to defer for additional information. Approved applications are assigned a priority score which enters into the Institutes' decision process as to whether or not to make an award.

A summary of the IRG's discussion and final recommendation is prepared for each application by review staff. This document (referred to informally as the "pink sheet") is sent automatically to each applicant as soon as feasible after the IRG meeting. The summary statements provide a critique of the research proposal and have the recommendation of the IRG. It is not uncommon for applicants who did not receive awards to revise their applications, using the summary statement as guidance, and resubmit them for another review.

The summary statements are forwarded to the national advisory council of each Institute, which usually meets 6 to 8 weeks following the review. The national advisory council, composed of 12 individuals expert in science, education, and public affairs, and lay citizens with special interests in Institute missions, serves as an advisory body to the Institute Director. Council members are appointed by the Secretary of HHS and serve staggered terms of 4 years. The council reviews the recommendations of the IRGs, paying special attention to questions of general policy or program guidelines which may be involved. The deliberations of this group provide a second formal review of the applications previously evaluated by the IRGs. By law, the council's recommendation of approval is required before an Institute may award research grants or cooperative agreements. In those cases where recommendations of council differed from that of the IRG, the applicant is notified. The applicant may choose to revise and resubmit the application, or the application may be deferred for a re-review.

IRG and council recommendations, as well as monies available, Institute priorities, and current public health issues, are all considerations used by Institute staff in determining which projects will be funded.

For those applicants who feel their review was flawed for whatever reason, ADAMHA has instituted an appeals process. The appeals process is not intended to resolve purely scientific disputes between peer reviewers and the investigator, nor is it a mechanism for allowing investigators to submit information that should have been presented in the original proposals. But if serious shortcomings are found to have occurred in the review of an application, they will be rectified by either allowing a re-review by the same or another IRG, special consideration by the advisory council, or administrative action by the Institute director or staff. Investigators are encouraged to discuss their concerns with the appropriate program staff before requesting an examination under the appeals process.

Applications for research support are reviewed by ADAMHA Initial Review Groups and the National Advisory Councils three times a year. The entire research grant review process, from receipt of the application through the awarding of grant funds, may take nine months or longer. An exception is the ADAMHA Small Grants Program. Small grant applications are usually processed within a 6-month period and have no specific receipt date.

The usual schedule for regular research grant applications is shown in the following chart.

NIH and ADAMHA Application Receipt and Review Schedule*

Application Receipt Dates		Initial (Peer) Review	Advisory Council Review	Earliest Start Dates
Research Grants				
(New*)	(Renewal)			
Feb. 1	Mar. 1	May–June	Sept.– Oct.	Dec. 1
June 1	July 1	Oct.– Nov.	Jan.– Feb.	Apr. 1
Oct. 1	Nov. 1	Feb.–Mar.	May–June	July 1
Fellowships (NRSA)**				
Jan. 10		May	Aug.	Sept. 1
May 10		Sept.	Dec.	Jan. 1
Sept. 10		Jan.	Apr.	May 1

These are the regular deadlines and review schedules used for grant applications. For special initiatives, different receipt dates and a somewhat shorter review cycle may be involved.

*Also all new and competing Program Project and Center Grants.

**Fellowship applications are reviewed by the Institute Training Boards rather than Institute Advisory Councils.

Chapter 5

Federal Sources of Research Support

Contents

DEPARTMENT OF AGRICULTURE

Cooperative State Research Service

John Patrick Jordan, Administrator
304-A Administration Building
14th Street and Independence Avenue, SW
Washington, DC 20250
(202/447–4423)

The Cooperative State Research Service (CSRS) administers several federal formula funding programs to more than 100 state institutions. Formula funds are appropriations approved by Congress and allocated to eligible institutions by statutory formula or by an administratively determined formula approved by the Secretary of Agriculture. These formula funds help maintain the basic and applied research programs of state research units.

CSRS supports research in the food and agricultural sciences. It includes studies in agricultural economics and rural sociology and, to a lesser extent, communications, political science, psychology, history, geography, and regional science. Since CSRS funds are awarded directly to state land-grant institutions, investigators must be affiliated with these institutions to receive funding. A large proportion of funds are earmarked for special projects.

CSRS has five principal funding mechanisms. Of interest to social and behavioral scientists are:

1) Hatch Act funding (the largest component of CSRS, these funds support research for agriculture, forestry, and rural life generally; 25% of funds are set aside for the Regional Research program, supporting topics such as interstate marketing and transportation);

2) Special Grants (funds are awarded either competitively or designated by appropriations language; some funds go to economics research);

3) Competitive Research Grants (a competitive, peer-reviewed awards process not limited to land-grant institutions; most funds are for biotechnology research);

4) Evans-Allen funds (funds are restricted to historically Black land-grant institutions; priority research areas include human nutrition, small farm production, human resources, energy, and transportation).

Most CSRS awards are grants to state land-grant institutions. The Competitive Research Grants are administered by the CSRS Office of Grants Program Systems.

Economic Research Service

Kenneth L. Deavers (Human and Community Resources, 202/786–1530)
T. Kelley White (International Agricultural Trade, 202/786–1700)
Kenneth C. Clayton (Production Agricultural Economics, 202/786–1876)
John A. Miranowski (Natural Resource Economics, 202/786–1455)
1301 New York Avenue, NW
Washington, DC 20005–4788

The Economic Research Service (ERS) provides economic and other social science information to aid public policy officials and program managers in developing and administering agricultural and rural development policies and programs and to aid the public at large in making decisions.

The Service carries on an active program of cooperative research with universities and other research organizations throughout the nation. Essential to such projects is that they be developed and conducted jointly by ERS and the university (or other organization) staff. Current projects are in a broad range of disciplines, but tend to concentrate in economics, sociology, and demography. Four main substantive areas are stressed in the ERS program: production agricultural economics, international agricultural trade, community and human resource development, and natural resource economics.

The purpose of the cooperative agreements program is to (1) foster collegial relationships between ERS and other researchers, (2) extend the subject matter and geographic breadth of the ERS program, (3) benefit from research expertise and special knowledge of social scientists working in strategic locations, and (4) complement ERS national-level analyses with in-depth research on issues of particular socioeconomic environments.

Agreements are either initiated by unsolicited proposals from researchers outside of ERS, or by direct solicitation of proposals from researchers who have particular capabilities or who are located in areas of special interest to the Service. Competitive solicitation of proposals is also used. In all cases, cooperative research agreements are only initiated when they are judged to have a high probability of contributing materially to the ongoing or emerging ERS research agenda. This agenda is identified through ERS's annual program planning activities.

Food and Nutrition Service

OFFICE OF ANALYSIS AND EVALUATION

Michael Wargo, Director, Program Evaluation Staff (703/756–3117)
Christy Schmidt, Director, Analysis Staff (703/756–3133)
1017 Park Center Building
3101 Park Center Drive
Alexandria, VA 22302

Program: The function of the Office of Analysis and Evaluation (OAE) is to provide unbiased analysis and evaluation information to aid the Food and Nutrition Service (FNS) in making decisions regarding policy, legislative, budgetary, regulatory, and program management processes. The OAE is primarily concerned with three programs administered by the FNS: child nutrition programs; the Women, Infants, and Children (WIC) supplemental food program; and food stamps. Although OAE does not support basic research in the social sciences, it does award contracts for program evaluations and some applied multidisciplinary research.

OAE comprises two functional divisions: the Analysis Staff and the Program Evaluation Staff. The Analysis Staff are largely concerned with short-term policy analyses performed primarily in-house. The Analysis Staff review legislative and regulatory reports and assess the impact of budgetary and congressional initiatives. The Program Evaluation Staff assess the effectiveness and efficiency of FNS food programs and provide technical assistance to other FNS staff. The current emphasis is on the operation and management of federal food programs and methods of detecting waste, fraud, and abuse, rather than the analysis of their nutritional impact on participants.

General research priorities for the food stamp program are announced annually in the *Federal Register* as required by Congress. Requests for applications (RFAs) for specific projects appear in the *Commerce Business Daily.* Although unsolicited proposals are accepted and reviewed, they seldom receive funding.

Few academic researchers choose to compete for OAE funds. OAE contracts require that principal investigators spend at least 50% of their time on the project. Most projects require a large field staff and the ability to collect and analyze extensive data sets. Traditionally, most OAE contractors are large research and development firms familiar with FNS programs. Both profit and nonprofit enterprises are eligible for OAE contracts.

Budget: The FY 1985 budget for OAE was $10.6 million, with an increase to $14.0 million anticipated for FY 1986.

Application/Review Process: Applications in response to an RFA are reviewed by a panel composed of OAE staff, technical experts, and other federal staff. A Board of Awards (contracting officers and other USDA staff) reviews applications and recommendations for procedural compliance.

Funding Mechanisms: Most OAE awards are contracts. Some cooperative agreements are made with other agencies. Grant awards are possible but rare. Contracts average between $1 million and $2 million.

Examples of Funded Research:
1) "Evaluation of State Efforts to Investigate and Prosecute Food Stamp Fraud."
2) "Evaluation of the Child Care Food Program."
3) "Report on the Feasibility of an Electronic Benefit Transfer System for the Food Stamp Program."
4) "An Assessment of Nutrition Assistance Programs Including the Procedures Required to Reinstate Direct Commodity Distribution to Needy Households."
5) "Multiple Benefits and Income Adequacy for Food Stamp Participant and Nonparticipant Households."

DEPARTMENT OF COMMERCE

Economic Development Administration

The Economic Development Administration (EDA) provides assistance through grants and loans to economically distressed areas for economic development planning purposes. EDA was created in 1965 to generate new jobs, to protect existing jobs in distressed areas, and to foster the development of economic programs on the state and local level.

RESEARCH AND EVALUATION DIVISION

David H. Geddes, Chief
Room 7865
Main Commerce Building
Washington, DC 20230
(202/377–4085)

Program: EDA supports research and evaluation projects in three areas: (1) the causes and impacts of economic dislocation (e.g., the causes of unemployment, underemployment, underdevelopment, chronic depression); (2) the formulation and implementation of national, state, and local economic development programs; and (3) the evaluation of approaches and techniques employed to alleviate economic distress. Individuals as well as universities and nonprofit and profit-making organizations are eligible for project grants.

Currently, priority consideration is given to several broad topics, including regional and local growth, employment and unemployment, rural and other nonmetropolitan economic development, industrial location, private sector participation, state and local government efforts, migration, export development, minority business development and minority employment, productivity and technology, and income and poverty.

Most EDA research funds are awarded to economists, although agency priorities have broad applicability for the social sciences.

Budget: The budget for extramural research and evaluation projects in FY 1985 was approximately $2 million, a level which has remained nearly constant over the past few years.

Application/Review Process: Application procedures and deadlines are published in the *Federal Register* each fall. Applicants must first submit a brief concept paper which includes a description of the project and the workplan, funding sought, vita, and general corporate capability data. Concept papers are reviewed by EDA staff who then select applicants to submit formal proposals. Most applicants invited to submit formal proposals do receive funding. Awards are subject to approval by the Assistant Secretary for Economic Development and Commerce's Financial Assistance Review Board. In 1985, 187 applications were reviewed, of which 20 were funded.

Funding Mechanisms: EDA awards primarily grants. Projects generally do not exceed 15 months in duration. In FY 1985 grants ranged from $25,000 to $170,000, with an average grant size of $100,000. EDA will provide up to 100% of the proposed project costs.

Examples of Funded Research:
1) "Banking and Small Business."
2) "Congruencies and Conflict in Regional Industrial Policy."
3) "Coping with the Loss of a Major Employer."
4) "Corporations in the Community."
5) "A Handbook for Local Export Promotion Programs."
6) "Dimensions of Urban Economic Distress."
7) "Public Works Investment in the U.S."

Minority Business Development Agency

The Minority Business Development Agency (MBDA) is the only federal agency designed specifically to assist in the creation and expansion of businesses owned by American minorities. A business must be at least 51% owned, controlled, and operated by a member of an economically and socially disadvantaged group (including Blacks, Hispanics, Native Americans, Asian-Pacific Americans, and Asian-Indian Americans) to be eligible for assistance. Through the MBDA, minorities receive assistance in obtaining financing; in identifying new business opportunities; and in marketing, management, and technical areas. Established by Presidential Order in 1969, the MBDA provides all services through a consortium of 100 business centers around the United States. The research program, however, is administered by the Office of Advocacy, Research, and Information in Washington, DC.

OFFICE OF ADVOCACY, RESEARCH, AND INFORMATION

Richard Stevens, Chief, Research Division
Room 5701
Main Commerce Building
Washington, DC 20230
(202/377–4671)

Program: The research program of the MBDA, begun in 1981, emphasizes analyses and studies which can be used to improve national minority business development policies and programs. Projects covering business formation, expansion, and failure, or the potential contribution of minority-owned firms to socioeconomic development are encouraged. Specific topics funded in 1985 included equity capital formation and use, governmental regulatory barriers to minority business development, and attitudes of minority youth toward entrepreneurship.

Although past projects have concentrated on economic and business development, an attempt is being made to strengthen the link between economics and sociology through the research program. Socioeconomic analysis of not only specific business problems but also investigation of the impact of those problems on the community (e.g., projects exploring the sociological, demographic, institutional, and other variables affecting minority business development) are encouraged.

Budget: In FY 1985 approximately $600,000 was available for extramural projects. The FY 1986 budget was projected to remain about the same.

Application/Review Process: The annual competition for contracts is generally announced in the *Commerce Business Daily* in December. Proposals are judged on their technical merit, policy relevance, and cost-effectiveness. A peer panel consisting of federal and nonfederal members reviews and ranks proposals. MBDA staff conduct a management review and make recommendations for funding to the director of the MBDA. These recommendations are then sent to the procurement office for review. Approximately 60 proposals are received per year, with an average of 6 funded.

The MBDA also has several databases useful for minority business and entrepreneurship research and generally makes them available to social scientists at little or no cost.

Funding Mechanisms: Research support from the MBDA is available to individuals, businesses, colleges and universities, and nonprofit and other organizations. All support is through contracts. The average amount of a contract is $75,000, with a limit of $250,000. Most contracts are for one year, although extensions are possible.

Examples of Funded Research:

1)   "Minority and Non-Minority Business Formation and Participation: Geographic Differences in Location and Community Environment" (awarded $92,965 in FY 1983).

2)   "Development of a Conceptual Framework for Minority Business Enterprise" (awarded $144,382 in FY 1983).

3)   "Demographic and Socio-Economic Characteristics Related to Minority Entrepreneurship" (awarded $108,991 in FY 1984).

4)   "Analysis of Formation and Failure Rates by Industry" (awarded $78,650 in FY 1984).

National Bureau of Standards

CENTER FOR FIRE RESEARCH

Robert Levine, Chief, Office of Fire Research Resources
Room A255, Building 224
Gaithersburg, MD 20899
(301/921–3845)

Program: The Center for Fire Research conducts both basic and applied research aimed at increasing knowledge of fire and at developing risk models that will reduce losses and costs due to fire. Research on data and tools for fire risk evaluation and on decision-making for the ultimate user are also supported by this program.

The extramural fire research program focuses on eight areas: (1) exploratory fire research; (2) fire toxicology; (3) furnishings flammability; (4) fire performance and validation; (5) smoke hazard calculation; (6) fire growth and extinction; (7) compartment fire models; and (8) fire safety performance. Of most interest to behavioral and social scientists is the fire safety performance division, in which research is supported on the behavior of persons at risk in fires and ways to calculate how rapidly persons can evacuate structures or otherwise find refuge.

Budget: In FY 1985 the budget of the Office of Fire Research Resources was $1.85 million; the budget was expected to remain approximately the same in FY 1986. Twenty-five grants were awarded in FY 1985, two of which were in the behavioral and social sciences.

Application/Review Process: All proposals are unsolicited, and prospective applicants are encouraged to discuss research topics with the program staff before submission. Once received, proposals are assigned to the relevant division leader. Peer reviewers evaluate the technical merit of proposals and its relevance to agency priorities. The division leader makes funding recommendations to the director of the Center for Fire Research.

Funding Mechanisms: Most funds are awarded to universities, though private and nonprofit organizations are eligible as well. All awards are grants.

Examples of Funded Research:

1) "Network Models of Building Evaluation."

2) "A Computerized Model for the Simulation of General Fire Emergency Evacuations."

3) "Continuation of Decision Analysis Studies in Fire Hazard Analysis."

4) "Economic Analysis of Residential Automatic Sprinkler Systems."

National Oceanic and Atmospheric Administration

The National Oceanic and Atmospheric Administration (NOAA) was established in 1970 to coordinate the federal civil programs related to the ocean and the atmosphere. Two concurrent trends in national science policy directed NOAA's development: increased attention to the planned development of oceanic resources and recognition that the oceans and atmosphere are interacting parts of the total environmental system. An important part of NOAA's mission relates to providing a basic understanding of the marine environment and developing information designed to produce rational, efficient, and equitable utilization, conservation, and development of the nation's oceanic and coastal resources.

NATIONAL SEA GRANT PROGRAM

Ned A. Ostenso, Director
6010 Executive Boulevard
Rockville, MD 20852
(301/443–8923)

Program: The National Sea Grant Program was created to accelerate national development of marine resources, including their conservation, proper management, and maximum social and economic utilization. Through this program, grants are made primarily to universities and other institutions of higher education for research, education, and extension activities. Most funds are awarded through the National Sea Grant College Program. Currently 29 Sea Grant Programs covering all coastal and Great Lakes states receive support.

The Sea Grant Program encourages broad participation of social scientists through the Marine Economics Program and the Marine Policy and Social Sciences Programs. Among the disciplines traditionally supported are cultural anthropology, economics, history, geography, political science, and sociology. Interdisciplinary scholarship with other disciplines such as the natural sciences, business, engineering, and law is encouraged. Research topics of interest include commercial and sports fisheries, aquaculture, marine recreation and coastal tourism, coastal zone resource use, ocean mineral and energy development, marine transportation, environmental risk assessment, and marine policy.

Research focusing on recreational and commercial fisheries and aquaculture accounted for over half of the Marine Economics Program in FY 1985. Increased attention is being given to coastal recreation development, marine transportation, and exploitation of seabed minerals. Future directions for research in marine economics include design of more efficient fisheries management systems, study of the economic performance of the marine industries, and expanding the base of economic information about the Exclusive Economic Zone (EEZ).

Priority topics for the Marine Policy and Social Science Program are social and institutional concerns in the development of EEZ, ocean disposal, development and use of bioengineered organisms, and social and culture issues in the development of aquaculture.

The Sea Grant Program recently instituted a Visiting Scholar Program. To be eligible for the program one must be a tenured professor (able to take sabbatical) and have had prior involvement with the Sea Grant Program. Prospective applicants should contact the director of a participating Sea Grant college in their area for more information.

Budget: The FY 1985 budget for the Sea Grant Program was approximately $39 million. Of that amount, about $1.3 million went to research in marine economics and another $1.2 million to other social science and marine policy research.

Application/Review Process: All proposals are unsolicited. Prospective applicants are encouraged to make their proposal through a participating Sea Grant College (a list of institutions may be obtained from the Sea Grant office) although they may apply directly to NOAA. Two thirds of the funds for a proposed project may come from the Sea Grant Program; the remaining one third must come from nonfederal sources.

Because most proposals are submitted to a participating Sea Grant institution (specific submission deadlines vary with institutions) the initial review is conducted by that institution. Sea Grant staff evaluate proposals using peer reviews and on-site visits. Final funding decisions are made within 90 to 180 days of receipt of proposals. Approximately 700 applications were received in FY 1985, of which 45 were funded.

Funding Mechanisms: This program awards grants to universities and institutes, laboratories, private or public organizations, state governments, and individuals. There are no dollar limits on awards, with $35,000 being the average award. Most grants are one to three years in duration. Individuals selected for the Visiting Scholar Program are provided a half-time salary for a period of up to 12 months.

Examples of Funded Research:
1) "Social and Economic Feasibility of Alternative Legal Frameworks for Developing Aquaculture" (awarded $29,541 in FY 1984).

2) "Job Satisfaction and Fishing: A Comparative Study" (awarded $24,400 in FY 1985).

3) "Population Policies in California's Coastal Zone" (awarded $14,625 in FY 1984).

4) "Economic and Legal/Political Implications of Mineral Resource Potential in the U.S. Exclusive Economic Zone" (awarded $57,200 in FY 1985).

5) "Biological Risks and Economic Consequences of Alternative Management Strategies" (awarded $116,700 in FY 1985).

6) "Congress and the Oceans: Change and Continuity, 1959–1984" (awarded $25,200 in FY 1985.

7) "The Role of Community-Level Resource Management Systems in Fisheries Conflicts" (awarded $35,700 in FY 1985).

8) "User Benefits and Economic Impacts of Artificial Reefs" (awarded $34,400 in FY 1985).

9) "Evaluating Public Policy Options for Increasing Production of Market Oysters" (awarded $22,300 in FY 1985).

NATIONAL MARINE FISHERIES SERVICE

Phyllis S. Bentz, Program Manager, Industry Development Program
Page Building 2, Room 325
3300 Whitehaven Street, NW
Washington, DC 20235
(202/634-7451)

Program: The National Marine Fisheries Services (NMFS) is concerned with the development and strengthening of the U.S. fishing industry and with increasing the supply of fish and fish products available to consumers. Under the Saltonstall-Kennedy Act of 1954, an amount equal to 30% of the gross receipts collected under the customs laws from duties on fishery products are available to the Commerce Department. At least 60% of these funds are set aside for research and development grants relating to commercial and recreational fishing in the United States, including, but not limited to, harvesting, processing, and marketing.

Each year NMFS publishes an announcement of its funding priorities in the *Federal Register.* Through an evaluation of fishing industry needs, regional directors and industry representatives formulate yearly priorities; separate priorities are established for national projects and the five regional divisions. Areas of interest to NMFS have included (1) domestic export and market promotion, (2) consumer education, (3) promotion of marine recreational fishing, (4) economic and market research, (5) vessel safety and insurance, (6) product development, and (7) product quality and safety research. Issues that have national significance are administered by the Washington office of NMFS. Projects related to specific geographic areas are administered by one of the five regional offices. NMFS research is most relevant to economics, marketing, and evaluation.

Budget: In FY 1985 approximately $9 million was available for extramural research.

Application/Review Process: Research announcements and application procedures are published in the *Federal Register* early in the calendar year. Proposal deadlines are 60 to 90 days after the announcement. The Washington office also maintains a mailing list of interested researchers. Proposals with national implications should be sent to the Washington office; those proposals relevant to a specific region should be sent directly to the regional office involved.

The initial technical review of proposals is conducted by a panel of federal and nonfederal individuals. A second panel of industry representatives evaluate the proposals to determine industrial significance. Based on technical and industry reviews, regional directors make funding recommendations to the administrator of NMFS, who makes the final decision. Proposals are subject to review and approval by the Commerce's Financial Assistance Review Board (FARB).

In FY 1985, 229 proposals were submitted, of which 56 were funded. Approximately one sixth of the FY 1984 budget was allocated to social science research, with most funds going to technical projects.

Funding Mechanisms: Both individuals and organizations may apply for NMFS funding. Specific eligibility requirements are detailed in the solicitation. Most awards are made through cooperative agreements (about 75%); the balance are grants. NMFS provides at least 50%, but not more than 80%, of the total costs of a project.

The NMFS also hires students for limited numbers of positions in the marine biology, economics, international affairs, and social science disciplines. The hiring is through the Summer Recruitment Program and the Student Recruitment Program. An Intergovernmental Personnel Assignment program is also administered by NMFS. For more information on these programs contact the NMFS Personnel Office (Room 318, 11420 Rockville Pike, Rockville, MD 20852).

Examples of Funded Research:
1)   "Marine Recreational Fishing Industry and Opportunities for Development" (awarded $133,000 in FY 1982).

2)   "Analysis of Seafood Consumption Patterns" (awarded $63,800 in FY 1982).

3) "Investing in the Fishing Industry: An Economic Prospectus for the Mid-Atlantic Region" (awarded $100,000 in FY 1983).

4) "The Spanish Market for Squid" (awarded $11,870 in FY 1983).

5) "Vessel Safety/Accident Reduction" (awarded $45,500 in FY 1984).

NATIONAL MARINE POLLUTION PROGRAM

Andrew Robertson, Director
610 Rockwall Building
11400 Rockville Pike
Rockville, MD 20852
(301/443–8823)

Program: The National Marine Pollution Program Office was established by NOAA to provide a focal point for coordinating federal efforts in marine pollution. A number of offices within the National Ocean Service of NOAA are directly involved in marine pollution research. They include the Ocean Use Impact Assessment Program, the Strategic Assessment Program, and the Coastal and Estuarine Assessment Program. Because of the diversity and number of research efforts, a comprehensive outline of all marine pollution programs is not available. Support is available through the various programs for social and behavioral research in such areas as demography, risk assessment, computer modeling, and development of socioeconomic data. Information requests should be directed to the National Marine Pollution Program Office in Washington.

Budget: The budget for the National Marine Pollution Program Office was $1.25 million in FY 1985. Figures are not available on the amount allocated to research in the social and behavioral sciences.

Application/Review Process: Proposals are unsolicited, and prospective applicants are strongly encouraged to contact the Marine Pollution Program Office concerning their particular interests.
    Each program within the National Ocean Service conducts its own review of proposals. All proposals are reviewed competitively.

Funding Mechanisms: Individuals, businesses, colleges and universities, and nonprofit and other organizations are eligible to receive research support. Funding is through both grants and contracts.

Examples of Funded Research:

1) "Estimation of Historic Sport Fishing Effort and Catch" (awarded $26,500 in FY 1983).

2) "The Development of Strategies for Managing the Social, Economic, and Environmental Impacts of Ocean Dumping in a Region" (awarded $76,000 in FY 1983).

3) "Demographic Methods for the Prediction of Toxic Substance Effects" (awarded $53,400 in FY 1984).

4) "Historical Assessment of Pollution Impacts on Fish and Shellfish in the Hudson-Raritan Estuary" (awarded $105,600 in FY 1984).

DEPARTMENT OF DEFENSE

The Department of Defense (DOD) research program includes basic research, exploratory development, advanced development, and operations systems development. Most social and behavioral science research is conducted in the first two categories at the Office of the Chief of Naval Research, the Army Institute for the Behavioral and Social Sciences, and the Air Force Office of Scientific Research. Some exploratory development, particularly of interest to behavioral scientists, is conducted at the technical laboratories supported by the Navy and the Air Force. Policy research of interest to political scientists, economists, sociologists, and others is supported by the Office of the Undersecretary for Policy. Although much of DOD's research and development is mission-related, unsolicited proposals are accepted by most of the offices described below. For social and behavioral scientists interested in DOD-sponsored research it is important to make informal contacts with program directors first. Another avenue of garnering support for research is to make contact with major contractors that often subcontract portions of their research contracts.

Office of the Undersecretary of Defense for Policy

POLICY RESEARCH PROGRAM

John P. Merrill, Director
Room 1E439
The Pentagon
Washington, DC 20301–2000
(202/697–6301 or 202/694–5249)

Program: The Policy Research Program provides support for the Office of the Assistant Secretary for International Security Affairs and 21 other offices within the Department of Defense. Of interest are political, social, and economic research related to defense matters. Program emphasis is on Soviet policies and perceptions, strategic theory, regional issues, and the integration of defense planning with other aspects of national security policy, including arms control.

Budget: The budget for FY 1985 was approximately $20 million, of which about one third went to unsolicited proposals.

Application/Review Process: Unsolicited proposals are welcome. Program staff encourage prospective applicants to submit brief concept papers explaining the study. Proposals are circulated to relevant offices within DOD for review. Depending on the nature of the study, security clearance may be necessary.

Funding Mechanisms: All research is funded by contract.

Examples of Funded Research:
1) "Strategic Analysis Ballistic Missile Defense" (awarded $30,000).

2) "Soviet Policies in the Asia-Pacific Region" (awarded $57,000).

3) "Cost Model for the Space Transportation System" (awarded $120,000).

4) "Impact of U.S. Policies on Terrorist Behavior" (awarded $99,000).

5) "Automated System for Assessing the Impact of Technology Transfer on Western Security" (awarded $350,000).

Secretary of the Air Force

AIR FORCE OFFICE OF SCIENTIFIC RESEARCH

The Air Force Office of Scientific Research (AFOSR) provides funding for basic research in several areas, including neuroscience, experimental psychology, and toxicology.

Life Sciences Directorate

R. K. Dismukes, Director
AFOSR/XOT
Bolling Air Force Base
Washington, DC 20332
(202/767–4278)

Programs in the Life Sciences Directorate are focused on basic research that will ultimately lead to a better understanding of the nature of skilled human performance, better matching of equipment to human characteristics, and better ways to protect Air Force personnel. These programs emphasize research on fundamental mechanisms underlying biological and behavioral functions, rather than applied studies.

Application/Review Process: Scientists are encouraged to contact the appropriate AFOSR program manager to determine whether their research interests match the needs of a particular program before submitting a formal proposal. Interdisciplinary research approaches are particularly welcome. Proposals are evaluated by ad hoc peer review panels. Final funding decisions are made by the program manager.

Funding Mechanisms: Both grants and contracts are used to fund investigator-initiated proposals.

VISION RESEARCH PROGRAM

John Tangney, Program Manager
AFOSR/XOT
Bolling Air Force Base
Washington, DC 20332
(202/767–5021)

Program:　The Vision Research Program primarily supports psychophysical research on normal human adults. Other approaches may be funded if the primary objective of the research could lead to the discovery and quantitative modeling of those featural processing mechanisms that underlie visual recognition. Multidisciplinary projects are encouraged, particularly if research results can be clearly linked to human behavioral data. In this regard, collaboration between psychophysicists and scientists of other disciplines is especially valuable.

The program currently supports research on a variety of topics related to featural processing, including mechanisms of contrast, detection and discrimination, motion, eye movement, color, and stereopsis. Other mechanisms that can be shown to influence recognition would be considered.

Budget:　Approximately $2.5 million will be available for this program in FY 1986.

Application/Review Process:　See the general discussion of the Air Force Office of Scientific Research above.

Funding Mechanisms:　See the general discussion of the Air Force Office of Scientific Research above.

Examples of Funded Research:
1) "Human Information Processing of Targets and Real-World Scenes."

2) "The Interaction of Sensory and Perceptual Variables."

3) "Visual Representations of Texture."

AUDITION PROGRAM

John F. Tangney, Program Manager
AFOSR/XOT
Bolling Air Force Base
Washington, DC 20332
(202/767–5021)

Program:　The Audition Program was recently instituted to support psychophysical research on the perception of complex, non-speech sounds in normal human adults. Other approaches, including electrophysiological studies and mathematical modeling of sensory processing, are welcome if results can be clearly linked to human behavioral data. Topics currently supported include research on those mechanisms that underlie recognition, pitch, localization, and speech. Other topics on featural processing mechanisms and sensory processing could be considered.

Budget: The FY 1986 budget for this program is approximately $1.5 million.

Application/Review Process: See the general discussion of the Air Force Office of Scientific Research above.

Funding Mechanisms: See the general discussion of the Air Force Office of Scientific Research above.

Examples of Funded Research:
1)   "Levels of Analysis of Complex Auditory Stimuli."
2)   "Complex Auditory Signals."
3)   "Mechanisms Mediating the Perceptions of Complex Acoustic Patterns."

COGNITIVE SCIENCE PROGRAM

Irving Biederman and Alfred R. Fregly, Program Managers
AFOSR/XOT
Bolling Air Force Base
Washington, DC 20332
(202/767–5021)

Program: A new program to support basic research in cognitive science will start in late 1986. This program will support basic theoretical and experimental work on human cognitive processing, including areas such as representation and utilization of perceptual knowledge, attention, memory representation, and judgment. Biological approaches that advance research on these topics will also be considered. This program will also provide funding for researchers for collaborative work with scientists at the Air Force Human Resources Laboratory, located at Brooks Air Force Base, Texas, where a large test facility has been built for research on human learning abilities.

Budget: Approximately $1.5 million will be available for this program in FY 1987.

Application/Review Process: See the general discussion of the Air Force Office of Scientific Research above.

Funding Mechanisms: See the general discussion of the Air Force Office of Scientific Research above.

Examples of Funded Research: (not applicable)

AIR FORCE HUMAN RESOURCES LABORATORY

Hope Galan, Unsolicited Proposals Coordinator
Brooks Air Force Base, TX 78235–5601
(512/536–3876)

The Air Force Human Resources Laboratory (AFHRL) is charged with planning and executing the Air Force exploratory and advanced development programs for research projects related to manpower and personnel, manned aircraft simulation, logistics, and technical training. Although managed by Brooks Air Force Base in Texas, intramural research is actually conducted in four divisions located at Air Force bases around the country: (1) Logistics and Human Factors Division, (2) Manpower and Personnel Division, (3) Operations Training Division, and (4) Training Systems Division. Contracts awarded for extramural research complement the intramural programs of the four divisions.

Budget: Approximately $39 million is available in FY 1986 for "obtaining the expertise and capabilities of industry and universities in the development of new technologies for personnel selection, training and universities." Figures on exactly how much of this money goes to unsolicited contracts for basic and applied research are not available.

Application/Review Process: Proposals and pre-proposals (short concept papers) should be submitted to the unsolicited proposal coordinator at Brooks Air Force Base. Program officers review proposals to determine the appropriate division for the project. The formal technical and scientific review is conducted by the division staffs, and funding recommendations are then made to central headquarters.

Funding Mechanisms: All extramural research is funded through contracts.

LOGISTICS AND HUMAN FACTORS DIVISION

Dr. William B. Askren, Acting Technical Director
Wright-Patterson Air Force Base, OH 45433–6503
(513/255–6797)

Program: This division supports research and development aimed at improving the performance of non-flying crews, groups, teams, and units; developing technology to improve maintenance capability for deployed combat operations; and developing new analysis techniques and automating logistics models and databases for the support of new systems.

Budget: See the general discussion of the Air Force Human Resources Laboratory above.

Application/Review Process: See the general discussion of the Air Force Human Resources Laboratory above.

Funding Mechanisms: All extramural research is funded through contracts.

MANPOWER AND PERSONNEL DIVISION

Nancy Guinn, Division Chief
Brooks Air Force Base, TX 78235
(512/536–2244)

Program: This division is concerned with developing management tools, procedures, and associated technologies to improve procurement, selection, classification, utilization, productivity, and retention of Air Force personnel. Developing and refining personnel management techniques is another focus for this division. Also of interest are computer-based models for skill requirement projections, retention analyses, training decisions, and assignment/reassignment decisions.

Budget: See the general discussion of the Air Force Human Resources Laboratory above.

Application/Review Process: See the general discussion of the Air Force Human Resources Laboratory above.

Funding Mechanisms: All extramural research is funded through contracts.

OPERATIONS TRAINING DIVISION

Milton Wood, Technical Director
HRL-OTP, Building 558
Williams Air Force Base, AZ 85240–6457
(602/988–6561)

Program: This division focuses on assessing the effectiveness of both current and future approaches to aircrew training. The development of flight simulators to provide greater training capability is also a priority research area.

Budget: See the general discussion of the Air Force Human Resources Laboratory above.

Application/Review Process: See the general discussion of the Air Force Human Resources Laboratory above.

Funding Mechanisms: All extramural research is funded through contracts.

TRAINING SYSTEMS DIVISION

Joseph Yasutake, Technical Advisor
Lowry Air Force Base, CO 80230
(303/370–4387)

Program: This division develops improved methods and strategies for initial skills development and enhanced job performance by upgrading individual and unit training. Specifically, improved training methods, instructional and learning strategies, and training design and evaluation techniques are developed and demonstrated. In addition, research on computer-based training and job-aiding systems is supported.

Budget: See the general discussion of the Air Force Human Resources Laboratory above.

Application/Review Process: See the general discussion of the Air Force Human Resources Laboratory above.

Funding Mechanisms: All extramural research is funded through contracts.

Secretary of the Army

ARMY RESEARCH INSTITUTE FOR THE BEHAVIORAL AND SOCIAL SCIENCES

The Army Research Institute for the Behavioral and Social Sciences (ARI) is the Army's focal point for research and development efforts in these fields. The Institute is problem- and product-oriented, responding to and working with agencies and commands throughout the Army. The core program is divided into three major areas: manpower and personnel research, systems research, and training research. Three specialized laboratories associated with each technical area administer the research program. The Office of Basic Research conducts an extramural program that cuts across all three areas.

OFFICE OF BASIC RESEARCH

Milt Katz, Director
5001 Eisenhower Avenue
Alexandria, VA 22333
(202/274–8641)

Program: The purpose of the ARI basic research program is to develop the behavioral science base for future applied research to improve the effectiveness of Army systems and soldiers. ARI gives priority support to proposals in defined critical areas. They are:

1) planning, problem solving, and decision-making (how knowledge is used; the effects of stress on cognitive processes; the impact of incomplete and dynamic information; the process of developing expertise, including both knowledge and strategies; establishing foundations for the design of decision heuristics);

2) unit performance (models of goal-directed unit performance as foundations for developing training, assessment, and evaluation methods; instructional theory to train teams for coordinated action; metacognition theories; the role of computers, particularly simulations, intelligent tutoring systems, and interactive videos);

3) skill-building technologies (knowledge acquisition in complex technical domains and the use of that knowledge to operate, maintain, and troubleshoot complex systems; the role of contextual factors in learning and performance; research on knowledge acquisition, theories of tasks and explanations, tutoring

principles, and student strategy models; increasing cognitive flexibility and creativity in problem-solving situations; mental workload enhancement, particularly under stress and time pressures);

4) designing systems for people (the design of systems to provide personnel information that integrates skills and capabilities and quantitative and qualitative indicators of pertinence, acceptability, and utility of information delivered).

Budget: Approximately $5 million will be available for extramural research in FY 1986. The majority of FY 1986 funds, however, are committed for support of continuing research projects.

Application/Review Process: Unsolicited proposals are no longer welcome at ARI. In accordance with the April 1985 revision of the Federal Acquisition Regulation, ARI now issues a basic research announcement in the *Commerce Business Daily* two or more times annually. This announcement describes ARI's mission and current research needs and calls for brief concept papers or preliminary proposals in the stated areas of interest. In response to requests, ARI supplies a current broad agency announcement which gives further program information and directions for submitting informal and formal proposals. Based on internal review, offerors may be encouraged to submit formal proposals. Planning should allow for a minimum of 6 to 9 months from receipt of formal proposals to execution of contract.

Funding Mechanisms: Contracts are used for the support of all basic research, with the possible exception of grants for the support of conferences and symposia. Contracts may be written to cover periods of 1 to 5 years. The average size of contract awards is $80,000 per year.

Examples of Funded Research:
1) "Components of Verbal Intelligence."
2) "Dynamic Personnel Job Management Modeling."
3) "Macroprocesses and Adaptive Instruction."
4) "Tests of the Stabilization-Error Theory of Retention."
5) "Methodology for Assessing Organization of Information."
6) "Aiding the Human Decision Maker Through Knowledge Based Sciences."
7) "The Assessment of Knowledge: Theory and Algorithms."
8) "Semi-Automatic Synthesis and Refinement of Knowledge."

Secretary of the Navy

OFFICE OF NAVAL RESEARCH

The Office of Naval Research (ONR) supports basic and applied research and exploratory developmental projects which offer the potential for advancement and improvement of naval operations. ONR carries out its research through intramural laboratories and through research contracts to universities, private industry, and nonprofit organizations.

Contract Research Program

The ONR Contract Research Program supports primarily basic research projects. Most research contracts are awarded for unsolicited proposals. A comprehensive statement of research needs is published annually in the *Commerce Business Daily*. ONR scientific officers also develop "Accelerated Research Initiatives" that specify areas of research that will receive special priority, usually for a five-year period. In addition, ONR publishes a *Selected Research Opportunities* (SRO) bulletin that designates specific fundamental research areas of importance to the Navy to encourage applications from multidisciplinary university research teams.

The ONR Young Investigators Program offers young faculty members stipends of no less than $50,000 per year for up to 3 years to support their research. Twelve awards are made annually to U.S. citizens who hold tenure-track positions and who received their graduate degrees on or after January 1980. Individuals wishing to apply for a Young Investigators award should submit a research proposal and a supporting letter from their university directly to the ONR program most relevant to the proposed project.

Life Sciences Programs Directorate

PSYCHOLOGICAL SCIENCES DIVISION

ENGINEERING PSYCHOLOGY PROGRAM

Willard S. Vaughan, Program Manager
800 N. Quincy Street
Arlington, VA 22217
(202/696–4290)

Program: The Engineering Psychology Program is concerned with assuring effective performance by personnel operating and maintaining the high technology equipment characteristic of the modern Navy and Marine Corps. The major focus of the program for the foreseeable future will be on studies of perception. Computational models, psychological experiments, and neurological findings about how characteristics of the perceived visual world are inferred from information received by the senses will be an increasingly important part of the research agenda for this program. In addition, this program sponsors research on decision-making, emphasizing studies that develop integrative models of the psychological mechanisms that produce behavioral phenomena in deductive and inductive inference, risk assessment, and preference and choice behavior. Another area of interest is research on user-systems interface. The Accelerated Research Initiative for this program concerns research on decision-making in distributed systems.

Budget: An estimated $3 million to $4 million was awarded in FY 1985.

Application/Review Process: See the general discussion of the ONR Contract Research Program above. Proposals may be submitted at any time. Researchers are encouraged to submit 3-to-4-page concept papers and to contact the program officers by letter or telephone. Proposals are reviewed by the program staff within ONR.

Funding Mechanisms: All research is funded by contract. Most awards are for 3-year periods.

Examples of Funded Research:
1) "Human-Computer Interaction and Decision Behavior."
2) "Computerized Speech Recognition and Synthesis."
3) "Inferences from Images."
4) "Discriminality of Signals from Noise in a Dynamic Stereoscopic Space."
5) "Effort and Accuracy in Decisions."

6) "Decisions and Judgment."

7) "Models of Group Dynamics in Distributed Tactical Decision-Making."

8) "Modeling Human Decision Processes in Command and Control."

9) "Human Factors in Expert Systems."

GROUP PSYCHOLOGY PROGRAM

Bert King, Program Director
800 N. Quincy Street
Arlington, VA 22217
(202/696–4209)

Program: In 1985 this program replaced the Organizational Effectiveness Program, signaling a change in emphasis to small-group task performance. The new program supports basic research using formal models and theory-driven, controlled experimentation on performance in small groups, especially those which work under stressful conditions or are hierarchically organized.

Topics for research in this program include learning and training, motivation, social modeling, productivity, information processing, decision-making, conformity/non-conformity, cooperation and competition, exchange processes, coalition formation, and bargaining and negotiation. The program will no longer support projects which focus on organizational theory or behavior variables that determine job performance, morale, retention, and quality of working life of members of work organizations.

Budget: In FY 1985, $1.3 million was available to support 12 to 15 contracts.

Application/Review Process: See the general discussion of the ONR Contract Research Program above. Proposals may be submitted at any time. Researchers are encouraged to submit 3-to-4-page concept papers and to contact the program officers by letter or telephone. Proposals are reviewed by the program staff within ONR.

Funding Mechanisms: All research is funded by contract. Most awards are for 3-year periods.

Examples of Funded Research:
1) "Survey and Theory of Patterns of Interaction."

2) "The Effects of Different Group Reward Systems upon Group Performance."

3) "Influence Processes, Divergent Thinking, and Performance."

4) "Development and Validation of a Mathematical Model of Group Performance."

5) "Short-Term Effects of Psychological Stress on Productivity, Information Processing, and Cohesion in Groups."

PERSONNEL AND TRAINING RESEARCH PROGRAM

Susan Chipman, Program Manager
800 N. Quincy Street
Arlington, VA 22217
(202/696–4209)

Program:　The Personnel and Training Research Program emphasizes theory-based research on human learning and instruction within the framework of cognitive science. Research should have long-term promise of contributing to improvements in the Navy's selection, training, and utilization of personnel.

Current program emphases include model-based measurement techniques, issues relevant to intelligent computer-assisted instruction (such as diagnosis of student knowledge states or principled selection of instructional and interactional strategies), problem-solving in complex domains, and models of human memory and attention. A possible future program priority involves more formal theories of human knowledge and skill and of the processes of acquisition and change.

Budget:　The FY 1985 budget for this program was approximately $6 million.

Application/Review Process:　See the general discussion of the ONR Contract Research Program above. Proposals may be submitted at any time. Researchers are encouraged to submit 3-to-4-page concept papers and to contact the program officers by letter or telephone. Proposals are reviewed by the program staff within ONR.

Funding Mechanisms:　All research is funded by contract. Most awards are for 3-year periods.

Examples of Funded Research:
1) "On-Line Item Calibration During Adaptive Testing."
2) "The Latent Trait Dimensionality of Psychological Tests."
3) "Computer Simulation Models of Human Visual Problem Solving."

4) "Attention and Performance."

5) "Interactive Activation Models of Speech Perception."

6) "Principles of Intelligent Computer-Based Instruction for Basic Skills."

7) "Human Understanding of Complex Systems."

8) "Dynamic Skill Acquisition."

Engineering Sciences Programs Directorate

INFORMATION SCIENCES DIVISION

ARTIFICIAL INTELLIGENCE PROGRAM

Alan Meyrowitz, Program Director
Office of the Chief of Naval Research
800 N. Quincy Street
Arlington, VA 22217
(202/696–4312)

Program: The Artificial Intelligence Program is oriented toward the development of automated aids to decision-making and intelligently controlled robotic systems. The program seeks to develop the scientific theory of computer-based mechanisms capable of exhibiting intelligent behavior. It is expected that such theory will enable the development of mechanisms capable of approximating and possibly exceeding human abilities to perceive, learn, reason, and act on their environment.

Emphasis in the program is placed on the fundamental issues of how knowledge about situations, facts, agents, and problem-solving strategies can be acquired, represented, and organized; how to automate various types of reasoning such as deduction, induction, reasoning by analogy, and distributed reasoning; how a system might learn from its experience, from examples, or from a teacher; and how to facilitate man-machine communication. Of particular interest is how to represent and reason about a dynamic world containing multiple agents, each with their own goals, capabilities, and incomplete and uncertain knowledge of the state of the world.

Budget: Approximately $1.5 million was available in FY 1985.

Application/Review Process: See the general discussion of the ONR Contract Research Program above. Proposals may be submitted at any time. Researchers are encouraged to submit 3-to-4-page concept papers and to contact the program officers by letter or telephone. Proposals are reviewed by the program staff within ONR.

Funding Mechanisms: All research is funded by contract. Most awards are for 3-year periods.

Examples of Funded Research: (not available)

Mathematical and Physical Sciences Programs Directorate

MATHEMATICAL SCIENCES DIVISION

MATHEMATICAL AND COMPUTATIONAL STATISTICS PROGRAM

Douglas J. DePriest, Program Manager, Statistics and Probability Group
Office of the Chief of Naval Research, Code 1111
800 N. Quincy Street
Arlington, VA 22217
(202/696–4961)

Program: The Mathematical and Computational Statistics Program sponsors a broad range of research projects on topics in statistics and probability. The program in statistical theory has two components: studies of small to moderate sample sizes and studies of large to very large sample sizes. In the former, statistical efficiency is of primary interest and research is focused on developing more efficient methods. Emphases are on nonparametric and robust methods, order-preserving methods, methods exploiting smoothness, asymptotic theory, and sequential and recursive methods. A second area of interest is research on specific applied probability problems related to naval logistics and stores. In studies of large to very large sample sizes, questions of computational efficiency or feasibility dominate the methodology.

A current priority for this program is the analysis of large, high-dimensional data sets. In addition, there is strong interest in issues of quality assurance, reliability, and logistics research. The focus here is on introducing modern statistical theory into those areas, with special interest in Bayesian methods for quality and reliability analysis as well as construction of a theoretically satisfactory treatment of multi-attribute sampling.

Budget: In FY 1985 approximately $3 million was available for extramural research. The FY 1986 budget is expected to be somewhat lower.

Application/Review Process: See the general discussion of the ONR Contract Research Program above. Proposals may be submitted at any time. Researchers are encouraged to submit 3-to-4-page concept papers and to contact the program officers by letter or telephone. Proposals are reviewed by the program staff within ONR.

Funding Mechanisms: All research is funded by contract. Most awards are for 3-year periods.

Examples of Funded Research:
1) "Robust Inference."
2) "Statistical Decision Theory and Bayesian Analysis."
3) "Large Data Set Research."
4) "Simulation Methodology."
5) "Reliability and Maintenance Policies for Complex Systems."
6) "Screening Variables."

OPERATIONS RESEARCH PROGRAM

Neil Glassman, Program Manager
Office of the Chief of Naval Research, Code 1111
800 N. Quincy Street
Arlington, VA 22217
(202/696–4313)

Program: The Operations Research Program is directed by the Navy Department interest in decision-making in a command and control environment. Thus, a major area of research is in the decision sciences. Studies are funded on topics such as the theoretical underpinnings of the decision sciences, Bayesian methods, statistical decision theory, game theory, and economic warfare. Another area for investigation is the practical implementation for naval use of a number of operations research techniques. Of particular interest to this program is research applicable to the production and logistical problems encountered by the Navy and the Marine Corps.

Budget: In FY 1985 this program's budget was approximately $1.8 million. The budget was expected to remain at the same level in FY 1986.

Application/Review Process: See the general discussion of the ONR Contract Research Program above. Proposals may be submitted at any time. Researchers are encouraged to submit 3-to-4-page concept papers and to contact the program officers by letter or telephone. Proposals are reviewed by the program staff within ONR.

Funding Mechanisms: All research is funded by contract. Most awards are for 3-year periods.

Examples of Funded Research:
1) "Project Center for Competitive and Conflict Analysis."
2) "Framing and Evaluation of Risk Analysis."
3) "Decision-Making in Conflict Situations."
4) "Studies in Applied Game Theory."
5) "Strategic Interaction in Complex Environments."
6) "Decision Control Models in Operations Research."

STATISTICAL SIGNAL ANALYSIS PROGRAM

Neil Gerr, Program Manager
Office of the Chief of Naval Research, Code 1111
800 N. Quincy Street
Arlington, VA 22217
(202/696–4321)

Program: The primary research interest of the Statistical Signal Analysis Program is stochastic process theory and its applicability to signal and noise models. Emphasis continues to be on the characterization and inference problems associated with non-Gaussian stochastic processes; of particular interest is detection theory associated with non-Gaussian processes. In addition, there is strong interest in inference procedures associated with time-series models, both in the time and frequency domain. Also under development is a research initiative that will focus on communications over networks.

Budget: Approximately $2 million was available for this program in FY 1985.

Application/Review Process: See the general discussion of the ONR Contract Research Program above. Proposals may be submitted at any time. Researchers are encouraged to submit 3-to-4-page concept papers and to contact the program officers by letter or telephone. Proposals are reviewed by the program staff within ONR.

Funding Mechanisms: All research is funded by contract. Most awards are for 3-year periods.

Examples of Funded Research:
1)   "Stochastic Signal Analysis for Naval Surveillance Systems."

2)   "Spatio-Temporal Stochastic Processes."

3)   "Changing Time Series Analysis."

4)   "Robust Statistical Methods for Time Series."

TECHNOLOGY PROGRAMS

MANPOWER RESEARCH AND DEVELOPMENT PROGRAM

Stanley C. Collyer, Chairman, Manpower R&D Planning Committee
Office of Chief of Naval Research, Code 222
800 N. Quincy Street
Arlington, VA 22217
(202/696-4713)

Program: The Manpower Research and Development Program is the ONR focal point for applied contract research in the areas of manpower, personnel, and training. The program encourages proposals in five areas:

1)   recruiting and retention (developing new sources of officer and enlisted personnel, assisting the recruiting force, and enhancing the understanding of economic and other exogenous factors that influence the supply of personnel; increasing the retention rate of women in nontraditional occupations; understanding the influences of nonmonetary factors, e.g., family matters, in retention);

2)   personnel selection (improving the predictive power of tests and other instruments, linking enlistment standards to performance; enhancing the process of matching abilities to jobs);

3)   manpower planning and policy support (determining the impact of policy decisions on manning levels; predicting and/or measuring the effects of manpower resource allocation on readiness; measuring the effects of quality-of-life programs);

4)   personnel management (socializing members of ethnic subpopulations; enhancing productivity; improving appraisal systems; improving the transfer and acceptance of new technology);

5) training (remediation of basic-skills deficiencies, e.g., the English usage of non-native speakers; improving the link between individual and team training; developing embedded or on-the-job training methods; advancing intelligent computer-aided instructional technology).

Proposals in these areas may pertain to active-duty personnel and also to other categories of naval manpower, i.e., reservists and civilian employees. Proposals whose main objectives are to conduct analyses, literature reviews, or program evaluations are not encouraged.

Budget: Approximately $1 million was available in FY 1985.

Application/Review Process: Researchers may submit proposals or concept papers at any time. An annual announcement of research interests is published in the *Commerce Business Daily.* The Planning Committee for the Manpower R&D Program evaluates proposals in conjunction with appropriate Navy user offices.

Funding Mechanisms: All research is funded by contract. Most projects are funded for 1 year, although additional funding is sometimes provided.

Examples of Funded Research:
1) "An Automated Aid for Personnel Retention."
2) "Artificial Intelligence Research in Navy Personnel Assignment."
3) "Research on a Constancy-Velocity Explanation of Long-Term Organizational Effects in Navy Units."
4) "Understanding Work Facilitation and Unit Effectiveness."
5) "Development of Computer-Based Instructional Systems for Training Essential Components of Reading."

NAVY PERSONNEL RESEARCH AND DEVELOPMENT CENTER

James W. Tweeddale, Technical Director
San Diego, CA 92152
(619/225–7364)

The Navy Personnel Research and Development Center (NPRDC) is the principal Navy center for manpower, personnel, education, training, and human factors research and development. Most of the work is done in-house, but there is contract money available for outside researchers to work on R&D topics concurrently with the NPRDC. NPRDC research tends to be focused more on "development" than on basic research. Three major laboratories conduct research, development, testing, and evaluation: (1) Training Laboratory, (2) Manpower and Personnel Laboratory, and (3) Human Factors and Organizational Systems Laboratory.

Budget: In FY 1985 the total funding for NPRDC was $30 million, of which approximately $10 million went to external contracts.

Application/Review Process: Most research contracts are solicited through requests for proposals (RFPs) published in the *Commerce Business Daily.* Unsolicited proposals will be considered and should be directed to the Contract Support Office.

All technical proposals, whether unsolicited or in response to an RFP, are reviewed internally. Unsolicited proposals must also be reviewed by a Noncompetitive Contract Review Board.

Funding Mechanisms: Most contracts are competitively awarded. Contract support for research programs is usually obtained for a 3-year period. Contracts range in size from $25,000 to $2 million.

TRAINING LABORATORY

Joe McLachlan, Director
San Diego, CA 92152
(619/225–7105)

Program: The Training Laboratory is divided into two departments: Training Technology and Training Systems. The Training Technology Department includes applications of computer technology, development of cognitive science/theory applications, and special warfare areas such as training in chemical and biological warfare defense. The Training Systems Department includes developing advanced computer-based training simulation systems; relating training systems to curriculum design, development, and implementation of land and air navigation training courses; individualization of professional military education courses; establishing performance criteria; developing individualized career structures; and developing a system of lateral entry for technically trained personnel.

The Training Laboratory also has two additional program areas: future technologies and reserve training and reimbursable projects. The first program deals with advanced computer-aided training tools and is co-located with the cognitive science laboratory at the University of California-San Diego. The second program deals with direct support of the Chief of Naval Reserves and the Naval Sea Systems Command.

Budget: See the general discussion of the Navy Personnel Research and Development Center above.

Application/Review Process: See the general discussion of the Navy Personnel Research and Development Center above.

Funding Mechanisms: See the general discussion of the Navy Personnel Research and Development Center above.

Examples of Funded Research:
1) "Utilization of Bilingual Naval Personnel."
2) "Collective Training Standards."
3) "Low-Cost Microcomputer Training Systems."
4) "Enlisted Personnel Individualized Career Systems."

MANPOWER AND PERSONNEL LABORATORY

Martin F. Wiskoff, Director
San Diego, CA 92152
(619/225-7759)

Program: The Manpower and Personnel Laboratory is concerned with developing technology and procedures that will enable the Navy to obtain and deploy the most effective qualitative and quantitative mix of personnel to meet force requirements, and to employ these personnel to achieve maximum military performance and readiness. This laboratory comprises three departments: Manpower Systems, Personnel Systems, and Computerized Testing Systems.

The Manpower Systems Department develops techniques and systems for determining manpower requirements, allocating manpower resources, and controlling personnel inventories. It also develops comprehensive manpower planning techniques for rapid, effective response to fluctuations in personnel resources and commitments.

The Personnel Systems Department develops methods and procedures for assessing the capabilities of applicants and on-board Navy and Marine Corps personnel; recruiting and acquiring high-quality officers and enlisted personnel; and classifying and assigning personnel to maximize their performance, utilization, and career longevity.

The Computerized Testing Systems Department focuses on development and evaluation of a computerized adaptive testing (CAT) version of the Armed Services Vocational Aptitude Battery (ASVAB) for personnel selection and classification.

Budget: See the general discussion of the Navy Personnel Research and Development Center above.

Application/Review Process: See the general discussion of the Navy Personnel Research and Development Center above.

Funding Mechanisms: See the general discussion of the Navy Personnel Research and Development Center above.

Examples of Funded Research:
1)   "Fleet Demand for Support Manpower."
2)   "Marine Corps Officer Loss Forecasting."
3)   "Dimensions of Job Performance."
4)   "Models for Calibrating Multiple-Choice Items."
5)   "Computerized Executive Networking Survey System."

HUMAN FACTORS AND ORGANIZATIONAL SYSTEMS LABORATORY

Robert E. Blanchard, Director
San Diego, CA 92152
(619/225–2232)

Program: The Human Factors and Organizational Systems Laboratory is concerned with developing and conducting an R&D program to advance the behavioral technologies supporting an improved understanding of humans'interaction with others and with complex hardware systems. The program addresses social, technical, and physical environmental factors for enhancing performance and improving the quality of working life. Major program activities include providing human factors support to the development of command and control systems, and improving the effectiveness of individuals and teams by application of principles of human performance.

The second concern of this laboratory is the development of programs to maximize the productivity of Navy personnel. The Organizational Systems program includes: identifying and developing appropriate measures and reporting systems for both individual and organizational performance; investigating the factors and policies that facilitate or inhibit the Navy's organizational functioning; examining the impact of new technologies on workers; and studying trends within society that may affect the Navy.

Budget: See the general discussion of the Navy Personnel Research and Development Center above.

Application/Review Process: See the general discussion of the Navy Personnel Research and Development Center above.

Funding Mechanisms: See the general discussion of the Navy Personnel Research and Development Center above.

Examples of Funded Research:
1) "Human Factors Engineering Technology in Shipboard Combat Systems."
2) "Enhanced Interfaces for Combat Decision Support."
3) "Improving Individual Unit Productivity."

DEPARTMENT OF DEFENSE HISTORY OFFICES

The Air Force, Army, Marine Corps, Navy, and Joint Chiefs of Staff all maintain history offices. These offices conduct historical research and prepare book-length monographs on battles, campaigns, and specific military components (e.g., a history of the Army's 24th Infantry), policy-related studies, and studies of lineage and honor. Most work is performed by in-house staff; however, some projects are contracted out. Outside contracts are frequently let to former employees on a sole-source basis.

Both the Army and the Navy are considering reviving their past practice of using outside researchers. The Air Force has a fellowship program that provides dissertation support to two historians per year. Work for the Joint Chiefs is usually classified.

Listed below, for informational purposes, are the addresses and phone numbers of the offices.

Office of Air Force History
Grant M. Hales, Senior Historian
Building 5681
Bolling Air Force Base
Washington, DC 20332
(202/767–5088)

U.S. Army Center of Military History
David F. Trask, Chief Historian
Casimir Pulaski Building
20 Massachusetts Avenue, NW
Washington, DC 20314
(202/272-0293)

Naval History Office
Dean Allard, Senior Historian
Building 57
Washington Navy Yard Annex
Eighth & M Streets, SE
Washington, DC 20374
(202/433-3224)

Marine Corps Historical Center
Henry B. Shaw, Chief Historian
Building 58
Washington Navy Yard Annex
Eighth & M Streets, SE
Washington, DC 20374
(202/433-3837)

DEFENSE ADVANCED RESEARCH PROJECTS AGENCY

1400 Wilson Boulevard
Arlington, VA 22209
(202/694-3032)

The Defense Advanced Research Projects Agency (DARPA) supports research designed to help maintain U.S. technological superiority over its potential adversaries. Its goals are to pursue those highly imaginative and innovative research ideas and concepts offering significant military utility. DARPA programs focus on proof-of-concept demonstrations of revolutionary approaches for improved strategic, conventional, rapid deployment, and seapower forces, and on scientific investigation into advanced basic technologies of the future.

Although most DARPA activities focus on the physical sciences, the Information Processing Techniques Office supports, among other things, basic research on artificial intelligence. Of interest are how machines can replicate or expand the capabilities of human intelligence and how this knowledge can be best represented and utilized in a computer.

The System Sciences Division supports research on understanding human behavior and the application of that understanding to military technologies. Topics of interest include improving man-machine interaction, mapping, improving group decision-making, and matching human capabilities to the design and functioning of unconventional vehicles.

Unsolicited proposals are accepted. Evaluation usually takes 4 to 6 weeks.

DEFENSE INTELLIGENCE COLLEGE

DEFENSE ACADEMIC RESEARCH SUPPORT PROGRAM

Robert O. Slater, Director, Language and Area Studies Program
Defense Intelligence College, DIC-R
Washington, DC 20301
(202/373-3342)

Program: The Defense Academic Research Support Program (DARSP) is an integral part of the Defense Language and Area Studies Program managed by the Defense Intelligence College, a professional, accredited, degree-granting Department of Defense education, training, and research institution. The purpose of DARSP is to provide a vehicle for direct contact and scholarly exchange between Defense analysts, college faculty, and noted experts on Third World issues. The goal of DARSP is to upgrade and sustain the quality of foreign language and area expertise available to the Defense intelligence community.

The program concentrates exclusively on the Third World (defined as Africa, the Middle East, Latin America, South Asia, and Southeast Asia) and includes roundtable discussions, conferences, research studies, and the development of materials to improve training in uncommonly taught Third World languages. Individual topics for discussion or research may cover regional, subregional, or national issues addressed from a variety of social science perspectives. Research projects may involve extensive data collection, analysis, and/or the application of innovative research approaches. DARSP will support both brief issue papers and in-depth research studies. All supported research is unclassified.

Budget: In FY 1985 approximately $600,000 was available for research.

Application/Review Process: Unsolicited proposals are welcome. Review is done in-house.

Funding Mechanisms: Funding is provided through basic ordering agreements (contracts). The average contract awarded is $30,000.

Examples of Funded Research: (not available)

DEPARTMENT OF EDUCATION

Office of Educational Research and Improvement

[Editor's Note: The Office of Educational Research and Improvement was scheduled to move from its present location by June 1, 1986. The new address will be 555 New Jersey Avenue, NW, Washington, DC 20208.]

In 1985 the research, dissemination, and statistics functions at the Department of Education underwent a major reorganization. The new structure places most of these functions in the Office of Educational Research and Improvement (OERI). OERI comprises five units: (1) Office of Research, (2) Center for Statistics, (3) Programs for the Improvement of Practice, (4) Information Services, and (5) Library Programs. Most research programs in the former National Institute of Education (NIE) are now located in the Office of Research. A description of the Center for Statistics is included in chapter 6.

Office of Research

The mission of the Office of Research (OR) is to generate knowledge that will increase understanding of the education system and contribute to improvements in the quality of education. OR supports research on fundamental educational processes at all levels and in all settings. The emphasis of OR research is on factors that contribute to, or detract from, the achievement of excellence in education for all individuals. Research is also designed to strengthen the scientific and technological foundations of education with the intent of advancing the practice of education as an art, science, and profession. Research is conducted primarily by scholars outside of government. It may be initiated by the field or solicited, or some combination of these processes. The Office of Research has four divisions: Learning and Instruction, Schools and School Professionals, Higher Education and Adult Learning, and Education and Society.

The research divisions have not, as of this writing, completed their program plans. It is anticipated that funding opportunities will be available for both field-initiated and Department-initiated studies. In FY 1986 a modest $500,000 was allocated for the Unsolicited Proposal Program. To date, no specific guidelines or priorities have been developed for unsolicited proposals.

Official agency descriptions of the four divisions are given below.

LEARNING AND INSTRUCTION DIVISION

John Taylor, Acting Director
Mail Stop 1805
555 New Jersey Avenue, NW
Washington, DC 20208
(202/357–6021)

Program: The Learning and Instruction Division supports basic and applied research for which learning and its relationship to the instructional process are the central focus. It addresses such issues as how youngsters acquire information, values, and character, and develop their knowledge of content areas; how human thought processes develop; how youngsters develop intellectually and become mature citizens; and what the implications of these findings might be for instruction. It also addresses the efficacy and efficiency of various instructional practices; examines interaction among teachers and students within classrooms; and studies the role of textbooks, workbooks, tests, and technology in the instructional process. The work of this division is currently focused on three major areas: content, learning, and instruction.

Application/Review Process: An announcement of OR research priorities will be published in the *Federal Register.* Applications are reviewed by panels of federal and nonfederal members.

Funding Mechanisms: Funding is provided through both grants and contracts.

SCHOOLS AND SCHOOL PROFESSIONALS DIVISION

Frank Sobol, Acting Director
Mail Stop 1817
555 New Jersey Avenue, NW
Washington, DC 20208
(202/357–6207)

Program: The Schools and School Professionals Division sponsors basic research that has the larger elementary-secondary educational system as its focus.

It spans the practices and policies of school building principals, school districts, state governments, and teacher preparation programs that bear on the nature of local educational practices. It investigates systems of incentives and standards that may influence education practices, and aspects of the organization of the education system as a whole which bear on how well it functions. The work of this division is presently concentrated on the teaching profession, schooling, and school leadership.

Application/Review Process: An announcement of OR research priorities will be published in the *Federal Register.* Applications are reviewed by panels of federal and nonfederal members.

Funding Mechanisms: Funding is provided through both grants and contracts.

HIGHER EDUCATION AND ADULT LEARNING DIVISION

Arthur Sheekey, Acting Director
Mail Stop 1819
555 New Jersey Avenue, NW
Washington, DC 20208
(202/357–6239)

Program: The Higher Education and Adult Learning Division supports basic and applied research on the educational aspects of the transition from youth to adulthood, as well as education occurring beyond high school. It supports studies on the wide range of institutions that educate adults, including colleges and universities, trade schools, community colleges, institutions offering advanced degrees, and corporate education and staff development programs. Research addresses the characteristics of adult learners, and problems associated with achieving quality in higher education. This division also addresses the problem of adult illiteracy and the education of high-risk, low-income youth and school dropouts. Current emphases are on institutions of higher education, education and employment, and adult learning.

Application/Review Process: An announcement of OR research priorities will be published in the *Federal Register.* Applications are reviewed by panels of federal and nonfederal members.

Funding Mechanisms: Funding is provided through both grants and contracts.

EDUCATION AND SOCIETY DIVISION

Oliver Moles, Acting Director
Mail Stop 1805
555 New Jersey Avenue, NW
Washington, DC 20208
(202/357–6223)

Program: The Education and Society Division supports basic and applied research and analytic activities that focus on the interaction between education and the community at large. Topics of inquiry range from the involvement of parents in the education of their children, the influence of parents and communities on local schools, the social context of education, and state and local responsibilities of education. Methods of inquiry range from contemporary empirical investigations to historical studies and philosophical analyses.

Application/Review Process: An announcement of OR research priorities will be published in the *Federal Register.* Applications are reviewed by panels of federal and nonfederal members.

Funding Mechanisms: Funding is provided through both grants and contracts.

Secretary's Discretionary Program for Mathematics, Science, Computer Learning, and Critical Foreign Languages

Patricia Alexander, Coordinator
555 New Jersey Avenue, NW
Washington, DC 20208 [after June 1, 1986]
(202/732–3599)

Program: The Education for Economic Security Act (EESA) was enacted "to improve the quality of mathematics and science teaching and instruction in the United States." The act addresses the importance of mathematics, science, computer learning, and foreign languages; it authorizes the Secretary of Education to make grants to state and local educational agencies, institutions of higher education, and nonprofit organizations, including museums, libraries, educational television stations, and professional mathematics, science, and engineering societies and associations to fund projects designed to have nationwide impact in these areas. In FY 1986 the Secretary reserved funds from this program for projects that enhance the professionalism and improve the qualifications of teachers and that improve instruction in these areas at the elementary and secondary school levels.

Funds from the Discretionary Program may be used for a variety of projects, including research, demonstrations, dissemination, and development. A set-aside of 25% of the budget is reserved for projects to improve instruction in critical foreign languages and may be awarded only to institutions of higher education (IHEs). In FY 1986 the first IHE and general competitions were held.

EESA requires the Secretary to give special consideration to local educational agencies proposing to establish or improve magnet school programs for gifted and talented students and to applicants proposing to provide special services to historically underserved and underrepresented populations in the fields of mathematics and science.

Budget: Approximately $4.5 million is available for this program in FY 1986.

Application/Review Process: Funding priorities are established for this program each year and announced in the *Federal Register.* The deadline for the next IHE competition will likely be in early summer of 1986. The deadline for the next general competition is scheduled for late summer or early fall of 1986. Review teams generally consisting of two nonfederal and one federal member read applications and provide a rating. Review results are forwarded to the Secretary of Education for final award decisions.

Funding Mechanisms: In FY 1986 grants could range from $50,000 to $150,-000 for projects lasting up to 18 months. These guidelines may change each year, depending on budget allocations.

Examples of Funded Research:
The results of the first competitions had not been announced at the time of this writing.

Assistant Secretary for Postsecondary Education

Fund for the Improvement of Postsecondary Education

Charles Karelis, Director
Room 3100
Regional Office Building 3
Washington, DC 20202
(202/245–8091)

Program: The Fund for the Improvement of Postsecondary Education (FIPSE) awards grants and cooperative agreements to institutions of post-secondary education and other public and private educational institutions for the purpose of improving postsecondary educational opportunities.

Current priorities span several broad areas:

1) ensuring that undergraduate curricula provide the knowledge and skills that an educated citizen needs, including knowledge of our intellectual and cultural heritage;

2) ensuring that recent increases in access to postsecondary education are made meaningful by improving retention and completion rates without compromising program standards;

3) improving the quality of undergraduate education;

4) improving the education of school teachers;

5) reforming graduate education by fostering the teaching skills of PhD candidates planning teaching careers and by broadening the social and ethical perspectives of students in professional graduate programs;

6) strengthening postsecondary educational institutions by providing incentives to develop the abilities of their leaders, administrators, faculty, and staff;

7) providing education for a changing economy by offering programs and services for workers, unemployed individuals, businesses, and communities;

8) developing educational uses of technology, including computers, television, and other electronic media.

The Secretary of Education intended to solicit suggestions from the field to assist in the development of priorities for FY 1987 and beyond.

Budget: The FY 1986 budget for FIPSE is $12.7 million, of which approximately $5.3 million is available for new awards.

Applications/Review Process: FIPSE employs a two-stage application process. Preapplications are required and are reviewed by nonfederal field readers. Preapplications are judged primarily on significance of the project, and less weight given to feasibility and appropriateness. Applicants who receive favorable reviews at this stage are then invited to submit final applications. Final applications are also reviewed by field readers, with equal weight given to significance, feasibility, and appropriateness. Final funding decisions are made by FIPSE staff.

Annual funding priorities and application procedures are announced in the *Federal Register.* Interested individuals may also contact the FIPSE office to have their name placed on a mailing list for announcements.

Funding Mechanisms: Awards may be made for project periods of up to 36 months. Awards range from $5,000 to $200,000 per year.

Examples of Funded Projects:
The descriptions that follow are for projects funded in FY 1985.

1) Develop and implement a preservice civic education program by introducing social science faculty to law related education content and materials.

2) Develop and teach a multidisciplinary, multicultural series of courses on women's role in health care. The project will serve graduate students in the health professions, the social sciences, and community practitioners in order to bridge the gap between conventional graduate and continuing professional education.

3) Create 10 research training teams of graduate and undergraduate minority students working with faculty mentors. Expected outcomes include more minority students with extramural research skills in early graduate careers, and exposure of undergraduates to research and alternative career options.

4) Help faculty understand the development of reasoning skills in students and how their teaching might further that process. This faculty development program draws extensively on Perry's theory of intellectual and ethical development in the college years.

5) Develop a curriculum on economic literacy which will be used by the residents of Appalachia. The curriculum will enable area residents to better understand the changing economy of their region and its impact on their future.

6) Incorporate modules on international education in 13 liberal arts and methodology courses for preservice teachers. Conduct faculty seminars and use experiential learning to strengthen student understanding of international issues.

7) Establish a national research clearinghouse on racial minority women and working class women in the South and use the clearinghouse to facilitate the revision of courses by women's studies and social science faculty.

8)   Create a center for bilingual studies with curriculum providing a viable educational alternative for Hispanics; a strong liberal arts emphasis; cultural sensitivity; equitable treatment; and replicability.

Office of Higher Education Programs

DIVISION OF HIGHER EDUCATION INCENTIVE PROGRAMS

NATIONAL GRADUATE FELLOWS PROGRAM

Louise White, Acting Executive Officer
P.O. Box 44367, L'Enfant Plaza Station
Washington, DC 20026
(202/732–2945)

Program: The National Graduate Fellows Program (NGFP) was authorized by Congress in 1980 to award fellowship support to students of superior ability, as demonstrated by their achievements and exceptional promise to pursue graduate study in the arts, humanities, and social sciences. The Program did not actually receive funding until FY 1985, with the first awards made in January 1986.

To be eligible, applicants must be enrolled in or seeking admission to a graduate program with the expressed intent of obtaining a doctorate or other graduate degree. The NGFP does not support students seeking master's degrees, except where such a degree is an integral preparatory step to a doctorate or where the doctorate is not commonly recognized to be the terminal degree. Continued support beyond the initial year is contingent upon the availability of funds and satisfactory academic progress.

Some eligible fields of support are architectural history, anthropology, economics, ethnomusicology, foreign languages and literature, geography, history, linguistics, political science, psychology, and sociology.

The National Graduate Fellowship Board has responsibility for program procedures, policies, and selection criteria. Members of the board are presidentially appointed and include representatives of both public and private institutions of higher education. Although no priorities among the eligible fields were designated for the 1986 competition, it is likely that in future years the Board will select priority areas based on national needs and other existing programs of fellowship support.

Budget: The FY 1986 budget for the NGFP was $2.5 million. At the time of this writing, pending congressional budget actions indicated that future support for this program is uncertain.

Application/Review Process: An annual competition for fellowship awards is held. The next deadline is anticipated to be in January 1987. Fellows are chosen on the basis of demonstrated academic ability, academic transcripts, letters of recommendation, personal statement, and proposed plan of study. Applicants are evaluated by panels of scholars chosen by the National Graduate Fellowship Board.

Funding Mechanisms: Fellows receive a stipend of up to $10,000 per year. The institution in which the fellow is enrolled may receive up to $6,000 to cover costs associated with graduate school tuition and fees. The total fellowship period may be up to a maximum of 48 calendar months.

Center for International Education

The Center for International Education (CIE) administers a number of programs that promote foreign language and area training, curriculum development, and research.

INTERNATIONAL RESEARCH AND STUDIES PROGRAM

Robert R. Dennis, Program Manager
Room 3053, ROB-3
400 Maryland Avenue, SW
Washington, DC 20202
(202/732-3296)

Program: The International Research and Studies Program supports research designed to improve and strengthen instruction in modern foreign languages, area studies, and other related fields needed to provide full understanding of the places in which the languages are commonly used.

Current priorities for this program include (1) the use of computers for improving foreign language instruction, (2) foreign language acquisition, (3) improved teaching methodologies for foreign languages, (4) foreign language proficiency testing, and (5) instructional materials development for uncommonly taught languages. Prospective applicants should consult *A Survey of Material Development Needs in the Less Commonly Taught Languages in the U.S.,* since reviewers use this publication as a guide to the critical shortages in language materials. (This book is available from the Center for Applied Linguistics, 1118 22nd Street, NW, Washington, DC 20037; 202/429–9292.)

In recent years this program has become increasingly focused on the study of uncommon languages and materials development rather than area studies. While proposals in area studies are considered, they are seldom funded, with the exception, perhaps, of an occasional curriculum guide. The program is "product oriented" and tends to fund more applied and developmental research than basic linguistics.

Budget: The FY 1986 budget for this program was approximately $1.5 million.

Application/Review Process: Applications are mailed to peer reviewers according to specialty areas. Applications receiving the most favorable ratings are then given, together with mail comments, to a panel with more general expertise who perform a second review and rank applications. Panel ratings and comments are then reviewed by CIE program staff and funding recommendations made to the Assistant Secretary for Postsecondary Education.

The deadline for proposals varies, but it is generally in November.

Funding Mechanisms: Grants are awarded for project periods of one to three years. In FY 1985 the average award was $58,000.

Examples of Funded Research:
1) "Proficiency-Based Curriculum and Materials Development in Chinese, Japanese, and Russian" (awarded $56,342 in FY 1985).

2) "Himalayan History and Anthropology: A Syllabus and Comprehensive Bibliography" (awarded $48,694 in FY 1985).

3) "Application of Learning Strategies to Foreign Language Education" (awarded $89,623 in FY 1985).

4) "Analysis of Secondary School Students' Proficiency Levels in Reading Unedited Materials in French, Spanish, and German" (awarded $50,525 in FY 1985).

5) "Text Processing Strategies of Readers in Foreign Languages" (awarded $43,089 in FY 1985).

FULBRIGHT-HAYS TRAINING GRANTS

The Fulbright-Hays Training Grants support the promotion, improvement, and development of modern foreign languages and area studies. Two programs, Doctoral Dissertation Research Abroad and Faculty Research Abroad, have broad applicability for the social and behavioral sciences.

This Fulbright-Hays program defines area studies as the comprehensive study of the aspects of a society or societies, including their geography, history, culture, economy, politics, international relations, and languages. Funding priorities are not established per se, although projects focusing on Western Europe will not be considered.

DOCTORAL DISSERTATION RESEARCH ABROAD PROGRAM

John Paul, Program Manager
Regional Office Building 3
400 Maryland Avenue, SW
Washington, DC 20202
(202/732-3298)

Program: The Doctoral Dissertation Research Abroad Program provides assistance for graduate students to engage in full-time dissertation research abroad in modern foreign languages and area studies. This program is designed to aid teachers and prospective teachers and scholars in increasing their research knowledge and capability in world areas not widely included in American curricula and to enhance understanding of those areas, cultures, and languages.

Applicants must be planning a teaching career in higher education in the United States and have adequate language skills for the country where the proposed research will take place.

Budget: In FY 1985, 31 institutional grants and 113 individual fellowships were awarded totaling $1.75 million.

Application/Review Process: Applications are reviewed by peer panels generally composed of nonfederal members. Panel ratings and comments are then reviewed by CIE program staff, who make funding recommendations to the Assistant Secretary for Postsecondary Education.

The deadline for applications is generally in November.

Funding Mechanisms: Graduate students may receive fellowships for periods of 6 to 12 months for full-time dissertation research. Awards averaged $15,473 in FY 1985.

Examples of Funded Research:

1) "The Influence of Cultural Values on Economic Behavior: An Analysis of a Japanese Department Store."

2) "Congress and the Role of Ideology in the Making of U.S. Foreign Policy Toward Costa Rica and Honduras."

3) "Social Complexity, Exchange, and Demography in the Colombian Andes."

4) "The Functions of Narrative Discourse in Shavante Society: A Study of Language Use in Context (Brazil)."

5) "Family and Factory: Italian Immigrant Women and Children in the Sao Paulo Textile Industry, 1900–1920."

6) "The Social Processes of Local Capital Accumulation in Northwestern Tanganyika, 1920–1960."

7) "Japanese Coastal Fishermen in Transition: Government Policy and Socioeconomic Change."

8) "The Soviet Foreign Trade Monopoly: Forecasting, Planning, and Adjustment in an Open Economy."

9) "Sociolinguistic Variation and Social Change in Tunisia."

10) "The Education of Afghan Refugees in Pakistan: A Case Study in Factors Affecting Socialization and Assimilation."

FACULTY RESEARCH ABROAD PROGRAM

Merion Kane, Program Manager
Regional Office Building 3
400 Maryland Avenue, SW
Washington, DC 20202
(202/732-3301)

Program: The Faculty Research Abroad Program is designed to assist higher education institutions in strengthening their foreign language and area studies programs by enabling faculty members to maintain their language and area studies expertise by conducting research abroad. Its overall objective is to strengthen research knowledge and capabilities in world areas not widely included in American curricula.

Applicants must have been engaged in teaching relevant to their foreign language or area studies specialization for the two years immediately preceding the date of the award.

Budget: The FY 1986 budget for this program was $700,000.

Application/Review Process: Applications are reviewed by peer panels generally composed of nonfederal members. Panel ratings and comments are then reviewed by CIE program staff, who make funding recommendations to the Assistant Secretary for Postsecondary Education.
  The deadline for applications is generally in November.

Funding Mechanisms: Grants for full-time research of 3 to 12 months are available. Stipends are generally equal to one's academic salary.

Examples of Funded Research:
1)   "Presidency, Bureaucracy, and Policy Making in Mexico, 1970–1985."

2)   "Ethnohistory and Population Dynamics of the Black Carib of Central America."

3)   "Women and Politics in Colombia: The Process of Change."

4)   "The History of the Jewish Settlement at Sosua in the Dominican Republic."

5)   "Patterns of Protest: Workers and Unions in Postwar Japan."

6)   "Siberia in the Soviet Economy: Regional Diversity and Prospects."

7)   "Church and Society in Imperial Russia, 1750–1914."

8)   "A Social History of the Lower Ranks in the Russian Army, 1796–1855."

9)   "The Political Culture of Senior Civil Servants in Israel."

BUSINESS AND INTERNATIONAL EDUCATION PROGRAM

Susanna C. Easton, Program Director
Regional Office Building
400 Maryland Avenue, SW
Washington, DC 20202
(202/732–3291)

Program: The Business and International Education Program makes institutional awards to pay up to 50% of the costs of projects designed to promote linkages between institutions of higher education and American businesses engaged in international economic activities. The purpose of each grant is both to enhance the international academic programs of the institution and to provide appropriate services to the business community to enable it to expand its capacity to engage in commerce abroad.

Eligible activities include:

1) innovation and improvement in international education curricula, including the development of new programs for nontraditional, mid-career, or part-time students;

2) development of programs to inform the public of increasing international economic interdependence and the role of American business within the international economic system;

3) internationalization of curricula at the junior and community college level, and at undergraduate and graduate schools of business;

4) development of area studies programs and interdisciplinary international programs;

5) establishment of export education programs through cooperative arrangements with regional and world trade centers and councils, and with bilateral and multilateral trade associations;

6) research for and development of specialized teaching materials, including language materials, and facilities appropriate to business-oriented students;

7) establishment of student and faculty fellowships and internships for training and education in international business activities;

8) development of opportunities for faculty of junior business and other professional schools to acquire or strengthen international business activities;

9) development of research programs on issues of common interest to institutions of higher education, private sector organizations, and associations engaged in or promoting international economic activity.

Budget: The Program awarded $2.1 million for 35 new projects in FY 1985.The same level of funding was anticipated for FY 1986.

Application/Review Process: An annual competition for awards is held, with the deadline for proposals occurring in late winter to early spring. Proposals are evaluated by peer review panels.

Funding Mechanisms: Grants are used to fund projects. Awards may range from $15,000 to $120,000.

Examples of Funded Projects:
1) $50,000 to a university department of agricultural business management to assist U.S. businesses in establishing trade relations with developing Third World nations. Activities include development of a research program and database for an international business center and development of a training program that recognizes the social, political, and cultural diversity of target countries.

2) $62,000 to a university to provide resources for businesses involved in trade with countries in the Caribbean Basin. Activities include faculty research and the development of case studies and occasional publication in monograph form of research findings.

3) $150,000 continuation award to a university for strengthening East Asian studies in the international business and education department. Activities include research and preparation of teaching materials on the Pacific Basin Trade Environment and on non-joint venture forms of technology transfer between the United States and the People's Republic of China.

4) $50,000 to a university's graduate school of business and department of Slavic languages and literature to develop a seminar for teaching international negotiations to middle managers. Topics include principles of negotiation and analysis of cross-cultural transactions.

Assistant Secretary for Special Education and Rehabilitation Services

National Institute of Handicapped Research

The National Institute of Handicapped Research (NIHR) provides support for national and international research on the rehabilitation of disabled individuals. The overall mission of the Institute research program is to (1) identify the causes and consequences of disability; (2) maximize the healthy physical and emotional status of disabled persons, including their functional ability, self-sufficiency, and personal autonomy; (3) prevent or minimize the mental, social, educational, vocational, and economic effects of disability on individuals and families; and (4) reduce barriers that restrict disabled persons in the course of their daily life.

Categories of grant funding include Rehabilitation Research and Training Centers, Rehabilitation Engineering Centers, Research and Demonstration Projects, Information Utilization Projects, and Field-Initiated Research Grants. In addition, NIHR administers a program of research fellowship awards.

Application/Review Process: An annual announcement of NIHR funding priorities and requests for applications are published in the *Federal Register.* Different priority areas are established each year. Grant and fellowship applications undergo both staff and peer review to evaluate scientific, administrative, and technical merit. Peer reviewers are drawn from an NIHR-maintained computer roster of nonfederal scientists and other experts. Federal employees qualified in specific areas may also be included on peer review panels.

Funding Mechanisms: NIHR awards grants, contracts, fellowships, and cooperative agreements. Individuals may apply for fellowships; other awards are made to an agency or institution.

REHABILITATION RESEARCH AND TRAINING CENTERS

Betty Jo Berland, Director of Planning and Evaluation
3070 Switzer Office Building
330 C Street, SW
Washington, DC 20202
(202/732–1139)

Program: Research and Training Centers (RTCs) have been established to conduct coordinated and advanced programs of rehabilitation research and to providing training to personnel engaged in research or the provision of services. RTCs must be operated in collaboration with institutions of higher education and must be associated with a rehabilitation service program. The specific mission of each RTC is to conduct research in priority core areas and to transfer research knowledge into tangible products useful to rehabilitation practitioners. Center training programs disseminate and promote the utilization of new rehabilitation knowledge through such means as undergraduate and graduate texts and curricula, in-service training, and continuing education.

Competitions for new centers are held usually once a year, although in some years all funds go to continuation awards. Specific areas of need are identified for each competition. Recent priorities have included cardiovascular rehabilitation, rehabilitation of blind and severely visually-impaired individuals, and rehabilitation of deaf and hearing-impaired individuals.

Budget: NIHR anticipated making new awards totaling approximately $1.5 million in FY 1986.

Application/Review Process: See the general discussion of NIHR above. In years when a competition is held for new centers, the deadline for applications is generally in December.

Funding Mechanisms: See the general discussion of NIHR above. Awards may be made for up to 60 months.

Examples of Funded Research:
1) "Psychosocial and Medical Rehabilitation of Elderly Handicapped Individuals" (5-year project; awarded $336,282 from NIHR and $150,000 from NIMH in FY 1985).

2) "Improving the Psychosocial Environment and Eliminating Social and Attitudinal Barriers" (5-year project; awarded $500,000 in FY 1985).

3) "Research and Training Center to Improve Vocational Rehabilitation at the Worksite and Increase Employment of Severely Disabled Individuals" (5-year project; awarded $349,268 in FY 1985).

4) "Research and Training Center for the Study of Psychological and Linguistic Aspects of Deafness" (5-year project; awarded $400,000 in FY 1985).

REHABILITATION RESEARCH AND DEMONSTRATION PROJECTS

Betty Jo Berland, Director of Planning and Evaluation
3070 Switzer Office Building
330 C Street, SW
Washington, DC 20202
(202/732-1139)

Program: Applications for Rehabilitation Research and Demonstration Projects are solicited annually for specific areas. Projects may include scientific, technical, and methodological areas of interest. Topics of investigation might include studies and analyses of industrial, vocational, social, physical, psychiatric, psychological, economic, and other factors affecting the rehabilitation of handicapped individuals, including the special problems of the homebound and institutionalized.

Some eligible activities include international research and training, joint projects with other federal agencies and with private industry, research related to disabled children and the elderly, and projects related to persons living in rural areas.

Budget: Approximately $2.5 million is available for new awards in FY 1986.

Application/Review Process: See the general discussion of NIHR above. The deadline for applications is generally in April.

Funding Mechanisms: See the general discussion of NIHR above.

Examples of Funded Research:
1) "Enhanced Understanding of the Economics of Disability" (5-year project; awarded $200,000 in FY 1985).

2) "Economic-Behavioral Assessment and Intervention in Families" (4-year project; awarded $150,000 in FY 1985).

3) "Factors Affecting the Well-Being of Elderly Mentally Retarded" (3-year project; awarded $200,000 in FY 1985).

4) "Model to Improve Rehabilitation to Urban Minority Groups" (3-year project; awarded $199,728 in FY 1985).

FIELD-INITIATED RESEARCH PROGRAM

Betty Jo Berland, Director of Planning and Evaluation
3070 Switzer Office Building
330 C Street, SW
Washington, DC 20202
(202/732–1139)

Program: Field-initiated research proposals are solicited by NIHR to encourage the input of original and innovative ideas from the research community. Established in 1984, awards may be made for projects in any area having a direct bearing on the development of methods, procedures, and devices to assist in the provision of vocational and other rehabilitation services to handicapped individuals, especially the most severely handicapped.

Budget: Approximately $1.5 million is available for new awards in FY 1986.

Application/Review Process: See the general discussion of NIHR above. The deadline for applications is generally in February.

Funding Mechanisms: See the general discussion of NIHR above. The average award for this program is $75,000; projects may be supported for up to three years.

Examples of Funded Research:
1) "Community Integration and Adjustment of Mentally Retarded: Longitudinal, Cross-Residential Analysis" (3-year project; awarded $100,000 in FY 1985).
2) "Social Skills Training for Older and Younger Persons with Severe Disabilities" (3-year project; awarded $96,123 in FY 1985).
3) "Community-Based Research on Behaviorally Disordered, Handicapped Youth" (3-year project; awarded $117,530 in FY 1985).
4) "Disability Management and Rehabilitation: An Analysis of Programs, Costs and Outcomes" (3-year project; awarded $78,187 in FY 1985).
5) "Family Factors and Work Adjustment of Handicapped Mexican Americans Disabled by Stroke or Brain Trauma" (3-year project; awarded $86,045 in FY 1985).
6) "Psychological Intervention: An Aid to Rehabilitation of Low Back Pain Patients" (3-year project; awarded $101,785 in FY 1985).
7) "Parental Decision-Making in the Treatment of Newborns with Disabilities" (3-year project; awarded $92,861 in FY 1985).
8) "Predictors of Transition Problems Among Learning Disabled Adolescents and Young Adults" (3-year project; awarded $70,231 in FY 1985).

9) "Dialogue with Deaf Children: Its Relation to Intellectual and Personal Growth" (1-year project; awarded $74,566 in FY 1985).

10) "A Cross-Disability Study of Mother-Infant Attachment" (1-year project; awarded $76,574 in FY 1985).

MARY E. SWITZER FELLOWSHIP PROGRAM

Rheable Edwards, Program Director
3522 Switzer Office Building
330 C Street, SW
Washington, DC 20202
(202/732–1200)

Program: The Mary E. Switzer Fellowship Program was established to provide support to individuals to perform research on the rehabilitation of disabled persons. Fellows are expected to devote full time for one year to the fellowship activity and must work in a setting related to the proposed research. Fellowships are awarded in two categories: Distinguished Fellowships for individuals who have a doctorate and seven or more years experience, and Merit Fellowships for individuals with less experience and some graduate training.

Budget: NIHR anticipated awarding approximately $400,000 in new fellowships in FY 1986.

Application/Review Process: See the general discussion of NIHR above. An annual announcement of fellowship availability is published in the *Federal Register.* The deadline for applications is generally in April. NIHR has the option either to designate priority areas for the fellowship program or to leave the competition open to any topic. In recent years the Institute has done both.

Funding Mechanisms: See the general discussion of NIHR above. Fellowship awards offer a stipend of up to $50,000 plus travel expenses.

Examples of Funded Research:
1) "Telecommunications and an Interactive Process Approach to Literacy in Deaf Young Adults."

2) "The Development of an Instrument to Assess Personality in Mildly Mentally Retarded Adults."

3) "Impact of International Exchanges of Information on Innovative Responses to Disability."

4) "The Future of Disability: Epidemiology and Corporate Resources."

5) "Barriers to the Rehabilitation of Mildly Handicapped Youth: Social and Vocational Incompetency During the Postsecondary School Transition."

Special Education Programs

DIVISION OF INNOVATION AND DEVELOPMENT

RESEARCH IN EDUCATION OF THE HANDICAPPED

James Johnson, Chief, Field-Initiated and Student-Initiated Research Programs (202/732–1123)
Nancy Safer, Chief, Directed Research Program (202/732–1109)
400 Maryland Avenue, SW
Washington, DC 20202

Program: The Research in Education of the Handicapped program supports applied research, surveys, and demonstration projects relating to the educational needs of handicapped children. Research and related activities should be designed to increase knowledge and understanding of handicapping conditions, and teaching, learning, and education-related practices and services for handicapped children and youth, including physical education and recreation.

Two categories of projects supported by the program, Field-Initiated Research and Student-Initiated Research, are of particular interest to social and behavioral scientists.

Field-Initiated Research projects may cover a broad range of topics proposed by professionals and/or faculty that fall outside the areas of interest of the directed research activities of the Special Education Programs. The FIR program has two basic characteristics: (1) investigators in the field initiate the areas, thus the program is reactive to the the needs and new ideas of the field; and (2) since any topic of applied research in educating the handicapped is eligible, it allows maximum flexibility for consideration of a wide variety of ideas for research. Internal coherence and technical quality of the project plan serve as the primary basis for evaluating applications.

Student-Initiated Research projects support research training for students (primarily graduate-level) by funding projects initiated and directed by the student and carried out under the supervision of a professor. Awards may cover the cost of such items as data collection, data analysis, travel, materials, necessary equipment, communications, and report preparation. General salary or stipend support for the student is not permitted. Consultant fees must be justified.

Both categories are limited only by the mission of the program—the support of applied research related to the education of handicapped children and youth. Proposals from any discipline may be considered; multidisciplinary projects are encouraged.

In addition to these two funding categories, Research in the Education of the Handicapped also has a directed (solicited) research program. Different priorities are designated for each competition, although a competition may not be held every year.

Budget: In FY 1986 approximately $1.8 million was available for new Field-Initiated Research projects. Approximately $150,000 was available for new Student-Initiated Research projects.

Application/Review Process: A general announcement for Research in Education of the Handicapped is published in the *Federal Register,* usually in July. Specific program deadlines vary. Proposals are reviewed by ad hoc peer panels.

Funding Mechanisms: Field-Initiated Research projects may be funded for a period of up to 60 months, although most projects are for 1 to 3 years. Awards and generally range from $30,000 to $130,000 for the first year. Student-Initiated Research projects may be funded for up to 18 months; awards are typically under $10,000.

Examples of Funded Research: Field-Initiated Research projects:

1) "Improving the Sociolinguistic Behavior of Retarded Children in Relation to Nonhandicapped Peers" (awarded $83,475 in FY 1985).

2) "Experimental Comparison of Alternative Types of Parent Involvement in Early Intervention" (awarded $114,120 in FY 1985).

3) "Interaction Between Mothers and Handicapped Infants" (awarded $80,768 in FY 1985).

4) "Validation of Social Skills for Successful Performance in Community Environments by Learners with Moderate and Severely Profound Disabilities" (awarded $118,006 in FY 1985).

5) "The Experimental Acquisition of Sociocommunicative Skills in Young Children with Severe Handicaps" (awarded $107,384 in FY 1985).

6) "The Modification of Attitudes Toward Handicapped Persons: A Comprehensive Integrative Review of Research" (awarded $79,613 in FY 1985).

7) "The Prevalence of Handicapping Conditions Among Juvenile Offenders" (awarded $86,447 in FY 1985).

Student-Initiated Research projects:

1) "Componential Analysis of Analogical Reasoning Processes of Learning Disabled Children" (awarded $7,207 in FY 1985).

2) "Achievement, Motivation, Coping Processes, and Sports Participation of Elite Athletes with Physical Handicaps" (awarded $14,713 in FY 1985).

3) "Prenatal Diagnosis of Child Impairment: Parental Adaptation to Prior Knowledge of Impairment" (awarded $17,108 in FY 1985).

4) "Comparative Effects of Computer-Assisted Instruction on Motivation and Achievement of Learning Disabled and Non-Learning Disabled Students" (awarded $7,752 in FY 1985).

5) "Siblings as Communication Trainers for Prelinguistic Infants with Down's Syndrome" (awarded $8,253 in FY 1985).

OFFICE OF BILINGUAL EDUCATION AND MINORITY LANGUAGES AFFAIRS

Edward Fuentes, Deputy Assistant Director
Reporters Building, Room 421
7th and D Streets, SW
Washington, DC 20202
(202/245–2600)

Program: The Office of Bilingual Education and Minority Languages Affairs (OBEMLA) is responsible for managing the substantial sums appropriated annually to support bilingual education programs and certain other activities aimed at school children with limited English proficiency and other groups. While the bulk of OBEMLA administered funds goes to local education agencies for the operation of instructional programs, the Office does support research and evaluation activities of interest to psychologists, linguists, anthropologists, and other social and behavioral scientists involved in educational research.

The research and evaluation activities of the Office include (1) evaluating the educational programs sponsored by OBEMLA and (2) sponsoring research aimed at determining the most effective classroom procedure for teaching limited-English-speaking children in American schools. Perhaps more so than most educational issues, federally supported bilingual education has been a highly political issue for two decades. Consequently the programs administered by OBEMLA have been buffeted by controversy and policy changes over the years.

After a period when almost all OBEMLA research activities were farmed out to other agencies, the newly reorganized Research and Evaluation staff anticipate a return in FY 1987 to a competitively awarded contract research program. Research topics are likely to parallel the ongoing research supported by the Office in FY 1986, which includes: (1) immersion studies, (2) a longitudinal survey (begun in 1983), (3) evaluation model studies, and (4) parent preference surveys.

Budget: In FY 1986 approximately $3.8 million was allocated for research and evaluation, of which approximately 80% was committed to ongoing projects. While the FY 1987 budget for evaluation and research is likely to be lower, the ongoing commitments will require less than $1 million.

Application/Review Process: Most research will be contracted for on the basis of Requests For Proposals (RPFs). While all RFPs are announced in the *Commerce Business Daily,* OBEMLA maintains a standing mailing list of potential applicants; interested social scientists may request that their names be placed on this list. Applications are evaluated by a two-track process. Technical and programmatic evaluation is performed by a review panel (frequently formed around the core staff who prepared the RFP). A separate budget review is conducted by an OBEMLA contract officer. Review panels are formed for each RFP competition. The Office negotiates with the applicants considered to be technically capable of performing the work. Final decisions are taken by the director of OBEMLA based on recommendations of the review panel and the contract officer.

Funding Mechanisms: Research and evaluation projects are funded through contracts. Specific guidelines are established for each competition.

Examples of Funded Research:
1)   "Tense Marking in Second Language Learning: Patterns of Spoken and Written English in a Vietnamese Community" (awarded $50,891 in FY 1983).

2)   "The Causal Relationship Between Bilingualism, Cognition, and Social Cognitive Skills" (2-year project; awarded $135,000).

3)   "Nonverbal Factors in the Education of Chinese American Students" (awarded $14,476 in FY 1981).

4)   "Investigation of Language Behavior Among Puerto Ricans in the U.S." (awarded $62,180 in FY 1981).

5)   "Improving the Functional Writing of Urban Secondary Students" (awarded $136,000 in FY 1981).

DEPARTMENT OF HEALTH AND HUMAN SERVICES

Office of the Secretary

Assistant Secretary for Planning and Evaluation

Gerald Britten, Deputy Assistant Secretary, Office of Program Systems
447-D HHH Building
200 Independence Avenue, SW
Washington, DC 20201
(202/245–9774)

Program: In addition to the principal function of policy development, the office of the Assistant Secretary for Planning and Evaluation (ASPE) has two support functions within the Department of Health and Human Services: the conduct of research on policy issues of interest to both the executive and legislative branches and evaluations of HHS programs and policies. Evaluations are performed by this office usually in cross-cutting areas germane to more than one program, in cases where an agency does not have sufficient staff or resources to conduct its own evaluation, or in cases where an objective, external evaluation of a program is necessary.

The ASPE policy research program has moved from long-term, high cost projects to smaller and more targeted studies. This change in the nature of ASPE research has occurred concurrently with the steady decline in its research budget. The FY 1986 budget represents a 75% decrease from its FY 1980 level. A number of ASPE research projects are mandated or suggested by the Congress; in some cases the performer of the research is also mandated.

Most ASPE research interests fall in one of four broad categories:

1) income security and employment (principally welfare and retirement policy, addressing questions such as: What is the nature of welfare dependency and how is it affected by such factors as female-headed households, minorities, adolescent pregnancy? What are appropriate public and private sector interventions? How effective are employment programs for minorities? Do family issues and a history of family welfare dependency contribute to its perpetuation? What is the proper balance between social security and private pensions? How could federal policies encourage or stimulate increased private sector participation?);

2) health policy (principally to explore changes in the health care system and the impact of HHS policies on that system, addressing questions such as: What incentives will encourage prudent "buying" of health care? What are the be-

nefits of free enterprise? What geographic variances occur in health care costs/ delivery? What effect do preventive efforts such as anti-smoking campaigns and prenatal care have on health care costs?);

3) social services policy (examining questions such as: What incentives found effective in the private sector can be introduced in the public sector? How can increased private sector service provision, such as employer-provided day care, be encouraged? How can social services be made more effective and efficient? What are the effects of voucher systems and competitive bidding?);

4) long-term care policy (addressing questions such as: What are the policy implications and costs of alternative long-term care systems, e.g., home-delivered care and case management? What are possible new ways to organize/ deliver long-term care? What are the barriers to/incentives for private insurance?).

Budget: In FY 1986 ASPE will have approximately $7 million available for evaluation projects and $6 million for policy research. About 20% of the research funds were expected to be available for new projects. In future years ASPE officials hope to make more of the budget available for new starts.

Application/Review Process: ASPE issues very specific requests for proposals in each of the four priority areas, usually in the *Federal Register* or the *Commerce Business Daily.* Proposals are reviewed by ad hoc panels convened according to topic and generally composed of federal staff. Review panel recommendations are only advisory; final funding decisions are made by the program officers and the Assistant Secretary.

ASPE has a fairly well-defined grantee network. Because research dollars are scarce, awards are most likely to go to researchers known for the quality of their work. Contact with program staff prior to submitting proposals is encouraged.

Funding Mechanisms: ASPE awards grants, contracts, and task orders (competitively awarded purchase orders, usually up to $600,000 each, which contract for multiple short-term studies in a particular subject area).

Examples of Funded Research:
1) "Causes of Growth in Payments for Medicare Part B, Physician Services" (awarded $222,000 in FY 1985).

2) "Poverty and Family Structure" (awarded $50,000 in FY 1985).

3) "Factors in AFDC Participation Rates" (awarded $77,000 in FY 1985).

4) "Study of Preferred Provider Organizations as Alternative Financing and Delivery System Models" (awarded $638,000 in FY 1985).

5) "Hospital Capital Financing Practices in a Variety of Settings" (awarded $340,000 in FY 1985).

Health Care Financing Administration

OFFICE OF RESEARCH AND DEMONSTRATIONS

Michael Hoban, Director of Operations Support
2226 Oak Meadows Building
6325 Security Boulevard
Baltimore, MD 21207
(301/594-7370)

Program: The Office of Research and Demonstrations (ORD) of the Health Care Financing Administration (HCFA) provides funds for research and demonstration projects that will help to resolve major health care financing issues or to develop innovative methods for the administration of Medicare and Medicaid. Supported are studies of program impact on beneficiary health status, access to services, utilization, and out-of-pocket expenditures. The organizational behavior and economic impact of health care providers and the overall health care industry are also topics of investigation. Currently the ORD has more than 300 research, demonstration, and evaluation projects of which approximately 200 are either cooperative agreements or grants, and 100 are either contracts or intramural projects.

The Office of Research conducts and supports data collection efforts and research on health care providers, reimbursement, beneficiary behavior, and health care utilization. The Office of Demonstrations and Evaluations supports and manages demonstrations and evaluates demonstration projects that test new delivery and financing systems for Medicare and Medicaid services.

The HCFA research program comprises seven broad priority areas:

1) hospital payment (prospective payment systems, hospital and subacute care, voucher systems and their impact on hospitals, development of systems to combine physician and hospital payments, etc.);

2) physician payment (physician payment appropriate for Medicare and Medicaid, effects of voucher system on physician participation in Medicare, development of competitive-bidding payment models, etc.);

3) state programs for long-term care (promotion of home care by family or community support arrangements, study and analysis of predictors of institutionalization, new approaches to financing and delivering long-term care, prospective payments and competitive bidding for skilled nursing homes, etc.);

4) alternate payment systems (health maintenance organizations, preferred provider organizations, voucher systems, HMO performance, long-term effects of competition, adjusted average per capita cost, etc.);

5)   program analysis and evaluation (geographic variations in medical care use and costs, relationship between work history and health, effects of the prospective payment system on beneficiaries, impact of program changes and factors influencing program performance, etc.);

6)   quality and coverage (development of valid quality-of-care measurements, coverage of alcoholism and mental health services, cost effectiveness of new technology, etc.);

7)   beneficiary awareness and prevention (effectiveness of self-care training for patients, health education and behavior modification projects, impact of prenatal care on Medicaid costs, etc.).

HCFA funds pragmatic, applied research with a strong empirical emphasis. Applications for cooperative agreements and grants may be submitted by private or public nonprofit agencies or organizations, including state agencies that administer the Medicaid program. Private for-profit organizations may apply for cooperative agreements or grants (discretionary funds).

The HCFA research program is strongly affected by political processes; congressionally mandated studies constitute a significant portion of the research portfolio. HCFA staff anticipate that "coverage and quality" will receive the highest priority in the future.

Budget: The FY 1985 budget of the ORD was $34 million. Approximately $6.5 million was available for new cooperative agreements and grants, and approximately $6.1 million was awarded for new contracts.

Application/Review Process: Annual announcements of priority areas and application procedures are published in the *Federal Register.* Awards are made approximately 5 to 6 months after the closing date. Deadlines are generally established in November of each year; the deadline for FY 1987 funds is November 3, 1986. Proposals are reviewed by ad hoc peer review panels selected by the ORD director. The panels provide a rating for each application; final review and final funding decisions are made by the ORD director.

Contracts are awarded through regular federal procurement procedures. Requests for proposals for contracts are announced in the *Commerce Business Daily.*

Funding Mechanisms: Cooperative agreements and grants range from $35,000 to $275,000. Project periods generally do not exceed three years.

Examples of Funded Research:
1)   "Allocation of Resources Under the Budget Constraints Imposed by the British National Health Service" (4-year project; total costs $127,794).

2)   "Creating Diagnosis-Related-Group-Based Physician Reimbursement Schemes: A Conceptual and Empirical Analysis" (2-year project; total costs $503,424).

3) "Assess (State) Tax Incentives as a Means of Strengthening the Informal Support System for the Elderly" (3-year project; total costs $167,168).

4) "Systematic Examination of Factors That Promote Home Care by the Family" (3-year project; total costs $393,153).

5) "Test of the Out-of-Pocket Cost Savings as an Incentive for Changing Beneficiary Choice Behavior" (3-year project; total costs $709,316).

6) "Study of Medicare-Funded Heart Transplants" (3-year project; total costs $1,626,294).

7) "Impact of Psychological Intervention on Health Care Utilization and Costs: A Prospective Study" (5-year project; total costs $955,000).

8) "Prenatal Care and Its Relationship to Medicaid Costs" (2-year project; total costs $78,679).

Office of Human Development Services

The Office of Human Development Services (OHDS) is divided into four programmatic units: the Administration for Children, Youth, and Families; the Administration on Developmental Disabilities; the Administration on Aging; and the Administration for Native Americans. Since 1981, OHDS has focused its efforts on three goals: (1) increasing family and individual self-sufficiency and independence through social and economic development strategies; (2) targeting federal assistance to those most in need; and (3) improving the effectiveness and efficiency of state, local, and tribally administered human services. The OHDS research agenda is driven by these goals. One method OHDS has used to target research efforts on very specific administration goals has been to coordinate most competitive funds from the four programs into one comprehensive program, the Coordinated Discretionary Funds Program. Very little basic research is now supported by OHDS, and the amount is not expected to increase. OHDS officials feel that, instead, resources should be concentrated on demonstration, application, and replication projects.

COORDINATED DISCRETIONARY FUNDS PROGRAM

Ramon Garcia, Chief, Analysis and Review Branch
721-B HHH Building
200 Independence Avenue, SW
Washington, DC 20201
(202/245–6233)

Program: The Coordinated Discretionary Funds Program (CDP) is the major research and demonstration effort of OHDS. The overriding theme of the CDP is to promote self-sufficiency utilizing an increasing proportion of private sector resources and initiatives. Toward this goal, proposals which propose the use of volunteers or involve the private sector are favored. A new component of the FY 1986 CDP solicitation is the inclusion of proposals which entail joint projects with private foundations. All CDP proposals must clearly target one or more OHDS populations: the elderly; children, youth, and families; Native Americans; the poor; and the developmentally disabled.

Current research priorities for the CDP include:

1) promotion of economic independence of individuals;

2) support for families and community-based care;

3) promotion of housing alternatives and living arrangements;

4)   preparation for an aging society;

5)   foundations/OHDS partnerships;

6)   strengthening the function of state and local agencies and tribal governments;

7)   improving the management of human services;

8)   child welfare services training;

9)   education, awareness, and training in aging;

10)   transfer of international innovations.

According to OHDS staff, few evaluation proposals are submitted. Proposals for state-of-the-art assessments by academics who are experts in their fields would be welcome.

Budget: The FY 1985 budget for CDP research was approximately $33 million.

Application/Review Process: OHDS has experimented with several application and review procedures since the inception of the CDP program. For FY 1986 the program reverts back to a single-stage application submitted to the OHDS Division of Research and Demonstration. OHDS senior staff select some proposals for administrative review; most proposals reviewed this way do receive funding. The balance are referred for competitive review by panels of federal and nonfederal members. A list of approved reviewers is maintained from which senior OHDS staff make panel selections. Results of the panel reviews are considered by the OHDS staff in making funding decisions.

An announcement of CDP research priorities and application procedures are published in the *Federal Register,* generally in August or September, with a November deadline.

Funding Mechanisms: CDP will award grants and cooperative agreements. Proposals may be submitted for project periods of up to 3 years, although awards are made for one year at a time. Grants may range from $10,000 to $200,000. The average award is $100,000. At least 25% of the total cost of a proposed project must come from nonfederal sources, except projects funded under the Native Americans Act, where the grantee share must be 20%.

Examples of Funded Projects:

1)   "One Company—One Kid" (a demonstration program directed by a major university designed to involve corporations, local government, and community resources in placing special needs children with adoptive parents).

2)   "Runaway and Homeless Youth Post Institutional Services."

Public Health Service

ALCOHOL, DRUG ABUSE, AND MENTAL HEALTH ADMINISTRATION

National Institute on Alcohol Abuse and Alcoholism

The National Institute on Alcohol Abuse and Alcoholism (NIAAA) provides support for basic and applied alcohol research. The long-range goal of the research program is to develop new knowledge that will facilitate the achievement of two broad objectives: to reduce the incidence and prevalence of alcohol abuse and alcoholism and to reduce the morbidity and mortality associated with alcohol use, alcohol abuse, and alcoholism.

NIAAA supports alcohol-relevant research in many disciplines, including anthropology, economics, epidemiology, psychology, and sociology. Studies must be clearly related to the etiology, prevalence, prediction, diagnosis, prognosis, treatment, management, or prevention of alcoholism, or other alcohol-related problems.

Most proposals funded by NIAAA are submitted in response to a general program announcement. In addition, NIAAA issues announcements of special research interests, as well as joint program announcements with the National Institute on Drug Abuse, the National Institute of Mental Health, and the National Institutes of Health. Two special program announcements which will remain open through FY 1986 concern the prevention of alcohol, drug abuse, and mental health disorders at the worksite, and community prevention research in alcohol and drug abuse.

The research program of NIAAA is administered through the Extramural Research Division, the Biometry and Epidemiology Division, and the Intramural Clinical and Biological Research Division. Most social and behavioral science research is located in the Clinical and Psychosocial Research Branch of the Extramural Research Division.

CLINICAL AND PSYCHOSOCIAL RESEARCH BRANCH

Ernestine Vanderveen, Chief
14C-17 Parklawn Building
5600 Fishers Lane
Rockville, MD 20857
(301/443–4223)

Program: The NIAAA research program is divided into six areas, all of which can be addressed by the Clinical and Psychosocial Research Branch. The areas are:

1) biomedical and genetic factors, including neuropharmacology and biological-behavioral linkages and animal models;

2) psychological and environmental factors, including social, cultural, environmental and familial factors, and psychosocial aspects of special populations;

3) alcohol-related problems and medical disorders, including accidents and violence, birth defects, and central nervous system disorders and cognitive impairment;

4) treatment, including diagnostic classification, psychological and behavioral intervention, special population treatment issues, outcome monitoring, efficacy and access, and diagnostic tools;

5) prevention, including risk precursors and high-risk groups, health promotion as a prevention modality, and influence of law and policy;

6) epidemiology, including patterns of use and abuse and models of incidence and prevalence.

Research priorities also include studies of traffic safety, injury and death due to alcohol use/abuse, and the problems of special populations (the elderly, women, youth, and minorities).

Most grantees supported by this branch are psychologists, sociologists, and public health professionals. Few applications are received in the areas of prevention and epidemiology, although these areas have wide applicability for the social and behavioral sciences.

Application/Review Process: See the general descriptions of NIH and ADAMHA in chapter 4.

Funding Mechanisms: See the general descriptions of NIH and ADAMHA in chapter 4.

Budget: This branch had an FY 1985 budget of $6 million. Except for some funding of collaborative projects with other Institutes, the branch budget goes to extramural research in the social and behavioral sciences.

Examples of Funded Research:
1) "Alcohol Affect and Aggression" (awarded $85,762 in FY 1984).

2) "Adolescent Drinking Patterns in Puerto Ricans" (awarded $55,116 in FY 1984).

3) "Patterns of Alcohol Abuse and Family Stability" (awarded $59,414 in FY 1984).

4) "Prenatal Alcohol Exposure and Development in Early Childhood" (awarded $64,547 in FY 1984).

5) "Environmental Treatment of Alcohol Abusers" (awarded $255,810 in FY 1984).

6) "Social Psychological Aspects of Alcoholism in Women" (awarded $53,974 in FY 1984).

7) "Behavioral-Economic Analysis of Alcoholic Relapse" (awarded $81,386 in FY 1984).

8) "Structure and Content of Employee Alcoholism Programs" (awarded $374,124 in FY 1984).

9) "Prevention Research: Server Intervention and the Law" (awarded $56,468 in FY 1984).

10) "Black and Hispanic Alcohol Problems: A National Study" (awarded $477,173 in FY 1984).

National Institute on Drug Abuse

The research programs of the National Institute on Drug Abuse (NIDA) are aimed at increasing knowledge of narcotic addiction and drug abuse and at developing improved methods for the assessment, treatment, and prevention of these problems. Research support ranges from fundamental studies on the mechanisms of action of abused drugs to applied research and development activities. Because of the broad mission of NIDA, to study "the nature and extent of drug abuse in the U.S.," support is available for a wide range of social and behavioral science disciplines. Traditionally grantees have included epidemiologists, ethnographers, psychologists, sociologists, and social workers. NIDA research would also be particularly appropriate for other anthropologists, criminologists, economists, historians, and statisticians.

Research announcements are issued to stimulate proposals in areas of general or special Institute interest. Joint program announcements with the National Institute on Alcohol Abuse and Alcoholism and the National Institute of Mental Health are released periodically soliciting proposals in cross-cutting areas. All NIDA programs are currently placing a high priority on studies of cocaine and marijuana use.

It is estimated that approximately 50% of applications submitted to NIDA are approved for funding; 25% are actually funded.

The NIDA extramural research program is administered by three divisions: Clinical Research, Epidemiology and Statistical Analysis, and Preclinical Research.

DIVISION OF CLINICAL RESEARCH

CLINICAL AND BEHAVIORAL PHARMACOLOGY BRANCH

J. Michael Walsh, Chief
10A-16 Parklawn Building
5600 Fishers Lane
Rockville, MD 20857
(301/443-1263)

Program: The Clinical and Behavioral Pharmacology Branch supports studies ranging from basic research using animal models to experimental treatment programs. Areas supported include abuse liability and behavioral mechanisms of action, effects of drugs on performance, behavioral intervention strategies in treatment and evaluations of new agents and new uses for extant drugs. In addition, the branch has a large smoking cessation program and a pain and analgesics program. In keeping with Institute-wide priorities, the branch may fund studies related to cocaine, marijuana, and Acquired Immune Deficiency Syndrome (AIDS).

The principal new interest of this branch is in the area of drug use and human performance: effects on school children in learning situations; effects on worker productivity in industry; and effects on individual performance in team situations. Studies to develop "assessment batteries" to determine fitness for duty are also encouraged.

Most of the research in this branch is primarily of interest to psychologists and psychiatrists. Branch staff are encouraging researchers to become more involved with medical schools, incorporate more human subjects into their research, and propose more rigorous clinical research.

Budget: This branch had an FY 1985 budget of $11 million for extramural research. Approximately 80% of the budget goes to the behavioral sciences.

Application/Review Process: See the general descriptions of NIH and ADAMHA in chapter 4. Preliminary contact with the appropriate program manager before submitting applications is strongly encouraged.

Funding Mechanisms: See the general descriptions of NIH and ADAMHA in chapter 4.

Examples of Funded Research:
1)   "Effects of Drugs on Group Behavior" (funded for 6 years; total direct costs, $548,677).

2) "Smoked Marijuana: Motivational and Performance Effects" (funded for 3 years; total direct costs, $259,329).

3) "Maintaining Non-Smoking" (funded for 6 years; total direct costs, $561,591).

4) "Psychopharmacology of Drug Abuse" (career development award; funded for 8 years; total direct costs, $326,580).

5) "Opiates: Mechanisms of Action on Learning" (funded for 2 years; total direct costs, $89,315).

6) "Behavioral Pharmacology of Addiction Treatment" (funded for 1 year; total direct costs, $209,089).

7) "Interaction of Abused Drugs with Interpersonal Behavior" (funded for 3 years; total direct costs, $179,974).

TREATMENT RESEARCH BRANCH

Frank M. Tims, Chief
10A-30 Parklawn Building
5600 Fishers Lane
Rockville, MD 20857
(301/443-4060)

Program: In the past, a major portion of the budget of the Treatment Research Branch has gone to studies of heroin and methadone and long-term assessments of traditional treatment models. The branch would like to expand its focus and move toward developing new integrated, innovative treatment models with attention to social, biological, environmental and individual behavioral characteristics. Studies which assess the effectiveness of a variety of treatment strategies (pharmacological and behavioral) in a broad range of settings (private clinics, family doctors, mental health centers) would be welcome.

Special emphasis should be placed on antecedents to treatment, the mechanisms of treatment, and the direct effects of treatment during relatively brief follow-up periods. Proposals should include clearly defined and finite follow-up conditions and clear control conditions, and they should focus on the reliability and validity of the data obtained in terms of extension to treatment in non-research settings.

Topics of interest to the branch include in-patient versus out-patient treatment; interactions between drugs-behavior-environment; interactions between prescribed drugs and illicit drugs, alcohol, and tobacco; antecedents to stimulant use; commonalities across treatments of drug abuse and other bio-behavioral disorders; and treatment models for different socioeconomic groups.

Budget: The FY 1985 budget for this branch was approximately $6 million for all extramural research.

Application/Review Process: See the general descriptions of NIH and ADAMHA in chapter 4. Preliminary contact with the appropriate program manager before submitting applications is strongly encouraged.

Funding Mechanisms: See the general descriptions of NIH and ADAMHA in chapter 4.

Examples of Funded Research:
1) "Adolescent Drug Abuse Treatment and Early Intervention" (funded for 4 years; total direct costs, $815,188).

2) "Treatment Utilization and Treatment Needs" (funded for 3 years; total direct costs, $460,057).

3) "Methadone Treatment: A Study of a County Policy Change" (funded for 3 years; total direct costs, $447,217).

4) "Addicts' and Agencies' Expectations of Treatment" (funded for 3 years; total direct costs, $452,026).

5) "National Survey of Outpatient Drug Abuse Treatment" (funded for 3 years; total direct costs, $401,923).

6) "Intergenerational Family Therapy with Drug Abusers" (funded for 2 years; total direct costs, $117,485).

7) "Careers of Opioid Users" (funded for 3 years; total direct costs, $244,615).

8) "Relapse to Three Abused Drugs" (funded for 3 years; total direct costs, $332,794).

PREVENTION RESEARCH BRANCH

Catherine Bell, Chief
10A-16 Parklawn Building
5600 Fishers Lane
Rockville, MD 20857
(301/443–1514)

Program: The Prevention Research Branch supports studies of (1) primary disease prevention and health promotion interventions aimed at reducing the incidence of drug abuse, (2) outreach and early intervention programs for novice drug users and abusers who have not been clinically identified, (3) methods for early identification and screening of persons at risk for drug abuse, and (4) risk factors as a basis for the design of preventive interventions.

Four areas of research are identified as ongoing priorities for this branch:

1) risk factors in drug experimentation, including identifying subpopulations at risk, interpersonal risk factors, efficacy of parental limit-setting, social and environmental factors conducive to drug abuse;

2) methodology development, including new research protocols, methods, and assessment techniques (cost/benefit analysis, community impact, etc.);

3) intervention research, including social skills, inoculation training, and community intervention;

4) secondary data analysis of existing large data bases and large-sample studies which compare different populations or explore interrelationships among various risk factors.

Future priorities of this branch include the study of drug abuse etiology (behavioral and family genetics, psychological, environmental, and social influences), research on high-risk individuals (particularly minorities), and early intervention strategies. Applications in the area of small and tightly controlled studies of individual behavior such as early precursors, attitudes, and beliefs are also encouraged.

Budget: The FY 1985 budget for this branch was $4.5 million, all going to extramural support of the social and behavioral sciences.

Application/Review Process: See the general descriptions of NIH and ADAMHA in chapter 4. Preliminary contact with the appropriate program manager before submitting applications is strongly encouraged.

Funding Mechanisms: See the general descriptions of NIH and ADAMHA in chapter 4.

Examples of Funded Research:
1) "Family Therapy for Drug Abusing Adolescents" (funded for 5 years; total direct costs, $901,406).

2) "Childhood Etiologic Determinants of Adolescent Drug Use" (funded for 3 years; total direct costs, $446,248).

3) "Effects of Drug Abuse Message Styles" (funded for 3 years; total direct costs, $142,999).

4) "Cigarette Smoking and Public Policy" (career development award; funded for 5 years; total direct costs, $182,392).

5) "Drug Abuse, Stress, and Adaptation in Old People" (funded for 4 years; total direct costs, $538,623).

6) "Drug Abuse Prevention and Black Parent Training" (funded for 3 years; total direct costs, $674,033.

7) "Drug Abuse Assessment in Industry: Phase II" (funded for 2 years; total direct costs, $215,185).

8) "A Value Approach to Reducing and Preventing Smoking" (funded for 4 years; total direct costs, $438,616).

DIVISION OF EPIDEMIOLOGY AND STATISTICAL ANALYSIS

EPIDEMIOLOGIC RESEARCH BRANCH

Michael Backenheimer, Research Sociologist
11A-55 Parklawn Building
5600 Fishers Lane
Rockville, MD 20857
(301/443-2974)

Program: Research grants are relatively new to the Division of Epidemiology and Statistical Analysis. All are administered through the Epidemiologic Research Branch.

Five research areas are identified as being of particular interest to the branch:

1) population trends in drug abuse with particular emphasis on measures of incidence and prevalence, including new methods, studies, techniques, and other epidemiologic approaches to trend measurement, and studies of high-risk populations (minorities, youth);

2) consequences of drug abuse/addiction, including indicators such as crime, family disintegration, motivation, subcultures, and longitudinal studies which seek measurement of consequences and change over time;

3) risk factors associated with drug abuse/addiction, including the use potential of selected social indicators and demographic variables and trends as predictors;

4) epidemiologic methods employed in drug abuse/addiction, including the development of innovative and imaginative approaches to the study of epidemiologic phenomena, and the development of reliable and valid sampling frames within high risk populations;

5) the natural history of drug abuse/addiction, including the processes and mechanisms by which individuals advance through the varied stages and drugs

involved in the phenomenon, particularly career patterns of minority populations.

Other special interests of the Epidemiologic Research Branch are studies of the nature and extent of drug abuse in industry, drug use by the elderly (particularly how physicians prescribe for the elderly), the economic costs of drug abuse, and studies by criminologists. The branch is also seeking to encourage the involvement of minority researchers in the drug abuse field.

Budget: Nine new grants were funded by this branch in FY 1985, ranging in size from $1.2 million to less than $70,000. Typical awards are under $200,000 for direct costs.

Application/Review Process: See the general descriptions of NIH and ADAMHA in chapter 4. Preliminary contact with the appropriate program manager before submitting applications is strongly encouraged.

Funding Mechanisms: See the general descriptions of NIH and ADAMHA in chapter 4.

Examples of Funded Research:
1)   "Drug Use and Lifestyle in American Youth" (awarded $1.2 million for direct costs for FY 1985).

2)   "Economic Behavior of Street Opiate Addicts" (awarded $67,000 for direct costs for FY 1985).

3)   "Drug Use Among Young Indians: Epidemiology and Correlates" (awarded $258,000 for direct costs for FY 1985).

DIVISION OF PRECLINICAL RESEARCH

NEUROSCIENCES RESEARCH BRANCH

Roger Brown, Chief
10A-31 Parklawn Building
5600 Fishers Lane
Rockville, MD 20857
(301/443-6975)

Program: The Neurosciences Research Branch encourages investigations into the basic mechanisms underlying the action of abused drugs and substances, including tobacco and inhalants, on the central nervous system at the neuronal level or higher. Research which focuses on the relationship between drug and substance abuse and the central nervous system mechanisms which underlie behavioral processes is specifically encouraged. Priority areas for this branch include brain-reward mechanisms, brain function-drug-environment interactions, drug-induced neuropathology, drug influences on brain development, and pain mechanisms.

The Neurosciences Branch particularly encourages multidisciplinary research by teams of natural and behavioral scientists. If appropriate neural models have been developed, joint efforts by biochemists and experimental psychologists would be particularly welcomed.

Another area of growing interest for this branch is the developmental consequences of drug abuse. Of particular interest would be studies of the consequences of drug abuse on prenatal and postnatal development and the behavioral methodology to determine the effects of maternal drug use on offspring.

Budget: The FY 1985 budget of this branch was approximately $10 million, of which about 50% went to behavioral science research.

Application/Review Process: See the general descriptions of NIH and ADAMHA in chapter 4. Preliminary contact with the appropriate program manager before submitting applications is strongly encouraged.

Funding Mechanisms: See the general descriptions of NIH and ADAMHA in chapter 4.

Examples of Funded Research:
1) "Effects of Abused Drugs on Neuronal Integration."
2) "Neuronal Substrate of Opiate Analgesia."
3) "Conditioning of Tolerance to Morphine."
4) "Opiate Actions in Brain Reward Mechanisms."
5) "Action of Marijuana on Brain Metabolism."
6) "Environmental Modulation of Opiate Reward."

National Institute of Mental Health

[Editor's note: In 1985 the National Institute of Mental Health underwent a major reorganization aimed at clarifying the function and primary mission of NIMH as a research Institute. Existing divisions (except intramural research) were abolished and new ones created, based more on function than on topical areas. The reorganization entailed numerous programmatic, staff, and logistical changes that were not made final until the end of 1985; some changes may still occur in 1986. A special note of thanks goes to Dr. Frank Sullivan, NIMH Deputy Director, and his staff for providing the program descriptions for NIMH.]

The National Institute of Mental Health (NIMH) is the focal point for federal support of basic research and training in mental health. Thus, the Institute is a significant source of support for social and behavioral scientists in a number of disciplines.

The reorganization of NIMH in 1985 was effected to align the structure of the Institute in emphasizing its mission of research, dissemination of research findings, and technical assistance in the promotion and improvement of mental health services. Although well over half of the total budget is expended for extramural research, the Institute also has a distinguished intramural program, as well as dissemination, education, and services programs.

The Institute's extramural research effort comprises three divisions: the Division of Basic Sciences, the Division of Clinical Research, and the Division of Biometry and Applied Sciences. Descriptions of the major branches within each division of interest to social and behavioral scientists are included below.

DIVISION OF BASIC SCIENCES

NEUROSCIENCES RESEARCH BRANCH

Stephen H. Koslow, Chief
11–105 Parklawn Building
5600 Fishers Lane
Rockville, MD 20857
(301/443–1504)

Program: The Neurosciences Research Branch supports brain research focusing on behavioral studies on the neural mechanisms underlying specific behavior; molecular biology research including developmental, behavioral, and functional neurobiology using recombinant DNA approaches, DNA cloning techniques, and hybridization methods; and neurobiological research on the biological mechanisms underlying regulation and modulation of normal and abnormal brain function.

A major interest is understanding, at the neurobiological level, the pathological mechanisms in states such as schizophrenia, depression or other psychoses, neuroses, organic brain syndromes and other behavioral disorders; and psychopharmacological research in preclinical areas for studies on the effects, sites, and mechanism of action of psychoactive drugs. Projects are also supported in behavioral pharmacology, drug metabolism, and related fields, including drug development, synthesis, toxicology, pharmacogenetics, and chronopharmacology.

Budget: The FY 1986 budget for this branch was projected to be approximately $36 million.

Application/Review Process: Applications are submitted to the Division of Research Grants (DRG) of the National Institutes of Health. A detailed description of the DRG and the Alcohol, Drug Abuse, and Mental Health Administration review process is included in chapter 4.

Funding Mechanisms: See the general description in chapter 4.

Examples of Funded Research:
1)   "Learning Mechanisms in Abdominal Galion of Aplysia."

2)   "Biochemistry of Neurotransmitter Receptors."

3)   "Antidepressants and Monoamine Receptors and Responses."

BEHAVIORAL SCIENCES RESEARCH BRANCH

Joy Schulterbrandt, Chief
11C10 Parklawn Building
5600 Fishers Lane
Rockville, MD 20857
(301/443-3942)

Program: The Behavioral Sciences Research Branch provides support for the development of knowledge regarding correlates of behavior relevant to normative mental health and as they relate to the precursors of mental disorders. This includes basic research projects which elucidate psychological, psychosocial, psychobiological, and environmental factors which singly or in interaction influence the development and modification of adaptive and maladaptive behavior. Of particular interest are studies focusing on behaviors which clarify the development and maintenance of effective coping and psychological adjustment, as well as those that explain how normal processes become become maladaptive and dysfunctional with the potential for serious adverse mental health consequences.

Also of interest are developmental and normative studies of behavior and their various mediators throughout the lifespan, particularly studies targeting periods in the life cycle which involve heightened vulnerability to mental and emotional distress or behavioral dysfunctions for all populations other than the aged or groups already psychiatrically diagnosed. Such studies focus on normative and non-normative transitions in normal populations and involve basic behavioral research efforts with individuals and groups whose vulnerability to behavioral dysfunctions at such targeted periods may help to clarify change mechanisms and important antecedents or precursors of maladaptive or dysfunctional outcomes.

Budget: The FY 1986 budget for this branch was projected to be approximately $20 million.

Application/Review Process: Applications are submitted to the Division of Research Grants (DRG) of the National Institutes of Health. A detailed description of the DRG and the Alcohol, Drug Abuse, and Mental Health Administration review process is included in chapter 4.

Funding Mechanisms: See the general description in chapter 4.

Examples of Funded Research:
1) "Human Learning and Retention."
2) "Origins of Mental Health Problems in the Family."
3) "Emotion, Facial Expression and ANS Activity."

HEALTH AND BEHAVIOR RESEARCH BRANCH

Ellen Simon Stover, Acting Chief
11–103 Parklawn Building
5600 Fishers Lane
Rockville, MD 20857
(301/443–3563 or 443–4337)

Program: The Health and Behavior Research Branch supports studies of the biological, psychological, and psychosocial aspects of stress and other psychological states, immunology, sleep and rhythmic behaviors, nutrition, ingestive behavior, exercise, physical disorders, and health-related attitudes and practices.

Topics of interest include studies on the development of objective measures of stress and coping capacities and the relationship of these variables to mood, cognition, and behavior. Also of interest are studies examining homeostatic processes and alterations in normal behavioral processes; biological, behavioral, psychological, and social factors in normal and abnormal patterns of ingestive behaviors and sleep/waking behavior, including the development of obesity, anorexia nervosa, bulimia, and sleep disorders; health consequences of disruptions of the normal sleep-wake cycle and abnormal work schedules; and the effect of seasonal change and nutrient intake on normal behavioral processes and how they may be altered.

Of special interest is research on the biological, behavioral, and psychosocial aspects of immune function and dysfunction; development and testing of psychological and behavioral measures to assess mental health status as related to acquired immune deficiency syndrome (AIDS); the development of methods for coping with AIDS and related diseases; research on understanding the interrelationships between psychological, social, and behavioral processes and immune function and disease; and the development of methods to assess altered immune function as a result of stressful behavior states.

Budget: The FY 1986 budget for this branch was projected to be approximately $7 million.

Application/Review Process: Applications are submitted to the Division of Research Grants (DRG) of the National Institutes of Health. A detailed description of the DRG and the Alcohol, Drug Abuse, and Mental Health Administration review process is included in chapter 4.

Funding Mechanisms: See the general description in chapter 4.

Examples of Funded Research:
1) "Adolescent Development Sleeping and Waking Behavior."
2) "Studies of Stress Resistant Children and Adults."

DIVISION OF CLINICAL RESEARCH

MENTAL DISORDERS OF THE AGING BRANCH

Barry D. Lebowitz, Acting Chief
11C-03 Parklawn Building
5600 Fishers Lane
Rockville, MD 20857
(301/443–1185)

Program: The Mental Disorders of the Aging Branch plans, supports, and conducts programs of research, research training, clinical training, and resource development in the classification, assessment, etiology, genetics, clinical course, outcome, and the pharmacologic, somatic, and psychosocial treatment and rehabilitation of organic and other mental disorders affecting the elderly, with particular emphasis on Alzheimer's disease; reviews and evaluates research development in the field; and recommends new program directions.

Major topics of interest include causes, treatment, and prevention of Alzheimer's disease, major depressive disorder, schizophrenia, and other mental disorders of elderly; the relationship between physical illness and mental disorder in the elderly; chronically mentally ill elderly; families, support systems, and self-help in the care of the elderly; and prevention of pathology among those at risk for disorder.

Budget: The FY 1986 budget for this branch was projected to be approximately $9 million.

Application/Review Process: Applications are submitted to the Division of Research Grants (DRG) of the National Institutes of Health. A detailed description of the DRG and the Alcohol, Drug Abuse, and Mental Health Administration review process is included in chapter 4.

Funding Mechanisms: See the general description in chapter 4.

Examples of Funded Research:
1) "Informed Consent in Aging Psychiatric Patients."
2) "Memory and Mental Health in Aging."
3) "Parent Care, Sibling Relationships, and Mental Health."
4) "Caring for Demented Spouses: Crisis Versus Adaptation."
5) "Social Supports, Aging, and Psychiatric Disturbances."

CHILD AND ADOLESCENT DISORDERS BRANCH

Jack D. Burke, Jr., Acting Chief
10–104 Parklawn Building
5600 Fishers Lane
Rockville, MD 20857
(301/443–5944)

Program: The Child and Adolescent Disorders Branch plans, supports, and conducts programs of research, research training, and resource development in the classification, assessment, etiology, genetics, clinical course, outcome, and the pharmacologic, somatic, and psychosocial treatment and rehabilitation of disorders affecting children and adolescents. The branch also reviews and evaluates research developments in the field and recommends new program directions.

Major topics of interest include autism, attention deficit disorder/hyperactivity, conduct disorder, affective disorders, anxiety disorders, suicide, and the emotional disorders manifested by the mentally retarded.

Budget: The FY 1986 budget for this branch was projected to be approximately $10 million.

Application/Review Process: Applications are submitted to the Division of Research Grants (DRG) of the National Institutes of Health. A detailed description of the DRG and the Alcohol, Drug Abuse, and Mental Health Administration review process is included in chapter 4.

Funding Mechanisms: See the general description in chapter 4.

Examples to Funded Research:
1) "Behavioral Assessment Battery for Children."

2) "Investigation of Cognitive Dysfunction in Autism."

3) "Attention Deficit Children: A Dimensional Analysis."

4) "Childhood Depression—Nosologic/Developmental Aspects."

5) "Treatment Process for Antisocial/Aggressive Behavior."

PREVENTION RESEARCH BRANCH

Joyce B. Lazar, Chief
14C-02 Parklawn Building
5600 Fishers Lane
Rockville, MD 20857
(301/443–4283)

Program: The major programs of the Prevention Research Branch include four research programs and one public education and professional training program:

1) Prevention of Development Disorders Among Infants at High Risk.

2) Prevention of Conduct Disorders in School Aged Children.

3)   Prevention of Anxiety and Depression Resulting from Stressful Life Conditions.

4)   Development of Coping Mechanisms.

5)   Depression Awareness, Recognition, and Treatment Campaign.

The Prevention Research Branch recognizes that preventive intervention research in the field of mental health traverses populations, research settings, disciplines, diagnostic categories, and scientific methods. Specifically, the branch is interested in supporting biological and psychosocial research that attempts to intervene in the development of mental disorders and behavioral dysfunctions, as well as research that develops interventions to promote mental health and mental well-being.

To this end, the branch has supported research in the psychosocial, cognitive, psychological, developmental, and, recently, biological areas. The Prevention Research Branch is currently funding investigators from diverse backgrounds and training, including community psychology, psychiatry, pediatrics, developmental psychology, nursing, industrial psychology, social psychology, anthropology, and social work. The focus of the work is on assessing preventive intervention trials which occur in a variety of settings, ranging from neonatal intensive care units to homes, schools, community work sites, and university and hospital laboratories.

Budget: The FY 1986 budget for this branch was projected to be approximately $7 million.

Application/Review Process: Applications are submitted to the Division of Research Grants (DRG) of the National Institutes of Health. A detailed description of the DRG and the Alcohol, Drug Abuse, and Mental Health Administration review process is included in chapter 4.

Funding Mechanisms: See the general description in chapter 4.

Examples of Funded Research:
1)   "Assessment and Intervention with Premature Infants" (funded for 3 years; total direct costs, $855,627).

2)   "Prediction and Primary Prevention of Child Maltreatment" (funded for 5 years; total direct costs, $711,419).

3)   "Prevention with Black Pre-adolescents at Social Risks" (funded for 4 years; total direct costs, $660,000).

4)   " Prevention of Antisocial Behavior in Children" (funded for 5 years; total direct costs, $1,987,075).

5)   "Physical Illness, Depression and Elderly American Indians" (funded for 3 years; total direct costs, $156,798).

6) "Hispanic Social Network Prevention Intervention Study" (funded for 3 years; total direct costs, $1,442,901).

7) "Prevention Intervention for Unemployed Vietnam Vets" (funded for 3 years; total direct costs, $1,053,432).

SCHIZOPHRENIA RESEARCH BRANCH

Samuel J. Keith, Chief
10C-06 Parklawn Building
5600 Fishers Lane
Rockville, MD 20857
(301/443-3524)

Program: The Schizophrenia Research Branch plans, supports, and conducts programs of research, training, and resource development in the classification, assessment, etiology, genetics, clinical course, outcome, pharmacologic, somatic, and psychosocial treatment and rehabilitation of schizophrenic and related disorders. The branch also reviews and evaluates research developments in the field and recommends new program directions.

There are four programs within this branch: Pharmacologic and Somantic Treatment, Resources and Analysis, Biological and Clinical Factors Research, and Psychosocial Treatment Rehabilitation.

Major topics of interest in the Pharmacologic and Somatic Treatment Pro gram include clinical development of new pharmacologic agents; clinical trials of psychotropic drugs for the treatment of schizophrenia and related conditions, and tardive dyskinesia; mechanisms, prevalence, and treatment of side effects; clinical application of pharmacologic methodology to psychotic symptomatology; and efficacy of combined treatment approaches in schizophrenia.

The Resources and Analysis Program is concerned with the development and application of statistical methodology, computer-based clinical assessment, and computer software for clinical trial design, conduct, management, and analysis.

Major topics of interest in the Biological and Clinical Factors Research Program include biochemical research on biochemical, neuroanatomical, and neuroendocrine factors as they relate to the etiology and pathophysiology of schizophrenia and related conditions; psychiatric, psychological, and socio-cultural research on the description, classification, and measurement of psychopathological states in conditions relevant to schizophrenia; the methodology of cross-cultural and cross-ethnic research on schizophrenic psychopathology; and the putative spectrum of schizophrenia-related disorders, including borderline, schizoid, and schizotypal personality disorders.

Major topics of interest in the Psychosocial Treatment Rehabilitation Program include psychosocial factors relating to etiology, course, and prognosis in schizophrenia and related conditions; development of psychosocial treatment and rehabilitation approaches; assessment of process and outcome of specific psychosocial treatments in schizophrenia and related conditions; and combined treatment strategies in schizophrenia.

Budget: The FY 1986 budget for this branch was projected to be approximately $14 million.

Application/Review Process: Applications are submitted to the Division of Research Grants (DRG) of the National Institutes of Health. A detailed description of the DRG and the Alcohol, Drug Abuse, and Mental Health Administration review process is included in chapter 4.

Funding Mechanisms: See the general description in chapter 4.

Examples of Funded Research:
1) "Social Skill and Schizophrenia" (support approved for 3 years; awarded $151,606 for FY 1985).

2) "Outpatient Treatment: Targeted Versus Maintenance Medication" (support approved for 5 years; awarded $87,353 for FY 1985).

3) "The Course of Dyskinesia" (support approved for 4 years; awarded $195,210 for FY 1985).

4) "NMR Imaging in the Major Psychoses" (support approved for 3 years; awarded $139,898 for FY 1985).

5) "Prospective Study of Children of Schizophrenic Parents" (support approved for 3 years; awarded $505,675 for FY 1985).

6) "Biology of Schizophrenia Subtypes" (support approved for 3 years; awarded $193,789 for FY 1985).

7) "Environmental-Personal Treatment of Schizophrenia" (support approved for 2 years; awarded $208,631 for FY 1985).

EPIDEMIOLOGY AND PSYCHOPATHOLOGY BRANCH

Ben Z. Locke, Chief
10C-05 Parklawn Building
5600 Fishers Lane
Rockville, MD 20857
(301/443-3774)

Program: The Epidemiology and Psychopathology Branch plans, supports, and conducts programs of research, research training, and resource development in the epidemiology of mental disorders, including risk factors and population genetics; and the classification, assessment, etiology, genetics, clinical course, outcome, and treatment of general psychopathology and other mental disorders not assigned elsewhere. The branch also reviews and evaluates research developments in the field and recommends new program directions.

Major epidemiologic topics of interest include studies of the incidence and prevalence of specific mental disorders, including their co-occurrence with other mental or physical disorders. Relevant risk factors include urbanization, population density, social class, employment status, education, race, and religion. Included are studies of (1) the relationship of community disorganization to prevalence and incidence of mental illness and (2) the relationship of stress, social supports, and mental illness. General psychopathology research includes cross-cultural or cross-ethnic studies including studies of family and cultural factors in the etiology, expression, diagnosis, and outcome of mental disorders. The Emergencies and Disasters program focuses on studies of mental health sequela resulting from exposure to traumatic life crises and catastrophic events, including natural disaster, technological emergencies, mass violence, and other collective emergency situations.

Budget: The FY 1986 budget for this branch was projected to be approximately $10 million.

Application/Review Process: Applications are submitted to the Division of Research Grants (DRG) of the National Institutes of Health. A detailed description of the DRG and the Alcohol, Drug Abuse, and Mental Health Administration review process is included in chapter 4.

Funding Mechanisms: See the general description in chapter 4.

Examples of Funded Research:
1) "National Survey of Child and Adolescent Disorders."
2) "A Psychiatric Epidemiology Study of Blue Collar Women."
3) "Social Stress—Social Selection and Psychiatric Disorders."
4) "Predictors of Depressive Symptoms in Urban Black Adults."
5) "Dyadic Responses to Stress: A Study of Married Couples."

AFFECTIVE AND ANXIETY DISORDERS RESEARCH BRANCH

Robert M.A. Hirschfeld, Chief
10C-24 Parklawn Building
5600 Fishers Lane
Rockville, MD 20857
(301/443–1636)

Program: The Affective and Anxiety Disorders Research Branch plans, supports, and conducts programs of research, research training, and resource development in the classification, assessment, etiology, genetics, clinical course, outcome, and pharmacologic, somatic, and psychosocial treatment and rehabilitation of affective and anxiety disorders, including suicidal behavior in adults. The branch also reviews and evaluates research developments in the field and recommends new program directions.

Programs within the Affective and Anxiety Disorders Research Branch are:

1) Clinical and Biological Studies of Affective Disorders (i.e., depression, mania, manic-depressive illness, mood disturbances, grief, death, and stressful life events);

2) Clinical and Biological Studies of Anxiety Disorders (anxiety disorders such as panic attacks, agoraphobia, and obsessive-compulsive behavior);

3) Somatic Treatments of Affective and Anxiety Disorders (focusing on pharmacologic or somatic treatment, e.g., electroconvulsive therapy, clinical trials of pharmacologic agents thought to be effective for the Affective, Anxiety Personality and Somatoform disorders);

4) Psychosocial Treatments of Affective and Anxiety Disorders (focusing on assessing the efficacy, safety, and efficiency of particular psychosocial therapies applied to Affective, Anxiety, Somatoform and Personality, the development and improvement of methods for evaluating the processes, mechanism, and efficacy of psychosocial treatments of the above disorders, etc.).

Budget: The FY 1986 budget for this branch was projected to be approximately $27 million.

Application/Review Process: Applications are submitted to the Division of Research Grants (DRG) of the National Institutes of Health. A detailed description of the DRG and the Alcohol, Drug Abuse, and Mental Health Administration review process is included in chapter 4.

Funding Mechanisms: See the general description in chapter 4.

Examples of Funded Research:
1) "Social Skills Training and Notriptyline Treatment of Affective Disorders" (support approved for 3 years; awarded $96,000 for FY 1985).

2) "Couples Treatment of Agoraphobia" (funded for 5 years; total award $422,454).

3) "Factors in Divorce-Related Depression and Its Treatment" (awarded $108,177 for FY 1985).

4) "Fear Modification, Imagery, Cognition and Control" (support approved for 4 years; awarded $110,245 for FY 1985).

5) "Depression, Explanatory Styles and Learned Helplessness" (funded for 4 years; total award $555,853).

DIVISION OF BIOMETRY AND APPLIED SCIENCES

BIOMETRIC AND CLINICAL APPLICATIONS BRANCH

Lawrence Chaitkin, Chief, Extramural Programs
18C-06 Parklawn Building
5600 Fishers Lane
Rockville, MD 20857
(301/443-4233)

Program: The Biometric and Clinical Applications Branch is placing special emphasis on mental health services research in three areas: mental health economics, primary care, and the organization and delivery of services in the health and mental health specialty sectors.

The mental health economics program focuses on studies which assess the role of economic factors in mental health services and analyze benefit coverage for such services. The primary care research program seeks to improve understanding of the current relationship between the primary care and specialty mental health sectors; improve recognition, diagnosis, and management of mental and emotional problems by primary care providers; and improve coordination of care and increase referrals to mental health specialists for these patients. Mental health services research is supported in two major areas: (1) systems research on the scope, distribution, adequacy, appropriateness, and use of mental health services; and (2) clinical services research that examines the diagnosis and management of patients in health and specialty mental health treatment settings.

Related topics of interest to the Biometric and Clinical Applications Branch include studies of the effectiveness of consultation-liaison psychiatry; studies of the prevalence, distribution, and associated features of mental disorders in various types of clinical settings; studies of the need for mental health treatment; studies which investigate the diagnostic, treatment, and referral patterns of patients seen in clinical settings; studies of methods to improve clinical care;

studies of the prescribing of psychotropic medication; studies to assess and improve the administration and management of local and state mental health service organizations; and studies which focus on the relationships and interactions among components of the mental health service system.

Budget: The FY 1986 budget for this branch was projected to be approximately $7 million.

Application/Review Process: Applications are submitted to the Division of Research Grants (DRG) of the National Institutes of Health. A detailed description of the DRG and the Alcohol, Drug Abuse, and Mental Health Administration review process is included in chapter 4.

Funding Mechanisms: See the general description in chapter 4.

Examples of Funded Research:
1) "Psychiatric Hospitalization Versus Emergency Housing" (funded for 3 years; total direct costs, $487,767).

2) "Federal Employee Health Benefits Plan: The Impact of Changes in Mental Health Benefits" (funded for 2 years; total direct costs, $249,437).

3) "Management of Psychosocial Problems by Pediatricians" (funded for 3 years; total direct costs, $360,645).

4) "Mental Health Services for Youth: Comparing Two Systems" (funded for 3 years; total direct costs, $220,069).

5) "Effectiveness of Local Mental Health Delivery System" (funded for 3 years; total direct costs, $232,573).

6) "Physician Response to Psychosocial Problems in Primary Care" (funded for 1 year; total direct costs, $44,626).

7) "Service Needs of the Homeless Mentally Ill" (funded for 3 years; total direct costs, $531,101).

8) "Psychiatric Inpatient Episodes in General Hospitals" (funded for 2 years; total direct costs, $201,415).

ANTISOCIAL AND VIOLENT BEHAVIOR BRANCH

Saleem A. Shah, Chief
18–105 Parklawn Building
5600 Fishers Lane
Rockville, MD 20857
(301/443–3768)

Program: The Antisocial and Violent Behavior Branch is the focal point in NIMH for research and research training in the areas of antisocial behavior, individual violent behavior, rape and sexual assault, and law and mental health interactions. The objectives of this branch are to improve understanding of mental health issues and needs in the foregoing areas and to assist in the development of improved strategies for prevention, management, treatment, and evaluation. The scope of the branch's program encompasses biological, behavioral, psychosocial, and empirical legal studies.

Specific areas of priority interest include:

1)   longitudinal studies that can contribute to improved understanding of mental health processes reflected in the development, maintenance, and cessation of antisocial and violent behaviors among children, youths, young adults, and mentally ill persons, as well as studies of those factors which assist most youths in avoiding serious antisocial behavior;

2)   research designed to increase knowledge of biological, behavioral, and psychosocial processes associated with individual violent behaviors, and to develop improved methods for management and treatment of such behaviors;

3)   studies on the etiology, incidence, prevalence, and mental health effects of rape and sexual assault (including child sexual abuse and incest);

4)   the careful conceptualization, development, testing, refinement, and evaluation of new and more effective treatment models for use with children, youth, and adults who manifest antisocial, delinquent, criminal, violent, and criminally deviant sexual behaviors;

5)   the development of improved and empirically based criteria to aid decision-making with respect to a number of law and mental health issues—e.g., pretrial competency, exculpatory insanity, sexual psychopathy, psychopathy, dangerousness, and involuntary commitment.

Support is also provided for studies of major statutory changes and other legal developments pertaining to the civil and criminal commitment, handling, and treatment of the mentally ill. A portion of the branch's available funds is also used to support important investigator-initiated projects that do not fall within any of the noted priority areas but are nonetheless relevant to the NIMH and branch mission.

Budget: The FY 1986 budget for this branch was projected to be approximately $7 million.

Application/Review Process: Applications are submitted to the Division of Research Grants (DRG) of the National Institutes of Health. A detailed description of the DRG and the Alcohol, Drug Abuse, and Mental Health Administration review process is included in chapter 4.

Funding Mechanisms: See the general description in chapter 4.

Examples of Funded Research:

1) "The Dynamics of Delinquent Behavior—A National Survey" (funded for 11 years; total direct costs, $3,600,000).

2) "The Prediction of Violent Behavior" (funded for 3 years; total direct costs, $310,000).

3) "Medical Contexts and Sequelae of Domestic Violence" (funded for 5 years; total direct costs, $174,000).

4) "The Rape Victim: Her Response and Treatment" (funded for 7 years; total direct costs, $351,000).

5) "The Evaluation of Child Molesters" (funded for 5 years; total direct costs, $1,249,000).

6) "Sequelae of Child Maltreatment: A Longitudinal Study" (funded for 2 years; total direct costs, $240,000).

7) "Early Intervention for Antisocial Behavior in Children" (funded for 3 years; total direct costs, $239,000).

8) "Mental Disorder in an Urban Jail" (funded for 3 years; total direct costs, $228,000).

9) "Assessing the Impact of Insanity Defense Reform" (funded for 5 years; total direct costs, $996,000).

10) "Civil Commitment Evaluation: Individual Outcome" (funded for 2 years; total direct costs, $186,000).

MINORITY RESEARCH RESOURCES BRANCH

James R. Ralph, Chief
18–101 Parklawn Building
5600 Fishers Lane
Rockville, MD 20857
(301/443–2988)

Program: The Minority Research Resources Branch (MRRB) provides support for research and research training. Small Grant applications dealing with minority issues are funded by the Branch as are the Minority Fellowship Program, Minority Access to Research Careers Program, the Minority Biomedical Research Support Program, research and development centers for minority research, and conference grants.

The Minority Access to Research Careers (MARC) Program consists of two training activities: the Honors Undergraduate Research Training Program and the Faculty Fellowship Research Training Program. The objectives of this program are (1) to increase the number of well-prepared students from institutions with substantial minority enrollment who can compete successfully for entry into Ph.D. degree programs in disciplines related to mental health, alcoholism, and drug abuse; and (2) to develop and strengthen biological, psychological, behavioral, and/or public health sciences curricula and research training opportunities in these academic institutions. Currently, support is provided to 11 minority-based institutions throughout the nation including four Historically Black Colleges and Universities. The objective of the MARC Faculty Fellowship Program is to enhance research capabilities of faculty at institutions with substantial minority enrollment by providing fellowships for selected individuals for advanced research training in specified areas of research related to alcoholism, drug abuse, and mental health. It is intended that the recipients of these awards will return to their home institutions following such training, to teach and conduct research, and to inspire and assist students to prepare for research careers in these areas.

The Minority Fellowship Program (MFP) provides predoctoral support for research training to minority students through four professional associations. They are the American Psychological Association, American Sociological Association, American Nurses Association, and Council on Social Work Education.

The Minority Biomedical Research Support Program (MBRS) provides support to minority faculty conducting mental health research and to undergraduate and graduate students obtaining research experience through a Reimbursable Agreement with the Division of Research Resources, NIH. The objectives of the program are to increase the numbers and quality of minority health and mental health scientists and to strengthen the capability of minority (eligible) institutions to provide health and mental health research career opportunities to their students and to conduct research in the health and mental health sciences. This program is currently funding 45 undergraduates and 15 graduate students in 16 separate academic institutions having a substantial percentage of minority enrollment.

Four Minority Research and Development Centers are also supported by this branch:

1) Spanish Speaking Mental Health R&D Center, University of California, Los Angeles

2) Fanon R&D Center, Charles R. Drew Medical School, Los Angeles

3) Pacific Islander/Asian American R&D Center, University of Illinois, Chicago

4) Hispanic R&D Center, Fordham University, Bronx, New York

Budget: The FY 1986 budget for this branch was projected to be approximately $6 million.

Application/Review Process: Applications are submitted to the Division of Research Grants (DRG) of the National Institutes of Health. A detailed description of the DRG and the Alcohol, Drug Abuse, and Mental Health Administration review process is included in chapter 4.

Funding Mechanisms: See the general description in chapter 4.

CENTERS FOR DISEASE CONTROL

National Institute for Occupational Safety and Health

Roy M. Fleming, Associate Director for Grants
Room 3053, Building 1
1600 Clifton Road, NE
Atlanta, GA 30333
(404/329-3343)

Program: The National Institute for Occupational Safety and Health (NIOSH) funds extramural research and demonstrations relating to occupational safety and health. NIOSH programmatic interests are divided into 12 broad research categories covering a wide range of work-related physical and mental disorders and safety concerns. Two categories are of particular interest to social and behavioral scientists: (1) psychologic disorders (e.g., neuroses, personality disorders, alcoholism, drug dependency) and (2) control technology research (e.g., application of scientific principles to control strategies, preconstruction review, technology forcing/new source performance concepts, technology transfer, substitution, unit operations approach).

NIOSH staff encourage proposals in any area that will lead to pragmatic effects on the workplace, i.e., any research that could have practical implications for eliminating workplace factors in illness and injury. Besides an interest in specific psychologic disorders, NIOSH can support studies on the behavioral components of prevention of any occupational injury or disease, including lung disease, musculoskeletal injuries, occupational cancers, and cardiovascular disease.

Budget: In FY 1985 NIOSH supported three grants in the psychologic disorders category totaling $225,000. NIOSH staff estimate that this represents only one third of their total support for the behavioral sciences.

Application/Review Process: Applications to NIOSH are submitted to the NIH Division of Research Grants in accordance with regular NIH procedures and deadlines. (See the general description of NIH in chapter 4.)

Although preliminary telephone inquiries are not encouraged, NIOSH staff will review and comment on preliminary proposals or concept papers.

Funding Mechanisms: NIOSH funds research through several standard NIH mechanisms, including research project grants, demonstration grants, Special Emphasis Research Career Awards, small grants, and, on occasion, program project grants. The maximum project period that can be supported is 5 years.

Examples of Funded Research:
1) "Occupational Stress and Health of Women LPN's and LSW's" (4-year project).

2) "Neuropsychological Effects of Chronic Solvent Exposure" (3-year project).

3) "A Behavioral Evaluation of Toluene and Ethanol" (2-year project).

4) "Compliance with OSHA Health Standards: Methods and Cases" (1-year project).

5) "Ethical Issues in Identifying and Protecting High-Risk Persons in Workplaces" (1-year project).

HEALTH RESOURCES AND SERVICES ADMINISTRATION

Bureau of Health Care Delivery and Assistance

DIVISION OF MATERNAL AND CHILD HEALTH RESEARCH GRANTS PROGRAM

Gontran Lamberty, Chief
6–17 Parklawn Building
5600 Fishers Lane
Rockville, MD 20857
(301/443–2190)

Program: Officially called the Maternal and Child Health and Crippled Children's Research Grants Program, this program has been traditionally oriented toward applied research in areas of maternal and child health. Program staff emphasize that support is available for a broad range of research questions, ranging from very applied clinical research to broad behavioral science topics. General topics of interest include validation of currently accepted health care practices; studies of innovation before they are widely adopted; family, economic, cultural, and environmental factors in disease etiology; effects of federal and state health care policies; continuation and expansion of on-going data collection programs; and improvement of research methods.

Program staff anticipate that a future direction will be the support of more social-behavioral health questions and more disease-specific studies. Studies of this nature would provide a basis for "tailor-made" interventions appropriate for specific diseases or genetic disorders. There is also increasing interest in infant mortality differentials such as race, social, and ethnic variables, and social stratification. Research should focus not on documenting differences but rather on explaining the causes.

Much of the research supported by this program is appropriate for the social and behavioral sciences, including psychology, sociology, anthropology, and health economics. Child development psychologists have been particularly successful in obtaining funding from this program. First-time applicants are advised to consult with program staff prior to submitting proposals. Scientific reviewers look for proposals which are methodologically strong, well-grounded in biostatistics, demonstrate an understanding of the medical profession, and contain little jargon specific to a particular discipline.

Research priorities are established annually, a list of which is included in the application package. The staff would also welcome creative and innovative research agenda initiated by the research community.

Budget: The research program of the Division of Maternal and Child Health had an FY 1985 budget of $6.5 million. Of that amount, $2.5 million was available for new and competing renewal grant applications.

Application/Review Process: Submission deadlines for proposals are March 1 and August 1. The program uses standard form PHS-398, which must be submitted to the Grants Management Branch, Bureau of Health Care Delivery and Assistance, 7A-08 Parklawn Building, 5600 Fishers Lane, Rockville, MD 20857. Applications are reviewed by a standing research review committee composed of 11 nonfederal members knowledgeable in maternal and child health issues. The recent experience has been that, while only 15% to 25% of reviewed proposals are approved for funding, nearly all of those approved do in fact receive funding. The average grant award is $90,000 (including indirect costs) per year; project periods are generally 2 to 3 years. While there are no limitations on the size of grants, smaller proposals are more likely to receive funding.

Funding Mechanisms: This program makes grant awards to public or non-profit organizations or institutions of higher education. Individuals are not eligible.

Examples of Funded Research:
1) "Neurobehavioral Assessment of Premature Infants" (awarded $147,362 for FY 1983).

2) "Psychosocial Aspects of Genetic Counseling" (awarded $112,999 for FY 1983).

3) "SIDS Loss: Psychosocial Impact and Predictors of Coping" (awarded $192,287 for FY 1983).

4) "Regionalized Perinatal Services Planning for Evaluation" (awarded $209,531 for FY 1983).

5) "Prematurity, Mother-Infant Interaction, and Language" (awarded $82,723 for FY 1983).

6) "A Case Comparison of Teenage Fathers" (awarded $46,627 for FY 1983).

NATIONAL CENTER FOR HEALTH SERVICES RESEARCH AND HEALTH CARE TECHNOLOGY ASSESSMENT

The National Center for Health Services Research and Health Care Technology Assessment (abbreviated hereafter as NCHSR) is the primary source of federal support for research on problems related to the quality and delivery of health services. NCHSR responds to the need for better data and information, new techniques, and innovative methods for improving health care delivery. NCHSR programs evaluate health services, assess technologies, and improve access to new scientific and technical information for research users. NCHSR research is targeted to the needs of health care policymakers, those who operate hospitals and other health care institutions, and individuals who are responsible for health care expenditures.

The intramural research program, staffed primarily by social and behavioral scientists, is more policy-oriented than the extramural program. Intramural staff perform on-going studies of hospital use and costs, long-term care, health status and health promotion, and health care expenditures. The National Health Care Expenditures Study, a large national survey which examines how Americans use and pay for health care services, has evolved as a major source of data for both researchers and policymakers.

DIVISION OF EXTRAMURAL RESEARCH

Norman Weissman, Director
Room 318, Park Building
5600 Fishers Lane
Rockville, MD 20857
(301/443-2345)

Program: The role of NCHSR extramural research is to contribute to the health services knowledge base from which empirically based information can be derived by policymakers—both immediately and over the coming decades. Equally important is the development of the methodological foundation for addressing the next generation of policy issues.

Most NCHSR research is multidisciplinary social/behavioral science or has a social science component (i.e., socio-environmental factors influencing adaptation or efficacy of new devices). While most support goes to basic research projects, development and evaluation projects can be considered for funding.

Four areas are likely to remain of primary importance:

1) primary care/health promotion and disease prevention (including expanding the role of primary care practitioners; improving the effectiveness of specific interventions; analyzing the risks, costs, and benefits of preventive interventions; clinical and epidemiological studies; organizational, regulatory, and economic studies; and methodological studies);

2) technology assessment (including the development, diffusion, and utilization of medical technology; the development of new methods for evaluating medical technology; and the development of methodologies for assessing the costs/benefits, cost-effectiveness, and social and ethical implications of technology applications);

3) role of market forces in health care delivery (including economic incentives and the supply of health care services; alternative delivery systems; competition in providing health care for the elderly and publicly insured; quality of health care and barriers to competition; the market for health care information; and multihospital systems);

4) state and local health problems (including the development of state and local administration of health care programs; resource allocation methods; and the role of public hospitals).

In addition to awarding grants and contracts for research, NCHSR provides grants for research projects undertaken in conjunction with the preparation of a dissertation. Students are eligible to apply if they are enrolled in an accredited doctoral degree program in the social, medical, management, or health sciences and intend to conduct dissertation research on the organization, delivery, financing, or quality of health care services. All requirements for the doctoral degree other than the dissertation must be completed by the time of the grant award.

Budget: The FY 1985 budget for extramural research was approximately $12 million.

Application/Review Process: Although NCHSR is located in the Office of the Assistant Secretary for Health, grant proposals are submitted to the Division of Research Grants at the National Institutes of Health. (See the general description in chapter 4.) Scientific review by NIH study sections are particularly rigorous, in part because NCHSR does not have a national advisory body to perform a second review of applications. Recent experience has been that approximately 20% of applications are approved for funding. A final funding decision is made by NCHSR staff. Proposal deadlines for applications are February 1, June 1, and October 1.

Applications for grants for health services dissertation research should be submitted directly to NCHSR on PHS Form 398. Deadlines for receipt of proposals are November 1 and March 15. Applications are reviewed by both NCHSR staff and nonfederal reviewers.

Funding Mechanisms: NCHSR will award research project grants and contracts as well as grants for dissertation research. Research projects may be from 1 to 5 years. Approved grants generally do not exceed $250,000. Grants to support dissertation research may not exceed $20,000 in total direct costs and are generally made for a period of 1 year.

Examples of Funded Research:
1) "Methods to Improve Quality of Physician Prescribing" (4-year project).

2) "Analysis of the Utilization and Economic Impact of the State of Kentucky's Generic Drug Substitution Legislation" (1-year project).

3) "Behavioral Outcome in Head Injury" (3-year project).

4) "U.S. Health Care Delivery Policy and Distributive Justice" (4-year project).

5) "Private Health Insurance for Long-Term Care of the Elderly: An Exploratory Study" (1-year project).

6) "The Cultural Context of Childhood Diarrhea" (15-month project).

7) "Ethical and Social Dilemmas of Government Policy" (16-month project).

8) "Stress and the Amish Community in Transition" (2-year project).

9) "Verbal Interactions and Health Outcomes by Age Group" (3-year project).

10)   "Development of Population Based Health Planning Areas" (2-year project).

NATIONAL INSTITUTES OF HEALTH

National Cancer Institute

Of the 11 NIH institutes, the National Cancer Institute (NCI) is the largest and most organizationally complex. Technically a bureau and not an institute, NCI has a total research budget of approximately $1 billion, about half of which goes to extramural research grants. Although the social and behavioral sciences do not have a high visibility at NCI, these disciplines are integrated into the biomedical research efforts of many divisions and programs. No programs provide support exclusively for the social and behavioral sciences, nor are there study sections which review applications from these disciplines separately. Social and behavioral scientists therefore compete with biomedical scientists for funding; thus, they must have a good understanding of current medical theory, of cancer in particular, and, in many cases, knowledge of a particular form of cancer.

It is difficult to determine exactly how much of the NCI budget goes to support of the social and behavioral sciences. Most NCI staff are unwilling to make estimates or give a breakdown of their program budgets because they do not want to discourage social and behavioral scientists from submitting applications. Although the percentage of total funds awarded to these disciplines is relatively small, the actual dollar amount available for extramural support, even based on the NIH average of 4%, is probably close to $20 million. The programs highlighted below were selected as the most likely sources of support for social and behavioral scientists; they are not the only sources.

Application/Review Process: See the general description of NIH review procedures in chapter 4. NCI has a total of 21 advisory committees and councils that review grant and contract proposals and advise the NCI director on matters of policy and direction. The National Cancer Advisory Board, the committee that performs the final review of research grant applications, had no social or behavioral scientists among its members in 1985.

Funding Mechanisms: See the general description of NIH in chapter 4.

Examples of Funded Research:
1)   "Expanding the Patient's Role: Effecting Health Outcomes."
2)   "Collaborative Epidemiologic Cancer Research in China."

3) "Informal Self-Help Approaches to Smoking Cessation."
4) "School and Family Oriented Cancer Prevention Program."
5) "Cancer Risk Reduction Through Smoking Prevention."
6) "Patterns of Medical Care in Elderly Patients."

DIVISION OF CANCER PREVENTION AND CONTROL

PREVENTION PROGRAM

Peter Greenwald, Acting Associate Director
6A07 Blair Building
9000 Rockville Pike
Bethesda, MD 20892
(301/427–8731)

Program: The emphasis in this program is on research studies to identify, evaluate, and implement techniques and approaches for the prevention and early detection of cancer. Those studies capable of achieving these objectives with minimal risk and cost are preferred. Specific interests include risk assessment, diet and nutrition, occupational cancer control, and screening and early detection of cancer.

Application/Review Process: See the general description of NCI above.

Funding Mechanisms: See the general description of NCI above.

Examples of Funded Research: See the general description of NCI above.

CENTERS AND COMMUNITY ONCOLOGY PROGRAM

Carolyn Gotay, Program Director, Community Oncology and Rehabilitation Branch
732 Blair Building
9000 Rockville Pike
Bethesda, MD 20892
(301/427–8708)

Program: Of most interest in this program is the Community Oncology and Rehabilitation Branch (CORB). Evaluation and research projects on the impact of social and emotional factors on cancer diagnosis, treatment, and follow-up are funded by this branch. CORB also encourages research on the lifestyle adaptations of those individuals who have been cured of cancer or have been identified as having progressive disease. All research projects identify needs and problems associated with cancer; most propose an intervention strategy.

Specific areas of interest include:

1) pain management and control and methods to transfer current knowledge in these areas to practitioners;

2) quality of life assessments;

3) occupational stress experienced by those caring for cancer patients in hospices and other facilities;

4) insurance benefits/coverage for cancer patients;

5) problems of daily living;

6) pediatric oncology, follow-up of survivors, and later interventions;

7) bereavement;

8) interventions to reduce social, psychological, physical, and economic consequences for patients and their families.

Application/Review Process: See the general description of NCI above.

Funding Mechanisms: See the general description of NCI above.

Examples of Funded Research: See the general description of NCI above.

CANCER CONTROL SCIENCE PROGRAM

CANCER CONTROL APPLICATIONS BRANCH

Thomas Kean, Chief
1A01 Blair Building
9000 Rockville Pike
Bethesda, MD 20892
(301/427-8777)

Program: The purpose of the Cancer Control Applications Branch (CCAB) is to identify opportunities for and facilitate the application of effective measures for preventing and controlling cancer. Future interests of this branch include cancer prevention and control activities in state health departments, cancer control among minority populations, evaluation of cancer control interventions, and demographic projections and assessments.

The CCAB also provides two funding mechanisms of particular interest to social and behavioral scientists. The Cancer Control Small Grants Research Award is designed to encourage scientists from a variety of academic disciplines to apply their skills in the field of human cancer control intervention research. The Cancer Control Science Associates Program provides a three-year period of duty; two years working at NCI and a third year at one of the NCI-supported cancer prevention and control programs. Social and behavioral scientists with a doctoral degree and a minimum of one year of postdoctoral training or experience are eligible for this program.

Application/Review Process: See the general description of NCI above.

Funding Mechanisms: See the general description of NCI above.

Examples of Funded Research: See the general description of NCI above.

HEALTH PROMOTION SCIENCES BRANCH

Lillian Gigliotti, Chief
414A Blair Building
9000 Rockville Pike
Bethesda, MD 20892
(301/427–8656)

Program: The Health Promotion Sciences Branch (HPSB) supports research needed to develop, implement, and evaluate programs that offer target populations the opportunity to adopt behaviors which reduce cancer risk, facilitate early detection and appropriate treatment, and/or improve the quality of life of people afflicted with cancer. Established in August 1983, the HPSB relies on the social and behavioral sciences, education research, information/communication sciences, health economics, and evaluation research to provide support for its program and collaboration with other programs in this division.

Future research priorities for the HPSB include:

1)   strategies to modify and assess nutrition behavior;

2)   communication strategies for health promotion;

3)   evaluations of health promotion interventions;

4)   development of a health services research program;

5)   integrating cancer education into the school system;

6) social and psychological study of women with breast cancer;

7) ethics in health promotion research;

8) occupational health promotion.

Application/Review Process: See the general description of NCI above.

Funding Mechanisms: See the general description of NCI above.

Examples of Funded Research: See the general description of NCI above.

OCCUPATIONAL CANCER BRANCH

Veronica Conley, Acting Chief
630 Blair Building
9000 Rockville Pike
Bethesda, MD 20892
(301/427–8633)

Program: A relocation from the Prevention Program to the Cancer Control Science Program is pending for the Occupational Cancer Branch. This branch supports research in cancer prevention and control in target populations who are at high risk of developing cancer due to occupational exposures. Toward this end, the Occupational Cancer Branch compiles clinical, laboratory, and epidemiological data on work-related carcinogenic agents. Several program emphases have been identified for the future: developing a viable occupational research network, developing and evaluating occupational cancer education programs, collaborative work with the National Institute for Occupational Safety and Health on hazard evaluation, and research on prevention practices of workplace health personnel in cancer hazardous settings.

Application/Review Process: See the general description of NCI above.

Funding Mechanisms: See the general description of NCI above.

Examples of Funded Research: See the general description of NCI above.

SMOKING, TOBACCO, AND CANCER PROGRAM

Thomas J. Glynn, Program Director for Smoking Research
632 Blair Building
9000 Rockville Pike
Bethesda, MD 20892
(301/427–8620)

Program: The Smoking, Tobacco, and Cancer Program (STCP) is an NCI-wide program coordinated by the Division of Cancer Prevention and Control. Major program emphasis has been placed on intervention research and its applications aimed at reducing cancer incidence related to smoking and tobacco use.

Specific topics of interest include prevention programs targeted to school-age youth, use of mass media to influence and reinforce prevention and cessation behaviors, "self-help" programs for smoking cessation, the role of health professionals (particularly physicians) as exemplars and intervenors in prevention/cessation efforts, smoking/tobacco patterns and interventions in minority populations, prevention/cessation of smokeless tobacco use, cessation programs aimed at high-risk populations (e.g., heavy smokers, underserved populations), and research into the methodology of the applications of smoking research.

Application/Review Process: See the general description of NCI above.

Funding Mechanisms: See the general description of NCI above.

Examples of Funded Research: See the general description of NCI above.

CANCER ETIOLOGY DIVISION

EPIDEMIOLOGY AND BIOSTATISTICS PROGRAM

John A. Cooper, Chief, Extramural Programs Branch
8C18 Landow Building
7910 Woodmont Avenue
Bethesda, MD 20892
(301/496–1882)

Program: The Extramural Programs Branch (EPB) of the Epidemiology and Biostatistics Program supports a program of basic and applied research in cancer epidemiology, biometry, and related multidisciplinary activities. The Program mainly utilizes grant mechanisms, but contracts and cooperative agreements are also awarded. EPB consists of program areas in biometry (including genetics) and epidemiology, and the specific areas of AIDS research, nutrition, tobacco and health, and biochemical epidemiology.

In biometry, topics of interest include statistical techniques useful in evaluating the effects of potential carcinogens and determining the effects of patient characteristics on survival analysis or the analysis of competing risks; record linkage for investigations involving special population groups; and the design of statistical techniques to evaluate carcinogen screening tests and procedures.

Research areas of interest in epidemiology include investigations of the natural history of specific cancers, the incidence and prevalence of various cancers as a function of geographic location, etiologic factors related to cancer, opportunities for preventive action, and improved methodologies for the design and conduct of epidemiologic studies.

National Eye Institute

Constance Atwell, Chief, Strabismus, Amblyopia, and Visual Processing Branch
6A49 Building 31
9000 Rockville Pike
Bethesda, MD 20892
(301/496–5301)

Program: The National Eye Institute's mission is to support and conduct research on the prevention, treatment, and rehabilitation of disorders of the visual system. A major thrust of the NEI scientific program is to describe the normal functioning of the human visual system and the ways in which it becomes abnormal as a result of various diseases or developmental disorders. As a result, an important area of research is the use of behavioral techniques that capitalize on the observers' subjective or reflexive responses to carefully defined visual stimuli. By using standardized tests of visual function, the effects of newly developed intervention strategies or treatments can be assessed more reliably. Behavioral tests are also important for diagnosing or predicting the progression of some eye diseases. In addition, NEI supports epidemiologic investigations and research on the rehabilitation of the visually handicapped.

The Strabismus, Amblyopia, and Visual Processing program of NEI encompasses a broad range of studies concerned with the structure and function of the neural pathways from the eye to the brain, the central processing of visual information, visual perception, optical properties of the eye, functioning of the pupil, and control of the ocular muscles. Of particular interest are studies of the normal development of visual capacity in the infant and the effects of early sensory deprivation on the development of visual function.

Budget: Figures are not available on the percentage of NEI'S budget that is spent on the social and behavioral sciences. In FY 1985 the Institute spent approximately $98,000 on health and behavior research; however, that amount is only a small portion of the total spent on behavioral science research.

Application/Review Process: See the general description of NIH in chapter 4.

Funding Mechanisms: See the general description of NIH in chapter 4.

Examples of Funded Research:
1) "Psychophysiological Studies of Ocular Abnormalities."
2) "Visual Direction with Normal and Immobilized Eyes."
3) "The Visual Requirements of Everyday Tasks."

National Heart, Lung, and Blood Institute

The National Heart, Lung, and Blood Institute (NHLBI) plans, conducts, and supports research, clinical trials, and demonstrations relating to the causes, prevention, diagnosis, and treatment of heart, blood vessel, lung, and blood diseases. The research is performed both in NHLBI laboratories and through grants and contracts for extramural projects. In addition, NHLBI provides support for the training and development of new scientists.

BEHAVIORAL MEDICINE BRANCH

Stephen Weiss, Chief
Room 604, Federal Building
7550 Wisconsin Avenue
Bethesda, MD 20892
(301/496–9380)

Program: The Behavioral Medicine Branch (BMB) is the only branch within the Division of Clinical Applications and Prevention that has a basic science function. Although the branch is concerned with general health aspects of the heart, lungs, and blood, the primary focus is on the heart. The core of the BMB program is the interface between the biomedical and behavioral aspects of health and disease. Generally, projects which lack a multidisciplinary approach do not receive funding. Projects should address health questions using the knowledge of both the biomedical and behavioral sciences. Since the study section reviewing most BMB proposals is representative of both fields, proposals should be methodologically strong in both areas.

The Behavioral Medicine Branch enjoys a high profile within the NHLBI and its programs are very much in the mainstream of the Institute's research agenda. This is reflected in the success rate for proposals submitted to the BMB: 71% of submitted proposals are approved; 37% are funded. The branch relies on unsolicited proposals submitted in response to general NHLBI research announcements as well as special Institute initiatives. BMB research is appropriate not only for psychologists, but also sociologists and anthropologists. In addition to research grants, the branch has 12 training programs providing multidisciplinary training in biobehavioral medicine.

BMB research is generally divided among three areas: basic research, clinical studies and disease prevention, and health promotion.

Basic research questions include the understanding of basic brain-body mechanisms, environmental stressors, coping mechanisms, and health and disease states.

Treatment research seeks to identify those techniques and combinations of techniques (both behavioral and pharmacological) that are most efficacious in preventing or controlling disease states.

Health promotion involves three levels of inquiry: (1) health behavior development (health-enhancing behavior in children, smoking prevention, good dietary patterns, proper physical exercise, stress management techniques); (2) health behavior change (strategies for modifying patterns of unhealthy behaviors); and (3) health behavior maintenance (strategies for maintaining healthy diets, exercise regimens, smoking cessation, etc.).

Budget: In FY 1984 the NHLBI spent approximately $31 million (about 4% of its total budget) on social and behavioral science research. About one third of those funds are awarded through the Behavioral Medicine Branch.

Application/Review Process: See the general description of NIH in chapter 4.

Funding Mechanisms: See the general description of NIH in chapter 4.

Examples of Funded Research:
1) "Psychosocial Factors in Essential Hypertension" (awarded $106,182 in FY 1984).

2) "Psychosocial Stressors, Smoking Cessation and CV Risk" (awarded $85,123 in FY 1984).

3) "Joint USSR-USA Behavioral Hypertension Treatment Study" (awarded $130,375 in FY 1984).

4) "Caffeine Influences on Exercise and Psychological Stress."

5) "Biracial Studies of Children's Cardiovascular Reactivity" (awarded $91,011 in FY 1984).

6) "Speech Characteristics in Coronary Heart Disease" (awarded $24,220 in FY 1984).

National Institute on Aging

The National Institute on Aging (NIA) was established in 1974 with a congressional mandate to conduct and support "biomedical, social and behavioral research and training related to the aging process and the diseases and other special problems and needs of the aged." The NIA conducts laboratory and clinical research at its Gerontology Research Center in Baltimore and at the National Institutes of Health campus in Bethesda. The Epidemiology, Demography, and Biometry Program conducts intramural research and supports some outside investigators through research contracts. Most NIA extramural research is conducted by the Biomedical Research and Clinical Medicine Program and the Behavioral Sciences Research Program.

BEHAVIORAL SCIENCES RESEARCH PROGRAM

Matilda White Riley, Associate Director
Room 4C32, NIH Building 31
9000 Rockville Pike
Bethesda, MD 20892
(301/496-3136)

Program: The Behavioral Sciences Research (BSR) Program is concerned with the social, cultural, economic, and psychological factors that affect both the process of growing old and the place of older people in society. A broad range of basic research topics in psychology, sociology, anthropology, economics, political science, and social epidemiology fall within the purview of BSR. The BSR program is divided into three broad categories: cognitive and biopsychological aging; social psychological aging; and older people and society.

While continuing to accept and fund applications across a broad spectrum of topics, several areas of particular interest have been identified for FY 1986 and FY 1987:

1) cognitive aging (mechanisms of age-related changes in intelligence, learning ability, memory, and sensorimotor function, including visual perception and hearing);

2) biopsychology of aging (relationships between behavioral aging and the neural and other physiological aspects of aging);

3) behavioral geriatrics research (broad questions on the relationship between health, behavior, and aging; health-related attitudes and behaviors of older people and their families and friends; the social context of daily living; change with age; means for positive modification);

4) effects of gender on health and longevity (sources of gender differences; implications for the quality of life for both sexes; ability to function independently; societal costs);

5) oldest old—those over 85—(morbidity, mortality, and causes of death; changes in social structures to accommodate their needs; social and economic conditions; psychological functioning);

6) changing age composition of the population (modeling the societal impact on the health and status of older people, including migration patterns);

7) economic well-being of the elderly (accurate estimations of the impact of taxation, monetary, and nonmonetary public benefits; cross-generational transfers; sources of income);

8) influences of social institutions on health and functioning (formal health care systems; patient-provider interactions);

9) research methods and data resources (development and application of social science research methods to research on aging; identification and support of human study populations and data archives; cross-national comparisons);

10) productivity in the middle and later years (relationships among age, work incentives, health, and productivity; motivation; cognitive and sensorimotor abilities and job skills; phased retirement and flexible work schedules; health and early retirement).

BSR has traditionally supported studies of social networks, interpersonal relations, and social support. Other topics currently undersupported because of the lack of applicants include personality, coping, and attitude formation and change. Special emphasis is given to research and training on the role of social and behavioral factors in health and effective functioning in the middle and later years of life.

Budget: Since the NIA does not make specific budget allocations to the different components of the extramural research program, applications for research and training compete for a common pot of funds. Thus, the percentage of the NIA budget spent on social and behavioral science research depends primarily on the number of fundable applications submitted in those disciplines. Currently the NIA spends approximately 25% of its extramural budget, or $15 million, on social and behavioral science research.

Application/Review Process: See the general description of NIH in chapter 4.

Funding Mechanisms: See the general description of NIH in chapter 4. Special Emphasis Research Career Awards for social and behavioral scientists in behavioral geriatrics research (three years' salary and modest research support for developing interdisciplinary research knowledge and skills) are also available. Application deadlines for these awards are February 1, June 1, and October 1.

Examples of Funded Research:
1) "Choice of Living Arrangements for the Elderly" (awarded $162,984 in FY 1984).

2) "Social Networks and the Care of Frail Elders" (awarded $181,531 in FY 1984).

3) "Longitudinal Studies of Adult Cognitive Development" (awarded $332,705 in FY 1984).

4) "Coping and Health Among Older Urban Widows" (awarded $124,333 in FY 1984).

5) "Autobiographical Memory Across the Adult Lifespan" (awarded $52,292 in FY 1984).

6) "Health, Labor Market Activity, and Income Security" (awarded $81,628 in FY 1984).

7) "Life Course Patterns and Well-Being in Educated Women" (awarded $76,775 in FY 1984).

8) "Precursors of Psychological Well-Being in Old Age" (awarded $82,769 in FY 1984).

9) "Political Orientations Over the Life-Span" (awarded $207,644 in FY 1984).

10) "Demographic Study of Multiple Causes of Death" (awarded $75,040 in FY 1984).

11) "Identity Structure and Retirement" (awarded $24,370 in FY 1984).

12) "Economic Well-Being in Later Years: A Longitudinal Study" (awarded $98,197 in FY 1984).

EPIDEMIOLOGY, DEMOGRAPHY, AND BIOMETRY PROGRAM

Joan Cornoni-Huntley, Acting Associate Director
Room 612, Federal Building
7550 Wisconsin Avenue, NW
Washington, DC 20814
(301/496–1178)

Program: The Epidemiology, Demography, and Biometry Program (EDBP) conducts and supports research on the epidemiology of health and disease as well as the interaction of demographic, social, and economic factors as they affect the health of the elderly.

Epidemiologic approaches include analysis of data from longitudinal studies and development of reference populations for integrated studies of medical, socioeconomic, and behavioral aspects of health. EDBP is also developing descriptive studies of events attendant to the last days of life. Special emphasis in epidemiologic research is given to senile dementia. Another objective of EDBP is the development of an age structured macroeconomic model of the U.S. economy. Included in the program are studies of intergenerational income transfers and lifetime spending patterns of the elderly. Other EDBP research focuses on aspects of the institutionalization of the elderly, differential effects of socioeconomic and demography variables on the aged, and differential survival and mortality patterns.

EDBP does not award grants. It does, however, contract out some data collection projects. Requests for contract proposals are announced in the *Commerce Business Daily.*

National Institute of Arthritis, Diabetes, and Digestive and Kidney Disease[1]

Walter Stoltz, Director, Extramural Activities Division
Room 657
5333 Westbard Avenue
Bethesda, MD 20892
(301/496–7277)

Program: The National Institute of Arthritis, Diabetes, and Digestive and Kidney Disease (NIADDK) supports research on a number of diseases charac-

---

[1]Editor's note: In late 1985 the Congress approved a reauthorization of NIH creating a separate National Institute of Arthritis and a National Institute of Diabetes, Digestive, and Kidney Disease. The change will officially take place on October 1, 1986.

terized by chronicity and long-term disabling effects rather than mortality. Areas of interest include arthritis and related tissue diseases, musculoskeletal disease, skin disease, diabetes and related metabolic disorders, diseases of the gastrointestinal tract, endocrine disorders, disease of the blood and bone, and kidney and urological diseases.

Although social and behavioral research is a small part of the NIADDK portfolio, support is available on the behavioral factors that influence the development, treatment, and prevention of diseases targeted by the Institute's mission. Diagnostic and therapeutic concerns related to the research areas supported by NIADDK depend upon a better understanding of the behavioral and social factors involved. One topic of particular concern to all NIADDK programs is research on patient compliance with required preventive or therapeutic regimens.

NIADDK research interests include:

1) psychosocial and behavioral concerns of diabetics who must restrict or alter their lifestyles because of dietary changes and the necessity for a closely regulated time schedule for meals, exercise, and insulin shots;

2) the relationships between psychological stress and fluctuations in the course of diabetes;

3) psychological origins of gastrointestinal disorders;

4) neurohormonal control of gastrointestinal functions, including motility, transport, and such phenomena as vomiting and diarrhea.

Budget: In FY 1985 NIADDK spent $6.52 million for 58 projects in the area of health and behavior.

Application/Review Process: See the general description of NIH in chapter 4.

Funding Mechanisms: See the general description of NIH in chapter 4.

Examples of Funded Research:
1) "Epidemiology of Back Pain in Nursing Personnel."
2) "Irritable Bowel Syndrome: Characterizing the Patient."
3) "Psychophysiology of Irritable Bowel Syndrome."
4) "Behavioral and Metabolic Correlates of Genetic Obesity."
5) "Psychosocial Factors in Diabetes Compliance and Control."

National Institute of Child Health and Human Development

The mission of the National Institute of Child Health and Human Development (NICHD) is to conduct and support research in the reproductive, developmental, and behavioral processes that determine the health of children, adults, families, and populations. NICHD administers a multidisciplinary program of research, research training, and public information. The Institute has four major components: the Center for Population Research and the Center for Research for Mothers and Children, both extramural programs supporting research through grants and contracts; the Intramural Research Program; and the Epidemiology and Biometry Research Program.

The Center for Population Research (CPR) conducts the federal government's central effort in population research. Because population research is inherently interdisciplinary in nature, CPR was created to treat the subject in a systematic manner and to fill in the gaps left by other federal agencies. CPR supports basic research, while other agencies support primarily applied population research or data-gathering activities.

CPR comprises four branches: Reproductive Sciences, Contraceptive Development, Contraceptive Evaluation, and Demographic and Behavioral Sciences. Most social and behavioral science research is supported by the Demographic and Behavioral Sciences Branch.

The Center for Research for Mothers and Children (CRMC) is the primary extramural program supporting research and research training on the special health problems of mothers and children at NICHD. The CRMC was reorganized in 1984. Five branches now administer the CRMC research program: (1) Human Learning and Behavior, (2) Mental Retardation and Developmental Disabilities, (3) Endocrinology, Nutrition and Growth, (4) Pregnancy and Perinatology, and (5) Genetics and Teratology Branch. The first three branches support research in a variety of topics in the social and behavioral sciences; the latter two are largely biomedical in nature.

The National Advisory Child Health and Human Development Council serves as an advisory body for NICHD on matters of policy and funding. This council is unique among NIH advisory councils in that among its 15 members are three behavioral scientists and one social scientist.

CENTER FOR POPULATION RESEARCH

DEMOGRAPHIC AND BEHAVIORAL SCIENCES BRANCH

Wendy Baldwin, Chief
7C25 Landow Building
7910 Woodmont Avenue
Bethesda, MD 20892
(301/496–1174)

Program: The Demographic and Behavioral Sciences Branch (DBSB) funds studies on the social, psychological, economic, and environmental factors governing population growth and structure, as well as the impact of population changes on individuals, families, and societies. The program funds mainstream studies of changes in family and household structures, understanding why changes have occurred, how these new population units function in the modern world, and what these changes imply for children, adults, and society. Another set of interests are the social and behavioral factors which influence the initiation of sexual activity, effective use of contraceptives, parenting of babies, and delayed childbearing.

DBSB also funds research in less obvious areas. Research is encouraged on the relationship between economic change and fertility. U.S. immigration policy has stimulated research questions on forces affecting population movement and the impact of migration on the United States; how population changes in foreign countries directly affect the United States; and the ties between U.S. population growth and that of other countries. Studies of data from foreign countries are needed as models to determine how U.S. population processes fit into a universal behavior pattern. Finally, historical demographic studies test the validity of theories relating to contemporary human experience.

The *Inventory and Analysis of Federal Population Research* provides information on all of the population research projects funded by the federal government each fiscal year. This publication may be obtained from the DBSB.

The branch does issue some requests for applications (RFAs) in order to stimulate proposals in areas in which there is particular agency interest. The staff rely, however, on unsolicited, investigator-initiated proposals for the core of the branch portfolio.

Budget: DBSB awarded approximately $20 million for research grants in FY 1985. The branch also had an FY 1985 budget of about $2.5 million for contract research. A large portion of the contract funds currently go to interagency agreements to maintain or supplement large data sets (such as the National Longitudinal Survey Youth Cohort and the Panel Study of Income Dynamics).

Application/Review Process: See the general description of NIH in chapter 4.

Funding Mechanisms: See the general description of NIH in chapter 4.

Examples of Funded Research:
1) "Migration, Adaptation, and Health: A Cross-Cultural Study" (awarded $120,843 in FY 1984).

2) "Socioeconomic Determinants of Contraceptive Choice" (awarded $99,496 in FY 1985).

3) "Metropolitan Migration in Europe and North America" (awarded $145,170 in FY 1984).

4) "Life Cycle Fertility and Female Labor Force Experience" (awarded $98,199 in FY 1985).

5) "Shift Work, Child Care, and Fertility" (awarded $25,123 in FY 1984).

6) "Quantitative History of Modern Fertility Control" (awarded $155,450 in FY 1984).

7) "Employment, Earnings, and Fertility of Immigrants" (awarded $81,152 in FY 1985).

8) "Family Structure, Marital History, and Child Development" (awarded $73,089 in FY 1984).

CENTER FOR RESEARCH FOR MOTHERS AND CHILDREN

HUMAN LEARNING AND BEHAVIOR BRANCH

Norman Krasnegor, Chief
7C18 Landow Building
7910 Woodmont Avenue
Bethesda, MD 20892
(301/496–6591)

Program: The Human Learning and Behavior Branch (HLB) has as its primary mission the development and support of research that maximizes knowledge of child health. The HLB research portfolio in the aggregate is designed to determine how the interaction of biological, psychological, and socio-environmental factors result in normative development. Processes and behaviors from the prenatal period to the beginning of adulthood are investigated across a wide diversity of research. A major focus of the HLB Branch will continue to be descriptive and experimental studies in developmental psychology. Special consideration will be given to research on children born at biological risk for a variety of behavioral disabilities and to investigations of accidental injuries and risk-taking behavior.

The Human Learning and Behavior Branch is divided into five programmatic areas:

1) behavioral pediatrics (applying principles of human learning to health and illness behaviors of children);

2) developmental behavioral biology (studies of brain/behavior relationships, the biochemical, physiological, and hormonal bases of behavior, sensory motor processes, and comparative animal behavior);

3) learning and perception (research on basic learning mechanisms necessary for optimal behavior development, studies of perception, cognition, and memory—primary emphasis on infants, secondary emphasis on children and adolescents);

4) communication (research on the acquisition and development of speech, language, and reading ability in children—special emphasis on factors involved in dyslexia);

5) social and affective development (understanding basic behavioral, psychological, and genetic mechanisms involved in normal social and emotional development).

A limited number of requests for applications (RFAs) are issued by the HLB Branch. The FY 1986 research program will focus on learning and cognition, prenatal behavioral development, and behavioral pediatrics.

Budget: The HLB Branch spent approximately $16 million in support of research grants and research training in FY 1985.

Application/Review Process: See the general description of NIH in chapter 4.

Funding Mechanisms: See the general description of NIH in chapter 4.

Examples of Funded Research:
1) "Processes of Learning and Memory in Infancy" (awarded $48,432 in FY 1984; 1-year project).

2) "Development and Maintenance of Creativity in Children" (awarded $54,983 in FY 1984; 2-year project).

3) "Marriage, Parenting and Infant Development" (awarded $115,508 in FY 1984; 1-year project).

4) "Teen Social Behavior and the Prevention of Smoking" (awarded $129,778 in FY 1984; 1-year project).

5) "Adolescent Social Networks as Predictors of Development" (awarded $54,488 in FY 1984; 1-year project).

6) "Early Computer Access: Social and Psychological Effects" (awarded $198,121 in FY 1984; 3-year project).

7) "Cross-Linguistic Development Studies of Language" (awarded $57,117 in FY 1984; 2-year project).

8) "Effects of Mother's Education on Offspring Achievement" (awarded $53,664 in FY 1984; 1-year project).

MENTAL RETARDATION AND DEVELOPMENTAL DISABILITIES BRANCH

Theodore Tjossem, Chief
7C09 Landow Building
7910 Woodmont Avenue
Bethesda, MD 20892
(301/496–1383)

Program: The Mental Retardation and Developmental Disabilities Branch (MRDD) supports research and research training related to the biological, behavioral, and social processes that contribute to or influence the development of retarding disorders. MRDD Branch research on the causes, prevention, and amelioration of mental retardation also contributes to the understanding of other developmental disabilities, including autism, epilepsy, and cerebral palsy.

A large part of the mental retardation research funded by the MRDD Branch is conducted at 12 federally supported Mental Retardation Research Centers (MRRCs) across the country. These centers provide facilities for multidisciplinary and collaborative research between the biomedical, behavioral, and social sciences in laboratory and field settings.

MRDD research focuses on three areas:

1) Individual Processes: Studies of individual processes include cognition and learning, memory, perceptual and attentional processes, language and communication, and personality and adaptation.

2) Family Processes: Research on family processes is an increasing priority for the MRDD Branch. Topics of current interest include family dynamics, coping strategies of families with retarded children, relationships among siblings, adaptive behavior, retarded parents' caregiving skills, the transition from adolescence to young adulthood, and problems of the aging retarded.

3) Behavior in Educational, Residential, and Community Settings: Research on retarded individuals in residential and educational settings tends to be applied rather than basic, with findings that often have important policy implications. Research in this area is generally divided into four categories: social interaction, educational settings, institutions, and group homes. The branch is particularly interested in research in the social interaction of retarded adolescents, the role of microcomputers in educational programs for retarded children, determining the age at which intervention is effective for handicapped infants, institutional staff turnover, and factors that determine which individual/setting interactions are optimal.

In general, the MRDD Branch staff is interested in funding any research concerned with the prevention and amelioration of mental retardation and developmental disabilities. Traditionally MRDD research has been dominated by cognitive psychology. The branch would like to expand its support in other disciplines such as sociology, anthropology, and political science. Program announcements and requests for applications are listed in the *NIH Guide for Grants and Contracts*. Staff also rely heavily on direct communication with the research community to stimulate proposals in areas of particular interest.

Budget: In FY 1985 the MRDD Branch awarded a total of $36.4 million in grants and contracts. About 40% of the research budget goes to support of the social and behavioral sciences. Currently, all contract research is in biomedical areas.

Application/Review Process: See the general description of NIH in chapter 4.

Funding Mechanisms: See the general description of NIH in chapter 4.

Examples of Funded Research:
1) "Cognition, Affect, and Human Response in the Retarded" (new investigator research grant; awarded $50,242 in FY 1984).

2) "Influences, Competence, and Death of Retarded People" (awarded $236,549 in FY 1984).

3) "Exploratory Behavior of the Profoundly Multi-Handicapped" (awarded $68,131 in FY 1984).

4) "Automated Teaching Programs for the Severely Retarded" (awarded $81,614 in FY 1984).

5) "Effect of Schooling Severely Impaired on the Family" (awarded $113,292 in FY 1984).

6) "The Social Acceptability of Mentally Retarded Children" (awarded $130,940 in FY 1984).

7) "Infants' Perception and Brain Organization" (awarded $118,785 in FY 1984).

8) "Environmental Influences on Self-Injurious Behavior" (awarded $88,678 in FY 1984).

ENDOCRINOLOGY, NUTRITION, AND GROWTH BRANCH

Gilman D. Grave, Acting Chief
7C17 Landow Building
7910 Woodmont Avenue
Bethesda, MD 20892
(301/496–5593)

Program: The Endocrinology, Nutrition, and Growth Branch (ENG) supports research and training on developmental aspects of nutrition, endocrinology, and physical growth. A small proportion of the Branch's budget supports research on the behavioral and social aspects of nutrition. Research in this areas focuses on cultural and behavioral determinants of nutritional individuality and studies of eating habits, taste, olfaction, and food avoidances. Specific topics of interest include studies of social/environmental factors affecting nutrition, breast-feeding, formation of food habits, sociocultural changes as they affect nutritional status, and behavioral aspects of obesity. Also emphasized are anthropological and epidemiological studies of individuals' interaction with their nutritional environment.

A future priority for the ENG Branch will be the behavioral, neurological, and physiological development of low birth-weight babies when fed special diets. In FY 1986 the branch is planning to issue a joint request for applications with the Human Learning and Behavior Branch on the topic of nutrition and behavior.

Budget: The FY 1985 budget for the ENG Branch was $22 million. Less than 10% of this amount goes to support for the social and behavioral sciences.

Application/Review Process: See the general description of NIH in chapter 4.

Funding Mechanisms: See the general description of NIH in chapter 4.

Examples of Funded Research:
1) "Behavioral Factors Influencing Infant Weight Control" (awarded $186,040 in FY 1984).

2) "Social Psychology of Food Choice Development in Adolescence" (awarded $81,296 in FY 1984).

3) "Ache Foraging" (an anthropological study of the nutritional intake of an isolated tribe) (awarded $163,254 in FY 1984).

EPIDEMIOLOGY AND BIOMETRY RESEARCH PROGRAM

Heinz Berendes, Director
8A04 Landow Building
7910 Woodmont Avenue
Bethesda, MD 20892
(301/496–5064)

Program: The Epidemiology and Biometry Research Program (EBRP) provides services in the areas of biometry, computer sciences, and epidemiology. The Biometry Branch provides statistical analyses for both intramural and extramural investigators, and conducts research of its own in biometry and biostatistics. It also serves as the coordinating and data center for multi-institution clinical trials supported by NICHD. The Epidemiology Branch studies factors that contribute to or inhibit the occurrence of disease, and attempts to identify preventive measures.

The EBRP does not provide grants; all research funded by the program is conducted under contract.

National Institute of Dental Research

Patricia S. Bryant, Health Scientist Administrator
Room 506, Westwood Building
5333 Westbard Avenue
Bethesda, MD 20892
(301/496–7807)

Program: The National Institute of Dental Research (NIDR) supports a wide range of research and training activities aimed at improving dental health. Areas of support include both basic and applied research related to the etiology, pathogenesis, diagnosis, treatment, and prevention of dental and orofacial diseases and conditions. In the NIDR long-range research plan, behavioral research and pain research are identified as areas of program emphasis. Other priorities include prevention and epidemiology, both of which will provide opportunities for social and behavioral scientists.

Most NIDR behavioral and social science research is supported by the Craniofacial Anomalies, Pain Control, and Behavioral Research Branch in the Extramural Research Program. This branch supports studies of normal and abnormal craniofacial growth, development, and function; basic and clinical studies of acute dental and chronic orofacial pain and improved pain control; and studies on social and behavioral factors influencing oral diseases/disorders, dental treatment, or oral health. Particular emphasis is placed on research related to oral health promotion and to the adoption/long-term continuation of preventive measures.

Current topics of interest at NIDR include:

1) behavioral, social, and cultural factors related to the incidence, prevalence, and distribution of oral diseases and conditions;

2) relationships between emotional states, such as stress, and oral psycho-physiological responses and pathologies (e.g., peridontal diseases and apthous ulcers);

3) causes and treatment of clinically significant oral-motor behaviors, such as tooth clenching and bruxism;

4) measures of the impacts of oral diseases and conditions and their treatments (e.g., the psychosocial impacts of orthodontic treatment or orthognathic surgery);

5) factors that determine whether and how individual oral health-promoting behaviors are learned from early childhood to old age;

6) characteristics and processes within institutions and communities which influence the adoption and maintenance of preventive strategies to reduce oral diseases;

7) critical factors influencing dental professionals to adopt and integrate appropriate preventive procedures into practice;

8) behavioral and social factors which influence patient anxiety or satisfaction, pain responsivity, continuity of care, and patient compliance during dental treatment;

9) predictors and determinants of utilization of services;

10) behavioral or social factors relevant to acute dental pain and its control (e.g., "placebo" responses, cognitive therapies, anxiety-pain relationships);

11) behavioral or social factors in the etiology, diagnosis, or treatment of chronic orofacial pain conditions (e.g., temporomandibular joint disorders, "burning mouth" syndrome, myofascial pain dysfunction).

Budget: Approximately $3.9 million was spent on extramural research in the social and behavioral sciences in FY 1985.

Application/Review Process: See the general description of NIH in chapter 4.

Funding Mechanisms: See the general description of NIH in chapter 4.

Examples of Funded Research:
1) "Children's Acceptance of Caries Preventive Procedures" (2-year project; FY 1985 award, $220,405).

2) "Control of Stress During Dental Procedures" (1-year project; FY 1985 award, $99,511).

3) "Dental Disease and Work Loss" (1-year project; FY 1985 award, $101,192).

4) "Psychosocial Factors in Orthognathic Surgery" (2-year project; FY 1985 award, $72,602).

5) "Myofascial Pain-Dysfunction Syndrome and Life Stress" (1-year project; FY 1985 award, $148,333).

6) "Promoting Adherence to a Dental Regimen" (1-year project; FY 1985 award, $74,632).

7) "Interdependence in the Dentist-Patient Relationship" (1-year project; FY 1985 award, $7,801).

8) "Patient Response to Student Dentists' Affective Behavior" (2-year project; FY 1985 award, $51,180).

9) "Effects of Orthodontia on Psychosocial Functioning" (1-year project; FY 1985 award, $103,424).

10) "Effects of Physiological Feedback on Dental Fear" (2-year project; FY 1985 award, $47,419).

National Institute of Environmental Health Sciences

Robert A. Goyer, Associate Director, Extramural Program
P.O. Box 12233
Research Triangle Park, NC 27709
(919/541-7723)

Program: The National Institute of Environmental Health Sciences (NIEHS) is the only one of the National Institutes of Health (NIH) located outside the Washington, DC area. NIEHS is the principal federal agency for the support of research and training on the effects of chemical, physical, and biological environmental agents on human health. NIEHS pursues its mission by supporting basic and applied research on the consequences of the exposure of humans and other biological systems to potentially toxic or harmful agents in the environment.

NIEHS provides limited support for research and research training in the behavioral sciences in such areas as behavioral anomalies, behavioral toxicology, and the effects of environmental agents on learning and behavior.

NIEHS also conducts research in statistics, biomathematics, epidemiology, and risk estimation directed at estimating the probable risks for cancer, reproductive effects, and other adverse effects from environmental hazards. The major emphases are on refining existing methods for estimating human risk from data derived from studying laboratory animals and on examining quantitative issues involved in designing short-term tests. Epidemiological research focuses on the relationships between environmental exposures and human disease. Included are field studies of human disease, environmental pollutants, and the effects of toxins on fetal and child development. The Institute has an active interest in the development of laboratory, epidemiological, and statistical methods that help make field studies more feasible and interpretable.

Budget: The total research budget for NIEHS for FY 1985 was approximately $194.6 million, with approximately $4 million awarded for research grants in biometry and risk estimation.

Application/Review Process: See the general description of NIH in chapter 4.

Funding Mechanisms: See the general description of NIH in chapter 4.

Examples of Funded Research:
1) "Controlled Psychologic Study of Asbestos Exposure."
2) "Statistical Procedures for Censored Survival Data."
3) "Behavioral Effects of Lead Exposure in Children."

National Institute of Neurological and Communicative Disorders and Stroke

John D. Dalton, Director, Extramural Activities Program
1016A Federal Building
7550 Wisconsin Avenue
Bethesda, MD 20814
(301/496–9248)

Program: The mission of the National Institute of Neurological and Communicative Disorders and Stroke (NINCDS) is to identify, stimulate, and support research and research training on the prevention, diagnosis, and treatment of disorders of the nervous system. Although most NINCDS research is biomedical in nature, there are behavioral science components of many areas of inquiry. Areas of research interest include: speech, language, and cognitive disorders; speech and language processes; pain control; and disorders of taste, smell, and touch.

NINCDS extramural research is divided into five programs: (1) Communicative Disorders; (2) Convulsive, Developmental, and Neuromuscular Disorders; (3) Demyelinating, Atrophic, and Dementing Disorders; (4) Fundamental Neurosciences; and (5) Stroke and Trauma. Most behavioral science and linguistic research is located in the Communicative Disorders Program.

Budget: The total FY 1985 budget for extramural research for NINCDS was approximately $326 million.

Application/Review Process: See the general description of NIH in chapter 4.

Funding Mechanisms: See the general description of NIH in chapter 4.

Examples of Funded Research:
1) "Analysis of Acoustical Communication."
2) "Psychological Treatment of Headache."
3) "The Role of Vasopressin on Learning and Memory."
4) "Secondary Visual Mechanisms and Selective Attention."
5) "A Psychophysical Analysis of Stress-Induced Analgesia."
6) "Sensory and Perceptual Dysfunction in Autism."
7) "Cognitive and Neural Mechanisms of Tactile Perception."
8) "Behavioral Differentiation of the Dementias."
9) "Language and Cognitive Flexibility in Deaf Children."
10) "A Study of the Rhythm of Spoken Language."

National Library of Medicine

Associate Director, Division of Extramural Program
5N505 Building 38
8600 Rockville Pike
Bethesda, MD 20894
(301/496–6921)

Program: The mission of the National Library of Medicine (NLM) is to assist the health community in finding ways for more rapid and widespread communication of biomedical information. The NLM supports extramural research on basic issues of health knowledge management, organization, and utilization.

Support is available for a variety of disciplines, particularly information, computer, and cognitive sciences.

Areas of interest include:

1)   the role of knowledge in the health professional's working life (how professionals understand and respond to their information needs);

2)   the effective integration of knowledge into clinical and related scientific activities (optimal organization and retrieval for better teaching and learning of material traditionally stored in libraries);

3)   the nature and analysis of medical bibliography;

4)   policies, structures, and processes for managing and delivery of health information;

5)   how health professionals process information for medical problem solving;

6)   the representation and organization of knowledge in computers;

7)   computer reasoning from medical knowledge, including artificial intelligence as applied to knowledge bases and "expert" systems.

Many of the above areas bear on NLM's research initiative on "medical informatics." This initiative seeks to explore fully the new and developing technologies required to accomplish the NLM mission.

The National Library of Medicine also supports research on the history of medicine and the health sciences.

Budget: In FY 1985 the NLM had a total extramural budget of $12 million, a large portion of which went to medical libraries. Approximately $5 million went to support extramural research projects. A similar amount or slightly less was expected to be available for FY 1986. Figures on the amount spent on social and behavioral science research are not available.

Application/Review Process: Applications are submitted to the NIH Division of Research Grants (see the general description in chapter 4). Applicants are encouraged to contact the NLM extramural staff before submitting a proposal.

Funding Mechanisms: See the general description of NIH in chapter 4. Research may be funded through traditional research project grants (RO1s), New Investigator Research Awards, and Research Career Development Awards.

Examples of Funded Research:
1)   "Physiology in the American Context, 1870–1940."

2)   "Patterns—Partial Knowledge and Test Interpretation."

3)   "Women and Childbirth in America, 1750–1950."

Fogarty International Center

The Fogarty International Center (FIC) is one of the "Research and Support Divisions" of the National Institutes of Health. It was created to further international collaboration in the health and behavioral sciences through programs, conferences, and seminars; postdoctoral fellowships for research in the U.S. and abroad; and exchange programs for U.S. and foreign scientists. FIC serves as the coordinating agency for NIH biomedical and behavioral research activities at the international level and serves as the focal point for distinguished foreign visitors to the NIH.

In theory, the various FIC programs can support projects on any topic that is appropriate to the NIH mission (of uncovering new knowledge to advance health) as long as it has an international component. Thus, FIC programs are open to social and behavioral scientists. (Although FIC program announcements specify support for the "behavioral sciences," the definition does include the social sciences.) Proposals in psychology are eligible unless the project is one that clearly addresses an area that falls under the Alcohol, Drug Abuse, and Mental Health Administration purview rather than that of NIH.

Application/Review Process: Although details vary within the individual programs, proposals to FIC are reviewed by the NIH Division of Research Grants (see the general description in chapter 4). Before assignment to study sections, however, FIC staff review applications to determine if they are eligible for FIC support. Social and behavioral scientists are advised to contact the appropriate program officer prior to submission to determine agency interest and also to make clear how their project relates to FIC and NIH missions. An appeals process has recently been instituted at NIH to resolve cases where scientists feel their applications have received unfair or inappropriate reviews. This is one mechanism social and behavioral scientists may utilize to ensure that their proposals are not denied because of a bias toward the biomedical sciences.

Funding Mechanisms: FIC funds a variety of fellowships, as well as providing support for international conferences and collaborative research projects.

SENIOR INTERNATIONAL FELLOWSHIPS

Marcus Hairstone, Fellowships Program Officer
Building 38A, Room 615
9000 Rockville Pike
Bethesda, MD 20892
(301/496–6688)

Program: The Senior International Fellowship (SIF) provides opportunities for study or research in a foreign institution by U.S. scientists whose professional stature is well recognized by their peers and nominating institution. The SIF is intended to enhance the exchange of ideas and information about the latest advances in the health sciences, both basic and clinical; permit U.S. scientists to participate abroad in ongoing study or research in the health sciences; and improve the research, educational, and clinical potential of the U.S. nominating institution.

Prospective applicants must have a clear understanding with the foreign host institution about the goals of the fellowship and the work to be pursued. Recipients of a fellowship will be expected to bring to the host institution the intellectual stimulation, knowledge, and professional background that will make it a mutually enriching experience for the fellow and the foreign host.

Senior International Fellowships are awarded for a period of 3 to 12 months. Awardees receive a maximum stipend of $15,000, plus a foreign living allowance of $15,000 per year, transportation costs, and a home institutional allowance of up to $2,000.

To be eligible, an applicant must have a doctoral degree in one of the biomedical, behavioral, or health sciences; have at least five years' postdoctoral experience; be nominated by the academic dean or appropriate U.S. institutional official; hold a full-time appointment on the staff of the nominating institution; and be invited by a nonprofit foreign institution.

Proposals are not accepted for brief observational visits, attendance at scientific meetings or formal training courses, independent research projects within the host country, or full-time clinical, technical, or teaching services.

Application/Review Process: See the general discussion of FIC above. Deadlines for proposals are January 10, May 10, and September 10.

Funding Mechanisms: See the general discussion of FIC above.

Examples of Funded Research:
In FY 1984, 5 of 53 SIF awards went to social and behavioral scientists, including 3 psychologists, 1 sociologist, and 1 demographer.

FOREIGN GOVERNMENT-SUPPORTED FELLOWSHIPS FOR U.S. SCIENTISTS

Bettie Graham, Chief, International Research and Awards Branch
Building 38A, Room 615
9000 Rockville Pike
Bethesda, MD 20892
(301/496–6688)

Program: FIC administers a number of fellowships similar in scope to the Senior International Fellowships but funded by foreign governments. They include:

1) Academy of Finland Postdoctoral Research Fellowships.

2) Alexander von Humboldt Foundation Postdoctoral Research Fellowships.

3) French National Institute of Health and Medical Research Postdoctoral Fellowships.

4) NIH-French National Center for Scientific Research Exchange Program.

5) Irish Medical Research Council Postdoctoral Fellowships.

6) Norwegian Research Council for Science and the Humanities Postdoctoral Fellowships.

7) Swedish Medical Research Council Fellowships.

8) Swiss National Science Foundation Postdoctoral Fellowships.

9) Visiting Scientists Program of the National Science Council, Taiwan.

The eligibility requirements of each program vary. At a minimum, however, each candidate must hold a doctoral degree in one of the behavioral, biomedical, or health sciences and have some postdoctoral experience.

Application/Review Process: See the general discussion of FIC above. With the exception of the Alexander von Humboldt Foundation and the National Science Council of Taiwan fellowship applications, FIC arranges for receipt and scientific merit review of applications and transmits the applications and summary statements to the awarding organizations for final selection.

Funding Mechanisms: See the general discussion of FIC above. The maximum period of support for all programs is 1 year.

SCHOLARS-IN-RESIDENCE PROGRAM

Peter G. Condliffe, Chief
Building 16, Room 202
9000 Rockville Pike
Bethesda, MD 20892
(301/496–4161)

Program: Although individuals may not "apply," social and behavioral scientists should be aware that they are eligible to participate in the NIH Scholars-in-Residence Program. The program invites a limited number of international scholars to come to NIH for advanced study in a scientific environment that fosters the development of innovative approaches to research. Fogarty Scholars in Residence have a unique opportunity to study subjects of their own choosing and to interact with NIH scientists. Ideas and information can be exchanged through collaborative research, lectures and seminars, and the preparation of books, monographs, or other reports.

Only NIH scientists or former Fogarty scholars may nominate candidates for the Scholars in Residence Program. A panel of senior NIH intramural scientists reviews the nominees. The panel then sends its recommendations to the FIC Advisory Board and the FIC Director. As openings in the program become available, the FIC invites approved nominees. About 12 scholars receive invitations each year.

Although most recent scholars have been biomedical and natural scientists, program participation is open to the full range of biomedical and behavioral sciences.

Office of Population Affairs

The Office of Population Affairs (OPA), directed by a Deputy Assistant Secretary of Population Affairs, was established by Congress in 1970 as a policy-coordinating office to advise the Secretary of HHS on population research and family planning services.

The OPA has two divisions: the Office of Family Planning and the Office of Adolescent Pregnancy Programs. Both divisions award grants and contracts for research appropriate for social and behavioral scientists.

The Office of Population Affairs also sponsors a Data Archive on Adolescent Pregnancy and Pregnancy Prevention at Sociometrics Corporation in Palo Alto, California. Through the Archive, researchers, practitioners, administrators, and policymakers have access to large-scale data on important issues in the fields of adolescent pregnancy, pregnancy prevention, and family planning.

OFFICE OF FAMILY PLANNING

Patricia Thompson, Director of Research
731-E HHH Building
200 Independence Avenue, SW
Washington, DC 20201
(202/245–1181)

Program: The Office of Family Planning (OFP) administers the federal Title X program aimed at improving the efficiency and effectiveness of family planning projects, keeping the cost per unit of service to a minimum, and encouraging the involvement of the family in the provision of family planning services. OFP provides funds to over 4,000 community family planning clinics across the country. A small portion of the budget is retained to support applied research on the improvement of family planning services delivery for low-income women, adolescents, and others in need of such services.

OFP first issued solicitations for competitive, peer-reviewed research proposals in FY 1983 and moved to a more routinized system in FY 1986. The Office now issues a general research announcement which is published in the *Federal Register* and the *NIH Guide for Grants and Contracts*. Preference is given to proposals in the priority areas announced by the agency. The Office will continue to issue requests for applications on specific topics on occasion.

The FY 1986 research announcement contained 10 priority areas: family planning client behavior; adolescent family planning clients; male family planning clients; targeting of family planning services to subgroups with special needs (i.e., low-income families, minorities, handicapped, etc.); clinic personnel behavior; organization and management of family planning services; the role of private physicians; natural family planning; infertility services; and counseling services (evaluation of role and effectiveness).

OFP encourages proposals from a variety of social and behavioral science disciplines. To date, most support has gone to sociologists, anthropologists, psychologists, economists, and epidemiologists. Proposals that are primarily studies of federal policies are not encouraged, although there is some interest in analyses of state and local policies. Proposals for historical studies could be considered, although, to date, few have been submitted.

Budget: OFP awarded approximately $1.5 million for extramural research in FY 1985. Approximately $1 million in new starts per year is now expected.

Application/Review Process: OFP staff invite preliminary contact by phone from prospective applicants to discuss research ideas, but will not review preliminary proposals or give technical assistance to applicants.

Grant applications are submitted on PHS Form 398 to the Division of Research Grants at the National Institutes of Health (see the general description in chapter 4). Deadlines are February 1, June 1, and October 1. After scientific review by DRG study sections, final funding decisions are made by the Deputy Assistant Secretary for Population Affairs with assistance from staff.

Funding Mechanisms: Researchers may apply for individual research project grants or New Investigator Research Awards (NIRA). Direct costs for investigator-initiated research projects should not exceed $100,000 per year. NIRA awards are limited to $37,500 per year. Awards can be made for a maximum of 3 years.

Examples of Funded Research:

1) "Private Physicians' Role in Family Planning for Poor Women" (18-month project; total costs, $299,473).

2) "Factors Affecting Poor Women's Choice of Family Planning Providers" (3-year project; total costs, $166,604).

3) "Rural Family Planning Services: An Interactionist View" (2-year project; total costs, $245,537).

4) "A Mathematical Model for Family Planning Clinic Staffing" (1-year project; total costs, $66,021).

5) "Research on Adolescent Marriage" (2-year project; total costs, $292,-189).

6) "Low Income Need for and Access to Infertility Services" (1-year project; total costs, $74,452).

7) "Factors Influencing Family Planning Clinic Acceptance and Drop-Out" (2-year project; total costs, $256,927).

OFFICE OF ADOLESCENT PREGNANCY PROGRAMS

Eugenia Eckard, Acting Director of Research
731-E HHH Building
200 Independence Avenue, SW
Washington, DC 20201
(202/245–1181)

Program: The Office of Adolescent Pregnancy Programs (OAPP) was established in 1978 and began awarding research grants in FY 1982. Like the Office of Family Planning, OAPP has begun issuing a general research announcement to stimulate investigator-initiated proposals in areas of agency interest. OAPP is primarily responsible for administering the Adolescent Family Life Act (AFL) enacted by Congress in 1981. Language contained in the Act permits OAPP to spend up to one third of AFL funds for research, although the agency has not chosen to utilize that amount to date.

OAPP supports demonstration and evaluation projects for delivery of services to prevent adolescent pregnancy and to care for pregnant adolescents, and research on topics including adolescent sexual activity, parenting, and childbearing. A fundamental basis of the AFL (and thus of the research program) is to encourage the delay of sexual activity among adolescents rather than promoting contraceptive use.

Five research topics of interest identified by OAPP are:

1)   influences on adolescent premarital sexual behavior (demographic, economic, social, and psychological characteristics; family, peer, and media influ-

ence; adolescent decision-making processes; different patterns of influence for males and females);

2) consequences of adolescent premarital sexual behavior (differing effects on development of males and females, including psychological, social, educational, moral factors; differing consequences for major population subgroups);

3) adoption option for unmarried adolescent mothers (social, psychological, legal, and service factors; role of counseling; social attitudes toward single parenthood; family involvement);

4) parenting by unmarried adolescent mothers (role of the extended family; factors influencing parenting behavior; role of the father);

5) adolescent pregnancy services (scope and impact of public and private sector services and policies; evaluations of strategies to eliminate adolescent premarital sexual relations; evaluations of strategies that might enhance service delivery).

Budget: OAPP spent about $1.5 million for extramural research in FY 1985. Approximately $1 million in new starts per year is now expected.

Application/Review Process: Grant applications are submitted on PHS Form 398 to the Division of Research Grants at the National Institutes of Health (see the general description in chapter 4). Deadlines are February 1, June 1, and October 1. After scientific review by DRG study sections, final funding decisions are made by the Deputy Assistant Secretary for Population Affairs with assistance from staff.

Funding Mechanisms: Researchers may apply for individual research project grants or New Investigator Research Awards (NIRA). Direct costs for investigator-initiated research projects should not exceed $100,000 per year. NIRA awards are limited to $37,500 per year. Awards can be made for a maximum of 3 years.

Examples of Funded Research:
1) "Short Term Consequences of Adolescent Sexual Behavior" (1-year project; total costs, $130,576).

2) "Sex and Pregnancy Among Mexican-American Adolescents" (3-year project; total costs, $420,084).

3) "The Antecedents of Early Premarital Intercourse" (2-year project; total costs, $116,945).

4) "Adoption Behavior and the Propensity to Adopt in the U.S." (2-year project; total costs, $66,930).

5) "Fathers of Infants of Adolescent Mothers" (4-year project; total costs, $352,399).

Social Security Administration

The Social Security Administration (SSA) conducts an integrated program of intramural and extramural research activities designed to provide accurate information and analyses concerning the major programs of SSA responsibility —Old Age and Survivors Insurance (OASI), Disability Insurance (DI), Supplemental Security Income (SSI), and Aid to Families with Dependent Children (AFDC). Research and statistical data are used to provide cost, revenue, and workload estimates, and to enhance program management and efficiency. They are also used to provide cost estimates and analyses for legislative initiatives.

In 1983 the SSA underwent a "realignment" motivated in part by an agency shift from social research to operational research. Staff were transferred from the Office of Research and Statistics to operating components where they now conduct operationally oriented studies. The primary research and statistical function, however, remains with the former office which has become the Office of Research, Statistics, and International Policy.

Although SSA has a general mandate to perform policy analysis and research, the level of social research is within the SSA Administrator's discretion. The Congress can—and does—mandate that SSA do particular studies that the Congress deems desirable or necessary.

SSA budget figures indicate that a total of $18.8 million was spent on intramural and extramural research in FY 1985, of which $1.2 million went to university-based researchers. By SSA definition, all research is "applied" rather than "basic" since it is focused on particular programs. Although areas of interest to SSA encompass a broad spectrum of social and behavioral science disciplines (including sociology, economics, political science, statistics, and demography), the amount of support available for academic researchers has been declining.

OFFICE OF RESEARCH, STATISTICS, AND INTERNATIONAL POLICY

Dan Graham, Program Analyst
Room 138, Altmeyer Building
6401 Security Boulevard
Baltimore, MD 21235
(301/597–2927)

Program: The Office of Research, Statistics, and International Policy (ORSIP) is responsible for providing information on the effects of Social Security Administration (SSA) programs and the interactions among these programs, other tax and income transfer programs, and economic, social, and demographic forces. ORSIP responsibilities are categorized in four functional areas: program statistics, policy research, legislative impact analysis, and technical assistance to others. Extramural funding is generally in the area of policy research.

In early 1986 ORSIP staff will have completed a congressionally mandated study on the effects of raising the retirement age on persons in ill health and/or physically demanding jobs. It is anticipated that this study will produce an agenda for future research and possibly generate extramural projects in this area. ORSIP is also funding the coding of data from the Framingham Heart Study to facilitate its use for analysis of the process by which persons become disabled. After coding and documentation have been completed, outside researchers will probably be solicited for help in data analysis.

ORSIP does conduct some contract research, most of which goes to applied research and development firms. Academic researchers seldom compete for these contracts, partly because the tasks are too ambitious for a small team of researchers to undertake.

Budget: ORSIP spent approximately $3.2 million on extramural research in FY 1985. A level of $600,000 to $700,000 is anticipated for extramural grants in FY 1986.

Application/Review Process: Requests for applications are announced in the *Federal Register* on an ad hoc basis. Applications are reviewed by panels of federal and nonfederal experts and by ORSIP staff. The rank order determined by the review panel is generally binding, although final funding decisions are made by the Associate Commissioner for Policy.

Funding Mechanisms: ORSIP may award both grants and contracts. Projects are generally funded for one year only, but may compete for renewal awards. There is no dollar limitation on awards, but most grants are small (under $70,000).

Examples of Funded Research:

In FY 1984 ORSIP awarded a total of five grants for research on the impact of raising the retirement age. In FY 1985 one grant was awarded to evaluate the reliability of estimates generated by microsimulation models.

OFFICE OF FAMILY ASSISTANCE

Elizabeth Barnes, Chief, Office of Policy and Evaluation
B424-C Trans Point Building
2100 2nd Street, SW
Washington, DC 20201
(202/245–3284)

Program: The research program of the Office of Family Assistance (OFA) is primarily concerned with the Aid to Families with Dependent Children (AFDC) program. Several broad areas of interest have emerged in recent years: (1) developing programs to aid AFDC recipients in becoming self-supporting, (2) evaluation of the WIN (Work Incentive) program, (3) AFDC program management and improvements in information systems, and (4) methods to detect and recover overpayments.

Although there are two categories of applicants eligible for OFA funds (Section 1115 for state and governmental units and Section 1110 for any nonprofit organization), all funds went to governmental units in FY 1984 and FY 1985. Because most projects are conducted in operational settings, grantees are typically agencies serving AFDC recipients. Applications for projects may include methodological studies or project evaluations by academic researchers.

Budget: More than half of the extramural research budget of OFA is set aside for state and governmental units. The amount available for nongovernmental units, including university-based researchers, was approximately $1 million in FY 1985, although most extramural funds went to continuation awards. It was anticipated, however, that more new awards would be made in future years.

Application/Review Process: OFA research priorities are announced annually in the *Federal Register,* usually in the spring. Unsolicited proposals are accepted, but are held to compete with those submitted in response to a research announcement. Ad hoc review committees composed primarily of federal staff are convened to review proposals. Final funding decisions are made by the Associate Commissioner for Family Assistance.

Funding Mechanisms: OFA awards grants, generally for projects of three years or less. There is no dollar limitation imposed, but awards average about $150,000.

Examples of Funded Projects:
1)   "Welfare Fraud/Early Prevention Detection Project" (16-month project).
2)   "Overpayment Recovery Project" (2-year project).
3)   "Fraud Prevention Profile" (2-year project).

OFFICE OF DISABILITY

Aaron Krute, Director, Division of Disability Studies
Room 2223, Annex Building
6401 Security Boulevard
Baltimore, MD 21235
(301/594–0301)

Program: The mission of the Division of Disability Studies is to plan and direct a continuing basic economic and social research effort to measure the size, nature, and effects of the private and social costs of disability and ill health on the population in general, and to evaluate the effectiveness of SSA disability programs, including trust-funded rehabilitation services and Medicare coverage for the disabled. The division also conducts national surveys of the disabled and conducts studies of significant disability policy issues. In addition, division staff conduct studies mandated by Congress as well as administer the extramural program.

Like other SSA divisions, this office focuses primarily on operating policy issues. The Division of Disability Studies is unique within the SSA, however, in that it still relies heavily on academic social and behavioral scientists for its extramural research program. Most grant recipients are university-based, and most research is interdisciplinary in nature. Typical grantees are psychologists, sociologists, and economists.

Division staff are hopeful that a future direction will be a return to basic, people-oriented research. Funding for a broad population-based survey is anticipated for FY 1987.

Budget: (figures not available)

Application/Review Process: Research interests are announced in the *Federal Register;* contract announcements appear in the *Commerce Business Daily.* Announcements are for specific funding opportunities and funds are set-aside for those projects. Review panels composed primarily of SSA staff are convened for each project. Review panels approve or disapprove proposals, but do not rank them. Final funding decisions are made by the Associate Commissioner for Disability and her staff.

Division staff will consider unsolicited proposals although few are received. Prospective applicants should submit a brief concept paper first.

Funding Mechanisms: The division normally awards grants for research and contracts for data collection. Most contracts go to private R&D firms.

Examples of Funded Research: (not available)

DEPARTMENT OF HOUSING AND URBAN DEVELOPMENT

Assistant Secretary for Policy Development and Research

OFFICE OF POLICY DEVELOPMENT AND RESEARCH

Kenneth J. Beirne, General Deputy Assistant Secretary
Room 8100
451 7th Street, SW
Washington, DC 20410
(202/755–5600)

Program: The Office of Policy Development and Research (PD&R) is responsible for the development, planning, execution, and evaluation of research and demonstration programs of the Department of Housing and Urban Development (HUD). In addition, PD&R has principal responsibility for providing program evaluation, economic and policy analysis, and staff assistance to the Secretary of HUD in determining national housing and community development goals, program priorities, and objectives. PD&R administer's HUD's research and technology appropriation, which is the Department's only funding source for carrying out research and evaluations.

In 1981 PD&R totally re-oriented its research priorities and increased its emphasis on policy development. PD&R's research was redirected toward projects that improve the efficiency, effectiveness, and equity of HUD programs and reduce costs.

PD&R comprises four programs: (1) Office of Economic Affairs, (2) Office of Housing Studies, (3) Office of Policy Development, and (4) Office of Urban and Community Studies. The latter two programs award very few outside research contracts. In the past, the Office of Housing Studies was the primary supporter of extramural research, funding topics such as modernization needs and voucher systems in assisted housing. Future extramural research monies will be concentrated in the Office of Economic Affairs, with a major emphasis on housing finance.

Two topics of particular interest to PD&R are the study of multi-family assisted and insured housing and the development of a design for comprehensive public housing management. It is anticipated that requests for applications will be issued for contract research on both topics.

PD&R staff are also interested in developing new data sources in areas such as fair housing and assisted-housing recipients and in improving the condition of current HUD databases.

Budget: The shift in PD&R priorities has been accompanied by dramatic decreases in the PD&R budget, going from $51.3 million in FY 1981 to $21.3 million the following year. The budget has continued to erode in subsequent years. A large portion of the budget is reserved each year to fund the Annual Housing Survey which carries a price tag of about $12 million. Thus, only about $5 million will be available for discretionary funding in FY 1986.

Application/Review Process: An announcement of general research interests as well as requests for applications for specific projects are published in the *Federal Register* and the *Commerce Business Daily.* HUD also maintains a Bidder's List for prospective applicants. Although unsolicited proposals are accepted, in recent years almost none have been funded.

Solicited applications are reviewed by panels selected by the Assistant Secretary for PD&R, generally from HUD staff. Final funding decisions are made by the PD&R staff.

Funding Mechanisms: Most PD&R research funding is done by contract, although occasionally grants are made. PD&R also procures a number of "Indefinite Quantity Contracts" from organizations able to complete information requests in a short amount of time. These contracts are awarded competitively in particular subject areas (e.g., housing finance, housing assistance) every three years. Contracts guarantee the recipient of a minimum $50,000 payment over the life of the contract and a maximum of $450,000.

Examples of Funded Research:
1) "Local Solutions for Housing Needs of the Elderly" (1-year project; total award, $83,601).

2) "Demonstration to Test Self-Sustaining Employment of Single Head of Households" (2-year project; total award, $210,000).

3) "Evaluation of the Congregate Housing Services Program" (5-year project, total award, $1,225,882).

4) "Case Studies of PHA Effective Management" (1-year project; total award, $320,576).

HOUSING SURVEY SMALL GRANT PROGRAM

Duane T. McGough, Director
Room 8208
451 7th Street, SW
Washington, DC 20410
(202/755–5630)

Program: In FY 1981 PD&R initiated a program of particular interest to new researchers. Located in the Office of Economic Affairs, the Housing Survey Small Grant Program encourages policy-relevant research using data from the Annual Housing Survey. Awards are limited to college or university researchers of instructor or assistant professor rank. Competitive proposals from women and minority researchers receive preference, because they are currently underrepresented as researchers in this field.

Priority is given to proposals that extend past research on programs and policies in the following areas:

1)   strategies for improving assisted and public housing programs;

2)   strategies for providing standard rental housing efficiently where it is needed;

3)   possible means of reducing housing costs;

4)   impacts of changes in housing affordability on low-income renters, first-time homebuyers, and household formation decisions;

5)   strategies to promote fair and nondiscriminatory housing.

HUD is especially interested in research that uses longitudinally linked Annual Housing Survey files from either the national or Standard Metropolitan Statistical Area (SMSA) samples.

Budget: PD&R anticipated a budget of approximately $144,000 for this program in FY 1986.

Application/Review Process: The deadline for applications is generally in late March; projects begin in June with a seminar in Washington. A review committee of PD&R staff evaluates proposals and forwards its recommendations to the Assistant Secretary for PD&R for a final decision.

Funding Mechanisms: Small grants of no more than $18,000 are awarded. The standard project period is 65 weeks. Nominal cost sharing by the sponsoring college or university is required.

Examples of Funded Research:
1)   "The Impact of the Housing Affordability Crisis on First-Time Buyers."

2)   "Housing Prices and Market Segmentation: An Analysis of White, Black, and Spanish Origin Households."

3)   "The Impact of Recent Changes in the Mobile Home Industry on the Quality, Affordability, Occupancy, and Location of Mobile Homes."

4)   "Estimating Bid Rents, Willingness-to-Pay, and the Cost Effectiveness of Housing Assistance Programs: A New Econometric Application of Rosen's Hedonic Price Theory."

DEPARTMENT OF JUSTICE

National Institute of Justice

The National Institute of Justice (NIJ) is a research branch of the Department of Justice. The Institute's mission is to develop knowledge about crime, its causes, and its control. Priority is given to policy-relevant research that can yield approaches and information that state and local agencies can use in preventing and reducing crime. NIJ reorganized its extramural program somewhat in FY 1986 in an effort to provide a more sustained, coordinated support base. The new Sponsored Research Program solicits proposals in several broad areas, with specific priorities established in each area. In addition, support is available through the visiting fellowships, graduate research fellowships, and summer research fellowships programs. Unsolicited proposals may be submitted, but because the targeted priority areas are so broad, most unsolicited proposals can be placed in one or more of the designated programs. All NIJ programs are appropriate for social and behavioral scientists.

SPONSORED RESEARCH PROGRAM

John Pickett, Director of Planning and Management
633 Indiana Avenue, NW
Washington, DC 20531
(202/724–2945)

Program: The Sponsored Research Program funds both basic and applied studies intended to bridge the gap between criminal justice theory and practice. All research is directed at improving the nation's ability to control crime and criminal behavior. Several topics have been established as ongoing priority areas, although specific topics within each may be designated each year.

Ongoing areas of interest are:

1) controlling the serious offender (including crime control theory and policy; offender classification and prediction of criminal behavior; violent criminal behavior; and drugs, alcohol, and crime);

2) aiding the victims of crime (including legislation and other changes affecting victims; police assistance to victims; and family violence and child sex abuse);

3) crime prevention (including partnerships between police; neighborhood actions against crime; and the private sector and prevention of specific crimes);

4) improving the criminal justice system (including police efficiency and effectiveness; police response to spouse assault; court effectiveness; corrections; and the system of criminal justice).

Budget: Approximately $9.3 million has been allocated for the sponsored research program for FY 1986.

Application/Review Process: An annual research announcement lists specific priority areas and staff contacts for each topic. Project periods, award amounts, and deadlines vary widely. Proposals are reviewed by peer panels chaired by NIJ program managers. Review panels made recommendations to the NIJ Director, who has final authority to make awards.

Funding Mechanisms: The NIJ will award grants or cooperative agreements to academic institutions, nonprofit organizations, public agencies, and individuals.

Examples of Funded Research:
1) "A Longitudinal Analysis of Neighborhood Delinquency Rates."

2) "Psychological Assessment of the Adult, Male Prison Inmate."

3) "Justifiable and Criminal Homicide of Family Members, Acquaintances, and Strangers: Regional, Cultural, and Environmental Factors."

4) "Modeling the Crime Reduction Effects and Economic Benefits of Drug Abuse Treatment."

5) "Effects of Criminal Court Testimony on Child Sexual Assault Victims."

6) "Fines as an Alternative to Incarceration: The Attitude and Practices of Trial Court Judges."

7) "The Impact of Rape Reform Legislation."

VISITING FELLOWS PROGRAM

Joseph Kochanski, Chairperson
633 Indiana Avenue, NW
Washington, DC 20531
(202/724–2962)

Program: The Visiting Fellows Program has two components that provide fellowship opportunities for researchers and for criminal justice practitioners. The principal aim is to increase understanding of crime and criminal behavior, the impacts of crime control policies, and the fairness, effectiveness, and efficiency of criminal justice operations. Fellows are expected to spend a minimum of 80% of their fellowship period at NIJ. While at the Institute, fellows also have the opportunity to participate in the development of plans for criminal justice research programs of national scope, interact with NIJ staff and other visiting fellows, and present seminars on their own research.

Fellowships for researchers are designed for individuals with broad and extensive criminal justice research experience and are awarded on the basis of this experience and their proposed research project.

Budget: This program has a budget of $250,000 for FY 1986 to provide six awards (three for researchers and three for practitioners).

Application/Review Process: An annual research announcement lists specific priority areas, deadlines, and staff contacts for the fellowship program. Proposals are reviewed by peer panels chaired by NIJ program managers. Review panels made recommendations to the NIJ Director, who has final authority to make awards.

Funding Mechanisms: Awards are made to individuals to cover salary and project costs for periods of 6 to 18 months. In addition, some relocation and travel expenses are covered. The fellowship salary is determined on the basis of the applicant's earned income.

GRADUATE RESEARCH FELLOWSHIPS PROGRAM

Joseph Kochanski, Chairperson
633 Indiana Avenue, NW
Washington, DC 20531
(202/724–2962)

Program: The Graduate Research Fellowships Program provides a limited number of fellowships awarded to doctoral candidates through sponsoring universities. Support is provided for students engaged in the research and writing of a doctoral dissertation in the areas of crime, crime prevention, criminal behavior, or criminal justice. Prior to the grant award, applicants must have completed all degree requirements except for the research, writing, and defense of the dissertation.

Budget: For FY 1986 a total of $150,000 was allocated for this program to support 13 to 17 fellowships.

Application/Review Process: An annual research announcement lists specific priority areas, staff contacts, and deadlines for the fellowship program. Proposals are reviewed by peer panels chaired by NIJ program managers. Review panels made recommendations to the NIJ Director, who has final authority to make awards.

Funding Mechanisms: The maximum amount of a fellowship is $11,000. Awards are for 1 year or less.

SUMMER RESEARCH FELLOWSHIPS PROGRAM

Winifred L. Reed, Program Manager
633 Indiana Avenue, NW
Washington, DC 20531
(202/724-7636)

Program: The Summer Research Fellowships Program is intended for senior researchers as well as relatively new Ph.D.s with strong quantitative skills and experience with machine-readable criminal justice data sets. This program of short-term projects is designed to build upon data analyses that have a potential for improving criminal justice policies.

Awards may be made for projects that address specific criminal justice policy questions of interest to federal, state, and local policymakers. Specific areas of interest may be designated each year. Currently, program emphasis is on the re-analysis of existing research data. The selection of data sets and of particular hypotheses to be investigated is left to the applicant. Relevant data sets are available from the Criminal Justice Data Archive at the Inter-University Consortium for Political and Social Research at the University of Michigan.

Budget: In FY 1986 the program anticipated making five awards of no more than $10,000 each.

Application/Review Process: An annual research announcement lists specific priority areas, deadlines, and staff contacts for the fellowship program. Project periods, award amounts, and deadlines vary widely. Proposals are reviewed by peer panels chaired by NIJ program managers. Review panels made recommendations to the NIJ Director, who has final authority to make awards.

Funding Mechanisms: The program is designed to serve as summer support for individuals; the inclusion of institutional indirect costs is strongly discouraged.

Office of Juvenile Justice and Delinquency Prevention

RESEARCH AND PROGRAM DEVELOPMENT DIVISION

Pamela Swain, Director
Room 780, Indiana Building
633 Indiana Avenue, NW
Washington, DC 20531
(202/724–7560)

Program: The Office of Juvenile Justice and Delinquency Prevention (OJJDP) supports research that will contribute to the prevention and treatment of juvenile delinquency. The Research and Program Development Division is organized in three major topical areas: (1) prevention of delinquent behavior and child exploitation, (2) improvement of the juvenile justice system, and (3) development of alternatives to traditional juvenile justice systems. The majority of resources in each area are focused on serious juvenile crime and protection of abused and exploited children. Support is available for basic research, policy studies, and program evaluation.

Different priorities are established for the three research areas each year, with requests for applications issued for specific topics. Current priorities include (1) research on the causes and correlates of delinquency, (2) school crime and discipline, (3) legal issues involving juvenile justice, (4) law enforcement agencies' policies and practices for handling missing children and homeless youth, (5) statistics on missing children, and (6) program and services for children and youth abusing drugs and alcohol.

Future topics of interest to OJJDP include missing children, child victims as witnesses, drug abuse among inner-city minority youth, longitudinal studies of causes of delinquency, and the impact of de-institutionalization of status offenders.

Program priorities are decided internally by OJJDP staff, but public and congressional interests are considered. Although Congress seldom mandates specific studies to be undertaken by OJJDP, it does suggest particular research themes for the agency to pursue.

Grantees in this program have traditionally included sociologists, psychologists, and political scientists. More proposals from anthropologists, economists, and psychiatrists are particularly encouraged. Program evaluations are more frequently being funded by the state agencies which receive juvenile justice formula [block] grants. Since evaluations are generally contracted out, interested researchers are encouraged to contact their appropriate state agency.

Budget: Approximately $5 million in extramural funds was awarded in FY 1985.

Application/Review Process: Strict regulations regarding the review and funding of competitive awards and peer review of unsolicited applications were issued in August 1985.

Requests for proposals are issued throughout the year with varying deadlines. Proposals are reviewed by peer panels composed of researchers and practitioners and the OJJDP staff. The results of both reviews are given to the Administrator of OJJDP for final funding decisions.

Funding Mechanisms: Competitive research projects are funded by grants. Some contracts are awarded for activities such as technical assistance with conferences or indefinite-quantity contracts for policy papers and monographs. Research funded through the Missing Children's Act is limited to nonprofit organizations; other grants may go to both profit and nonprofit groups.

Examples of Funded Research:
1) "The Impact of Residential Treatment: Adaptation in the Community Five Years Later."
2) "Dropping Out and Delinquency Among Puerto Rican Youths."
3) "The Young Criminal Years of the Violent Few."
4) "High Risk Early School Behavior for Later Delinquency."
5) "Delinquency in a Birth Cohort Replication."
6) "Juvenile Arrest Trends in the United States: The Years Between 1970 and 1981."
7) "Evaluation of the Habitual Juvenile Offender Program."

DEPARTMENT OF LABOR

Employment and Training Administration

PERFORMANCE MANAGEMENT AND EVALUATION DIVISION

Raymond Uhalde, Chief
8000 Patrick Henry Building
601 D Street, NW
Washington, DC 20213
(202/376–6660)

Program: The Employment and Training Administration (ETA) supports research and evaluation projects related to the Job Training Partnership Act, the Employment Service, the Job Corps, labor markets, and the technology of training. In addition, it continues to support the Job Training Longitudinal Survey and the National Longitudinal Survey of Labor Market Experiences and is conducting three experiments related to youth and adult training. Because most ETA research funds are earmarked for these and other departmental projects, little money is available for discretionary funding.

Application/Review Process: Notices for competitive contracts are published in the *Commerce Business Daily*. Unsolicited proposals are accepted, but limited resources make funding unlikely.

Funding Mechanisms: All awards are made through contracts.

Budget: Approximately $12 million was available for research and evaluation in FY 1985. Much of the budget goes to support ETA's nondiscretionary projects and research in other parts of the Department of Labor, notably the Assistant Secretary for Policy and the Bureau of International Affairs.

DEPARTMENT OF STATE

Bureau of Intelligence and Research

OFFICE OF LONG-RANGE ASSESSMENTS AND RESEARCH

E. Raymond Platig, Director
Room 6842
2201 C Street, NW
Washington, DC 20520
(202/647–1342)

Program: Located in the State Department's Bureau of Intelligence and Research (INR), the Office of Long-Range Assessments and Research (LAR) has
three functions: preparation of analytical assessments, management of the Department's program of extramural policy research, and interagency research
planning and guidance.

    The LAR program focuses on the underlying forces and longer-term trends
and prospects for U.S. foreign policy across all world areas. LAR is the main
instrument for bringing the expertise of nonfederal research scholars to bear on
the Department's foreign policy mission. Through the Commissioned Research
Division, LAR works with all policy bureaus and staffs in the Department to
identify their policy research requirements and helps to meet these needs
through the use of contracts, consultants, conferences, and contacts with the
private research sector. It also develops cooperative contract research projects
with other government agencies and manages research projects supported by
funds allocated to other bureaus of the Department.

    LAR does not encourage unsolicited proposals, nor does it provide primary
research support. Competitive contracts are announced in the *Commerce Business
Daily.* Most contracts awarded are small (under $10,000). Contracts may be for
specific topics or indefinite quantity contracts to produce brief policy papers
during a limited time period. LAR also conducts a number of small working
conferences throughout the year, inviting a small panel of academic researchers
to come to Washington to discuss policy issues.

Budget: The budget for external contracts at LAR has remained constant at
$600,000 for several years. That amount is usually supplemented through
interagency transfers, however, making the total amount of support approximately $1.2 million.

Application/Review Process: Competitive contract announcements are published in the *Commerce Business Daily.* Applications are reviewed by State Department staff.

Funding Mechanisms: All funding is by contract.

Examples of Funded Research:
A list of contracts awarded by LAR is not available to the public since many studies involve classified materials.

SOVIET AND EASTERN EUROPEAN STUDIES GRANTS PROGRAM

Paul K. Cook, Advisor
Room 6747
2201 C Street, NW
Washington, DC 20520
(202/647–6839 or 647–6842)

Program: The Soviet-Eastern European Research and Training Act of 1983 provides for U.S. government assistance to develop and maintain a national capacity for advanced research and training in the field of Soviet and Eastern European studies. Eligible activities under the Act include graduate training, advanced research, public dissemination of research data and results, contact and collaboration among federal and private specialists, and the acquisition of firsthand experience in the Soviet Union and the countries of Eastern Europe. Countries specified by the Act include Albania, Bulgaria, Czechoslovakia, German Democratic Republic, Hungary, Poland, Romania, USSR, and Yugoslavia.
Applications for funding under the Act are invited from organizations prepared to conduct national programs in the field of Soviet and Eastern European and related studies as follows:

1) programs for research on the Soviet Union and Eastern Europe at the postdoctoral level;

2) programs offering graduate, postdoctoral, and teaching fellowships for advanced training in Soviet and Eastern European studies, including language training;

3) programs to carry out advanced training and research on a reciprocal basis in the Soviet Union and Eastern Europe to provide greater access for U.S. specialists to research facilities and resources in those countries;

4) programs to facilitate dissemination of research methods, data, and findings in Soviet Union and Eastern European studies;

5) programs to facilitate research collaboration among specialists and between federal and private researchers by conducting seminars, conferences, etc.

Advanced research and training programs are to be conducted on a shared-cost basis by the sponsoring organization and State Department through institutions of higher education or nonprofit corporations. To be eligible for consideration, programs must be national in scope. Local or regional programs having a demonstrable national impact are also eligible. Programs that foster interdisciplinary studies and the development of secondary competencies are encouraged. Special emphasis is placed on those disciplines and topics where the existing base of expertise is weakest in light of national needs.

Budget: A budget of $4.8 million was anticipated for this program in FY 1986.

Application/Review Process: The deadline for proposals is generally in October or November. An announcement of the program and request for applications is published in the *Federal Register*. The Soviet-Eastern European Studies Advisory Committee was established to recommend grant policies and recipients. Final funding decisions are made by the Committee and State Department officials.

Funding Mechanisms: There are no specific guidelines on the size of grant that can be requested. Indirect costs are limited to 10% of the total grant amount. Project periods may extend up to 4 years.

Examples of Funded Projects:
1) $741,150 to two scholarly associations to fund a joint fellowship program designed to attract and retain junior scholars, including shared cost with universities for initial academic assignments and support for collaborative research projects, and to conduct a national competition for grants to American institutions that offer intensive training in the Russian language.

2) $83,333 to a university research center to organize and conduct a national competition among editorial boards of scholarly journals in the field for publication of works by young scholars.

3) $121,360 to a university to partially fund a Slavic reference service and summer research laboratory on Russia and Eastern Europe.

4) $1,399,950 to a nonprofit organization to augment existing programs designed to develop and sustain long-term fundamental research dealing with major Soviet and Eastern European policy issues.

DEPARTMENT OF TRANSPORTATION

UNIVERSITY RESEARCH PROGRAM

William F. Brown, Director
Room 10309-D, P-34
400 7th Street, SW
Washington, DC 20590
(202/426–0190)

Program: The University Research Program (URP) of the Department of Transportation (DOT) serves as the focal point for the support of basic and applied academic research for the various operating components of the Department. The primary purpose of URP is to assure that the resources of the higher education community are utilized effectively in DOT efforts to solve national transportation problems. URP research priorities concern all modes of local, state, regional, and national transportation by highway, rail, air, and waterways.

Four general areas of transportation research are on-going topics of interest to DOT:

1) regulation (deregulation opportunities, maritime policy);

2) investment and financing (trade facilitation, private industry trends);

3) safety (alcohol safety research, including enforcement and public involvement issues, prevention programs for youth, drug impairment measurement, detection, and behavioral tests; restraint system usage; behavioral aspects of moving and storing hazardous material; occupational stress);

4) technology (artificial intelligence; human factors in automated control systems; mathematical modeling of oil and hazardous chemical spills).

The Department determines specific priorities for each of the four categories and issues a request for proposals, generally biennially. The next solicitation will be for projects to be funded in FY 1987. Future priorities will include an ongoing interest in behavioral aspects of fatal accidents, studies of compliance, changing demographic patterns, more efficient use of computers, economic competitiveness of the United States, and more productive uses of capital.

The URP particularly encourages historically Black colleges and universities to compete for research funding.

Budget: The URP has a fairly stable budget of about $1 million each year to fund new projects.

Application/Review Process: Only proposals submitted in response to URP program announcements are considered for funding. The deadline for proposals is generally in mid-February. Applications are reviewed by panels of DOT and other federal staff and by the staff members directly responsible for the priority area involved. Applications and award recommendations are then reviewed by the Departmental University Research Review Board. The final award decisions are made by the Deputy Secretary of DOT.

A *Proposal Preparation Manual* is available upon request from the URP office.

Funding Mechanisms: All URP research is funded by contract. Contracts may range from $50,000 to $250,000; the average is $80,000-$100,000. Primarily multiyear contracts are awarded.

Examples of Funded Research:

1)   "Investment Strategies to Solve Rural Bridge Problems" (FY 1984 contract, $73,780).

2)   "Visual Process and Driving Safety" (FY 1984 contract, $36,000).

3)   "Transit Efficiency for Inner City Minorities" (FY 1984 contract, $184,489).

4)   "Intercity Passenger Transportation Demand" (FY 1984 contract, $14,060).

5)   "Industrial Policy for Maritime Industry" (FY 1984 contract, $39,582).

6)   "Safety Boat Legislation" (FY 1984 contract, $15,493).

URBAN MASS TRANSPORTATION ADMINISTRATION

UNIVERSITY RESEARCH AND TRAINING PROGRAM

James Bautz, Director, Office of Service and Management Demonstrations
Room 6100
400 7th Street, SW
Washington, DC 20590
(202/426–4995)

Program: The Urban Mass Transportation Administration (UMTA) awards grants to colleges and universities for research and training projects in areas of urban and rural transportation analysis, management, and operations. The

UMTA University Research and Training Program (UR&T) is designed to support basic and theoretical research within the academic community that will increase the knowledge base, improve decision-making and management processes, or assist transit professionals in anticipating significant national issues and trends. UR&T funds may not be used to conduct research on public transportation planning problems, feasibility studies, or demonstration projects that are site-specific. Principal investigators must be full-time teaching members of an educational institution and may not have appointments only in research or administration. Substantive participation by students in research projects is strongly encouraged.

The UR&T Program is interested in supporting research in several broad areas: (1) safety and security; (2) private sector participation; (3) transit assistance programs; (4) service and operations; (5) facilities, equipment, and maintenance; and (6) human and management resources. Future topics of interest may include marketing, suburban mobility, productivity, work rule reform, quality circles, and private sector initiatives.

UR&T research is appropriate for a wide range of social and behavioral sciences, including sociology, geography, statistics, demography, psychology, urban studies, and economics. It is not unusual for applications that are favorably reviewed but not funded by UR&T to receive funding from one of the other operating units of DOT.

Budget: Slightly less than $1 million was available for new research projects in FY 1985.

Application/Review Process: UR&T issues an annual announcement of its research priorities, listing contact persons for each topic. The deadline for applications is generally mid-November. Applications are reviewed by UMTA or other DOT staff. Recommendations from these reviews are made to the UMTA Administrator for final selection. Minority institution participation and geographic distribution are considered in the selection process.

Funding Mechanisms: Grants of up to $85,000 are awarded for 1-year projects only.

Examples of Funded Research:
1)   "Analysis of Bus Transit Accidents: Empirical, Methodological, and Policy Issues" (FY 1984 award, $74,482).

2)   "The Implications of User-Side Subsidies for Transit Financing" (FY 1984 award, $42,569).

3)   "A Study of the Impact of a Mandated Training Program on New Taxicab Drivers in New York City" (FY 1984 award, $71,766).

4) "Development of a Self-Instructive Course in Disaggregate Mode Choice Modeling for Practicing Transportation Professionals" (FY 1984 award, $74,221).

5) "A Study of Elderly and Handicapped Perception of a Transit Rider Program in Rural and Urban Communities in Northern Mississippi" (FY 1984 award, $43,000).

6) "Analysis of 1970 and 1980 Census Data on Transit Trips for the Journey to Work" (FY 1984 award, $57,330).

DEPARTMENT OF THE TREASURY

Internal Revenue Service

Frank M. Malanga, Director, Research Division
Room 3423, PM:PFR:R
1111 Constitution Avenue, NW
Washington, DC 20224
(202/566–6436)

The Research Division of the Internal Revenue Service (IRS) funds extramural research in a number of areas of interest to social and behavioral scientists. The IRS is concerned with topics such as voluntary compliance, tax form simplification, resource allocation models, discriminant analysis, demographic trends, opinion research, testing, and statistical methods.

On occasion the IRS will publish requests for proposals for specific projects in the *Commerce Business Daily,* but most outside research is secured through indefinite quantity contracts or task orders awarded competitively to organizations that can perform a series of studies over a period of several years.

The IRS also conducts annual conferences focused on particular research issues. Conference participants are generally academic researchers and are invited by the IRS to participate.

INDEPENDENT EXECUTIVE AGENCIES

Central Intelligence Agency

Office of Research and Development
Washington, DC 20505

The Central Intelligence Agency (CIA) conducts research to meet the intelligence needs of the United States. For obvious reasons of national security, the CIA does not issue an announcement of its research priorities, preferring instead to respond to individual requests for information from interested researchers.

Research contracts are available for social and behavioral scientists in many areas of Agency concern. Research projects may range from brief research papers to multiyear studies. Academic researchers interested in the CIA should contact the Academic Affairs Coordinator at 202/351–4449.

Budget figures and examples of funded research are not available.

International Development Cooperation Agency

AGENCY FOR INTERNATIONAL DEVELOPMENT

Floyd O'Quinn, Office of Research and University Relations
Room 309, Rosslyn Plaza Center
Washington, DC 20523
(703/235–8929)

Program: The research activities of the Agency for International Development (AID) are aimed at improving the well-being of the poor majority in developing countries. General fields of interest include:

1) agriculture and fisheries.

2) nutrition and food science.

3) health.

4) population and family planning.

5) education and human resources development.

6) economic development and distribution problems.

7) institutional and social aspects of development.

8) development administration.

9) rural development.

10) urban development.

11) women in development.

12) physical and engineering sciences and technology.

13) environment, natural resources, and energy.

Research projects can be funded from a variety of fields, including anthropology, demography, economics, education, and political science, among others.

Extramural research contracts are primarily initiated through the Bureau for Science and Technology, which has directorates for energy and natural resources, food and agriculture, health, human resources, and population. Other funding opportunities exist in the Bureau for Program and Policy Coordination, and the regional Bureaus for Africa, Asia and the Near East, and Latin America and the Caribbean.

AID also has a small research program for Historically Black Colleges and Universities (HBCUs). Through this program, AID seeks to involve researchers from these institutes in the problems of developing countries. Small research awards allow HBCUs to participate in AID programs without committing large personnel or financial resources to international work. AID will consider unsolicited proposals in any area of agriculture, nutrition, health, population, natural resources, energy, social science and economics, education, and rural development. Proposals should be for discrete research projects, not for general research support or for support of ongoing research partly funded by others. Proposals may be carried out in developing countries in collaboration with host scientists, or projects may be done entirely on HBCU campuses. The total cost of HBCU projects may not exceed $100,000, and project periods should be limited to 1 year.

Budget: Because research projects are funded through several AID Bureaus, figures on the total amount expended on social and behavioral science research are not available.

Application/Review Process: Contracts may be awarded competitively through solicitations in the *Commerce Business Daily* or may be awarded on the basis of unsolicited proposals submitted to one of the bureaus. Unsolicited proposals are welcome, but investigators are encouraged to contact the appropriate bureau staff first to discuss their research ideas. Proposals are reviewed by both AID staff and outside consultants.

Unsolicited proposals to the HBCU research program are reviewed by peer panels selected by National Science Foundation staff.

Funding Mechanisms: Extramural research is funded through both contracts and grants.

National Aeronautics and Space Administration

NASA HISTORY OFFICE

Sylvia Fries, Director
NASA Headquarters
Washington, DC 20546
(202/453–8300)

The History Office of the National Aeronautics and Space Administration (NASA) maintains archives, publishes historical and reference works, assists outside researchers, and advises staff throughout NASA on historical matters. Historical research at NASA is conducted both by NASA staff and through contracts to outside researchers. Contracts are awarded to produce book-length manuscripts which are published by the Government Printing Office. Topics of interest to NASA include aeronautical research and development, the development of space communications, international cooperation in space, and technology transfer. Requests for applications are published in the *Commerce Business Daily.*

POSTDOCTORAL FELLOWSHIPS IN AEROSPACE HISTORY

Office of the Executive Director
American Historical Association
400 A Street, SE
Washington, DC 20003
(202/544–2422)

Program: NASA, in cooperation with the American Historical Association (AHA), has recently instituted a program offering postdoctoral research fellowships in aerospace history. The program is administered by the AHA. Fellows are given the opportunity to spend one year as a part of the NASA History Office to work on a project of significant and sustained advanced research in NASA aerospace science, technology, management, or policy. The program will provide NASA with an improved base of qualified historians to conduct research and writing in support of its continuing program of commissioned NASA history monographs.

Applicants must be U.S. citizens and have a Ph.D. in history or in a closely related field. Fellows will spend a period of not less than 12 months in residence at NASA headquarters and/or various NASA centers. Fellows may not receive aid from another appointment, fellowship, scholarship, or similar grant or hold any other employment during the term of appointment.

Application/Review Process: Applicants must submit a proposal to conduct research in a NASA-related field. Selection will be made by a committee consisting of appointed members from the American Historical Association, the Society for the History of Technology, the History of Science Society, and the Economic History Association, in consultation with a designated officer of NASA. The deadline for applications is February 1.

Funding Mechanisms: The fellowship stipend is $23,000. An allowance of up to $1,000 is available for relocation and travel expenses.

National Archives and Records Administration

National Historical Publications and Records Commission

The National Historical Publications and Records Commission (NHPRC) was established by Congress in 1934 to make plans, estimates, and recommendations for the publication of important historical documents and to work with various public and private institutions in gathering, annotating, and publishing papers and records of national historical significance. In 1964 the Commission was authorized to make allocations to federal agencies and grants to state and local agencies, as well as to nonprofit organizations and institutions, for collecting, editing, and publishing significant historical documents.

The National Historical Records Program and the National Historical Publications Program, which can provide support for academic scholars and institutions of higher education, are described below.

NATIONAL HISTORICAL RECORDS PROGRAM

George L. Vogt, Director
National Archives Building
Washington, DC 20408
(202/523-5386)

Program: The National Historical Records Program encourages a greater effort by private organizations and government to preserve and make available for use those records that further an understanding and appreciation of American history. In addition to supporting projects relating directly to a body of records; the program also supports projects to advance the state of the art; to promote cooperative efforts among institutions and organizations; and to improve the knowledge, performance, and professional skills of those who work with historical records.

From time to time, the NHPRC issues priority statements and solicits proposals that address specific areas of concern. In recent years, the Commission has funded proposals falling within these broad categories: (1) arrangement, description, and preservation of historical records; (2) development of improved records for state and local governments and private organizations; (3) establishment of new archival programs at institutions that will support the programs on a continuing basis; (4) surveys of records not in archival repositories; (5) multi-institutional guides to historical records; (6) education and training of archivists, records custodians, and historical agency administrators; (7) improvement of archival techniques and processes in all areas; (8) feasibility studies leading to major project proposals; and (9) consultant grants.

In general, the program prefers to fund projects that hold promise of broad impact within the archival profession, that serve as a model for others in a similar situation, that contribute to new or improved records programs at the applicant institution, or that answer an urgent and critical need.

Budget: The Records Program has had a steady budget of $2 million for several years. It is often able to supplement that amount by securing additional funds from private sources.

Application/Review Process: The Commission meets three times a year to review applications. In FY 1986 the Records Program modified its review cycle somewhat by designating which categories of applications should be submitted for each Commission meeting. The deadline for proposals for archival projects for colleges, universities, and local governments, and those in response to the current initiative on Native Americans is October 1. Proposals from local governments, museums, and similar organizations are due February 1; proposals for state regrants are due June 1.

Prospective applicants are encouraged to contact NHPRC staff before submitting proposals. Proposals for state projects are reviewed by the appropriate State Historical Records Advisory Board. National and regional projects are reviewed by nonfederal panels that assist NHPRC staff in evaluating proposals. The Archivist of the United States awards grants based on the advice and recommendation of the Commission.

Funding Mechanisms: Grants may be outright or matching funds, or a combination of the two. Grants from this program range from $1,000 to over $200,000, but most awards are modest.

Examples of Funded Projects:
1) $25,100 to a college research center to collect and microfilm materials relating to Swedish-American immigration, history, and culture.

2) $19,700 to a university museum to produce a manual for anthropologists and archaeologists on the creation, care, and storage of field records to ensure archival permanence.

3) $46,835 to a college to establish and administer an archives and records management program for a local Native American tribe.

4) $36,268 to a university to make preservation copies of cellulose nitrate negatives documenting the urban and industrial history of Pittsburgh in the 1920s and 1930s.

5) $114,671 to a university library to conduct on-site surveys of the records of approximately 500 New York City labor organizations.

NATIONAL HISTORICAL PUBLICATIONS PROGRAM

Roger A. Bruns, Director
National Archives Building
Washington, DC 20408
(202/523-3092)

Program: The National Historical Publications Program is intended to ensure the dissemination and more general availability of documentary source material important to the study and understanding of U.S. history. Projects should be based on material of widespread interest among scholars, students, and the public. Documents should have historical value and interest that transcend local and state boundaries.

Grants are awarded in two categories: Book Editions and Microfilm Publications Projects. Book projects reproduce in print the text of the papers of outstanding U.S. citizens and other documents that may be important for an understanding and appreciation of U.S. history. Projects may involve collecting, compiling, editing, and publishing such papers or documents. Microform projects involve the arrangement and microcopying of papers of national significance; the preparation of appropriate printed guides and/or indexes; and the distribution of sale and interlibrary loan copies.

The Publications Program also considers applications from university and other nonprofit presses for subvention of printing and manufacturing costs in book publications that have been formally endorsed by the NHPRC. Grants generally do not exceed $10,000 per volume. Only a limited number of subvention grants are available annually.

Budget: The Publications Program has had a steady budget of $2 million for several years, much of which goes to continued funding of works in progress. In some cases the Program has been able to assist applicants in securing supplementary funds from private sources.

Application/Review Process: The customary deadlines for proposals are November 15, March 15, and July 15. Applicants are encouraged to submit a brief description of the proposed project at least 3 months before the deadline. Applications are distributed to outside reviewers for comment before the Commission meets to review them and make funding decisions. Awards are made by the Archivist of the United States.

Funding Mechanisms: Grants are awarded only to institutional sponsors of projects. There are no restrictions on the amount that can be requested; the average grant is $40,000. Funding may be through outright grants or matching grants. A cost-sharing of at least 50% is encouraged.

*Examples of Funded Projects:**

1) $50,000 to a research center for "The Papers of Dr. Martin Luther King, Jr." (an additional $50,000 was granted by the Ford Foundation).

2) $69,568 to a historical society for "Documentary History of the Supreme Court of the United States, 1789–1800."

3) $28,770 to a university for "The Journals of Diego de Vargas."

4) $27,610 to a university for "The Papers of John Paul Jones."

5) $73,390 to a university for "The Papers of Marcus Garvey and the Universal Negro Improvement Association, 1910–1940."

---

*amounts listed are for one year only

National Foundation on the Arts and Humanities

NATIONAL ENDOWMENT FOR THE ARTS

The National Endowment for the Arts (NEA), an independent federal agency, was created in 1965 to encourage and support American arts and artists. It fulfills this mission through grant support and through leadership and advocacy activities.

Social scientists approaching the NEA should be prepared to frame and discuss research plans within the program interests and priorities of the Endowment. NEA is not a major source of support for the professional activities of social and behavioral scientists. The vast majority of grants and fellowships are awarded to artists and arts organizations to support performance and other creative activities. A standard response of NEA officials to inquiries about social science research interests is to direct the inquirer to the NEA's sister agency, the National Endowment for the Humanities. However, several of the Endowment's programs make awards for work utilizing social science methods and expertise. Social scientists do compete successfully for grants in several NEA programs, and social scientists serve on NEA advisory councils and review panels.

Application/Review Process: The application procedures are standard for most grant-making programs. Each program issues separate application guidelines which are necessary to develop a fully responsive proposal. Most programs encourage letters of inquiry with informal descriptions of a project. NEA staff will provide advice on draft proposals. Peer review panels are formed for each competition. Final award decisions are made by the NEA Chairman based on recommendations of the peer review panels, the National Advisory Council on the Arts, and NEA staff.

Funding Mechanisms: With the exception of fellowships, most grants require matching contributions. Usually the NEA contribution must be matched one-for-one.

DANCE PROGRAM

Nigel Redden, Director
Room 621
1100 Pennsylvania Avenue, NW
Washington, DC 20506
(202/682-5435)

Program: The Dance Program provides support for professional choreographers, dance companies, and organizations that present and serve dance. Anthropologists, ethnomusicologists, semioticists, social historians, and other researchers concerned with documentation and recording of performances may find support for their work in this program.

Budget: This program awarded approximately $9.1 million in grants during FY 1984.

Application/Review Process: See the general discussion of NEA above.

Funding Mechanisms: See the general discussion of NEA above.

Examples of Funded Projects:

1) $5,000 to independent film makers for the filming of sacred Javanese dance *Bedoyo Ketawang* in Indonesia.

2) $8,000 to a nonprofit organization to document and preserve through film the recent reconstruction of Oskar Schlemmer's Bauhaus dances.

3) $5,000 to a nonprofit national council for a film documenting the Royal Khmer Classical Dance Company of Cambodia, now in residence as refugees in the United States.

DESIGN ARTS PROGRAM

Adele Chatfield-Taylor, Director
Room 625
1100 Pennsylvania Avenue, NW
Washington, DC 20506
(202/682-5437)

Program: The Design Arts Program supports projects that promote excellence in architecture, landscape architecture, urban design and planning, interior design, industrial design, graphic design, and fashion design. Of particular interest to social scientists are the Design Exploration/Research Grants which support investigation of design issues or concerns in any of the disciplines supported by the program. Grants up to $40,000 are intended to promote the understanding of aesthetic, utilitarian, economic, and social criteria used to achieve design quality and to evaluate the impact of design decisions on physical environment and human activity.

Budget: This program awarded approximately $4.7 million in grants in FY 1984.

Application/Review Process: See the general discussion of NEA above.

Funding Mechanisms: See the general discussion of NEA above.

Examples of Funded Projects:
1) $40,000 to a university for research into the problems and potential of vacant and derelict land in American cities.

2) $40,000 to a university for research on the potential uses of open space in blighted inner-city neighborhoods.

3) $12,500 to a university for research on international markets for U.S. design services.

4) $17,000 to a nonprofit research foundation to develop a plan and design guidelines for the revitalization of an historically significant Black neighborhood in a major city.

5) $10,000 fellowship to an individual to study examples of architect-selection procedures that have resulted in particularly good architecture and to inform public building clients about these architect-selection procedures and the importance of including public space in buildings.

6) $5,000 fellowship to an individual to study American heavy industrial manufacturing facilities for a book on the changing relationship among American manufacturing processes, American work ideals, and industrial architecture.

FOLK ARTS PROGRAM

Bess Lomax Hawes, Director
Room 725
1100 Pennsylvania Avenue, NW
Washington, DC 20506
(202/682-5449)

Program: The Folk Arts Program supports the traditional arts that have grown through time within the many groups living in the United States—groups that share the same ethnic heritage, language, occupation, religion, or geographic area. These folk arts include music, dance, poetry, tales, oratory, crafts, and various types of visual art forms. This program may be of interest to folklorists, cultural historians, ethnomusicologists, anthropologists, linguists, and other social scientists with research interests that include performance and ritual.

Budget: This program awarded approximately $3.3 million in grants in FY 1984.

Application/Review Process: See the general discussion of NEA above.

Funding Mechanisms: See the general discussion of NEA above.

Examples of Funded Projects:
1) $6,100 to a Native American group for a survey of tribal elders, documenting and translating traditional legends and cautionary tales, and making them available in small, low-cost bilingual publications.

2) $27,300 to a university to prepare a catalog of the Native American sound recordings in a museum and to disseminate duplicate recordings and other cultural materials to tribes and other Native American organizations in the state.

3) $15,000 to a nonprofit institute for a festival on dance, music, and cultural history of African and Afro-American performing arts.

4) $16,400 to a state arts council to survey and identify traditional artists and craftspeople of a region of the state and to coordinate the development of a slide/tape presentation, a teacher's guide, and a series of school programs based on the research.

RESEARCH DIVISION

Harold Horowitz, Director
Tom Bradshaw, Coordinator
Room 706
1100 Pennsylvania Avenue, NW
Washington, DC 20506
(202/682–5432)

Program: Within NEA's Office of Policy, Planning, Research and Budget is a small Research Division that conducts and contracts out studies that assist the Endowment, artists, arts organizations, and the public by developing, analyzing, and disseminating new information on the needs and conditions of the arts field. The division has been less active in funding research and survey projects in recent years due to sharply reduced budgets. The 1985 legislation reauthorizing the Endowment calls on NEA to plan and implement a data collection system which, beginning in 1988, will form a basis for biennial "state of the arts" reports. It is anticipated that the Research Division will play an important role in developing such a system, and will consequently become a more active contractor for extramural research.

Requests for proposals are announced in the *Commerce Business Daily*. No mailing list is maintained. Division staff will provide information on future plans by telephone.

Budget: In FY 1984 the division awarded over $500,000 for outside projects. In FY 1986 the division has approximately $100,000 available to support research.

Application/Review Process: See the general discussion of NEA above.

Funding Mechanisms: See the general discussion of NEA above.

Examples of Funded Projects:
1) $280,000 to a university survey research center to begin a 1985 survey of public participation in the arts (a follow-up of a 1982 survey).
2) $83,500 in 2 contracts to a nonprofit organization to conduct evaluation studies of 3 NEA grant-making programs.

NATIONAL ENDOWMENT FOR THE HUMANITIES

The National Endowment for the Humanities (NEH) supports scholarship, research, education, and public programs in the humanities. The 1965 act of Congress establishing the Endowment defines the humanities as the study of the following:

> language, both modern and classical; linguistics; literature; history; jurisprudence; philosophy; archaeology; comparative religion; ethics; the history, criticism, and theory of the arts; those aspects of the social sciences which have humanistic content and employ humanistic methods; and the study and application of the humanities to the human environment with particular attention to the relevance of the humanities to the current conditions of national life.

Within the terms of the NEH mandate, social science studies that have been awarded NEH support tend to be historical or philosophical in approach or attempt to cast light on questions of interpretation or criticism traditionally identified with the humanities. NEH also supports studies that use the disciplines of the humanities to interpret, analyze, or assess science and technology. Thus, within these constraints, social scientists are eligible for nearly all of the programs of the Endowment.

In order to compete effectively for NEH support, social scientists (unlike scholars from disciplines focused entirely within the humanities) generally have to clearly establish the humanistic nature of the proposed work as well as the soundness and import of the project. NEH officials suggest the following steps for social scientists considering applying for Endowment support:

1) frame description and arguments in language as free of disciplinary jargon as possible;

2) discuss the project idea with NEH program staff to determine whether the project will be deemed eligible under NEH guidelines;

3) construct proposals in a manner that will be illuminating to humanist reviewers who may not be familiar with the discipline of the applicant.

Application/Review Process: All NEH grant funds are awarded competitively. Each division or office of the Endowment has developed written guidelines and application instructions. While there are a number of aspects of these instructions which are more or less universally applied, there are also specifications tailored to each competition. In almost all cases, an effective application requires adherence to the guidelines—especially because answers to a series of questions about the relationship of the proposed project to NEH priorities must be included with the proposal. Particular requirements are mentioned in the program descriptions that follow, but the application procedure throughout NEH has certain characteristics in common:

1) NEH staff in all programs are assigned to be both helpful and candid with potential applicants throughout the development process. In addition to inviting interviews and telephone discussions of project ideas, applicants are encouraged to submit complete draft proposals (i.e., fully developed narratives and budgets). NEH staff will provide detailed comment and suggestions in response. Drafts should be submitted six weeks prior to the application deadline.

2) For most NEH competitions, applicants are either invited or required to suggest scholars familiar with their work who may be consulted in the external review process. Likewise, as appropriate, applicants should identify scholars who are known to be unfavorably disposed to their work.

3) Peer review panels are appointed for most competitions. In 1985 over 150 separate panels were used. New panels are formed for each competition; there are no standing panels. Panelists are selected to bring together an appropriate mix of scholars and professionals in the humanities. Following individual review of proposals, panelists meet in sessions chaired by NEH staff. In addition to panelist and staff review, NEH often consults additional independent outside reviewers.

4) The advice of panels and outside reviewers is assembled with NEH staff comments (on specific fact or policy issues not fully covered in the review) and presented to the National Council on the Humanities. The Humanities Council

meets four times a year and serves as an advisory body to the Chairman of NEH. Taking into account staff advice and panel reviews, final decisions are made by the Chairman.

5) For both successful and unsuccessful proposals, applicants receive both the reviewers' written comments (with reviewers' identities masked) and, as appropriate, summaries of comments by NEH staff and the Council. If resubmission is invited, NEH staff work with applicants to clarify problem areas identified by reviewers or others in the review process. NEH staff point out that a number of projects are funded after resubmission.

Funding Mechanisms: NEH funds can be awarded in three different ways: (1) through an outright grant, (2) through matching funds (i.e., NEH funds contingent upon raising a specified amount of qualified support), and (3) through a combination of outright and matching funds. In practice, most NEH awards require some level of cost-sharing from the applicant and/or other nonfederal sources.

SPECIAL INITIATIVES

In addition to the array of programs operated through the NEH's divisions and offices described below, the Endowment promotes Special Initiatives aimed at encouraging proposals on designated topics. Special Initiatives result from a wide consultative process including consideration by the National Council on the Humanities. In general, Special Initiatives solicit proposals for each NEH division where regular application procedures are followed. An exception to this is the current initiative on the Bicentennial of the U.S. Constitution which has a separately staffed office. (See separate entry for this office.) In addition to the Constitution Bicentennial, other current Special Initiatives are:

1) *The Columbian Quincentenary.* In anticipation of the 500th anniversary of the European discovery of the Western Hemisphere, NEH is inviting a wide range of projects to interpret "the transformations that created new societies and new forms of cultural expression through the encounters of native American, European, and African peoples."

2) *Understanding America* and *Understanding Other Nations.* These two parallel initiatives were launched in November 1985 in response to "increasing evidence that despite the resurgence of interest in basic education, young Americans know shamefully little about their own heritage and about the cultures of foreign nations." While a wide variety of projects will be invited under these two initiatives, NEH staff indicate that the strongest interest is in activities aimed at strengthening the study of American history and the teaching of foreign languages.

DIVISION OF FELLOWSHIPS AND SEMINARS

Guinevere L. Griest, Acting Director and Deputy Director
Room 316
1100 Pennsylvania Avenue, NW
Washington, DC 20506
(202/786–0458)

The Division of Fellowships and Seminars provides support for scholars, teachers, and others to undertake full-time independent study and research. Awards may support studies contributing to expanded scholarly knowledge, to the conception and substance of individual courses, or to the general public's understanding of the humanities. Projects may address broad topics or pertain to a specialized field.

The Endowment supports research principally through this division and through the Division of Research Programs. In general, applications for individual study and research are supported through the Fellowships Division and collaborative research through the Research Division. However there are major exceptions of special interest to social scientists (e.g., projects involving the production of reference works and scholarly tools as well as most archaeological projects should be submitted to the Division of Research Programs).

In addition to its regular programs, this division also participates in NEH special initiatives. Current special initiatives include Fellowships in the Foundations of American Society, Constitutional Fellowships, and Graduate Study Fellowships for Faculty at Historically Black Colleges and Universities. Awards under these categories are funded through regular program allocations.

Most competitions in the division follow regular NEH staff and peer review procedures. A significant difference, however, is that the staff are prepared to comment on the eligibility of a fellowship application but will not provide critiques or advice on draft proposals. Review panels are rarely organized around individual social science disciplines; applications are assigned to the panel deemed most appropriate (e.g., a proposal from a geographer might be assigned to a history panel).

NEH FELLOWSHIPS

Maben Herring, Assistant Director for Fellowship Programs
Room 316
1100 Pennsylvania Avenue, NW
Washington, DC 20506
(202/786–0466)

Program: NEH fellowships are awarded for independent study and research in the humanities. They free fellows from the day-to-day responsibilities of teaching and other work for extended periods of uninterrupted investigation, reflection, and, often, writing.

There are three standing categories of awards and one special initiative:

1)   Fellowships for College Teachers and Independent Scholars support both beginning and experienced college teachers and independent interpreters of the humanities in study and research directed toward scholarly publication or for work directed toward teaching. These fellowships are intended for teachers at 2-year, 4-year, and 5-year colleges and universities that do not have Ph.D. programs. Scholars and writers working independently or outside academic institutions are also eligible. For information, contact Karen Fuglie at 202/786–0466.

2)   Fellowships for University Teachers support teachers and scholars based at graduate universities and postgraduate professional schools to pursue independent study and research that will enable them to make significant contributions to thought and knowledge in the humanities. Offered to both scholars who have made significant contributions in the humanities as well as to younger scholars at the beginning of their careers, these fellowships are intended for individuals affiliated with academic institutions with extensive Ph.D. programs in the humanities. For information, contact Maben Herring at 202/786–0466.

For several years prior to December 1985 applications from independent scholars were administered through the university teachers program. Recently the programs were restructured with the intent of creating competitions in which scholars working outside academic institutions could compete more effectively.

3)   Summer Stipends provide support for faculty members in universities, 2-year and 4-year colleges, and independent scholars working in the humanities to undertake 2 consecutive months of full-time independent study and research. An eligible project may be one that can be completed during the stipend period or it may be part of a long-range endeavor. College and university teachers must be nominated by their institutions; others apply directly to the program. For information, contact Joseph Neville at 202/786–0466.

4)   Currently, as a special initiative, the Division is awarding Constitutional Fellowships to support study and research on the philosophical, literary, historical, or political origins of the Constitution; the relation of the structure of the Constitution to American political, social, or intellectual culture; or the connection between self-government and the purposes of human life. Awards for Constitutional Fellowships are made from the regular allocation for the fellowships programs but the review of applications is managed by the Office of the Bicentennial of the U.S. Constitution. For information, contact Joseph Phelan at 202/786–0332.

Budget: This program awarded approximately $6.7 million in fellowships in FY 1985 (109 Fellowships for College Teachers totaling $2.65 million; 136 Fellowships for Independent Study and Research totaling $3.36 million; and 219 Summer Stipends totaling $657,000).

Application/Review Process: See the general discussion of NEH above. The deadline for the two fellowships programs is June 1 for projects beginning after January 1. Applicants receive notification in approximately 6 months. Summer Stipend applications are due October 1 for projects beginning after June 1.

Funding Mechanisms: See the general discussion of NEH above. All grants are outright; no matching funds are used. Beginning in 1986 the range for fellowships in both categories is $18,000 to $27,500; the flat rate for Summer Stipends is $3,000.

Examples of Funded Projects:
Fellowships of $18,000 to $25,000 were awarded to:

1)   a research university scholar for "Language and Politics in a West African Chiefdom."

2)   a college teacher/researcher for "The Transformation of Work and Changes in the Sexual Division of Labor in the U.S. Printing Industry, 1800–1920."

3)   an independent scholar for "Portuguese-Asian Trade under the Habsburgs, 1580–1640."

4)   a research university scholar for "School, Culture and Society: Educating Minorities in Twentieth-Century America."

Summer Stipends of $3,000 were awarded to:

1)   a university scholar for "An Archaeological Investigation into the Expansion of the Aztec Empire."

2)   a university scholar for "A History of Coronary Heart Disease in Twentieth Century America."

3)   a university scholar for "Bilingualism and Correspondences in Spanish and Basque."

SUMMER SEMINARS PROGRAM

Kenneth Kolson, Assistant Director for Seminar Programs
Room 316
1100 Pennsylvania Avenue, NW
Washington, DC 20506
(202/786–0463)

Program: The Summer Seminars program provides opportunities for teachers to work with distinguished scholars on topics in the humanities. Awards are made in two categories: Seminars for College Teachers and Seminars for Secondary School Teachers.

Summer Seminars for College Teachers provide grants to institutions to conduct seminars for teachers in 2-year, 4-year, and 5-year colleges and universities and other qualified individuals. Senior scholars design and propose 8-week seminars related to their expertise and interests. Seminar participants work with the director and other distinguished scholars and teachers, pursuing advanced study and research in their own or related fields. The seminar theme, however, should be broad enough to accommodate a wide range of interests and should be central to the major ideas, texts, critical concerns, and approaches to the humanities. Applications to direct Summer Seminars are administered through this office. After the decisions have been made about seminars to be offered, NEH publicizes the complete list widely. Teachers interested in participating in a seminar apply directly to the seminar director at the host institution. Participation in each seminar is limited to 12 college teachers, each of whom receives a stipend of $3,500. For information, contact Kenneth Kolson at 202/786–0463.

Summer Seminars for Secondary School Teachers provide opportunities for teachers of grades 7–12 to work with distinguished teachers and scholars, studying seminal works in the humanities systematically and thoroughly. Teachers/scholars from colleges and universities design and propose seminars lasting 4, 5, or 6 weeks. Prospective seminar directors have wide latitude in designing seminars within the two essential elements of the program: focus on a limited number of major primary works in the humanities and a course of intensive study of the chosen works. Seminars may also be held overseas. After seminars are competitively chosen, the complete list of seminars is publicized widely by NEH. Secondary school teachers interested in participating apply directly to a seminar director. Participation in each seminar is limited to 15 teachers, each of whom receives a stipend of $2,000, $2,375, or $2,750, depending on the length of the seminar. For information, contact Steven S. Tigner at 202/786–0463.

Budget: The Summer Seminars program awarded approximately $6.5 million in FY 1985, of which approximately $440,000 was in matching funds.

Application/Review Process: See the general discussion of NEH above. The deadlines are as follows: Summer Seminars for College Teachers, March 1, 1986 for directors of 1987 seminars; Summer Seminars for Secondary Teachers, April 1, 1986 for directors of 1987 seminars. The deadline for prospective participants is March 1; applications are sent directly to seminar directors.

Funding Mechanisms: See the general discussion of NEH above.

Examples of Funded Projects:
1) $65,000 to a university to support a summer seminar for college teachers, "Language Maintenance and Language Shift among American Ethnolinguistic Minorities."
2) $55,000 to a university to support a summer seminar for college teachers, "Economic Growth, the State, and Ideology in Latin America, 1880–1980."
3) $57,500 to a university to support a summer seminar for college teachers, "Courts in American Society."
4) $52,500 to a college to support a seminar for secondary school teachers, "Churchill's History, the Second World War."
5) $62,000 to a university to support a summer seminar for secondary school teachers, "Classic Studies in American Ethnic and Racial History."
6) $62,000 to a university to support a summer seminar for secondary school teachers, "Technology and the Human Experience."
7) $21,600 to a university to support a seminar for secondary school teachers, "Wise, Locke, Adams: The American Constitution."

GRADUATE STUDY FELLOWSHIPS FOR FACULTY AT HISTORICALLY BLACK COLLEGES AND UNIVERSITIES

Maben Herring, Acting Program Officer
Room 316
1100 Pennsylvania Avenue, NW
Washington, DC 20506
(202/786–0466)

Program: Fellowships from this program are awarded to enable faculty members to devote one year of full-time study leading to a doctoral degree in the humanities, with preference given to those individuals who are at the dissertation stage of their work. This is the only NEH program that supports work leading to a graduate degree. The program is restricted to teachers in Historically Black Colleges and Universities.

Budget: This program is a special initiative, and awards are made from the regular fellowships allocation. In FY 1985, 10 grants totaling approximately $250,000 were awarded.

Application/Review Process: See the general discussion of NEH above. The deadline for applications is March 15 for awards beginning in September of the following year.

Funding Mechanisms: See the general discussion of NEH above. Grants are limited to $27,500 and are made through the applicant's institution.

TRAVEL TO COLLECTIONS PROGRAM

Gary Messinger, Program Officer
Room 316
1100 Pennsylvania Avenue, NW
Washington, DC 20506
(202/786-0463)

Program: Grants of $500 enable individual scholars to travel to the research collections of libraries, archives, museums, or other repositories.

Budget: In FY 1985, 411 grants were awarded for a total of $205,500.

Application/Review Process: See the general discussion of NEH above. The deadlines are January 15 for travel after June 1, and July 15 for travel after December 15.

Funding Mechanisms: See the general discussion of NEH above.

YOUNGER SCHOLARS PROGRAM

Leon Bramson, Program Officer
Room 316
1100 Pennsylvania Avenue, NW
Washington, DC 20506
(202/786-0463)

Program: The Younger Scholars program awards grants to promising college students and advanced high school students to conduct research and writing projects in the humanities. Younger Scholars work full-time for 9 weeks during the summer, researching and writing a paper under the close supervision of a humanities scholar. No academic credit may be given for these projects.

In 1986 and 1987, applications for research and writing projects on the Bicentennial of the U.S. Constitution are also invited.

Budget: In FY 1985 approximately $250,000 was awarded by this program.

Application/Review Process: See the general discussion of NEH above. November 1 is the deadline for submission of all Younger Scholar applications, including Bicentennial awards.

Funding Mechanisms: See the general discussion of NEH above. Awards are $2,200 for college students and $1,800 for high school students. Each award includes $400 for the project adviser.

Examples of Funded Projects:

1) $2,200 to a college student for a historical and archaeological survey of eighteenth and nineteenth century mills in an area of New York State.

2) $1,800 to a high school student for a project on the atomic bomb and Soviet-American relations, 1944–45.

3) $2,200 to a university student for a project on Islamic and other cultural traditions in West Sumatra.

DIVISION OF RESEARCH PROGRAMS

Richard Ekman, Director
Blanche Premo, Deputy Director
Room 318
1100 Pennsylvania Avenue, NW
Washington, DC 20506
(202/786–0200)

The Division of Research Programs seeks to strengthen the intellectual foundations of the humanities through the support of projects that will enable scholars to conduct research; that is, grants to support the research environment, such as bibliographies and other tools, as well as basic research projects. The work of the division is carried out through four major granting programs with several categories within each. In the descriptions that follow, readers should keep in mind that the division underwent a major reorganization in 1985, and as a consequence many familiar programs have been renamed and/or repositioned within the division.

TEXTS PROGRAM

Margot Backas, Acting Assistant Director
Room 318
1100 Pennsylvania Avenue, NW
Washington, DC 20506
(202/786–0207)

Program: The Texts Program supports the preparation for publication of manuscripts that promise to make major contributions to the study of the humanities.

The three granting categories are:

1) Editions grants support the preparation of authoritative and annotated editions of sources of significant value to humanities scholars and general readers. For information, call Margot Backas at 202/786–0207.

2) Translations grants support the translation into English of works that will provide insight into history, literature, philosophy, and artistic achievements of other cultures and that will make available the thought and learning of their civilizations; all translations must provide critical introductions and explanatory annotations that clearly establish the historical and intellectual contexts of the work involved. For information, call Susan Mango at 202/786–0207.

3) Publication Subvention grants are intended to assist the publication and dissemination of distinguished scholarly works in all fields of the humanities. Applicants must be established publishers or scholarly publishing entities. In all cases the scholarly work proposed for subsidy must have been formally accepted for publication. For information, call Margot Backas at 202/786–0207.

Budget: Grants and matching funds awarded by this program in FY 1985 totaled approximately $5.4 million.

Application/Review Process: See the general discussion of NEH above. The deadline for Editions and Translations is June 1, with notification in March. For Publication Subvention applications, deadlines are April 1 and September 1, with notification in September and March respectively.

Funding Mechanisms: See the general discussion of NEH above. Awards average $6,000 per volume—no award for a single volume can exceed $10,000. In a federal fiscal year, no publisher may receive more than $50,000 in outright and federal matching funds or support for more than five works, whichever is less.

Examples of Funded Projects:
1) $152,000 in matching funds to a university to provide continuing support for the microfilm and book edition of the papers of Thomas A. Edison.

2) $174,000 to a university to provide continuing support for the edition of the papers of Marcus Garvey and the Universal Negro Improvement Association.

3) $20,000 to an individual to support preparation of the original language text and translation of a book-length traditional oral history from Bambara Segou (Mali, West Africa), which spans the reigns of nine rulers, 1712–1827, and covers the most active years of the Atlantic slave trade.

4) $14,000 to a library to support translation and annotation of more than 160 German-language documents on the history and culture of Chicago's German workers from 1850 to 1920.

5) $7,800 to a university press to support publication of a volume in the chronological edition of the *Writings of Charles Sanders Peirce* covering the years 1872–1878.

6) $10,000 to a scholarly publishing enterprise to support publication of a book that traces the historical development of connected farm buildings, an architectural form common in rural New England, and relates them to the culture of the area.

REFERENCE MATERIALS PROGRAM

John Williams, Assistant Director
Room 318
1100 Pennsylvania Avenue, NW
Washington, DC 20506
(202/786–0358)

Program: The purpose of the Reference Materials program is to provide support for projects that promise to facilitate research in the humanities by organizing essential resources for scholarship and by preparing aids and reference materials that can improve scholarly access to information and collections.
There are two grant-making categories:

1) Tools grants support the creation of dictionaries, historical or linguistic atlases, encyclopedias, concordances, *catalogues raissonnes,* linguistic grammars, descriptive catalogues, databases, and other materials that serve to codify information essential to research in the humanities. Grants in this category generally require 20% to 25% cost-sharing. For information, call Helen Aguera at 202/ 786–0358.

2) Access grants support projects that promise to increase the availability of important research collections and other significant source material in all fields

of the humanities. Support is provided for such activities as archival arrangement and description projects; bibliographies; records surveys; cataloging projects involving print, graphic, film, sound, and artifact collections; indices; foreign microfilming; and other guides to humanities documentation. Under certain circumstances oral history projects may be supported. In addition, support may be provided for the development of national standards for access to different types of scholarly resources and projects that promise to improve ways in which libraries, archives, and other repositories make research documentation available. For information, call Marcella Grendler at 202/786-0358.

Budget: Grants and matching funds awarded by this program in FY 1985 totaled approximately $10.8 million.

Application/Review Process: See the general discussion of NEH above. The deadline for both categories is November 1, with notification in June.

Funding Mechanisms: See the general discussion of NEH above.

Examples of Funded Projects:
1) $70,000 to a university to support development of an English dictionary of the Tamil verb.

2) $150,000 to a university to support production of three bilingual volumes, which include the humanities portion of the multivolume U.S.-Mexico Borderlands Atlas, a historical atlas, a cultural atlas, and a statistical abstract.

3) $8,000 to a university to support the production of concordances to Darwin's *The Expression of the Emotions in Man and Animals; The Descent of Man and Selection in Relation to Sex;* and *The Origin of the Species,* 6th edition.

4) $90,000 to a research center to provide continuing support for the creation of a computerized database of historical statistics of Puerto Rico since 1900, containing time series of economic, social, and political statistics, available both in published form and computer tapes.

INTERPRETIVE RESEARCH PROGRAM

Dorothy Wartenberg, Assistant Director
Room 318
1100 Pennsylvania Avenue, NW
Washington, DC 20506
(202/786-0210)

Program: This program supports original research that will advance knowledge or deepen critical understanding in all fields of the humanities.

The two granting categories are:

1) Projects grants support major collaborative and coordinated projects in both individual disciplines and interdisciplinary areas. Awards include biographies; historical and analytical studies in literature and the arts; research in history, philosophy, and other humanities disciplines; focused interdisciplinary studies; humanistic research in political science, sociology, and cultural anthropology; and archaeological projects that promise to strengthen scholarly knowledge and understanding of history and culture, i.e., survey, excavation, materials analysis, laboratory research, artifact preservation, and preparation of monographs. Support for archaeology may also include grants for pre-expedition survey work. Grants average $50,000 in this category and generally require 20%-25% cost-sharing. For information, call David Wise at 202/786-0210.

2) Humanities, Science and Technology grants support research that employs the theories and methods of humanities to study science and technology, as well as research that broadens and deepens understanding of the fundamental concerns that underlie current issues about the conduct and applications of science and technology. Projects that promote collaboration of scientists and engineers with humanities scholars and projects that promise to improve interdisciplinary research methods are encouraged. Awards may be offered for projects in areas of inquiry that include the form, content, and purposes of scientific knowledge; the processes through which scientific knowledge is developed; the invention, innovation, and transfer of technology; the social, moral, and legal meaning of specific scientific and technological innovations; the interaction among sciences, technology, and other elements of culture; and the methods and concepts that the humanities use to study science and technology. For information, call Daniel Jones at 202/786-0210.

Budget: Grants and matching funds awarded by this program in FY 1985 totaled approximately $4.6 million.

Application/Review Process: See the general discussion of NEH above. The deadline for both categories is October 1, with notification in June.

Funding Mechanisms: See the general discussion of NEH above.

Examples of Funded Projects:
1) $6,500 to a college to support the excavation of a site in Turkey with unusual early Bronze and early Neolithic aceramic (pre-pottery) levels.

2) $75,000 to a university sociologist to support study of the industrial development of an agricultural community based on financial records, 1820-1915.

3) $85,000 to a university to support the study of the ethnography and folklore of a Hungarian-American community.

4) $88,000 to a university to support research by a cultural anthropologist on the adaptation of a southern African chiefdom to modern capitalism.

5) $65,000 to support collaborative research on the history of the synthetic rubber industry in the United States, 1942–1956.

6) $125,000 to a university to provide continuing support for collaborative research by resident and visiting scholars on the legal history of the American family.

REGRANTS PROGRAM

Eugene Sterud, Senior Program Officer
Room 318
1100 Pennsylvania Avenue, NW
Washington, DC 20506
(202/786–0204)

Program: This program awards funds to organizations that will then regrant those funds according to a plan that reflects a coherent and effective strategy for improving the state of research in particular areas of the humanities. Awards are made to learned societies, federations and committees of scholarly associations, major research libraries and centers, and colleges and universities. Through regrants to individuals, these institutions provide both short- and long-term support for American scholars to conduct individual and collaborative research projects, research planning and development activities, and major conferences both in the U.S. and abroad.
    There are four categories of awards:

1) Conference awards support conferences that enable both American and foreign scholars to advance the current state of research on topics in the humanities; supports costs of organizing and publicizing; travel and other expenses for presenters; stipends to participants for partial travel and per diem expenses; and publication of conference results. For information, call Crale Hopkins at 202/786–0204.

2) Centers for Advanced Study support coordinated research in well-defined subject areas at independent centers for advanced study, overseas research centers, independent research libraries, and research museums. For information, call David Coder at 202/786–0204.

3) Regrants for International Research awards funds to national organizations and learned societies to enable American scholars to pursue research abroad,

to attend or participate in international conferences, to engage in collaborative work with foreign colleagues, and to sponsor international scholarly exchange and collaborative international research endeavors. For information, call Eugene Sterud at 202/786–0204.

4) Regrants for Selected Areas support three kinds of regrants offered by the American Council of Learned Societies: ACLS fellowships (grants for research over 6–12 months), Grants-in-Aid (up to $3,000 to advance in-progress research projects), and Research Fellowships for Recent Recipients of the Ph.D. For information, contact ACLS, 228 East 45th Street, New York, NY 10017; 212/697–1505.

Budget: Grants and matching funds awarded by this program in FY 1985 totaled approximately $3.4 million.

Application/Review Process: See the general discussion of NEH above. Deadlines for applications by organizations seeking funds for regranting programs are available from NEH. In turn, each of the independent organizations regranting NEH funds has its own deadlines for individuals.

Funding Mechanisms: See the general discussion of NEH above.

Examples of Funded Projects:
1) $300,000 outright and $500,000 in matching funds to the American Council of Learned Societies to provide continuing support for the U.S. component of a scholarly exchange program in the humanities with the USSR and Eastern Europe.

2) $200,000 to the National Academy of Sciences to support scholarly exchanges with the People's Republic of China.

DIVISION OF GENERAL PROGRAMS

Donald Gibson, Director
Room 426
1100 Pennsylvania Avenue, NW
Washington, DC 20506
(202/786–0267)

The Division of General Programs supports projects that are aimed at increasing the public understanding and appreciation of the humanities through the interpretation of cultural works; the illumination of historical ideas, figures, and events; and the illustration of methods and learning in the disciplines of the humanities. In addition to housing most of the NEH's programs for the general public, this division tends to be an organizational home for activities which cross divisional lines and consequently do not fit in another division or office.

Social scientists interested in increasing public understanding of both the scholarly work and applications of their disciplines may find support in this division.

HUMANITIES PROJECTS IN MEDIA

James J. Dougherty, Assistant Director
Room 420
1100 Pennsylvania Avenue, NW
Washington, DC 20506
(202/786–0278)

Program: This program supports the planning, writing, or production of television and radio programs in the humanities intended for general audiences. The collaboration of scholars in the humanities with experienced producers, writers, and directors is required. Special initiatives are Children's Programming and the Bicentennial of the Constitution.

There are four categories of awards:

1) Planning Grants encourage collaboration between scholars and production personnel and the development of an approach and format to adapt material in the humanities for television and radio. Products of a grant should include program outlines—concept, themes, and final format. These grants do not exceed $20,000.

2) Scripting Grants support the writing of one or more scripts or detailed program treatments. These grants often follow successful utilization of a planning grant.

3) Production Grants support the production costs of a single program, a pilot program, or a series. Likewise these grants are frequently awarded for projects earlier supported by planning and scripting grants and are based on successful collaborations forged under the earlier phases of the project.

4) Talk Shows grants support projects that can take a variety of formats—a one-on-one interview, a thematic approach with several guests, or a nonstudio documentary.

The program will consider supporting promotional costs for completed projects. Grants may also be awarded after successful production for print materials (e.g., teachers' guides).

Budget: Grants and matching funds awarded by this program in FY 1985 totaled approximately $9.4 million.

Application/Review Process: See the general discussion of NEH above. The deadline in recent years has been mid-March for projects beginning in October, with notification of awards in September. NEH staff encourage submission of a 2-to-3-page letter outlining the project at least 6 weeks prior to deadline to determine eligibility. Review panels are composed of scholars and media professionals.

Funding Mechanisms: See the general discussion of NEH above.

Examples of Funded Projects:
1) $22,000 to a university to support planning of a TV film dealing with the emigration of European scholars and intellectuals to the United States prior to and during World War II, and the impact these emigres have had on American culture and in particular on the humanities disciplines and professions.

2) $39,000 to a university to support the writing of a script for a one-hour television pilot program on language, based on new research in linguistics, speech, and writing theory.

3) $177,000 to a consortium of colleges to support production of a 60-minute film exploring American fundamentalism and life from cultural and sociological perspectives through a portrait of an independent Baptist Church and its community in New England.

HUMANITIES PROJECTS IN MUSEUMS AND HISTORICAL ORGANIZATIONS

Sally Yerkovich, Assistant to the Division Director
Room 420
1100 Pennsylvania Avenue, NW
Washington, DC 20506
(202/786–0284)

Program: Grants from this program are aimed at strengthening exhibits at museums and historical organizations—to make possible exhibitions that give visitors an understanding and appreciation "of an object itself and also of its relationship to ideas, events, and aesthetic values." The NEH seeks to facilitate the groundwork of research and collections management that are the foundation for any intellectually substantial public exhibition. The program also supports the planning and implementation of exhibitions.

There are six categories of support in this program:

1)   Planning Grants support research and design elements for specific interpretive exhibitions and projects, both temporary and permanent.

2) Implementation Grants allow institutions to implement completely planned, full-scale projects of large and small scope. These grants can focus on temporary exhibitions, permanent installations, historic site interpretations, publications about permanent collections, or related educational programs.

3) Collections-Sharing Grants are awards to institutions with seldom exhibited or stored objects to lend these objects for use in interpretive humanities exhibitions and related programs at other institutions.

4) Self-Study Grants allow organizations to evaluate their resources for public programming in the humanities. There is a $15,000 award limit in this category.

5) Enhancement of Interpretive Skills Grants allow institutions and service organizations to sponsor workshops, seminars, and other training opportunities to enhance the interpretive skills of museum and historical organization personnel. Also supported are workshops and training programs to increase knowledge of collections management techniques.

6) Collection Study and Management awards were introduced experimentally in 1984 to help organizations study and manage collections. Within this category, NEH offers the following types of grants for documentation and conservation:

Documentation Grants to institutions to catalogue a defined body of objects that potentially lends itself to projects in the humanities;

Planning for Computerized Documentation Grants for one or two experienced professionals with broad knowledge of computerized collections management techniques and of museums to advise an institution on its needs;

Conservation Survey and Analysis Grants for institution conservators to develop condition and treatment reports for the objects in a defined body and to determine priorities for treatment;

Conservation Treatment for Objects in a Permanent Collection Grants to conservators to provide conservation treatment for an object or objects in a permanent collection.

Budget: Outright grants and matching funds awarded in FY 1985 totaled more than $9.5 million.

Application/Review Process: See the general discussion of NEH above. Deadlines are the end of April for projects beginning in January, and the end of October for projects beginning in July. The program encourages all applicants to submit a full draft proposal (including budget) 6 to 8 weeks prior to the deadline.

Funding Mechanisms: See the general discussion of NEH above.

Examples of Funded Projects:
1) $49,500 to an archaeological institute to support preparation and publication of a catalog on Native American woodsplint basketry in the northeastern

United States that explains how the processes of basket production were defined by ideas about society and kinship.

2) $132,000 to a museum to support a catalog on a northwest coast American Indian collection and its development at the museum.

3) $10,000 to a museum to support a self-study by six consultants in the humanities to evaluate the museum's anthropology collections as the basis for future exhibitions and programs.

4) $11,000 to a historic foundation to catalog part of a large collection of prints, drawings, and photos documenting the development of the U.S. iron and steel industries.

HUMANITIES PROJECTS IN LIBRARIES

Thomas Phelps, Assistant Director
Room 420
1100 Pennsylvania Avenue, NW
Washington, DC 20506
(202/786–0271)

Program: Humanities Projects in Libraries are designed to increase public understanding of the humanities through the discovery, interpretation, and greater appreciation of books and other resources in library collections

Projects should involve active collaboration among scholars and library staff both in planning and implementation. Projects may engage the public in an almost limitless range of humanities topics (e.g., explore language as a reflection of culture; history of systems of thought), and may use a variety of methods (conferences; lecture series; written materials such as thematic anthologies, essays on specific topics, annotated bibliographies, or reading lists).

There are two categories of support:

1)   Planning Grants support collaborative efforts of scholars and institutional administrative staff to design projects. Activities can include workshops, seminars, and the use of consultants to assist in planning public programs. Usually planning grants last no more than 6 months, with awards ranging between $5,000 and $15,000.

2)   Implementation Grants support presentation of fully developed public programs. Awards are usually for 1 to 3 years and range between $15,000 and $200,000.

Budget: Outright grants and matching funds awarded by this program in FY 1985 totaled approximately $2.8 million.

Application/Review Process: See the general discussion of NEH above. Deadlines for this program's annual competitions are early March for projects beginning in October, and early September for projects beginning in April.

Funding Mechanisms: See the general discussion of NEH above.

Examples of Funded Projects:

1) $143,000 to a department of libraries and archives (a state agency) to support a project to inform the public about historical materials held in the state archives through public programs, workshops for teachers and librarians, a traveling photographic exhibit, and a series of radio programs.

2) $266,000 to a major public library to support a 3-year series of programs on printing and censorship; an exhibit from the library's collections will be accompanied by materials developed from research and from lecture and public discussion programs.

3) $129,000 to an ethnic/cultural organization to support programs focused on themes reflecting the history, literature, arts, and culture of Poland and the Polish-American heritage; the programs are designed to promote an awareness and the use of humanities resources in the nation's libraries, and to provide opportunities to learn about Polish culture.

PUBLIC HUMANITIES PROJECTS

Malcolm Richardson, Assistant Director
Room 420
1100 Pennsylvania Avenue, NW
Washington, DC 20506
(202/786-0271)

Program: This program supports projects that enhance the appreciation and understanding of the humanities for out-of-school adult audiences, and those that cross divisional boundaries or that do not fit within other funding categories at NEH. The program does not treat these cross-divisional proposals as a category but does refer to them as "Exceptional Projects." These projects need not be directed primarily toward general audiences, though it is anticipated that most will contain elements that, directly or indirectly, are related to such audiences.

A variety of methods aimed at attracting general audiences are supported by this program, including lectures, discussions, conferences, films, radio broadcasts, ancillary exhibitions, dramatizations, and written materials, such as essays in newspapers and program notes.

Grants are awarded in two categories: Planning Grants and Implementation Grants. Both are identical to the categories for Humanities Programs in Libraries described above.

Budget: Outright grants and matching funds awarded in FY 1985 totaled approximately $1.7 million.

Application/Review Process: See the general discussion of NEH above. Deadlines are early February for projects beginning in October, and early October for projects beginning in April.

Funding Mechanisms: See the general discussion of NEH above.

Examples of Funded Projects:
1) $25,000 to a museum/cultural society to support planning for new programs of public education on the history and culture of selected Asian countries, including countries that are less familiar to the American public such as Burma, Malaysia, Pakistan, and Laos.

2) $57,000 to a university to support two related programs: an oral history of residents active in the South Bronx from 1960 to the present; and a library-related effort to bring major private collections of significant books, manuscripts, maps, and other records into the public domain.

3) $200,000 to a university to support a 3-year series of lectures and seminars on issues arising from the intersection of medicine and the humanities for audiences such as medical school faculty, students, employees, hospital patients, and visitors; each year two visiting humanities scholars are featured.

4) $54,000 to a public service organization to support an adult education program based on readings from classic texts in economics, political philosophy, and ethics which examine issues in daily economic life.

5) $150,000 to a university to support an 18-month program of public participation in the learning and doing of history; under the direction of scholars, archivists, and librarians, people collect, catalogue, archive, and display historical records about Black women in two midwestern states from 1866 to the present.

NOTE: Prior to a reorganization in late 1985, the Division also offered awards through a fifth program called "Humanities Programs for Youth/Youth Projects." The program was discontinued, but the Division continues to encourage the submission of proposals involving participation of young people (primarily junior and senior high school age) to work under the guidance of scholars and youth professionals. The "Younger Scholars" fellowship program is now administered through the Division of Fellowships and Seminars.

DIVISION OF EDUCATION PROGRAMS

Pamela Menke, Director
John F. Andrews, Deputy Director
Room 302
1100 Pennsylvania Avenue, NW
Washington, DC 20506
(202/786–0373)

The Division of Education Programs seeks to improve education in the humanities through grants to universities and colleges, academic and professional associations, and elementary and secondary schools. This division comprises four programs: Central Disciplines in Undergraduate Education, Humanities Instruction in Elementary and Secondary Schools, Exemplary Projects in Undergraduate and Graduate Education, and Humanities Programs for Nontraditional Learners.

In addition to the four core programs, several special initiatives are supported. Grants in this category are supported from funds allocated to regular NEH programs. The Education Division Director or Program Officers from the various programs may be approached as to whether a project idea falls under one of the special initiatives.

Current initiatives are (1) Improving the Preparation of Teachers in the Humanities (focuses on the problems of beginning elementary and secondary teachers, rather than those established in their careers); (2) High School Humanities Institutes at Historically Black Colleges and Universities (administered by the Humanities Instruction in Elementary and Secondary Schools Program, but provides for direct instruction of students and brings together high school and university teachers in a teaching program); (3) the Bicentennial of the U.S. Constitution (invites projects that would better educate students at any level about the philosophical, literary, historical, and political origins of the Constitution); (4) the Quincentennial of the Voyages of Columbus; (5) Understanding America; and (6) Understanding Other Nations.

CENTRAL DISCIPLINES IN UNDERGRADUATE EDUCATION PROGRAM

Martha Crunkelton, Acting Assistant Director
Room 302
1100 Pennsylvania Avenue, NW
Washington, DC 20506
(202/786–0380)

Program: Support from this program is restricted to colleges and universities. Grants are awarded to help establish or sustain the humanities in a central role in undergraduate education to help achieve long-term institutional improvements in the way the humanities are taught.

There are four categories of awards:

1) Improving Introductory Courses grants support institutional efforts to make introductory courses more effective. Contact Lyn Maxwell White at 202/786–0380.

2) Promoting Excellence in a Field grants support efforts of individual departments and programs within the humanities to foster greater depth of study and to implement other improvements in particular fields of the humanities. Contact Judith Ginsberg at 202/786–0380.

3) Fostering Coherence Throughout an Institution grants support comprehensive efforts to increase the coherence of an institution's offerings in the humanities. Contact Martha Crunkelton at 202/786–0380.

4) Planning Grants provide modest support for planning projects which fall into any of the three categories above.

Budget: Grants and matching funds awarded by this program in FY 1985 totaled approximately $4.9 million.

Application/Review Process: See the general discussion of NEH above. Deadlines for this program's two annual competitions are April 1 and October 1. Applicants receive notice in approximately 6 months.

Funding Mechanisms: See the general discussion of NEH above.

Examples of Funded Projects:
1) $57,000 to a college to support introduction of an integrated block of team-taught humanities, social science, and expository writing courses to satisfy general education requirements.

2) $95,000 to a university to support the costs of faculty release time for an interdisciplinary project on major cultural upheavals of the early twentieth century—through faculty development, preparation of materials, and the development of new courses.

3) $180,000 to a university to support development of an interdisciplinary core track involving required courses in philosophy, history, English, religious studies, and the social and physical sciences.

4) $15,000 to a university for partial support of a planning project to strengthen the foreign language and international studies program.

HUMANITIES INSTRUCTION IN ELEMENTARY AND SECONDARY SCHOOLS PROGRAM

Carolynn Reid-Wallace, Assistant Director for Humanities Instruction
Room 302
1100 Pennsylvania Avenue, NW
Washington, DC 20506
(202/786–0377)

Program: The purpose of the program is to strengthen instruction in elementary, middle, and secondary schools. Applicants may be individual schools, school systems, colleges, universities, museums, libraries, or collaborative groups representing different institutions.

Three grant categories administered by this program are:

1)   Institutes for Teachers and Administrators and Institutes for Principals provide opportunities for teachers and administrators to learn more about humanities fields and the most effective ways of teaching and/or supporting them by studying under the direction of leading scholars and master teachers.

2)   Collaborative Projects provide partial support for joint university and school system projects designed to strengthen the curriculum and to improve teaching in the basic disciplines of the humanities; occasionally Planning Grants are awarded to facilitate the cooperation necessary to plan this type of activity.

3)   High School Humanities Institutes at Historically Black Colleges and Universities provide opportunities for high school juniors to learn more about humanities disciplines by studying under the direction of college and university scholars during the summer; high school teachers may also participate. For information, call Jayme Sokolow at 202/786–0377.

Applications for the programs above are accepted in two cycles: May 15, with notification in January; and January 7, with notification in July.

A fourth category of awards, Independent Study in the Humanities, is administered by the Council on Basic Education (CBE), an independent non-profit organization. Awards are made to provide continuing support for three years to outstanding high school teachers with at least five years' teaching experience. The annual deadline for applications is December 1, with notification in April. For more information, contact the Council for Basic Education, 725 15th Street, NW, Washington, DC 20005; 202/347–4171.

Budget: Grants and matching funds awarded by this program in FY 1985 totaled approximately $8.0 million.

Application/Review Process: See the general discussion of NEH above.

Funding Mechanisms: See the general discussion of NEH above.

Examples of Funded Projects:

1) $295,000 to a nonprofit agency to support two 4-week institutes for social studies and Spanish teachers to study South American history and literature.

2) $110,000 to a university to support a 6-week institute for secondary school teachers from eight southeastern states to study African history in the context of world history, American history, and geography.

3) $85,000 to a university to support the introduction of a humanities-based approach to teaching social studies in 50 high schools of a major city and the development of materials to complement U.S. history textbooks.

4) $20,000 to a university to support planning meetings between the university and a local school system seeking to develop seminars in history and literature for secondary school teachers.

EXEMPLARY PROJECTS IN UNDERGRADUATE AND GRADUATE EDUCATION PROGRAM

Sara Chapman, Acting Assistant Director
Charles J. Meyers, Senior Program Officer
Room 302
1100 Pennsylvania Avenue, NW
Washington, DC 20506
(202/786–0384)

Program: This program supports the development and dissemination of projects in the humanities that build upon the best scholarship and are of value either in themselves or as models. Grants are awarded to colleges, universities, cultural institutions, and professional organizations in their efforts to strengthen faculty knowledge and thus teaching in the humanities. The three categories are:

1)   Institutes for College and University Teachers are designed to bring faculty members together for several weeks of intensive study on a subject central to the humanities and provide an opportunity for faculty to study under recognized scholars and to collaborate with colleagues from other institutions.

2)   Consortial Projects support inter-institutional collaboration to enhance the access to and quality of humanities teaching on more than one campus. NEH notes that because consortia typically are more successful as devices for increasing services than for reducing costs, the Endowment especially welcomes proposals for projects that promise greater cost-effectiveness than the participating institutions could achieve on their own.

3) Other Initiatives support a variety of activities that promise to increase the effectiveness with which the humanities are taught in a large number of institutions. Among the kinds of projects that are eligible for support are the collaborative development of model courses, workshops, conferences, and studies, and the organizing of inter-institutional faculty development programs.

Budget: Grants and matching funds awarded by this program in FY 1985 totaled approximately $5.0 million.

Application/Review Process: See the general discussion of NEH above. Applications are accepted in two competitions: May 1, with notification in January; and December 1, with notification in July.

Funding Mechanisms: See the general discussion of NEH above.

Examples of Funded Projects:
1) $80,000 to a university for a 4-week institute for 25 faculty members to introduce them to recent developments in "humanistic approaches to linguistic analysis."

2) $200,000 to a nonprofit research organization to support two 6-week institutes for 20 college and university teachers—the first on the ancient Near East from the third to first millennia B.C., the second on ancient Palestine from paleolithic to Islamic times.

3) $74,000 to a college to support a foreign-area studies curriculum for adult students with a focus initially on three geographic regions of the world; courses will be taught at off-campus sites in rural parts of the state.

4) $182,000 to a university to develop materials for the teaching of modern engineering as a integral part of the humanities; these will draw perspectives from three major disciplines and interpret contemporary ideas of engineering and society in terms of the history of science and technology.

5) $70,000 outright grant plus up to $30,000 matching funds to a professional association to support a comprehensive, 2-year project designed to clarify and strengthen the role of linguistics in the undergraduate curriculum.

HUMANITIES PROGRAMS FOR NONTRADITIONAL LEARNERS

Christine Kalke, Program Officer
Room 302
1100 Pennsylvania Avenue, NW
Washington, DC 20506
(202/786–0384)

Program: This program provides grants from funds allocated to the Exemplary Projects program (see above). Support is available for colleges, universities, libraries, and other organization for projects intended to make humanities education more accessible to nontraditional learners and to improve the quality of instruction in such programs.

Application/Review Process: See the general discussion of NEH above. Two competitions are held annually: April 1 and October 1, with notification in approximately 6 months.

Funding Mechanisms: See the general discussion of NEH above. Requirements include provision of at least 25% of project costs from nonfederal sources.

Examples of Funded Projects:
1) $150,000 to a university for an experimental project in teaching foreign languages through an individualized instruction program and the use of a telephone center; project includes development and refinement of courses for both commonly and uncommonly taught languages.

DIVISION OF STATE PROGRAMS

Marjorie A. Berlincourt, Director
Room 411
1100 Pennsylvania Avenue, NW
Washington, DC 20506
(202/786–0254)

Program: State humanities councils, mandated in the National Foundation on the Arts and Humanities Act, operate in all 50 states plus the District of Columbia, Puerto Rico, and the Virgin Islands. The state humanities councils are private, nonprofit organizations which receive grants from NEH to develop and support locally initiated humanities programs. Since 1976, state humanities councils have been authorized to support any project that is generally eligible for support from the NEH (including education and research projects and conferences). The special emphasis in state programs, however, is to make focused and coherent humanities education possible and available for adults. Within broad guidelines, each council develops its own guidelines, determines the emphasis of its programs, and selects its own council members and staff.

Social scientists may wish to approach state councils for support of certain types of professional activities. The following constraints/procedures should be kept in mind:

1) Grants from state councils average $3,000, with many less than $1,000.

2) Each state council is required to share the costs of its Endowment grant—both program and administrative funds. As a result, all state councils must require 50% cost-sharing from grantees (this may be provided by cash or services and materials supplied by the grantees).

3) NEH grants to state councils (granted biennially) range between $300,000 and $700,000 per year. In addition, the councils may apply to NEH for Treasury funds which permit "matching grants" parallel to NEH practice in other programs.

4) In several states, corporations, foundations, and other sources of private grants channel funds through the state councils, thus expanding financial resources for the granting programs.

Budget: Overall allocations in this area are declining somewhat. In FY 1985 the division awarded state councils approximately $24.4 million in outright and matching funds. This contrasts with nearly $26 million awarded in FY 1984.

Application/Review Process: See the general discussion of NEH above. Deadlines and application procedures are available from the individual state humanities councils. A directory of state humanities councils and other information can be obtained from this Division in Washington.

Funding Mechanisms: See the general discussion of NEH above.

OFFICE OF CHALLENGE GRANTS

James H. Blessing, Director
George Farr, Deputy Director
Room 429
1100 Pennsylvania Avenue, NW
Washington, DC 20506
(202/786–0361)

Program: The Office of Challenge Grants provides support for educational and cultural institutions and organizations to increase financial stability and to preserve or improve the quality of programs within institutions in which teaching and research in the humanities occur. Since the introduction of the program in 1979, grants have been awarded to institutions for work involving virtually every discipline in the social and behavioral sciences.

Budget: The FY 1985 budget was $19.6 million. There are no rigid subdivisions within the budget as to portions designated for categories of institutions.

Application/Review Process: See the general discussion of NEH above. There is a single competition each year with applications due (in recent years) by May 1. Detailed application guidelines are issued annually. Program managers stress that applicants receive valuable advice by submitting a full draft at least 6 weeks prior to the deadline. NEH staff will provide careful, detailed advice.

Funding Mechanisms: See the general discussion of NEH above. Grants for the federal portion of an overall challenge grant may range from $5,000 to $1,000,000. All funds granted to successful applicants are "offered" contingent upon grantee raising three dollars of eligible nonfederal funds for each federal dollar.

Examples of Funded Projects:
1) $415,000 to a museum to develop a $1,660,000 endowment to support basic research in cultural anthropology and archaeology in the southwestern United States.
2) $125,000 to a university to augment an endowment to support fellowships and faculty research in regional studies.
3) $1 million to a small college to establish a $4 million endowment to strengthen language and area studies, provide visiting professorships in international and cross-cultural studies, and other humanistic areas.

OFFICE OF PRESERVATION

Harold Cannon, Director
Room 802
1100 Pennsylvania Avenue, NW
Washington, DC 20506
(202/786–0570)

Program: In 1985, responding to rising concern about the imminent danger of destruction of many source documents because of the disintegration of paper or instability of other media, NEH created a new Office of Preservation. While a number of preservation projects have been supported in recent years by the

NEH's Research Division, the decision to institute a separate Office of Preservation was made with the intent of creating a flexible entity which can support grants for a variety of activities ranging from research to public information.

The Office's activities are very much focused on paper. Referring to "the brittle book problem," NEH staff estimate that 75 million books in major American research libraries are too brittle to be handled. Even with the new program in place, only 50,000 of the affected publications are being dealt with (e.g., microfilmed) annually. The Office actively seeks increased involvement by private philanthropy in the preservation of valuable print resources.

Grants are awarded by this Office to save informational content, improve research collection maintenance, develop preventive care practices, and train professional personnel. The program emphasizes the preservation of printed materials, archives, and manuscript collections. (It should be noted that NEH's Division of General Programs supports conservation and/or restoration of artifacts which may be used in public exhibition, and the Research Division supports organizing and cataloging projects in libraries and archives). Priority is given to U.S. imprints, Americana, and documents in an advanced stage of deterioration, principally materials produced between 1870 and 1920. The Office both administers and awards grants in support of the U.S. Newspaper Program, a major national effort to locate, catalog, and preserve newspapers published since 1690. Since 1983 some $3 million has been awarded to projects in 26 states in connection with the Newspaper Program.

Budget: In FY 1985 approximately $1.8 million was awarded for preservation projects. All grant funds were drawn from the Research Division's allocation. The new Office has high priority within NEH, and in FY 1986—the first year of operation as a separate office—the anticipated budget is $4 million.

Application/Review Process: See the general discussion of NEH above. The deadlines for proposals are June 1 and December 1; awards are announced 6 months later.

Funding Mechanisms: See the general discussion of NEH above.

Examples of Funded Projects:
1) $190,000 to a scholarly society to support a microfilming project for resources in classical studies; a selection of embrittled serials and books published between 1850 and 1918 will be chosen by a group of scholars.

2) $675,000 to a research library consortium to support the microfilming of 30,000 imprints (1876–1900) held in seven libraries and deemed fundamental to American studies.

OFFICE OF PLANNING AND BUDGET

Stephen Cherrington, Director
Room 402
1100 Pennsylvania Avenue, NW
Washington, DC 20506
(202/786–0428)

The Office of Planning and Budget provides internal support for all planning functions at the Endowment. These responsibilities include both the development and maintenance of internal statistical systems to track NEH grant-making activities and the commissioning of studies on trends and activities in the humanities, higher education, U.S. cultural institutions, etc. Many of these studies are statistically based and designed and carried out by social scientists.

HUMANITIES STUDIES PROGRAM

Jeffrey D. Thomas, Program Officer
Room 403
1100 Pennsylvania Avenue, NW
Washington, DC 20506
(202/786–0428)

Program: The Humanities Studies Program is the NEH's principal vehicle for policy studies, external data collection, and other activities aimed at informing the planning activities of the Endowment. The forerunner of this program was the Planning and Assessment Studies Program, which conducted studies that traditionally served as an important source of information about the humanities in America—notably in higher education. In FY 1985 Congress mandated a relocation of the program from NEH's program budget to its administrative budget because, in Congress's view, the work of the program is primarily intended to benefit NEH. In practice this has meant that the new Humanities Studies Program remains interested in the collection and analysis of information that will lead to a better understanding of the humanities, but work is more specifically tied to current concerns of NEH and is carried out through solicited research.

The Humanities Studies Program also provides ongoing support for national data collection projects, including the Survey of Earned Doctorates (through which the annual production of Ph.D.s is tracked by the National Academy of Sciences), and the Survey of Doctorate Recipients, a biennial assessment of the entire population of Ph.D.-holders. These surveys provide the agency with valuable information about the production and employment of humanities scholars. Support is also extended to the Higher Education Survey system (formerly the Higher Education Panel), a research program that can obtain policy-related information quickly from a representative sample of colleges and universities. The most recent survey documented the nature and extent of general education requirements in the humanities.

The 1985 legislation reauthorizing the Endowment calls upon the NEH to plan and implement a data collection system which, beginning in October 1, 1988, will form a basis for biennial "state of the humanities" reports. The legislation requires NEH, in consultation with other relevant agencies, to "develop a practical system of national information and data collection on the humanities, scholars, educational and cultural groups, and their audiences. Such system shall include cultural and financial trends in the various humanities fields, trends in audience participation. . . ." NEH must submit a plan and budget to relevant congressional committees in the fall of 1986. The Office of Planning and Budget (including contracts through the Humanities Studies Program) should play a central role in NEH's response to this congressional directive.

Budget: The Humanities Studies Program no longer has a separate budget line. In FY 1986 an estimated $650,000 is available for the program, of which approximately half will be expended for ongoing data collection projects.

Application/Review Process: See the general discussion of NEH above. Because of the structural changes described above, there are no grant competitions. Requests for proposals are published in the *Commerce Business Daily* as well as selected scholarly journals. A standing mailing list is maintained, however, and interested social scientists are encouraged to contact the Office of Planning and Budget to have their names placed on the list.

Funding Mechanisms: See the general discussion of NEH above. All funding is through contracts.

Example of Funded Projects:
1) $25,000 to a nonprofit research organization to support a study of factors contributing to the decline in the number of students entering the humanities and to the changing attitudes and background characteristics of those students.

2) $20,000 to a membership association to support research on the nature, level, and scope of funding provided by private and corporate foundations to support foreign language programs over the period 1974–1983.

3) $45,000 to a nonprofit research organization to analyze data from the National Longitudinal Survey of the High School Class of 1972 to assess the early career patterns of baccalaureate majors in the humanities, social sciences, and selected preprofessional fields. The study provides descriptive information

(e.g., types of jobs, activities, satisfaction, status, income) about the careers of humanities graduates, and analyzes the relative importance of family background, personal goals, collegiate accomplishments, and type of college attended for predicting early career destinations.

OFFICE OF THE BICENTENNIAL OF THE U.S. CONSTITUTION

Joseph Phelan, Officer in Charge
Room 504
1100 Pennsylvania Avenue, NW
Washington, DC 20506
(202/786–0332)

Program: In recognition of the 200th anniversary of the United States Constitution as a singular opportunity for scholarly and educational activities, NEH announced a Special Initiative to promote the study and public appreciation of the history and principles of the Constitution. The Office of the Bicentennial was established to assure focus on this Special Initiative.

Proposals focusing on the Constitutional Bicentennial may be submitted for all NEH grant-making divisions and offices. Proposals are invited on the philosophical, literary, historical, and political origins of the Constitution; relations of the structure of the Constitution to American political, social, and intellectual culture; and the connection between self-government and the purposes of human life.

NEH's general statement of "topics of special interest" lists (1) history of the period, (2) constitutional principles, (3) the U.S. Constitution and the world (e.g., comparison of the U.S. Constitution with the constitutions and laws of other countries), (4) individual rights, (5) the character of democracy (e.g., the relation of current American life and culture to the Constitution), (6) American federalism, (7) political institutions, and (8) constitutional interpretation.

Budget: There are no funds specifically allocated for the initiative. Grants are awarded from the regular program budgets.

Application/Review Process: See the general discussion of NEH above. Applicants should refer to the guidelines of the program for which submission of a proposal is contemplated. Information can be obtained from the programs directly or by contacting the Bicentennial Office. Standard NEH review procedures are followed with the exception that the Office of the Bicentennial directly manages the application process for certain competitions in the Divisions of

Education Programs, Fellowships and Seminars, and General Programs. For these divisions, the Bicentennial Office appoints special Bicentennial review panels.

Funding Mechanisms: See the general discussion of NEH above.

Examples of Funded Projects:
1) $56,000 to a university for a summer seminar for college teachers on Federalists and Anti-Federalists (an examination of the framing of the Constitution, focusing on the political philosophy of the proponents of the Constitution and their appeal to a "new science of politics," as contrasted with theories and opinions of Anti-Federalist opponents (funded by the Division of Fellowships and Seminars).

2) $270,000 to a college system for the research and publication of a 4-volume encyclopedia containing 2,000 alphabetically arranged articles covering the history and present state of American constitutional law, ranging from abolitionism to John Peter Zenger's case (funded by the Division of Research Programs).

3) $67,000 to a university for a summer institute for high school teachers on "The American Experience," a 4-week program on the meaning of the American Revolution and the "new political science" embodied in the Constitution; the institute featured lectures and discussions of readings from Locke, Montesquieu, *The Federalist,* and Tocqueville (funded by the Division of Education Programs).

4) $400,000 to an association for publication of a magazine that chronicles the Bicentennial of the Constitution by providing scholarly articles, resources, practical information, and suggestions for program planners (funded by the Division of General Programs).

National Science Foundation

Directorate for Biological, Behavioral, and Social Sciences

DIVISION OF BEHAVIORAL AND NEURAL SCIENCES

Richard T. Louttit, Director
Room 320
1800 G Street, NW
Washington, DC 20550
(202/357-7564)

The Division of Behavioral and Neural Sciences (BNS) is responsible for the support of research on nervous system activity and human and animal behavior that will further the understanding of the biological, environmental, and cultural factors that underlie behavior. Disciplines supported include anthropology, linguistics, psychology, and the neurosciences. Clinical research is not supported, although other applied research may be considered.

Programs within the division also fund proposals for specialized research facilities and equipment, doctoral dissertation research with special financial needs (not including stipends), and research conferences and workshops related to program areas.

Proposals may be submitted at any time, although specific target dates are established for each program.

ANTHROPOLOGY PROGRAM

John E. Yellen, Program Director, Archaeology and Physical Anthropology
Stuart M. Plattner, Associate Program Director, Social and Cultural Anthropology
(202/357-7804)

Program: The Anthropology Program supports all topics, geographic areas, and methodologies involving research in cultural and social anthropology, archaeology, and physical anthropology. Included are studies of human origins and the interaction of population, culture, and environment.

As with most NSF programs, the Anthropology Program does not have an established research agenda. However, there are two small specialized competitions within the program:

1) Support for Systematic Anthropological Collections provides assistance to systematic collections that are of outstanding research importance and in critical

need of restoration. The primary goal of these grants is to enhance the availability of such collections for scientific research. Proposals should be submitted by January 1 for awards the following summer.

2) An annual competition is held for two types of awards in anthropologically oriented archaeometry. Laboratory Support awards provide a modest but long-term core of funding for laboratories to acquire equipment and key personnel. Technique Development grants fund research that will develop and refine archaeometric techniques. Proposals are generally due by October 31 for awards the following spring.

Although dissertation research support is available for each BNS program, the Anthropology Program by far gives the largest number of these awards.

Budget: The total budget for the Anthropology Program was expected to be approximately $7.0 million in FY 1986.

Application/Review Process: See the general description of NSF in chapter 4. Proposals are first mailed to reviewers chosen by the program managers for their expertise in the specific area of research. A second review of proposals and the mail reviewers' comments is performed by standing advisory panels for each program. The advisory panels then make funding recommendations which are considered by the program manager and division director in making awards.

The target dates for proposals for the Anthropology Program are January 1 and August 1.

Funding Mechanisms: All research and related activities are funded by grants.

Examples of Funded Research:
1) "The Sex Ratio in Ecuador: Cultural Management and Cultural Change" (1-year project; FY 1984 award, $54,539).

2) "Socialization to Illness and Death Among American Children" (2-year project; FY 1984 award, $76,236).

3) "Family Resemblance for Longitudinal Measures of Growth" (2-year project; FY 1984 award, $23,058).

4) "Holistic Medicine as an Alternative Healing System: The Effect of Beliefs on Choice and Utilization" (dissertation grant) (18-month project; FY 1984 award, $7,704).

5) "New Techniques for Spatial and Statistical Understanding of Urban Society in Teotihuacan" (18-month project; FY 1984 award, $66,422).

6) "Ancient Maya Settlement and Community Patterns at the Site of Sayil, Puuc Region, Yucatan, Mexico" (1-year project; FY 1984 award, $163,667).

LINGUISTICS PROGRAM

Paul G. Chapin, Program Director
(202/357-7696)

Program: The Linguistics Program supports research into the syntactic, semantic, phonological, and phonetic properties of individual languages and of language in general. Studies of the acquisition of language by children, the psychological processes in the production and perception of speech, the biological foundations of language, the social influences on and effects of language and dialect variation, and the formal and mathematical properties of language models are also supported.

Budget: The FY 1986 budget for this program was expected to be approximately $3.1 million.

Application/Review Process: See the general description of NSF in chapter 4. Proposals are first mailed to reviewers chosen by the program managers for their expertise in the specific area of research. A second review of proposals and the mail reviewers' comments is performed by standing advisory panels for each program. The advisory panels then make funding recommendations which are considered by the program manager and division director in making awards.

The target dates for proposals for the Linguistics Program are February 1 and August 1.

Funding Mechanisms: All research and related activities are funded by grants.

Examples of Funded Research:
1) "Early Lexical Development: The Roles of Mother and Child" (1-year project; FY 1984 award, $30,000).

2) "Speech and Ethnic Identity Among the Saami of Northern Norway" (1-year project; FY 1984 award, $20,121).

3) "A Cross-Linguistic Study of Grammatical Categories" (2-year project; FY 1984 award, $80,000).

4) "Miscommunication: Doctors and Spanish-Speaking Patients" (dissertation grant) (1-year project; FY 1984 award, $6,842).

5) "Phonological Encoding in Language Production" (2-year project; FY 1984 award, $49,986).

MEMORY AND COGNITIVE PROCESSES PROGRAM

Joseph L. Young, Program Director
(202/357–9898)

Program: The Memory and Cognitive Processes Program supports research on complex human cognitive behavior, including learning, thought, and cognitive development. Included are such topics as memory, attention, concept formation, imagination, reading, problem-solving, decision-making, and intelligence. Projects in measurement or quantitative methods that relate to the study of cognition and applied cognitive research are also supported. The Program encourages proposals from a variety of theoretical perspectives.

Budget: The FY 1986 budget for the Memory and Cognitive Processes Program was expected to be approximately $3.0 million.

Application/Review Process: See the general description of NSF in chapter 4. Proposals are first mailed to reviewers chosen by the program managers for their expertise in the specific area of research. A second review of proposals and the mail reviewers' comments is performed by standing advisory panels for each program. The advisory panels then make funding recommendations which are considered by the program manager and division director in making awards.

The target dates for proposals for this program are February 1 and August 1.

Funding Mechanisms: All research and related activities are funded by grants.

Examples of Funded Research:
1) "Visual Images as Memory Structures" (1-year project; FY 1984 award, $12,000).

2) "Theoretical and Empirical Research in Human Information" (2-year project; FY 1984 award, $99,693).

3) "Numerical Concepts in Infancy" (3-year project; FY 1984 award, $235,658).

4) "Training for Formal Versus Programmatic Approaches to Reasoning" (1-year project; FY 1984 award, $46,058).

5) "Collaborative Processes in Reading Comprehension" (2-year project; FY 1984 award, $94,995).

PSYCHOBIOLOGY PROGRAM

Fred Stollnitz, Program Director
(202/357–7949)

Program: Serving as the link between biology and the behavioral sciences, the Psychobiology Program supports field and laboratory studies of behavior and its genetic, environmental, hormonal, neural, and motivational determinants, using a wide range of observational, experimental, theoretical, comparative, and quantitative approaches. Topics supported include animal learning and memory, conditioning and stimulus control, preferences and aversions, foraging and ingestive behavior, animal communication, migration and homing, and the social and reproductive behaviors of animals.

Budget: The FY 1986 budget for this program was expected to be approximately $4.7 million.

Application/Review Process: See the general description of NSF in chapter 4. Proposals are first mailed to reviewers chosen by the program managers for their expertise in the specific area of research. A second review of proposals and the mail reviewers' comments is performed by standing advisory panels for each program. The advisory panels then make funding recommendations which are considered by the program manager and division director in making awards.

The target dates for proposals for the Psychobiology Program are January 15 and July 15.

Funding Mechanisms: All research and related activities are funded by grants.

Examples of Funded Research:
1) "Modification of Aggressive Expression in Adolescent Males" (1-year project; FY 1985 award, $56,858).

2) "Developmental Determinants of Vocal Learning" (1-year project; FY 1985 award, $50,161).

3) "Quantitative Models of Choice in Human Self-Control" (2-year project; FY 1985 award, $81,496).

4) "The Relationship Between Acoustic Structure, Signal Message, and Receiver Response" (dissertation grant) (2-year project; FY 1985 award, $12,408).

5) "Learned Helplessness and Stressor Controllability: Behavioral and Neurochemical Consequences and Determinants" (1-year project; FY 1985 award, $80,000).

SENSORY PHYSIOLOGY AND PERCEPTION PROGRAM

Carol Welt, Program Director
(202/357–7428)

Program: The Sensory Physiology and Perception Program funds research on mechanisms and processes at the molecular, cellular, physiological, and behavioral levels involved in sensory transduction, neural coding and information processing, neurobiological and psychophysical correlates of sensory and perceptual phenomena, and development of perceptual systems.

Budget: Approximately $6.7 million was expected to be available for this program in FY 1986.

Application/Review Process: See the general description of NSF in chapter 4. Proposals are first mailed to reviewers chosen by the program managers for their expertise in the specific area of research. A second review of proposals and the mail reviewers' comments is performed by standing advisory panels for each program. The advisory panels then make funding recommendations which are considered by the program manager and division director in making awards.
     The target dates for proposals for this program are January 15 and July 15.

Funding Mechanisms: All research and related activities are funded by grants.

Examples of Funded Research:
1)   "Loudness Perception and Judgment: Individual Differences" (2-year project; FY 1984 award, $100,000).

2)   "Collaborative Research on Role of Anchors in Perception" (2-year project; FY 1984 award, $50,000).

3)   "Complex Auditory Processing in Human Infants" (3-year project; FY 1984 award, $53,215).

4)   "Perception and Orienting Responses" (3-year project; FY 1984 award, $45,133).

5)   "Chemical Senses, Hormones, and Behavior" (3-year project; FY 1984 award, $55,000).

SOCIAL AND DEVELOPMENTAL PSYCHOLOGY PROGRAM

Jean B. Intermaggio, Program Director
(202/357–9485)

Program: The Social and Developmental Psychology Program supports laboratory and field research in two broad areas: (1) human social behavior, including social perception, attitude formation and change, and social learning; and (2) human social development in children and adults, including personality and emotional developmental processes. Research to improve the conceptual and methodological base of social and developmental psychology is encouraged.

Budget: Approximately $2.9 million was expected to be available for this program in FY 1986.

Application/Review Process: See the general description of NSF in chapter 4. Proposals are first mailed to reviewers chosen by the program managers for their expertise in the specific area of research. A second review of proposals and the mail reviewers' comments is performed by standing advisory panels for each program. The advisory panels then make funding recommendations which are considered by the program manager and division director in making awards.
The target dates for proposals for this program are January 15 and July 15.

Funding Mechanisms: All research and related activities are funded by grants.

Examples of Funded Research:
1) "Daily Life Events, Coping, Mood, and Their Impact on Illness" (1-year project; FY 1984 award, $41,000).

2) "Self-Analysis and Attitude-Behavior Consistency" (2-year project; FY 1984 award, $95,329).

3) "Ambivalence and Behavior Toward Outgroups" (2-year project; FY 1984 award, $121,773).

4) "Modification of Gender-Stereotyped Behavior in Children" (2-year project; FY 1984 award, $125,519).

5) "Overjustification and Attitude Change" (1-year project; FY 1984 award, $40,016).

DIVISION OF SOCIAL AND ECONOMIC SCIENCE

Roberta Balstad Miller, Director
Room 316
1800 G Street, NW
Washington, DC 20550
(202/357-7966)

The Division of Social and Economic Science (SES) is probably the single most identifiable federal source of research support for basic research in the social sciences. SES provides support for disciplinary and multidisciplinary research, data collection, and measurement and methodological research in eight areas: economics, geography and regional science, history and philosophy of science, law and social science, political science, sociology, measurement methodology and data improvement, and decision and management science. The goal of the Division is to develop basic scientific knowledge of social and economic systems, organizations and institutions, and human interaction and decision-making. SES will also provide support for research to improve the quality and accessibility of social and economic databases, research conferences, doctoral dissertation research, the acquisition of specialized research and computing equipment, group international travel, and data resource development.

Programs in the Division are often able to expand their support base by arranging joint funding of projects with other SES programs or with programs in other divisions. Because of federal budget cuts in social science research, SES programs have maintained a relatively high success rate over the past several years by reducing the size of research awards. In the future, programs expect to increase the amount of awards, if necessary by decreasing the total number of awards.

ECONOMICS PROGRAM

Daniel H. Newlon, Senior Program Director
(202/357-9675)

Program: The Economics Program supports research on the processes and institutions of the U.S. economy and of the world system. The program emphasizes strengthening the theoretical foundations of economics and methods for analyzing and modeling economic behavior. Research areas currently supported include:

1) theory (mathematical economics; decision-making under uncertainty; information and incentive systems);

2) methods (foundations of econometrics; new quantitative techniques for analyzing economic behavior);

3) macroeconomics (microfoundations of economic aggregates; macroeconomic policies in open economies; modeling, testing, policy-making significance of rational expectations);

4) political economy and public finance (impact of taxes on savings and work effort; general equilibrium models of taxation; experimental investigation of individual and collective choice);

5) labor (U.S. labor force employment fluctuations; characteristics and macroeconomic effects of employment contracts; collection of longitudinal data on family income dynamics);

6) other topics, such as economic history, international economics, regulation, and the economics of resource depletion.

Budget: At the end of 1985 the NSF operating plan allocated a budget of approximately $10.5 million for this program in FY 1986.

Application/Review Process: See the general description of NSF in chapter 4. The target dates for proposals are January 15 and August 15.

Funding Mechanisms: All research and related activities are funded by grants.

Examples of Funded Research:
1) "International Productivity and Competitiveness" (1-year project; awarded $76,710).

2) "Econometric Studies of Aggregate Demand and Economic Fluctuations" (3-year project; awarded $152,043).

3) "Two Frameworks for the Theory of Organizations: Overlapping Games and Multiparty Contracts" (2-year project; awarded $51,028).

4) "The Influence of Fertility, Marriage, and Family Endowments on the Distribution of Income Equality of Opportunity" (1-year project; awarded $64,965).

5) "Integrated Theoretical and Experimental Studies of Auction Markets" (1-year project; awarded $23,828).

6) "Taxation, Corporate Investment and Merger Activity" (2-year project; awarded $62,500).

GEOGRAPHY AND REGIONAL SCIENCE PROGRAM

Ronald Abler, Program Director
(202/357-7326)

Program: The Geography and Regional Science Program supports research on location and its effects. The program promotes a deeper understanding of the causes and consequences of geographical differences in economic, social, cultural, and physical phenomena. The program supports research on the ramifications of location, on the interconnections and interactions among places and regions, and on interrelationships between man and the physical environment.

Principal topics of research include (1) migration and regional population change, (2) locational decision-making and locational processes, (3) regional economic growth and decline, (4) resource use and physical systems, (5) spatial methods and theory, and (6) urban and metropolitan processes and problems.

Budget: At the end of 1985 the NSF operating plan allocated a budget of approximately $1.2 million for this program in FY 1986.

Application/Review Process: See the general description of NSF in chapter 4. The target dates for proposals are January 15 and August 15.

Funding Mechanisms: All research and related activities are funded by grants.

Examples of Funded Research:
1) "Labor Market Competition Processes and Their Effects on Migration and Unemployment" (1-year project; awarded $32,352).

2) "Defense-Related Industrial Location and Regional Growth" (18-month project; awarded $64,103).

3) "The Effects of State Government Policies on the Start-Up of New Small Businesses" (1-year project; awarded $23,233).

4) "Channel and Floodplain Responses to Environmental Change" (1-year project; awarded $20,000).

5) "Consistent Multiregional Population Projections for 50 U.S. States, Puerto Rico, the District of Columbia, and Major Consolidated Metropolitan Statistical Areas" (2-year project; awarded $30,000).

6) "A Comparative Analysis of the Geography of Non-White Immigrants in Cities: Britain, Canada, and the United States" (1-year project; awarded $30,000).

MEASUREMENT METHODS AND DATA IMPROVEMENT PROGRAM

Murray Aborn, Program Director
(202/357–7913)

Program: The Measurement Methods and Data Improvement Program supports projects to improve the scientific quality and accessibility of social data, with an emphasis on improving survey data and increasing the usefulness of federal statistical data. Projects designed to enhance the reliability, validity, or utility of existing data sources, to make new data resources available, and/or to develop methods and models of broad utility in the analysis of social data may also be funded. The program will also support projects involving applications of cognitive science and information science to social measurement. Three general areas comprise this program: survey operations research, data improvement, and analytical methods.

Survey operations research is aimed at improving the scientific adequacy and reliability of procedures and practices involved in gathering data by surveys. Of interest are designs for making optimum apportionments of resources for reducing total survey error, development of computer-assisted survey technology, methods for assessing data quality and detecting errant survey practices, and applications of new advances in cognitive science to survey research methodology.

The data improvement element is particularly concerned with improving the scientific quality and research utility of governmental data series. A current initiative calls for applying principles of knowledge management from information science to the structuring of social science data files.

In projects involving analytical methods, priorities include the creation and development of tools with broad utility in analyzing social data; e.g., quasi-experimental techniques, time-series analytic methods, event-history analysis, categorical data analysis, social graphics, and meta-analysis.

Budget: At the end of 1985 the NSF operating plan allocated a budget of $2.77 million for this program in FY 1986.

Application/Review Process: See the general description of NSF in chapter 4. The target dates for proposals are January 15 and August 15.

Funding Mechanisms: All research and related activities are funded by grants.

Examples of Funded Research:
1) "Cognitive Processes in Survey Responding: Multiple Schemas and the Role of Affect" (3-year project; awarded $69,773).

2) "An Assessment of the Predictive Accuracy of Pre-Election Polls" (1-year project; awarded $59,910).

3) "Collaborative Research on the Design and Analysis Parallels Between Sample Surveys and Randomized Experiments" (1-year project; awarded $48,667).

4) "Wisconsin Longitudinal Study: Creation of Machine-Readable Archive of Data and Documents" (18-month project; awarded $88,912).

5) "Conference on the Use of Archival Data for Studying the Changing Life Experiences of American Women" (1-year project; awarded $19,988).

6) "A Unified Model of Individual Competence and Knowledge Aggregation" (2-year project; awarded $181,983).

SOCIOLOGY PROGRAM

Mark Abrahamson, Program Director
(202/357-7802)

Program: The Sociology Program supports basic research on macro problems
of social organization and micro problems of social interaction. The primary
objective of the program is to encourage theoretically focused empirical studies
of fundamental social processes, both within and among nations.

In addition to funding theoretical and methodological studies that transcend specialty areas within the discipline, topics in this program may be divided
in the following seven categories:

1)   communities (including community ethnography, factorial ecology, housing and transportation, rural and urban communities, spatial arrangements);

2)   demography (including fertility, mortality, and migration, and related processes);

3)   individuals and society (including attitudes and behavior, attribution, devi-
ance, roles and identities, socialization, status in small groups);

4)   organizations and markets (including bureaucratization, labor markets,
multinational corporations, occupations and professions, technology and organization);

5)   social institutions (including the organization of and behavior within
churches, families, governments, the military, prisons, schools, etc.);

6)   social processes (including collective behavior, conflict, development, mass
communication, social movements, voluntarism);

7)   stratification and mobility (including age, ethnic, race, and sex roles, attainment processes, class, status, power, voluntary and structural movement).

Budget: At the end of 1985 the NSF operating plan allocated a budget of
approximately $3.1 million for this program in FY 1986.

Application/Review Process: See the general description of NSF in chapter
4. The target dates for proposals are January 15 and August 15.

Funding Mechanisms: All research and related activities are funded by grants.

Examples of Funded Research:
1)   "Testing the Ability of Competing Criminogenic Theories to Explain
Crime Rate Trends and Distributions" (18-month project; awarded $66,000).

2)   "Collaborative Research on Higher Education, Social Structure and the
Labor Market" (18-month project; awarded $70,663).

3) "The Day Care Search and Women's Employment and Fertility" (2-year project; awarded $23,166).

4) "Coercive Tactics in Bargaining Relationships" (2-year project; awarded $58,118).

5) "Collaborative Research on Occupations, Organizations, and Inequality in Job Rewards: A Comparison of the United States and Japan" (18-month project; awarded $23,001).

6) "The Adaptation Process of Cuban and Haitian Refugees in The United States" (1-year project; awarded $71,047).

7) "The Political Consequences of Linkages Among Firms" (1-year project; awarded $17,689).

HISTORY AND PHILOSOPHY OF SCIENCE PROGRAM

Ronald J. Overmann, Program Director
(202/357-9677)

Program: The History and Philosophy of Science Program supports research relevant to the understanding of science (including the physical, biological, and social sciences), scientific change, and technological development. Included are studies of the nature and development of scientific theories and methodology, the interactions between science and technology, and social and intellectual factors that affect scientific development. Studies of the history of medicine generally are not supported. Research projects may include topics in the history and/or philosophy of science and technology in a general sense, the history and/or philosophy of a particular field of science, or studies of scientific developments during specific periods of history.

Budget: At the end of 1985 the NSF operating plan allocated a budget of approximately $1.6 million for this program in FY 1986.

Application/Review Process: See the general description of NSF in chapter 4. The target dates for proposals are January 15 and August 15.

Funding Mechanisms: All research and related activities are funded by grants. Awards by this program are limited to $9,000 for summer support and $30,000 for academic year support.

Examples of Funded Research:
1) "James Franck and the Social Responsibility of the Scientist" (1-year project; awarded $19,056).

2) "Ethnocentrism as a Source of Bias in Science" (1-year project; awarded $6,000).

3) "Edward Bradford Titchener and the Beginnings of Experimental Psychology in America" (1-year project; awarded $25,000).

4) "Relativity, Relativism, and Politics: The Reception of Einstein's Theories of Relativity" (1-year project; awarded $24,996).

5) "A History of Conservation and Community Ecology in Russia and the Soviet Union, 1900–1960" (1-year project; awarded $3,650).

6) "The History of Anthropological Thought and Institutions" (1-year project; awarded $18,350).

POLITICAL SCIENCE PROGRAM

Frank P. Scioli, Jr., and Lee Sigelman, Program Directors
(202/357-9406)

Program: The Political Science Program supports research on political institutions and processes, broadly defined. Topics of interest include (but are not restricted to) the interrelationships between political and social and economic phenomena; the causes and consequences of political change; elector and nonelectoral political behavior; the operation of political institutions such as executives, legislatures, courts, and parties; conflict and political instability; and decision-making and policy formation. Eligible research projects may be primarily analytic or empirical, and there is no programmatic preference for any one data collection method (observation, experimentation, quasi-experimentation, survey, archival research, etc.). Work supported by the program ranges across the traditional subfields of political science, including American politics, comparative politics, international relations and foreign policy, public policy and administration, and empirical theory. The program also actively supports work at the intersection of political science and related disciplines.

Budget: At the end of 1985 the NSF operating plan allocated a budget of approximately $3 million for this program in FY 1986.

Application/Review Process: See the general description of NSF in chapter 4. The target dates for proposals are January 15 and August 15.

Funding Mechanisms: All research and related activities are funded by grants.

Examples of Funded Research:
1) "Ideological Constraint, Issue Voting and the Nature of Political Reasoning" (2-year project; awarded $84,963).

2) "Verification and Deterrence in Arms Control: A Game-Theoretic Analysis" (14-month project; awarded $35,988).

3) "The Effects of Organization, Demand Making and Environmental Variables on State Legislative Policy Making" (2-year project; awarded $19,999).

4) "Secondary Analyses of Ideological Consistency in the National Election Studies" (18-month project; awarded $27,951).

5) "The Bureaucratic Elite in Israel" (15-month project; awarded $32,097).

6) "Structural Causes of Gender Inequality in Congressional Campaign Funding" (14-month project; awarded $44,928).

7) "The Domestic Context of American Foreign Policy: Elite and Mass Foreign Policy Attitudes, 1974–1982" (21-month project; awarded $25,997).

LAW AND SOCIAL SCIENCES PROGRAM

Felice J. Levine, Program Director
(202/357–9567)

Program: The Law and Social Sciences Program funds social scientific research on law and law-like systems of rules. Illustrative of the areas receiving support are studies of the processes that enhance or diminish the impact of law; causes and consequences of variations and changes in legal institutions; personal, social, and cultural factors affecting the use of law; dynamics and effects of dispute processing and alternative means of dispute resolution; determinants of decision-making in legal forums and contexts; and conditions and processes that create transformations between formal legal rules and law in action.

The program encourages theoretical development, empirical study, and methodological improvements aimed at advancing scientific knowledge about law, human behavior as it relates to law, and the dynamics of normative ordering in complex societies.

Research projects are clustered in five general areas:

1) dispute processing (litigation, mediation, arbitration, negotiation; legal mobilization; conflict resolution strategies);

2) impact of law (deterrence processes; social and economic consequences of variations in law; determinants of individual and organizational compliance);

3) legal decision-making (dynamics underlying deliberation and decision-making in legal forums; processes of information seeking; effects of courts, lawyers, enforcement, and regulatory agencies on rule and decision making);

4) legal and social change (social control; legal change and social, cultural, economic, and technological change; emergence, development, and transformation of law);

5) data resources and methods (development of data resources; improvements in techniques, measures, and models).

Budget: At the end of 1985 the NSF operating plan allocated a budget of approximately $1.6 million for this program in FY 1986.

Application/Review Process: See the general description of NSF in chapter 4. The target dates for proposals are January 15 and August 15.

Funding Mechanisms: All research and related activities are funded by grants.

Examples of Funded Research:
1) "The Effects of Evidence on Inferential Processes of Jurors and Juries" (2-year project; awarded $90,865).

2) "Determinants of Regulatory Enforcement and Compliance" (30-month project; awarded $95,618).

3) "The Impact of Partisan Judicial Elections on State Supreme Courts, 1850–1920" (18-month project; awarded $25,463).

4) "Creating a U.S. Data Resource on Capital Punishment" (1-year project; awarded $104,563).

5) "The Effect of Legal System Actions and Macroeconomic Conditions on Criminality" (2-year project; awarded $39,989).

6) "The Impact of Court-Ordered Reform on Social Control and Organizational Change" (1-year project; awarded $13,955).

7) "An Ethnographic Study of an Alternative Court in Yugoslavia" (1-year project; awarded $22,579).

DECISION AND MANAGEMENT SCIENCE PROGRAM

Trudi C. Miller, Program Director (202/357–7569)
Vincent Covello, Program Manager for Risk Assessment (202/357–7417)

Program: The Decision and Management Science Program (DMS) supports basic research on decision-making, management, and operational processes that would have implications for improving practice. Begun in 1982, this program considers proposals from all fields of science, and panel reviewers include social and behavioral scientists as well as natural scientists and engineers. The focus of DMS, however, is on the social and behavioral aspects of socio-technical systems. DMS research is characterized by (1) a reliance on models or formal theory, (2) systematic empirical observations in operational contexts, and (3) a focus on processes that are generalizable to contexts other than those in which observations are made.

To date, most support has gone to research on improvements in representing "rational" individuals in models. Projects cover evaluations of alternative models of problem-solving from psychology and artificial intelligence, estimates of the influences of often neglected factors (such as learning and contexts that determine salience), and appropriate uses of expected utility.

Another area of interest to DMS is game theory. Research in this category tests and extends game characterizations and solution concepts to fit real-world collective choice situations. Other models and methods of interest include stochastic process models, innovative uses of programming methods, applications of control theory, and axiomatic foundations for classes of methods.

A new component of the DMS program is research on risk assessment. The focus of this research is on quantifying and dealing with uncertainty in decision-making, management, and operational processes. The role of risk assessment in DMS is expanding because of its relevance to public and private sector decision-making in many areas, including biotechnology, nuclear energy, hazardous waste, toxic chemicals, computer security, and business failures.

Budget: At the end of 1985 the NSF operating plan allocated a budget of $1.56 million for this program in FY 1986.

Application/Review Process: See the general description of NSF in chapter 4. The target dates for proposals are January 15 and August 15.

Funding Mechanisms: All research and related activities are funded by grants.

Examples of Funded Research:
1) "An Exploratory Assessment of Compensation and Negotiation Methods for Managing Health, Safety, and Environmental Risks" (1-year project; awarded $103,680).

2) "A Decision Theoretic Analysis of Queuing Delays in Environments" (1-year project; awarded $104,536).

3) "The Flexibility-Efficiency Tradeoff in Alternative Organizational Forms" (6-month project; awarded $6,827).

4) "Collective Decision-Making When No One's Preference Need Be Convex" (1-year project; awarded $30,000).

5) "Research into Foundations, Uses and Extensions of Data Envelopment Analysis" (2-year project; awarded $83,763).

DIVISION OF INFORMATION SCIENCE AND TECHNOLOGY

Charles N. Brownstein, Director
Room 336
1800 G Street, NW
Washington, DC 20550
(202/357-9572)

The Division of Information Science and Technology (IST) is concerned broadly with the nature of information and how it is generated, represented, manipulated, and used. Research in this area is inherently multidisciplinary and reflects rapidly advancing high technology and socio-technical trends in advanced industrial economies. High priority areas are determined by special needs identified by unsolicited proposal trends, advisory groups, special studies, and program staff analyses.

Very strong emphasis is placed on basic research; applied work is supported only if it has broad, generic application potential. System development and the construction of information collections other than research databases are not generally supported.

Three research programs constitute the IST Division: Information Impact, Information Science, and Information Technology. The Program of Special Research Initiation Awards for New Investigators in Information Science provides support for new researchers in all three program areas. Each of the three programs has standing advisory panels to provide advice on issues of policy and program direction, but not to review applications.

Major opportunities and needs identified for IST for the future include:

1)   models of adaptive information processing, learning, searching, and recognition which underlie both understanding and automation of flexible information processing systems;

2)   knowledge resource systems, particularly intelligent systems beyond current rule-based systems, with capabilities for knowledge synthesis, changing rules and representations, and incorporating information of user performance;

3)   user-system interaction, with emphasis on fundamental principles of information exchange between individuals and visual displays, multiple media retrieval, data integration, flexible representation, and human performance;

4)   augmentation of human information processing, focused on use of technology to improve human performance in planning, decision-making, and communication at individual and organization levels of analysis;

5)   database resource improvement, especially data collections for research on the impact of information technology on activities such as investment, employment, productivity, and international trade (with particular attention to creating adequate databases for empirical research by many investigators);

6) empirical studies of information technology effects in experimental and natural settings, including firms and educational institutions (with emphasis on management of information and the role of technology in social and organizational behavior).

INFORMATION IMPACT PROGRAM

Laurence C. Rosenberg, Program Director
(202/357–9592)

Program: The Information Impact Program supports a wide range of theoretical and empirical research on information and information technology as a factor in economic and social processes; the structure, behavior, and performance of information industries (including telecommunications, computers, media, and financial services); and social and behavioral consequences of information technologies. The program also supports work designed to improve measurement and analysis methods relevant to these areas.

Of particular interest are topics such as improving understanding of the role of information processes in economic markets, productivity growth, measurement of productivity in service industries, information seeking and use behaviors, and new interactive technologies.

About half of the studies supported by this program are in economics, and many are co-funded by the Division of Social and Economic Science. The balance of the research supported is primarily in sociology, political science, and psychology. Policy studies may be supported if the focus is on policy impact rather than process.

Budget: A budget of approximately $2 million was anticipated for this program for FY 1986.

Application/Review Process: See the general description of NSF in chapter 4. All proposals are unsolicited. The division director and program directors will accept phone inquiries to discuss research ideas or review brief concept papers. It is important that applications for this division be clearly marked "IST"; otherwise they will likely be assigned to a disciplinary program in another division.

IST proposals are reviewed by peer reviewers by mail. Final funding decisions are made by the division director and program directors. About 40% of proposals to this division are successful.

Funding Mechanisms: Almost all awards are grants, although occasionally cooperative agreements are used. The average award is $75,000.

Examples of Funded Research:

1) "Collaborative Research on Informational Aspects of Distributed Computing and Decentralized Resource Allocation" (3-year project; total award, $423,785).

2) "A Study of Productivity Performance and Scientific and Technical Information" (1-year project; total award, $65,964).

3) "Industrial Robots in Japan and the U.S.: The Diffusion and Impact of a Major Application of Information Technology" (3-year project; total award, $53,583).

4) "Statistical Indicators of Scientific and Technical Communication in the U.S." (1-year project; total award, $76,327).

5) "A Longitudinal Analysis of the Social Impact of Computing in the Home" (2-year project; total award, $152,657).

INFORMATION SCIENCE PROGRAM

Joseph Deken, Program Director
Beth Adelson, Associate Program Director
(202/357–9569)

Program: The Information Science Program supports research on the properties of information and the dynamics of information aggregation and transfer. Emphasis is on investigation of information processing principles in tasks such as pattern recognition, learning, memory, decision-making, problem-solving, and issues related to knowledge-based systems such as the use of natural language, knowledge representation, complexity, uncertainty, inference, and knowledge retrieval. Support also goes to research on structural properties of information collection and on methods of document and knowledge retrieval.

The Information Science Program heavily supports the behavioral and cognitive sciences, as well as computationally oriented linguistics and neuroscience. Some proposals to this program may be co-funded by the Division of Behavioral and Neural Sciences and the Division of Computer Research.

It is anticipated that this program will be divided into two programs in the near future, with one of the new entities concentrated on cognitive aspects of information science.

Budget: The FY 1986 budget for this program was expected to about $5.5 million.

Application/Review Process: See the general description of NSF in chapter 4. All proposals are unsolicited. The division director and program directors will accept phone inquiries to discuss research ideas or review brief concept papers. It is important that applications for this division be clearly marked "IST"; otherwise they will likely be assigned to a disciplinary program in another division.

IST proposals are reviewed by peer reviewers by mail. Final funding decisions are made by the division director and program directors. About 40% of proposals to this division are successful.

Funding Mechanisms: Almost all awards are grants, although occasionally cooperative agreements are used. Grants made by the Information Science Program tend to be slightly higher than the division average of $75,000.

Examples of Funded Research:

1) "The Passing of Images" (1-year project; total award, $135,296).

2) "Fundamental Information Issues in the Theory of Measurement" (1-year project; total award, $95,505).

3) "A Normative Approach to Some Issues in the Theory of Computational Linguistics" (2-year project; total award, $28,913).

4) "A Single-Semantic-Process Theory of Passing" (3-year project; total award, $297,590).

5) "Problem-Solving Strategies in Program Comprehension and Generation" (2-year project; total award, $128,268).

INFORMATION TECHNOLOGY PROGRAM

Harold Bamford, Program Manager
(202/357–9554)

Program: The Information Technology Program funds research fundamental to the design of information processing systems that augment or supplant human information-processing activity. Encouraged are studies on the generation, integration, transfer, retrieval, and display of information resources; text, numerical, graphical, and vocal modes of interactions between human beings and information systems; and principles and methods of modeling the performance of information systems.

The program goes beyond the traditional question of "man-machine interface" to a more holistic approach to human factors in information systems. The majority of awards by this program are to highly technical, computer-oriented studies. There is support, however, for psychology and linguistics.

Budget: The FY 1986 budget was expected to be approximately $2 million.

Application/Review Process: See the general description of NSF in chapter 4. All proposals are unsolicited. The division director and program directors will accept phone inquiries to discuss research ideas or review brief concept papers. It is important that applications for this division be clearly marked "IST"; otherwise they will likely be assigned to a disciplinary program in another division.

IST proposals are reviewed by peer reviewers by mail. Final funding decisions are made by the division director and program directors. About 40% of proposals to this division are successful.

Funding Mechanisms: Almost all awards are grants, although occasionally cooperative agreements are used. The average award is $75,000.

Examples of Funded Research:
1) "Computer-Based Systems for Problem Structuring" (3-year project; total award, $267,400).

2) "Advanced Information Technology for Document Processing" (2-year project; total award, $222,900).

3) "Guided Computing and Graphics for Modeling in the Social Sciences" (co-funded by the Division of Social and Economic Science) (2-year project; total award, $110,030).

4) "Constructing a Self-Modifying Knowledge-Based Geographical Information System" (co-funded by the Division of Social and Economic Science) (18-month project; total award, $74,955).

PROGRAM OF SPECIAL RESEARCH INITIATION AWARDS FOR NEW INVESTIGATORS IN INFORMATION SCIENCE

Charles Brownstein, Division Director
(202/357–9572)

Program: The Program of Special Research Initiation Awards for New Investigators in Information Science (RI) is designed to develop new researchers in information science by providing opportunities for recent doctoral-level graduates. The program is directed toward full-time scientific faculty who have held the degree for four years or less and have not previously received awards for research in the information sciences. Grants are given to start projects in all areas supported by IST. Deadlines for proposals are the first Wednesday in February and the first Wednesday in August.

RI awards are funded by the three programs in IST; there is no budget set aside for this initiative. Ten to twenty RI awards are made each year.

Examples of Funded Research:

1) "The Role of Expertise in Human Information Processing and Decision Behavior" (co-funded by Division of Social and Economic Science) (1-year project; total award, $46,965).

2) "Heuristic Reasoning About Uncertainty: An Artificial Intelligence Approach" (1-year project; total award, $55,285).

3) "A New Data Structure for Text Processing and Pattern Recognition" (2-year project; total award, $99,796).

4) "Occupational Segregation Among Information Professionals" (1-year project; total award, $16,487).

ETHICS AND VALUES IN SCIENCE AND TECHNOLOGY

Rachelle Hollander, Cross-Directorate Program Coordinator
Room 310-D
1800 G Street, NW
Washington, DC 20550
(202/357–7567)

[Editor's Note: As this volume went to press, the status of the program for Ethics and Values in Science and Technology was uncertain. Although clearly authorized by the Congress in 1985, the corresponding appropriations bill did not include funding for EVIST. Thus, it is not clear at this writing what options the Foundation will have for continuing this program.]

Program: The program in Ethics and Values in Science and Technology (EVIST) coordinates the NSF effort to improve professional and public understanding of the ethical and value aspects of contemporary issues that involve science and technology and ethical, social, and professional standards that influence the conduct of scientific and technological activities. Proposals should focus on the roles of science and technology and their practitioners in areas of current social or professional concern and should clarify the ethical implications or value assumptions of those roles in order to contribute to the formulation of sound policy about them. Also supported are proposals to illuminate the roles of social and professional values in setting research priorities, selecting hypotheses, and developing and interpreting results for professionals and for the public.

In FY 1986 EVIST was relocated from the Directorate for Scientific, Technological, and International Affairs to the Directorate for Biological, Behavioral, and Social Sciences. EVIST no longer has a separate budget for funding proposals, but serves as a coordinating office for ensuring that the Foundation does support EVIST-related proposals with funds in the various research directorates.

Budget: Funding of EVIST proposals is provided by the research directorates. NSF has targeted $500,000 to be spent on this research in FY 1986 (a 50% reduction from FY 1985).

Application/Review Process: See the general description of NSF in chapter 4. Proposals are submitted to the EVIST office. Preliminary proposals (3 to 5 pages) are required. The standing deadlines are May 1 and November 1 for preliminary proposals, and August 1 and February 1 for final proposals. Mail reviewers are selected for each proposal by EVIST staff in cooperation with program officers in the related research directorate. A second review of all proposals is performed by a multidisciplinary EVIST advisory panel. Final funding decisions are made by EVIST staff and the relevant directorate staff.

Funding Mechanisms: The EVIST program can support both collaborative and individual research projects, dissertation research, and research-related activities such as conferences and symposia. It was anticipated that in light of upcoming budget restrictions, however, most emphasis would be placed on research projects.

Examples of Funded Research:
1) "Ethical and Value Issues for Information Sharing in Agencies with Research and Enforcement Missions" (18-month project; awarded $50,646).

2) "The Ethical Problems Raised by Fraud in Science and Engineering Publishing" (18-month project; awarded $56,000).

3) "Improving Technological Innovations for People with Physical Disabilities" (co-funded by Engineering Directorate) (dissertation award, $2,950).

4) "Values and Conflict Resolution in Policy Disputes Over Food" (co-funded by the Division of Social and Economic Science) (30-month project; awarded $74,995).

5) "A Value Analysis of Job Evaluation Systems Used for Comparable Worth Studies" (co-funded by Division of Social and Economic Science) (18-month project; awarded $59,998).

Directorate for Mathematical and Physical Sciences

DIVISION OF MATHEMATICAL SCIENCES

STATISTICS AND PROBABILITY PROGRAM

Peter Purdue and Bruce E. Trumbo, Co-Program Directors
Room 339
1800 G Street, NW
Washington, DC 20550
(202/357-9764)

Program: The Statistics and Probability Program supports research, as its name conveys, in the two areas of statistics and probability. Statistics research includes methods to collect, organize, and analyze data to uncover fundamental mathematical relationships among several variables. Major subfields include experimental design, parametric and nonparametric inference, robustness, decision theory, sequential analysis, multivariate analysis, and statistical computing.

Probability theory is concerned with the study of phenomena that are random, or modeled as random because of incomplete understanding. Major subfields include Markov processes, probability on Banach spaces, limit theorems, interacting particle systems, applied probability modeling, and stochastic processes.

The target date for proposals is generally in October, but proposals may be submitted at any time.

Budget: The FY 1986 budget for this program is approximately $6.2 million.

Application/Review Process: See the general description of NSF funding in chapter 4. Peer panel reviews are conducted by mail.

Funding Mechanisms: See the general description of NSF funding in chapter 4. The normal level for salary support is limited to 2 summer months.

Examples of Funded Research:
1) "Sequential Design, Quality Control, and Time Series."

2) "Estimation in Large Samples."

3) "Statistics and Game Theory."

4) Symposium on "Statistics, Law, and the Environment."

5) "Bayesian Statistics Theory and Methods" (co-funded by the Economics Program in the Division of Social and Economic Science).

6) "Sequential Allocation of Experiments: Bandit Problems."

7) "Interacting Particle Systems."

8) "Determining Band Width in Spectrum Estimation."

9) "Data Analysis Modeling and Inference."

Directorate for Scientific, Technological, and International Affairs

DIVISION OF INTERNATIONAL PROGRAMS

Bodo Bartocha, Director
Robert B. Hardy, Deputy Director
Room 1214
1800 G Street, NW
Washington, DC 20550
(202/357-9565)

The Division of International Programs (INT) encourages and supports U.S. participation in international science and engineering activities. The role of INT is to foster the exchange of information among scientists in the United States and foreign countries, initiate and support activities in matters relating to international cooperation, give U.S. scientists opportunities for scientific collaboration in developing countries, and provide support to U.S. institutions for research done abroad.

It is not the role of INT to provide primary research support. If a researcher demonstrates that he/she has primary support for a domestic project, INT will try to provide funding to internationalize the effort. INT generally will provide money for travel and supplies up to $20,000 for a 1- or 2-year effort. The Division does work to leverage support from other sources, including co-funding by NSF disciplinary programs.

International scientific research and related activities are supported through approximately 30 programs within INT. These programs are organized roughly in three areas: industrialized countries, developing countries, and socialist countries. Programs vary widely in structure and mechanisms of support. Generally, however, support is available for three types of activities: (1) cooperative research projects designed and conducted jointly by principal investigators from the United States and foreign country; (2) research-oriented seminars or workshops to exchange information, review the current status of a specific field of science, or plan cooperative research; and (3) scientific visits for planning cooperative activities or for research.

U.S. universities and colleges, professional societies, research institutes, and, in certain cases, individual scientists may apply for support. Principal investigators for most programs should be U.S. scientists with professional experience equivalent to at least five years of postdoctoral work. Because there has been a decline in the number of young U.S. scientists receiving research experience in other countries, INT is encouraging more young researchers to participate in a new exchange program with other industrialized countries.

Investigators are responsible for locating foreign colleagues for collaborative activities. Occasionally an INT-funded workshop will serve to introduce U.S. and foreign scientists with common research interests and thus initiate collaborative projects. Workshops of this nature may be the result of an unsolicited proposal, or they can be arranged by INT when either neglected or emerging areas of scientific inquiry are identified.

Much of the INT budget goes to the National Academy of Sciences, the International Council of Scientific Unions, and to the administration's Science and Technology Initiative with India. This, coupled with a major budget cut in 1981 (and only modest growth since then), has left little for discretionary funding. Because INT wishes to protect its bilateral programs with the industrialized countries, less money will be available for activities in developing countries.

It is INT policy to support any field of science that is generally eligible for NSF funding. In the case of the social and behavioral sciences, not all country programs will support these disciplines. In some countries, the host institution is not receptive to social and behavioral science research projects; in others, the government restricts research in these areas. If a program description does not mention the social sciences specifically as an area eligible for support, applicants should contact the program manager for that country or world area to determine whether a project could be considered.

Social scientists should be aware that they are now eligible to participate in INT-coordinated research in the People's Republic of China. This was not true in previous years, and the INT staff negotiated at length with their counterparts in the PRC to allow social science participation in collaborative and exchange programs.

A chart of the major INT programs accompanies this entry.

Budget: The total budget for this Division was $13 million in FY 1985. Less than $9 million was available for funding of specific country programs.

Application/Review Process: Proposals are unsolicited. Program announcements for each country or world area may identify specific priorities. Most country programs have target dates for submitting proposals.

The INT staff rely heavily on NSF disciplinary program managers when reviewing proposals. Most proposals from social and behavioral scientists are reviewed by program staff and peer panel members from divisions in the Direc-

Division of International Programs

Country or Region	Phone (202)	Cooperative Research	Seminars/ Workshops	Scientific Visits
Argentina	357-9563	D	D	A
Australia	357-9700	D	D	N
Austria	357-9700	D	D	N
Belgium	357-7554	A	D	N
Brazil	357-9563	D	D	A
Bulgaria	357-9516	A	A	N
China	357-7393	A	A	N
Finland	357-7554	D	D	N
France	357-7554	D	D	N
Germany (FRG)	357-9700	D	D	N
Hungary	357-9516	A	A	N
India	357-9402	A	A	D
Ireland	357-7554	D	D	N
Italy	357-7554	D	D	N
Japan	357-9558	D	D	N
Korea (ROK)	357-9537	D	N	D
Mexico	357-9563	D	D	A
New Zealand	357-9700	D	D	N
Pakistan	357-9402	A	A	D
Romania	357-9516	A	A	N
Spain	357-9550	D	D	D
Sweden	357-7554	D	D	N
Switzerland	357-9700	D	D	N

torate for Biological, Behavioral, and Social Sciences (BBS). Reviewers consider not only the technical merit of a proposals, but also comment on what priority a particular topic has within the discipline. INT program managers and senior staff consider these reviews in making final funding decisions.

Funding Mechanisms: Grants are made to support collaborative research projects, scholarly exchanges, scientific visits, and conferences and symposia.

Country or Region	Phone (202)	Cooperative Research	Seminars/ Workshops	Scientific Visits
United Kingdom	357-7554	D	D	N
Venezuela	357-9563	D	D	A
Africa Regional	357-9550	D	D	D
East Asia Regional	357-9537	D	D	D
Latin America	357-9563	D	D	A
Western Europe Regional	357-9700	D	D	N
Science in Developing Countries	357-9537	A	A	N
U.S.–Israel Binational Science Foundation*	357-7613	D	N	N
U.S.–Industrial Countries Exchange	357-7554	N	N	D

Notes: D = Consult program announcement for deadlines; A = Proposals may be submitted at any time; N = This category of support is not offered.
*This is not an NSF program, but information and applications may be obtained from INT.

Examples of Funded Research:

1) "Governmental Decentralization: Influence on Inter-Regional Settlement Patterns" (cooperative research project) (18-month project; awarded $9,737).

2) "A Study of Intermediate-Sized Cities in Indonesia" (cooperative research project) (1-year project; awarded $10,000).

3) "A Study of Chinese Language Change" (cooperative research project) (1-year project; awarded $19,986).

4) "A Study of Intermediate-Sized Cities in the Philippines" (cooperative research project) (1-year project; awarded $10,000).

5) "U.S.-Italy Workshop on Institutional Performance in Italy" (2-year project; awarded $15,889).

6) "U.S.-France Seminar on Work and the Family" (1-year project; awarded $20,000).

7) "U.S.-Federal Republic of Germany Workshop on Management of Risk" (10-month project; awarded $29,197).

8) "U.S.-Federal Republic of Germany Interdisciplinary Workshop on Constraints on Modeling Real-Time Language Processes" (6-month project; awarded $13,700).

9)   "Toward a Model of Municipal Waste Recycling Applicable to a National Economy" (cooperative research project) (9-month project; awarded $19,000).

10)   "U.S.-Australia-New Zealand Trilateral Seminar/Workshop on Decolonization: African Lessons and Pacific Experience" (6-month project; awarded $18,887).

DIVISION OF RESEARCH INITIATION AND IMPROVEMENT

Alexander J. Morin, Director
Room 1225
1800 G Street, NW
Washington, DC 20550
(202/357-7552)

The Division of Research Initiation and Improvement coordinates a number of NSF programs concerned with the resources of the scientific and technical community as a whole. Specifically, the division is charged with (1) increasing opportunities for women, minority, handicapped, and young investigators and for research faculty from predominantly undergraduate colleges to participate in the nation's scientific and engineering enterprise; and (2) improving access to scientific and technical resources by institutions that presently underuse those resources.

There are several programs within this division offering either individual research support or support for strengthening institutional research capabilities. Most are coordinated with the disciplinary programs within the various research directorates.

Three of the individual support programs are described below.

MINORITY RESEARCH INITIATION

Roosevelt Calbert, Program Director
Room 1225
1800 G Street, NW
Washington, DC 20550
(202/357-7350)

Program: The Minority Research Initiation (MRI) seeks to give greater access to scientific research support to minority groups that are underrepresented in science and engineering. The MRI program provides support for minority faculty members (or those with full-time research appointments) who wish to establish quality research efforts on their campuses, thereby increasing their ability to compete successfully for regular support from the Foundation and other sources. Proposals may be submitted in any field of science or engineering that is generally supported by NSF.

Proposals may be submitted by minority scientists who have full-time status at colleges or universities that have academic programs in the sciences or engineering, and who have not previously received federal research support as faculty members.

No specific deadlines or target dates apply to this program. Review and processing usually take from 6 to 9 months.

Budget: The anticipated budget for this program for FY 1986 was $2.5 million.

Application/Review Process: See the general description of NSF in chapter 4. Proposals are reviewed by the relevant disciplinary programs. Final funding decisions are made by MRI staff.

Funding Mechanisms: MRI projects normally will be supported for a period of up to 3 years and may be extended up to 2 additional years if warranted. The size of awards is generally consistent with the level of awards made by the relevant disciplinary program.

RESEARCH OPPORTUNITIES FOR WOMEN

Margrete S. Klein, Program Director
Room 1225
1800 G Street, NW
Washington, DC 20550
(202/357-7734)

Program: Research Opportunities for Women (ROW) is an NSF initiative to encourage and enable women scientists and engineers to undertake independent research. Women eligible to submit proposals are (1) those who have received their doctorates at least 3 years prior to the submission of a proposal and have not previously served as principal investigators on federally funded research projects, and (2) those with doctorates whose research careers have been interrupted for at least 2 of the past 5 years and who have not served as principal investigators since re-entering a research career.

Budget: Awards through this initiative are funded by the relevant NSF disciplinary program. The Foundation has targeted approximately $2 million for this effort in FY 1986.

Application/Review Process: See the general description of NSF in chapter 4. ROW research proposals are submitted to the relevant disciplinary program for evaluation and funding. Proposals should be submitted in accordance with their target dates or deadlines. Applicants are urged to discuss guidelines with the disciplinary program officer before submitting a formal proposal.

Funding Mechanisms: The size of ROW awards are consistent with the general level of awards in the relevant disciplinary program. ROW projects will be supported up to a maximum period of 3 years, although in exceptional circumstances an extension of up to 2 additional years is possible.

VISITING PROFESSORSHIPS FOR WOMEN

Margrete S. Klein, Program Director
Carol Erlebach, Program Specialist
Room 1225
1800 G Street, NW
Washington, DC 20550
(202/357–7734)

Program: The Visiting Professorships for Women program (VPW) addresses the need to develop full use of the nation's human resources for science and technology. The objectives of the program are to provide opportunities for women to advance their careers in the disciplines of science and engineering supported by NSF and to encourage women to pursue careers in science and engineering by providing greater visibility for women scientists and engineers employed in industry, government, and academic institutions.

Awards by this program enable women experienced in independent research to serve as visiting professors at academic institutions in the United States (and its possession and territories). Grantees undertake advanced research at a university or 4-year college. Research may be conducted independently or in collaboration with others. Grantees must also propose significant activities such as lecturing, counseling, and other interactive means to increase the visibility of women scientists in the academic environment and to provide encouragement for other women to pursue careers in science and engineering. The instructional and other interactive activities may be at the undergraduate or graduate levels, be directed to the community at large, or involve some combination thereof. To be considered, proposals must include substantial attention to these activities as well as to research.

Budget: The FY 1986 budget for this program is approximately $2 million. Supplementary funding by NSF disciplinary programs is possible.

Application/Review Process: See the general description of NSF in chapter 4. The applicant and the host institution are responsible for jointly developing a proposal. The deadline for submission is October 1. Proposals are submitted to the VPW office. The program officer of the disciplinary program most relevant to the proposal selects mail reviewers to evaluate and score the proposal. Once mail review is complete, all proposals, mail review results, and program officer evaluations are presented to a multidisciplinary panel for review and funding recommendations. Final funding decisions are made by NSF staff.

Funding Mechanisms: The usual award is for 1 year of full- or part-time professorship. Awards can be considered for one academic semester, or for periods up to 2 years. Awards generally range from $60,000 to $80,000.

Directorate for Science and Engineering Education

DIVISION OF RESEARCH CAREER DEVELOPMENT

Terrence L. Porter, Director
Room 414
1800 G Street, NW
Washington, DC 20550
(202/357-7536)

The Division of Research Career Development works to assure a steady flow of talented science and engineering students from all sectors and regions of the nation. Major programs of interest to social and behavioral scientists are presented below.

GRADUATE FELLOWSHIPS/MINORITY GRADUATE FELLOWSHIPS

Douglas S. Chapin, Program Director
Room 414
1800 G Street, NW
Washington, DC 20550
(202/357-7856)

Program: The Graduate and Minority Graduate Fellowships programs promote the future strength of the nation's scientific and technological base by offering recognition and support to outstanding graduate students in all fields of science and engineering. Fellowships are awarded for study or work leading to master's or doctoral degrees in the mathematical, physical, biological, and social sciences; engineering; and the history and philosophy of science. Awards are not made in clinical, law, education, or business fields, or in history or social work.

To be eligible, candidates must be U.S. citizens at or near the beginning of their graduate study. Specifically, applicants may not have completed more than 20 semester hours, or the equivalent, beyond the baccalaureate degree.

Graduate Fellowships and Minority Graduate Fellowships are identical except that Minority Fellowships are limited to U.S. citizens who are American Indian, Black, Eskimo or Aleutian, Pacific Islander, or Hispanic.

Budget: The FY 1986 budget for this program is approximately $27 million.

Application/Review Process: See the general description of NSF in chapter 4. Applications are generally due in November. Applicants are evaluated on the basis of academic records, recommendations, and Graduate Record Examination scores. Applications are reviewed by panels of scientists selected by the National Research Council. Final selection of awardees are made by NSF.

Funding Mechanisms: Fellows receive a stipend of $11,100 for each 12-month tenure. An annual cost-of-education allowance of $6,000 is made available to the fellow's institution for each year of tenure in lieu of tuition and fees. Support may be awarded for up to 3 years.

NATO POSTDOCTORAL FELLOWSHIPS IN SCIENCE

Terrence L. Porter, Division Director
Room 414
1800 G Street, NW
Washington, DC 20550
(202/357–7536)

Program: The North Atlantic Treaty Organization (NATO) offers a postdoctoral fellowship program to promote the closer collaboration among scientists in various nations. At the request of the State Department, the NSF administers the fellowship program. The fellowships support research and/or study by young scientists at institutions located in NATO member nations or other countries that cooperate with NATO.

NATO fellows must have a Ph.D. in a field of science that is generally supported by NSF and must devote full-time to scientific research at the postdoctoral level during the period of the fellowship. Applicants are evaluated on the basis of scientific competence, the potential for continued professional growth, and the potential for furthering international collaboration in science.

Budget: Funding for this program is provided by NATO. The program anticipates making approximately 50 awards in FY 1986.

Application/Review Process: The deadline for applications is generally November 1, with award announcements made the following February. Applications are reviewed by ad hoc peer panels primarily composed of European specialists.

Funding Mechanisms: Fellows receive a 1-year stipend of $18,000, plus dependent allowances, travel costs, and research-related expenses.

PRESIDENTIAL YOUNG INVESTIGATOR AWARDS

W. F. Oettle, Program Director
Room 414
1800 G Street, NW
Washington, DC 20550
(202/357-9466)

Program: The Presidential Young Investigator Awards are made to outstanding young science and engineering faculty. The awards are made to promising researchers near the beginning of their academic careers and are intended to help universities attract and retain outstanding young Ph.D.s who might otherwise pursue nonteaching careers.

Scholars from all fields of science supported by NSF may be nominated for these awards. To date few awards have been made to social and behavioral scientists; priority consideration has been given to the mathematical, physical, and biological sciences and engineering. The solicitation for 1986 nominees specified that at least half of the awards would be made in engineering fields.

Budget: The FY 1986 budget for this program allocated $6 million for 100 new awards.

Application/Review Process: U.S. institutions granting doctorates in at least one of the fields supported by NSF are eligible to participate. Nominations may be submitted from any science or engineering department in an eligible institution. Eligible institutions may nominate, for faculty awards, both current and prospective members of their faculty who are early in their careers and who are holding or have been offered tenure track positions at the time of nomination. Also eligible for nomination are promising graduate students and recent doctoral recipients for prefaculty awards.

The deadline for applications is usually in July. Applications are reviewed first in the appropriate NSF disciplinary program and then by staff of the Division of Research Career and Development.

Funding Mechanisms: Minimum awards are $25,000. In addition, NSF will provide up to $37,5000 of additional funds per year on a dollar-for-dollar matching basis for contributions from industrial sources (normally private, for-profit corporations), resulting in a total possible annual support of up to $100,000. Matching funds may be in either cash or permanent research equipment.

Nuclear Regulatory Commission

HUMAN FACTORS PROGRAM

Daniel Jones, Program Manager
Division of Human Factors Technology, AR-5200
Washington, DC 20555
(301/492–4846)

Program: The Human Factors Program of the Nuclear Regulatory Commission (NRC) supports research relating to the public understanding of nuclear safety, practical knowledge and technical information concerning nuclear technology, and the protection of public safety. The program includes, but is not limited to, support of professional meetings, symposia and conferences, as well as research projects. Projects are usually quite technical in nature.

Areas of research which may be of interest to social and behavioral scientists include behavioral observation/control, personnel evaluation and performance, psychological testing, value-impact analysis, and economic incentives. In recent years few awards have been made for social and behavioral science topics. However, research proposals in these areas are welcome. Changes in current regulations now under consideration may lead to a major effort in the area of psychological testing. Prospective applicants are encouraged to contact the Human Factors Office with proposal ideas.

Budget: In FY 1985 the Human Factors Program budget was approximately $2 million. The projected FY 1986 budget was approximately $1.2 million. Of this amount, 20% to 25% goes to unsolicited proposals. Much of the budget is allocated to the Department of Energy national laboratories; these labs frequently subcontract to private industry.

Application/Review Process: Most proposals are unsolicited. Periodically an announcement of funds available is published in the *Commerce Business Daily.* It is important, however, to contact the program manager to discuss prospective proposals.

The Division of Contracts of the NRC routes proposals to the proper offices. Often more than one office reviews incoming proposals. The review process is conducted by NRC staff and takes approximately 60 to 90 days. Final funding decisions are made by the branch chiefs.

Funding Mechanisms: Any person or organization is eligible to receive funding through this program. Most funds are awarded through contracts, although some grants are awarded as well.

Example of Funded Research
1)   "Standards for Psychological Assessment of Nuclear Facility Personnel."
2)   "Behavioral Reliability Program for the Nuclear Industry."

Smithsonian Institution

Established as a national museum under the trusteeship of the U.S. Congress nearly 150 years ago, the Smithsonian Institution is an archive complex and research organization of world importance.

Through its museums, research facilities, archives, and other reference resources, the Smithsonian has staff expertise and material holdings of central importance to the research interests of many social and behavioral scientists. The following summary is provided to identify areas in which Smithsonian activities and/or holdings are particularly strong:

1) American history, American material and folk culture, and the history of music and musical instruments;

2) history of science and technology;

3) history of art, design, and the decorative arts;

4) anthropology, archaeology, linguistics, and ethnic studies;

5) evolutionary, systematic, behavioral, environmental, and radiation biology;

6) geological sciences and astrophysics;

7) conservation, archeometry, museum studies, and other areas of museological concern.

Through the academic and grant programs managed by the Office of Fellowships and Grants, the Smithsonian encourages access to its collections, staff specialists, and reference resources by visiting scholars, scientists, and students. Most grants and awards are for research at the Smithsonian's own facilities. There are, however, a limited number of grants available for field study. Because of the broad scope of the Smithsonian's interests, virtually all the social and behavioral science disciplines have subfields with interests that would make them candidates to conduct research under the auspices of the Smithsonian.

OFFICE OF FELLOWSHIPS AND GRANTS

Roberta W. Rubinoff, Director
Jackie Thompson Rand, Academic Programs Specialist
Room 3300
L'Enfant Plaza
Washington, DC 20560
(202/287-3271 or 287-3321)

Program: The Office of Fellowships and Grants has the central management and administrative responsibility for Smithsonian research grants, fellowships, and visiting academic appointment programs. With the exception of a small number of awards reserved for physical scientists, all of the programs offer extensive opportunities for social and behavioral scientists. The offerings are as follows:

1) Smithsonian Fellowship Program

a) Graduate Student Fellowships are for students actively engaged in graduate study at any level to conduct research for 10-week periods under the guidance of Smithsonian staff members. (26 were awarded in 1985)

b) Predoctoral Fellowships are offered for periods of 6 to 12 months for scientists and scholars who have completed preliminary course work and examinations for the Ph.D. and are engaged in dissertation research. Candidates must have approval of their universities to conduct doctoral research at the Smithsonian. (22 were awarded in 1985)

c) Postdoctoral Fellowships are offered for 6 to 24 months for investigators who have completed the doctoral degree less than 7 years before the application deadline. Candidates with the equivalent of the doctorate in experience, training, and accomplishment may be considered. (46 were awarded in 1985)

d) Senior Postdoctoral Fellowships are offered for 3 to 12 months for persons more than 7 years beyond the doctoral degree. Applications may be made up to 2 years in advance of the starting date. Stipends are higher than the postdoctoral stipend, and are often matched by other sources such as sabbatical salary. (2 were awarded in 1985)

2) Other Fellowships and Visiting Awards (of interest to social and behavioral scientists)

a) Daniel and Florence Guggenheim Fellowship is awarded for research related to technology transfer, planetary exploration, or the history of aviation.

b) A. Verville Fellowship is awarded for analysis of major trends, developments, and accomplishments in aerospace history.

c) Fellowships in Materials Analysis support applications of techniques of the physical sciences to problems in art history, anthropology, archeology, and the history of technology.

d) Regents Fellowships are based on nomination from within the Smithsonian and offered to distinguished scholars and scientists for research in residence at any of the Smithsonian's bureaus. (3 were awarded in 1985)

e) The Charles A. Lindbergh Chair is awarded in the history of aeronautics.

f) The Martin Marietta Chair in Space History was established to attract scholars to carry on work at the Museum in the history of flight or other topics related to the history of space science and technology.

g) James E. Webb Fellowships are for development of management skills for cultural and scientific nonprofit organizations.

h) Faculty Fellowships provide opportunities for minority faculty members to conduct research in association with members of the Smithsonian professional research staff, using facilities and collections of the Institution.

i) The Rockefeller Foundation Residency Program in the Humanities awards postdoctoral fellowships for up to 12 months in residence at the National Museum of African Art and the Center for Asian Art to scholars in African art history and anthropology with an emphasis on material culture and Asian art history. (2 were awarded in 1985)

j) International Fellowships are for researchers from other countries to conduct internationally-oriented historical and scientific studies at the National Air and Space Museum.

3) Appointments for Visiting Scientists, Scholars, and Students. Support for investigators wishing to conduct research projects at Smithsonian facilities is sometimes offered by individual bureaus of the Institution. Scholars and students with outside sources of funding are also encouraged to utilize the Institution resources and facilities. The Office of Fellowships and Grants facilitates these visiting appointments.

a) Short-Term Visits are for scholars and students seeking access to Smithsonian facilities and staff for short periods of time—generally less than one month.

b) Short-Term Appointments at the Smithsonian Tropical Research Institute allow visiting researchers to work on any aspect of tropical biology and such allied subjects as the climates, ecology, and paleoecology of human populations, geology, paleobotany, and paleozoology of tropical regions.

c) Native American Program is open to North American Indians, Inuit, Aleut, Canadian Natives, Alaskan Natives, and Native Hawaiians to pursue research and internships at the Smithsonian.

4) Internships

a) Academic Internships for students and other qualified applicants are available in most of the Smithsonian bureaus and programs. They may range from a few weeks to a year and are generally arranged individually, directly with a bureau.

b) Internships in Museum Practices are for undergraduate and graduate students and museum professionals. Internships are individually arranged, usually for 3 to 6 months, and do not offer a stipend.

c) Summer Internships for High School Seniors.

5) Special Internship Programs

a) Minority Internships are available for undergraduate and graduate minority students.

b) Work/Learn Programs at the Smithsonian Environmental Research Center allow students to conduct studies on topics such as terrestrial or estuarine environmental research, resource planning and decision-making, and environmental education research and development. Programs are usually for 2 to 3 months.

c) Sidney and Celia Siegel Fellowship are summer appointments at the Cooper-Hewitt Museum, New York City.

d) Summer Internships at the National Museum of American Art are for upper division undergraduates with interests in areas such as art history and American Studies.

e) Graduate Internships at the National Museum of American Art are for graduate students in art history or American studies.

f) Internships at the National Museum of African Art are available for upper undergraduate or graduate students in areas such as art history, anthropology, or the study of African culture.

g) Internships at the National Air and Space Museum are available for both undergraduate and graduate students.

h) Research Traineeships at the National Zoological Park, Washington, DC, are summer programs for students.

6) Grants Program. The National Museum Act provides grants for training in conservation and museum practice.

[Note: In 1985 the administration of the Special Foreign Currency Program was transferred from the Office of Fellowships and Grants to the Smithsonian's Directorate of International Activities (see below).]

Budget: In 1985 the Office of Fellowships and Grants awarded approximately $1.7 million—$1.4 million from Smithsonian trust sources and $.3 million from federal sources.

Application/Review Process: Interested scholars should consult with the Office of Fellowships and Grants about deadlines and specific application procedures for the various awards and programs. Because the Smithsonian bureaus enjoy considerable autonomy, it is also recommended that scholars contact appropriate professional staff members directly. Such contacts are important not only to determine whether the Smithsonian's research and staff resources are appropriate for the proposed project, but also because the individual bureaus may have additional financial resources available internally. Office of Fellowships and Grants staff can be helpful in facilitating contact. The Office's annual publication, "Smithsonian Opportunities for Research and Study in History, Art, Science," details both the awards programs and the professional staff and resources of the Institution.

Most applications require two letters of recommendation which may not be provided by Smithsonian staff. Fellowship office staff screen for eligibility and completeness; Smithsonian professional staff from the appropriate bureau(s) review applications. On occasion, outside reviews are sought, but most decisions are based on recommendations of selection committees composed of Smithsonian staff members. Pre-application contact is recommended (though not required) since, in most instances, the Smithsonian researchers will be consulting, advising, or in other ways working with successful applicants.

Funding Mechanisms: Financial arrangements accompanying awards vary. In 1986 the range for 1-year fellowship stipends is: Predoctoral, $11,000; Postdoctoral, $18,000; Senior postdoctoral, $25,000. In addition, fellowship holders receive a $1,000 research expense allotment, plus transportation to and from Washington. A 10-week graduate summer fellowship carries a stipend of $2,500. Some awards permit additional grant support from non-Smithsonian sources and/or support from more than one Smithsonian source.

DIRECTORATE OF INTERNATIONAL ACTIVITIES

SPECIAL FOREIGN CURRENCY PROGRAM

Francine Berkowitz, Program Manager
Room 3300
L'Enfant Plaza
Washington, DC 20560
(202/287–3321)

Program: The Special Foreign Currency Program awards grants to U.S. institutions of higher education for studies in countries where the United States holds "excess" foreign currencies, derived largely from the sale of agricultural commodities under Public Law 480. Expenditures under the program require both "excess" currency and a cooperative agreement between the United States and the host country. In early 1986 the program offered awards for work in Burma, Guinea, Poland, and Pakistan. An agreement to resume projects in India in 1986 was a possibility.

The program supports individual or group research projects, research development, conferences and conference travel, exchange visits, publications, and museum professional programs. The program offers opportunities for social scientists from all disciplines but is particularly appropriate for anthropology, archaeology, cultural history, linguistics, and political science.

Budget: This program is authorized to grant up to $1.5 million in FY 1986.

Application/Review Process: There is one competition annually with proposals due November 1. Funding decisions are made by Smithsonian staff based on peer review panel recommendations. Peer review panels are composed of university-based scholars.

Funding Mechanisms: Awards may cover international and local travel, living allowances, and research expenses and are made entirely in local currencies. The program does not discourage grantees from seeking additional funds to cover dollar and or other hard currency expenses.

U.S. Arms Control and Disarmament Agency

The U.S. Arms Control and Disarmament Agency (ACDA) is charged with providing the Executive branch and Congress with recommendations concerning U.S. arms control and disarmament policy and assessing the effects of these recommendations on U.S. foreign policy, national security, and the economy. The Agency is concerned with essential scientific, economic, political, legal, social, psychological, military, and technological information on which arms control and disarmament policy is based. To this end, ACDA is authorized to conduct, support, and coordinate research for policy formulation. The Agency comprises four topical bureaus: Multilateral Affairs, Verification and Intelligence, Strategic Programs, and Nuclear and Weapons Control.

A portion of the Agency's research budget goes to extramural contracts. Requests for proposals are published in the *Commerce Business Daily.* On occasion, unsolicited proposals may be funded.

Two ACDA program described below, the Visiting Fellows Program and Humphrey Doctoral Fellowships, are particularly relevant for social and behavioral scientists.

VISITING SCHOLARS PROGRAM

Nancy Aderholdt, Personnel Management Specialist
Room 5722, ACDA
Washington, DC 20451
(202/647–2035)

Program: The ACDA administers a program for visiting scholars in the field of arms control and disarmament. Officially titled the William C. Foster Fellows Program, it is designed to give faculty members the opportunity to participate actively in the arms control and disarmament activities of the Agency and to give the Agency the perspective and expertise such persons can offer.

Visiting Scholars are assigned to one of ACDA's four topical bureaus. With the exception of the Bureau of Strategic Programs, which specifically seeks a physical scientist, appointments are possible for a broad range of social scientists. Candidates for the Bureau of Multilateral Affairs should be knowledgeable in areas of European political and military issues and NATO defense doctrine. The Bureau of Verification and Intelligence generally seeks a physical scientist, operations analyst, or an expert in Soviet strategy and doctrine. The Bureau of Nuclear and Weapons Control, responsible for ACDA's economic analysis work and research on nuclear nonproliferation issues, seeks candidates with a strong background in national security planning, weapons characteristics and capabilities, or political-military conditions in developing countries. Specific needs of the individual Bureaus are identified for each competition.

The selection of fellows is based on the expertise and service they can provide ACDA rather than a general interest in arms control or the pursuit of the scholars' own research.

Budget: The ACDA anticipated selecting four Visiting Fellows in FY 1986.

Application/Review Process: An annual announcement of the Visiting Fellows Program and specific needs for each Bureau is published in the *Federal Register.* Applications are reviewed by ACDA staff.

Applications should be made in the form of a letter indicating one's interest and expertise, a CV, and any other materials such as letters of reference and samples of published articles. The deadline for applications varies. For the FY 1986 competition, the deadline was January 31, 1986.

Funding Mechanisms: Fellows are selected for 1-year assignments with the agency and receive pay based on their regular salary rates plus travel and relocation costs.

HUBERT H. HUMPHREY DOCTORAL FELLOWSHIPS IN ARMS CONTROL AND DISARMAMENT

Matthew Murphy, Program Manager
Room 5847, ACDA
Washington, DC 20451
(202/647-8716)

Program: The Hubert H. Humphrey Doctoral Fellowships in Arms Control and Disarmament are designed to encourage specialized training and research in the arms control field. Students across a wide range of disciplines—including, but not limited to, political science, economics, law, sociology, psychology, public policy, operations research, and area studies—may apply. Research proposals should be designed to contribute to a better understanding of current and future arms control and disarmament issues. Although special consideration is given to research with direct policy or technical implications, innovative theoretical or empirical efforts will also be considered. Historical, quantitative, and policy analyses are all appropriate for this program.

Research topics that have traditionally been supported by ACDA include:

1)   strategic arms control;

2)   nuclear non-proliferation;

3) multilateral and regional arms control;

4) weapons development and acquisition;

5) conventional arms sales and technology transfer;

6) verification and compliance;

7) economics of arms production and sales;

8) the public and arms control;

9) arms control as a component of national security policy.

The program is open only to U.S. citizens or nationals who, by the date the fellowship begins, will have completed all academic requirements for the doctorate except their dissertation. Dissertation proposals must have been approved in accordance with university procedures. J.D. candidates preparing to enter their third or final year of law school are also eligible if the proposed research project would represent a substantial amount of credit toward their third-year requirements and would result in a paper that would, for example, be appropriate for publication in a law review.

Budget: The ACDA anticipated making five fellowship awards in FY 1986.

Application/Review Process: Applications are generally due in March. Proposals are evaluated on the basis of scientific merit, project feasibility, applicants' academic record, and the recommendations of references. A committee of ACDA staff and, on occasion, academic and private sector consultants review applications.

Funding Mechanisms: Fellowships are normally for a 1-year period, commencing either in September or January. Fellows receive a stipend of $5,000. In addition, the host institution receives up to $3,400 for tuition and fees.

Examples of Funded Research:
1) "The Emerging Structure of Strategic Arms Control Nuclear Weapon Policy, 1979–1983."

2) "The Politics of Deterrence: A Comparative Assessment of American and Soviet Defense Policy, 1960–1964."

3) "European Security and Domestic Politics in France, 1974–1984."

4) "The Application of Just War Principles to Nuclear War in Three Contemporary Theorists: Michael Walzer, Paul Ramsey, and William O'Brien."

5) "The Strategic Defense Initiative: Implications for NATO Strategy."

U.S. Information Agency

Fulbright Scholar Program

The Fulbright program was initiated by the Fulbright Act of August 1, 1946, which authorized the financing of educational exchange by the use of excess foreign currencies abroad. The purpose of the Fulbright program is "to enable the government of the United States to increase mutual understanding between the people of the U.S. and the people of other countries." Grants are made to U.S. citizens and nationals of other countries for university lecturing, advanced research, graduate study, and teaching in elementary and secondary schools.

The U.S. Information Agency (USIA) funds the Fulbright program and plans and administers the program with the help of binational commissions and foundations in over 40 countries that have executive agreements with the United States for continuing exchange programs, and with U.S. embassies in other countries—totaling about 120 countries each year. A number of cooperating agencies in the United States also assist USIA in administering the program. The Council for International Exchange of Scholars (CIES), affiliated with the American Council of Learned Societies, is the principal private cooperating agency for the administration of Fulbright scholar grants for advanced research and university teaching.

RESEARCH AWARDS AND LECTURESHIPS

Council for International Exchange of Scholars
11 Dupont Circle
Washington, DC 20036
(202/939-5401)

Program: The CIES administers Fulbright grants in five categories:

1) Research (approximately 300 awards are offered in most disciplines).

2) Lecturing (over 700 awards for university lectureships, many of which also offer some opportunity for research).

3) Lecturing/Research (awards are designed to combine both activities).

4) Junior Lecturing and Junior Research (designed primarily for younger scholars who are recent Ph.D.s or advanced Ph.D. candidates).

5) Travel (awards provide round-trip transportation to the country where the scholar will lecture or conduct research).

Grants are available for virtually all social and behavioral science fields and other related areas such as architecture and urban planning, business administration, communications and journalism, computer science, education, environmental sciences, library science, musicology, philosophy and theology, and social work.

For the 1986–87 academic year awards were available in approximately 100 countries. Countries vary as to the specific awards available, academic year, language requirements, benefits, and application deadlines. Prospective applicants should contact CIES to determine what opportunities exist in their field.

In addition to research and lectureship awards offered for individual countries, CIES also administers several regional awards:

1) African Regional Research Program (Awards are available in all academic fields for research in one or more African countries over periods of 3 to 9 months. African specialists are encouraged to apply, but applications are also welcome from scholars who may have limited or no previous experience in Africa. For information, call Ellen Kornegay, 202/939–5424.)

2) American Republics Research Program (For 1986–87, 20 research awards were available, each for 6 months, in any discipline for one or more countries of the Caribbean, Mexico, or South America. Applications are encouraged from scholars whose projects involve collaboration with colleagues in the host country and who are willing to give occasional lectures. For information, call Anne Carpenter, 202/939–5462.)

3) Central American Republics Research and Lecturing Program (This is an expanded program of awards for research and lecturing in Belize, Costa Rica, El Salvador, Guatemala, Honduras, Nicaragua, and Panama. Research awards are for 3 to 9 months in any field in one or several countries of the area. Lecturing awards are for 6 to 12 months in selected fields. For information, call Leslie Hunter, 202/939–5463.)

4) Islamic Civilization Research Program (Awards for 3 to 9 months are offered in any field for research on some aspect of civilization, society, or science in one or more Muslim countries or among Muslim communities of Africa, Asia, and the Middle East. Research may be on contemporary or historical topics; collaborative research with foreign scholars is encouraged. For information, call Renee Taft, 202/939–5468.)

5) Middle Eastern/South Asia Regional Lecturing Program (Applicants may propose a lecturing program of 4 to 9 months in any two of the following countries: Bahrain, Bangladesh, Mauritania, Nepal, Qattar, Saudi Arabia, Sri Lanka, and the United Arab Emirates. Some countries have expressed preference for certain fields, although scholars in any field may apply. For Middle East projects, call Gary Garrison, 202/939–5470; for South Asia projects, call Renee Taft, 202/939–5468.)

6) NATO Research Fellowship Program (Awards are limited to the social sciences on topics related to the North Atlantic Alliance. Research may be undertaken in one or more member countries. For information, call Steven Blodgett, 202/939–5416.)

7) Southeast Asian Regional Lectureships (Lecturing awards are available in broadcast journalism, TEFL/applied linguistics, and educational administration. For information, call Mary Ernst, 202/939–5475.)

8) Southeast Asian Regional Research Program (Awards are made for 3 to 9 months to conduct research on Southeast Asian society and culture. Eligible fields include the humanities, social sciences, communications, education, law, and business. Countries of study include Burma, Indonesia, Malaysia, Philippines, Singapore, and Thailand. Proposals for inter-country travel and collaborative research will be considered, except for Burma. For information, call Mary Ernst, 202/939–5475.)

9) Western European Regional Research Program (Awards are made for research on European politics, society, and culture, past and present. Applications are accepted in any discipline in the social sciences and humanities, with preference given to scholars with professional interest in European studies. For information, call Steven Blodgett, 202/939–5416.)

Application/Review Process: Deadlines and specific eligibility requirements for individual programs and world areas vary and may be obtained by contacting CIES. Applications undergo a two-stage peer review by CIES advisory committees, first by subject matter specialists and then by an interdisciplinary group of geographic area specialists. After scholars are nominated by CIES for awards, their applications are sent for further review to the Board of Foreign Scholarships, to Fulbright binational commissions or U.S. embassies abroad, and to prospective host institutions. The USIA or Fulbright commissions abroad notify candidates of award decisions.

Funding Mechanisms: Grant benefits include round-trip travel for the grantee and for a principal dependent of a grantee when the appointment is for a full academic year; a maintenance allowance determined by the grant category, country and duration of the grant, and family status; incidental allowances for baggage, essential books and services, and travel within the host country; housing or housing allowance in certain countries; and tuition allowance in certain countries for tuition costs of dependent children.

Examples of Funded Research:
1) "Research in Political Science: Relationship Between Elections and Economic and Political Development in Botswana" (9 months; University of Botswana, Gaborone, Botswana).

2) "Research in Educational Psychology" (10 months; Max Planck Institute of Psychological Research, Munich, West Germany).

3) "Lecturing and Research in Feminist Theology" (2 months; Lund and Uppsala Universities, Sweden).

4) "Research in Study of Justice" (7 months; University of Costa Rica, San Jose, Costa Rica).

5) "Research in Linguistics: Comparative Grammar of Highland East Cushitic and Acquisition of Amharic as First Language" (6 months; Addis Ababa University, Ethiopia).

6) "Research in Labor Law and Industrial Relations" (9 months; Germany, Sweden, and United Kingdom).

7) "Lecturing and Research on Women Workers in 20th Century Peru" (5 months; various institutions in Peru).

8) "Research on Innovation Process in Firms and Industries" (6 months; Massey University, Palmerston, New Zealand).

9) "Research in Economics: Alternative Development Strategies, Terms of Trade Between Industry and Agriculture" (5 months; University of Zagreb, Yugoslavia).

10) "Research in Detribalization Among Philippine Negritos" (9 months; Ateneo de Manila University, Philippines).

UNIVERSITY AFFILIATIONS PROGRAM

William Dant, Coordinator
E/AS - USIA
301 4th Street, SW
Washington, DC 20547
(202/485–8489)

Program: The University Affiliations Program, a component of the Fulbright program, is administered by the USIA to support institutional partnerships between U.S. and non-U.S. institutions of higher education. The goal of the program is to facilitate bilateral institutional relationships which promote mutual understanding through faculty and staff exchanges. Funding through this program is for projects that assign a U.S. faculty or staff member to the partner institution for teaching, lecturing, or research; maintain that person on full salary and benefits; and receive visiting faculty from the partner institution. Proposals may be funded either to establish new affiliations or for the enhancement of existing programs not previously funded by the University Affiliations Program. Grants are awarded on a one-time basis and are designed to serve as "seed money."

The annual announcement of funding opportunities specifies eligible world areas and disciplines to be supported. Most projects focus on the humanities, social sciences, education, and communication, although not all fields are eligible in some world areas. World areas are defined as Africa, American Republic, East Asia/Pacific, Europe, and Near East/South Asia. In addition, special initiatives may be designated. In FY 1986 special initiatives included projects on the Bicentennial of the U.S. Constitution, programs in Central American countries, and grants for community and junior colleges.

Budget: In FY 1986 funding was available for 25 grants through the general competition, 5 grants for the special competition for Central America, 5 grants for the Constitution Bicentennial, and 5 grants for community and junior colleges.

Application/Review Process: An annual announcement of the University Affiliations Program is published in the *Federal Register.* The deadline is usually in February. The review process is conducted in three stages—technical, academic, and Agency. Technically eligible proposals are forwarded to a nonfederal committee of academic peers for a substantive review. Proposals recommended by the academic committee are evaluated by USIA staff and funding decisions are made.

Funding Mechanisms: Grants are to be used only for participant travel costs and modest maintenance allowances. Institutional overhead is not allowable. The maximum grant amount ranges from $50,000 to $60,000, depending on the country involved. Support may be requested for a 2- or 3-year period.

United States Institute of Peace

The United States Institute of Peace was created by Public Law 98–525 to support the conduct of interdisciplinary research on the causes of war and the elements of peace and the successes and failures of diplomacy, and to promote peace education/research at graduate and postgraduate levels. In addition, the Institute is to devise public education and training programs, develop materials for publication, and appoint scholars from the United States and abroad for up to 2 years to pursue scholarly inquiry on international peace.

The Institute was appropriated $4 million in FY 1986. A Board of Directors was appointed and confirmed by the Senate in late 1985. As of January 1986, the Board had not met, no staff had been appointed, and no decisions had been made as to the allocation of funds. Individuals interested in the current status of the Institute are welcome to contact COSSA, 1200 17th Street, NW, Suite 520, Washington, DC 20036 (202/887–6166).

Woodrow Wilson International Center for Scholars

The Woodrow Wilson International Center for Scholars is the nation's official memorial to its 28th president. Established in 1968 to commemorate both the scholarly depth and public concerns of Woodrow Wilson, the Center seeks to carry out this mandate through a program of advanced research and communication to foster interaction between the world of ideas and the world of affairs.

Since its inception, the Wilson Center has been housed in the Smithsonian Institution, but operates as an independent agency.

RESIDENTIAL FELLOWSHIP PROGRAM

Ann Sheffield, Assistant Director for Fellowships, and Program Secretary for History, Culture, and Society
Room 331
Smithsonian Institution Building
Washington, DC 20560
(202/357-2841)

Program: The Wilson Center offers resident fellowships to advanced postdoctoral scholars in the humanities and the social sciences. The Center's fellowships are awarded in several programs:

1) History, Culture, and Society (general program).

2) American Society and Politics.

3) Kennan Institute for Advanced Russian Studies.

4) Latin American Program.

5) International Security Studies Program.

6) Asia Program.

7) East European Program.

8) West European Program.

Awards are for full-time research and/or writing.

For academic participants, eligibility is limited to those holding the doctorate. Successful applicants generally have published at least one book beyond the dissertation; for participants from nonacademic backgrounds, equivalent professional achievement is required.

Budget: In FY 1985 federal funding for fellowships was $1.2 million; the Center added approximately $100,000 from private sources. The federal contribution for FY 1986 is anticipated to be $1.2 million. Forty-five fellowships were offered and accepted in FY 1985.

Application/Review Process: The deadline for receipt of applications is October 1, with decisions by mid-February. Application requirements include identification of three to five scholars who are familiar with the applicants' work. A seven-member review panel meets in December. Final decisions are made by the Fellowship Committee of the Board of Trustees of the Wilson Center.

Funding Mechanisms: Fellowships vary from 4 months to 1 year, with most awards for 9 months. Fellowship awards average $2,500 to $3,000 per month. Applicants are encouraged to seek other sources of funding (e.g., foundation grants, sabbatical support, other fellowships).

CONGRESSIONAL AGENCIES

U.S. General Accounting Office

GAO DOCTORAL RESEARCH PROGRAM

Dominic G. DelGuidice, Coordinator
Room 7614
441 G Street, NW
Washington, DC 20548
(202/275-5495)

The U.S. General Accounting Office (GAO) is an independent agency in the legislative branch and provides Congress with information, analyses, and recommendations concerning operations of the government. The professional staff encompasses such diverse academic disciplines as accounting, business and public administration, engineering, economics, political science, operations research, and law. The GAO Doctoral Research Program funds research opportunities for up to five doctoral students who have completed all requirements for the doctorate except completing the dissertation. Selected students are actively involved in GAO work while conducting a project and gathering data for their dissertation.

Applicants whose area of dissertation research coincides with current GAO research interests are selected for the program. Participants come from virtually all academic disciplines. Areas of interest to the GAO include general government; human resources; national security and international affairs; resources, community, and economic development, accounting and financial management; information and technology management; program evaluation and methodology; privacy; national productivity; intergovernmental relations; science and technology policy, research, and development.

Students who have sufficient relevant work experience will receive temporary appointments at the GS-11 level ($26,381 per year). An assistantship in teaching or academic research may count toward this work experience. Other students are offered GS-9 level appointments ($21,804 per year).

The deadline for applications is generally in February.

Chapter **6**

The Federal Statistical Agencies

There are five major federal agencies that collect, analyze, and disseminate data on virtually all aspects of society and individuals within that society. They are the Bureau of the Census, the Bureau of Justice Statistics, the Bureau of Labor Statistics, the Center for Statistics (formerly the National Center on Education Statistics), and the National Center for Health Statistics.

The statistical agencies are particularly important to social and behavioral scientists—not because they are major funders of extramural research, but because they serve as important data resources for the research community. In addition, these agencies make contract agreements for data collection and analysis and, in varying degrees, seek input from academic and nonacademic researchers on ways to improve survey methodology.

Because all the major statistical agencies have unique and important relationships with the research community, we invited officials of each agency to prepare a statement describing their enterprises, focusing in particular on their interaction with social and behavioral scientists.

Bureau of the Census

The Bureau of the Census is known as the "Factfinder for the Nation." It collects demographic and economic data throughout the country, from year to year, and from one generation to the next; consequently, its statistics for different areas or time periods are useful for comparative study. Data collected from the censuses and surveys offer a rich supply of information for use in research.

The Census Bureau is responsible for taking all censuses authorized by law, including those of population, housing, agriculture, retail and wholesale trade, service industries, manufactures, mineral industries, transportation, construction industries, and governments. In addition, the Bureau conducts sample surveys on a monthly, quarterly, and annual basis. These surveys encompass some of the same subjects as the censuses, providing current information on social and economic conditions. The Bureau also tabulates and publishes monthly and annual statistics on U.S. foreign trade and produces annual county population estimates. The Census Bureau conducts research on specific subjects as well as basic and applied research on statistical methodology for censuses and surveys. Examples of research by subject are immigration, the family, fertility, the elderly, educational attainment, income, poverty, and economics of industry. Research on statistical methodology includes that on sampling, imputation, demographic methods, adjustment for census undercount, nonsampling errors, models for estimation, questionnaire design, alternative data collection methods, quality control, and cognitive factors in response.

Some ways the Bureau can provide research support to social and behavioral scientists are through (1) Joint Statistical Agreements, (2) the ASA/NSF/Census Research Program, and (3) the Annual Research Conference Series. Each of these programs cuts across many areas of Bureau activity.

Joint Statistical Agreements. Although the Census Bureau does not have grant funds for research, it supports research at nonprofit and educational institutions through Joint Statistical Agreements. The agency currently has agreements with several universities under which both parties share the costs and benefits, with the university paying from 25% to 50% of the costs. Joint Statistical Agreements are not solicited; most are initiated through discussions of mutual interests between researchers and Census Bureau staff.

Topics of current agreements include estimation of the sizes of a population and subpopulations to adjust for nonresponse, investigation of methodology to adjust for nonresponse in longitudinal surveys, and the development of models to estimate gross change tables for labor force classification when these changes are subject to various errors.

ASA/NSF/Census Research Program. The Program, which began in 1977, brings research fellows and research associates to the Census Bureau to do research with census data and to interact with Bureau staff. The program is jointly funded by the National Science Foundation and the Census Bureau and is jointly administered by the American Statistical Association (ASA) and the Bureau. Research fellows generally are university faculty, while research associates are advanced graduate students or recent Ph.D.s. Some 25 fellows and 24 associates have participated in the program to date, working on a broad range of research projects in statistics, economics, demography, and sociology.

Research projects have included analysis of missing data in sample surveys, effects of proxy- versus self-reporting on survey response variance, valuation of nonmoney income, models for a firm's productive capacity and its utilization, analysis of firm behavior in oligopolistic industries, cohort-of-entry analysis of data on the foreign-born, demography of American Indians, alternative household definitions in the Survey of Income and Program Participation, and studies of racial occupational and income inequality.

Research can be interdisciplinary, as in previous projects on economic-demographic modeling of interstate migration and time series methods for demographic projections.

Fellowship candidates submit research proposals to the Bureau describing in detail the project they wish to pursue as part of their application. Proposals are sought for applied research using Census Bureau operations or data. Further information on the program can be obtained by calling Arnold Reznek, Coordinator, at 301/763–3848.

Annual Research Conference Series (ARC). The ARC Series was established in March 1985 to provide a forum for academic, private sector, and government researchers, including those from other countries, to exchange and discuss current research and methods in areas relevant to Census Bureau programs. The first conference focused on methodological issues; the second one focused on nonsampling error, including a special track on issues of census undercount research. As themes are developed, researchers from around the world are invited to participate and prepare reports offering solutions or suggesting other avenues to further develop and improve on current research. Modest reimbursement for these reports and travel expenses to the conference are offered. For further information on the ARC Series, call Carolee Bush at 301/763–7976.

Information Services and Support. In addition to research opportunities, the Bureau offers a variety of user services and programs to researchers around the country, many at little or no charge. Activities include information services, training seminars and workshops, and consultation and technical assistance, to name a few.

The Bureau also has a College Curriculum Support Project designed to help university instructors integrate information on census concepts, methodologies, and products into their curricula. As part of this project, the agency prepares basic instructional materials, including textbooks, workbooks, case studies, instructors' guides, and bibliographies.

For information on the activities listed above, write to the Director, Bureau of the Census, Washington, DC 20233.

[Prepared by Barbara A. Bailar, Ph.D., Associate Director for Statistical Standards and Methodology, Bureau of the Census.]

Bureau of Justice Statistics

The Bureau of Justice Statistics (BJS) is the statistical agency of the U.S. Department of Justice. It is mandated by Congress to collect, analyze, publish, and disseminate statistics on crime, victims of crime, criminal offenders, and operations of justice systems at all levels of government throughout the United States. BJS obtains its statistics through periodic surveys and censuses, including:

National Crime Survey. This BJS survey, begun in 1973, produces annual national estimates of the amount of crime against persons and households, victimization rates, the characteristics of victims, criminal events and offenders, reporting of crime to the police, and the reasons for not reporting.

National Prisoner Statistics. An assortment of national censuses and surveys makes up this important component of the BJS statistical program. Censuses produce annual and semi-annual national and state-level data on the numbers of prisoners in state and federal facilities and their demographic characteristics. In addition, every 5 years census data are collected on detailed characteristics of state prisons, such as age of facility, security level, programs offered, confinement space, employment, and operating costs. Also at 5-year intervals, data are collected from a survey of state prisoners. Data collected include criminal histories, incarceration offense, and drug and alcohol use. The National Prisoner Statistics series dates to the early 1900s.

National Jail Statistics. This statistical series consists of two surveys and a census. A survey of jails produces annual estimates of the number of jail inmates and their demographic characteristics. A survey of jail inmates conducted every 5 years produces more extensive information about the jail population of the United States. In addition, a census of jails conducted at 5-year intervals produces detailed national and state-level data on jail facilities throughout the nation.

Capital Punishment. This BJS statistical series produces annual national and state-level data on the numbers and characteristics of persons sentenced to death and those executed. The Capital Punishment series dates to 1930.

Law Enforcement Data. Recognizing that very little national-level administrative and management data in law enforcement exist, BJS commissioned a study of the need for such data, including recommendations as to what types of data should be collected. Following a review of the final report of the study, *Law Enforcement Statistics: The State of the Art,* BJS asked the University of Maryland to submit an application for a research and development program for the collection of law enforcement management and administrative statistics on a national level. This project involves an analysis of existing data sets of police statistics, a survey of small police agencies about their data needs, the development of a survey questionnaire and handbook for a national collection effort, a discussion of various sampling designs, and a pretest of the proposed survey.

Prosecution and Adjudication Data. In 1981 BJS funded the first national survey of indigent defense services since 1973. Data were collected covering staffing levels, salaries, caseload, type of system, funding levels, organizational setting, legislative authority, method of compensation, and attorney selection. Prosecutor Management Information Systems (PROMIS) produces case-tracking data focused on the prosecution and trial of cases for selected municipalities and counties. In 1984 BJS published the second in a series of statistical descriptions of felony case flow in selected prosecutors' offices throughout the country that use PROMIS data. The report analyzed data from 14 jurisdictions for felony cases that reached final disposition in 1979. The next report in the series, covering 28 jurisdictions, was released in November 1985. A report on 1981 data from 38 sites is scheduled for release in 1986. Data in this series include number of felony cases screened, number of cases rejected or referred at screening, reasons for case rejections, number of cases filed, number of cases dismissed, reasons for case dismissals, number of guilty pleas, number of pleas to top charges, number of guilty verdicts at trial, number of sentences to incarceration, number of sentences to state prisons, and case processing times by type of disposition.

Federal Justice Statistics. A major recent priority is the development of a comprehensive Federal Justice Statistics Data Base tracking individual offenses from investigation through prosecution, adjudication, and correctional processing. Currently, the database includes input from the Federal Bureau of Investigation, the Drug Enforcement Administration, the Executive Office for U.S. Attorneys, the Administrative Office of the U.S. Courts, and the Bureau of Prisons, and covers calendar years 1979–81. This represents the first time that federal justice data have been incorporated in a single data series. Data from additional investigative agencies and covering additional years are now being obtained.

Justice Expenditure and Employment Data. The survey of justice expenditure and employment, begun in 1967, produces annual national and state-level data on the costs of the justice system and the numbers of persons employed by justice agencies.

BJS recognizes the high interest that social scientists have in its surveys and censuses. To meet the demand for time-series statistics, BJS has an extensive publication program for disseminating data from its data collection efforts.

Bulletins, Special Reports, Report to the Nation on Crime and Justice, Sourcebook of Criminal Justice Statistics—these are just a few of the BJS publications used by social scientists for instructional and research purposes. BJS distributes its reports through the National Criminal Justice Reference Service (NCJRS). The Reference Service notifies its mailing list of forthcoming publications, and users return a form requesting copies of desired publications. To get a registration form for the Reference Service mailing list or to order a BJS report, write to NCJRS, Box 6000, Rockville, MD 20850, or call 301/251–5500; or call toll-free 800/732–3277.

BJS Criminal Justice Data Archive. BJS sponsors the National Criminal Justice Data Archive at the Inter-university Consortium for Political and Social Research at the University of Michigan. Social scientists whose information needs are not met by BJS publications can turn to the archive which disseminates BJS data in machine-readable form. All BJS data are stored at the archive and are disseminated via magnetic tapes compatible with the user's computing facility. To get BJS data, contact the Criminal Justice Archive and Information Network, Inter-university Consortium for Political and Social Research, P.O. Box 1248, Ann Arbor, MI 48106, 313/763–5010.

Training in Criminal Justice Research. BJS sponsors month-long training in the quantitative analysis of BJS data. Social scientists gain exposure to the data, learn statistical analysis software, and become familiar with analysis techniques. For more information on how to apply for the training, contact the Criminal Justice Archive and Information Network (same address as above).

Solicitation for Research Proposals. BJS sponsors research conducted by social scientists. Through solicitations, BJS invites social scientists to submit research proposals on diverse topics in the criminal justice field. Proposals are evaluated by a peer review panel, and grant awards are made on the basis of the panel's recommendation. Announcement of the BJS solicitation is made in the *Federal Register.* Since there is no regular schedule for issuing solicitations, interested researchers should monitor that publication for announcements.

[Prepared by Steven R. Schlesinger, Ph.D., Director, BJS.]

Bureau of Labor Statistics

The Bureau of Labor Statistics (BLS) was originally established by the Congress in June 1884 as the Bureau of Labor to "collect information" on the earnings and workings of "laboring men and women." The Bureau's regular programs now include statistics on employment and unemployment, prices, wages and earnings, industrial relations, economic growth, productivity, and occupational safety and health.

BLS data are used in determining and analyzing fiscal and monetary policies; in allocating federal funds to states and local areas; to index wages in collective bargaining agreements; and to index pensions, transfer payments, long-term contracts, income tax brackets, and a host of private payments. (For example, a 1% rise in the Consumer Price Index occurring in July 1985, according to an OMB estimate, would trigger $2.8 billion in federal expenditures in 1987. In addition, the income of about one half of the U.S. population is affected, either directly or indirectly, by changes in the CPI.)

The Bureau is primarily organized along programmatic lines. The Offices of Employment and Unemployment Statistics, Prices and Living Conditions, Wages and Industrial Relations, Productivity and Technology, Economic Growth and Employment Projections, and Occupational Safety and Health Statistics are responsible for publishing and analyzing statistics based on a variety of sample surveys. These statistics are collected directly, or on a contract basis with the states or the Bureau of the Census.

Among the support offices, the Office of Research and Evaluation conducts research of general interest to the Bureau, evaluates the effectiveness of the Bureau's programs, and suggests improvements to existing procedures. This office also provides consulting and review services to other offices within the Bureau and, to a limited extent, other federal agencies.

BLS economists and statisticians maintain contact with the academic community in a variety of ways, including publishing in professional journals, participating in professional organizations and meetings, and making presentations to university colloquia. BLS often seeks the advice of statisticians, economists, and other social scientists, both informally and through the following types of arrangements:

1) In conjunction with the American Statistical Association (ASA), BLS sponsors a Research Fellow and Associate Program which provides academic scholars with access to BLS data and the opportunity to interact with BLS staff in discussing data and methodological problems that arise in a large-scale statistical agency. Not only will program participants be able to return to their academic institutions with ideas for further research, but BLS employees will broaden their perspectives through exposure to outside experts. The program is intended to encourage methodological research both at universities and at BLS on ways to collect and analyze data. Fellows are expected to become vital contributors to the Bureau's ongoing professional training programs, which include both economic and statistical seminar series. Persons interested in the Research Fellow and Associate Program should contact Cathryn Dippo, Coordinator, ASA-BLS Research Program (202/523–1874), for more information.

As part of the ongoing BLS seminar series, each year well-known economists and statisticians are invited to make presentations. During their visits to BLS, they have the opportunity to meet and discuss important issues with BLS staff members.

2) Through contracts for research consulting services, the Bureau addresses topics of special importance. Examples in the last few years include contracts on estimation procedures for the Current Employment Survey and on local area unemployment estimators. Requests for applications are published in the *Commerce Business Daily.*

3) Through the Department of Agriculture's cooperative agreement with the University of California at Berkeley, the Bureau is developing computer-assisted telephone interviewing (CATI) software. As a result of this agreement, a CATI system has been developed to accommodate longitudinal establishment surveys and to function in a personal computer environment.

4) To the extent possible within current budget constraints, BLS is interested in furthering its commitment to research. Topics of interest in the area of statistical methodology and computing include (a) the measurement and reduction of nonsampling errors through cognitive research on questionnaires and interviewing procedures, the development of expert systems using artificial intelligence techniques, and the implementation of statistical quality control programs; and (b) the development and evaluation of alternative estimators and statistical methods for data analysis. In the area of economic measurement and research, topics of interest include defining or refining concepts, particularly nonemployment and output definitions; incidence of injuries and illnesses; nonwage benefits; productivity; prices; and labor markets.

Social scientists seeking support for research related to the topics mentioned above may contact the Office of Research and Evaluation, Bureau of Labor Statistics, Room 2021, GAO Building, 441 G Street, NW, Washington, DC 20212 (202/523–1957). In addition to research in the fields of economics and statistics, BLS is interested in supporting research by other social scientists, such as cognitive psychologists and sociologists, on methods relating to improving the quality of data collected and analyzed by BLS.

[Prepared by Janet L. Norwood, Ph.D., Commissioner of Labor Statistics.]

Center for Statistics

[Note: In 1985, the Office of Educational Research and Improvement within the Department of Education was reorganized. Most functions and staff associated with the National Center for Education Statistics were transferred to the new Center for Statistics.]

The Center for Statistics (CS) is the primary federal source for collecting and analyzing statistics and other data related to education in the United States and in other nations. Its mission is to fulfill the congressional mandate to "collect, collate, and from time to time, analyze and report full and complete statistics on the condition of education in the U.S.; conduct and publish reports on specialized analyses of the meaning and significance of such statistics," assist state and local education agencies in improving their statistical systems, and review and report on educational activities in foreign countries. In addition, the Center responds to specific mandates from Congress.

The Center's activities are designed to (1) address high priority information needs; (2) provide consistent, reliable, complete, and accurate indicators of education status and trends; and (3) report to the Congress, the Department, and education policymakers at all levels on these findings in a timely manner with useful and high quality data.

The Center is under the supervision of a director who reports to the Assistant Secretary for Educational Research and Improvement. The Advisory Council on Education Statistics serves as an advisory body to the Secretary on technical matters.

There are four programmatic divisions in the Center: Condition of Education Division, Elementary and Secondary Education Statistics Division, Postsecondary Education Statistics Division, and Education Outcomes Division.

Condition of Education Division. CED conducts special analyses of statistical data at all levels of education. This Division is the focal point for data-based issues analyses of high priority topics within the education community. CED publishes the *Condition of Education,* an annual statistical report mandated by Congress, and the *Digest of Education Statistics,* an annual compendium of education statistics. The Division has responsibility for identifying continuing and emerging issues, determining data gaps, working with other divisions in the design and conduct of surveys to ensure that data needs are met, and extending the state-of-the-art knowledge of mathematical statistics, analysis techniques, and systems analysis.

CED is responsible for an ongoing research and analysis program to develop statistical indicators that can be used to measure the condition of education. In addition, it develops statistical projections of education time series and provides consultation on the methodology for making projections of education statistics.

Elementary and Secondary Education Statistics Division and Postsecondary Education Statistics Division. ESESD and PESD have similar responsibilities aimed at two levels of education. Both are responsible for developing and implementing systems and other special studies and surveys regarding educational institutions and individuals receiving services. They are responsible for the development of standardized terminology and data definitions and for training state and local personnel in reporting comparable, accurate, and timely data.

The principal institutional data systems of these two Divisions are the Common Core of Data (elementary/secondary statistics) and the Higher Education General Information System (postsecondary statistics). Redesign of the elementary/secondary system is under way while the redesign of the postsecondary system implementation began in 1985 with the phasing in of the Integrated Postsecondary Education Data System.

In addition to institutional records systems, both Divisions field surveys on individuals involved in the education process. Both private and public elementary/secondary teachers and administrators are surveyed, recent college graduates and, beginning in 1986, postsecondary students will be surveyed in the new National Postsecondary Student Aid Study.

Education Outcomes Division. EOD conducts longitudinal and cross-sectional assessment studies. The Division gathers, analyzes, and synthesizes qualitative and quantitative data related to the status of American education at all levels. EOD provides normative, descriptive, trend, growth, and comparative policy-relevant data concerning educational context, process, achievement, performance, and other outcomes. The principal data systems are the National Longitudinal Study of 1972 (NSL-72), the High School and Beyond Study (HS&B), the National Education Longitudinal Study of 1988 (NELS:88), and the National Assessment of Education Progress (NAEP).

EOD is also responsible for the review and analysis of educational activities in foreign countries, and for the coordination of data collection activities with foreign countries.

The Center interacts with the research community in many ways:

1)   Design: Planning and advisory committees are established for most projects. Researchers are an essential part of the process.

2)   Data Collection: The Center primarily collects data through contracts (although NAEP is a grant). Contracts vary in size and scope; all are advertised in the *Commerce Business Daily* (CBD).

3) Data Analysis: Most data analysis is done by contracts, which are announced in the CBD. Additionally, CS makes data tapes available to the public at a nominal cost. Center data is frequently cited in articles presented in scholarly journals and papers included in the Education Resources Information Center (ERIC). Researchers should contact the Center to be included on the mailing list for data tape announcements.

4) Associations: CS staff frequently participate at meetings of the American Educational Research Association and American Statistical Association, providing another opportunity for interchange of ideas.

5) ASA/CS/NSF Fellows Program: One of the major goals of the ASA/CS/NSF Fellows Program is to help bridge the gap between academic scholars and government social scientists by exposing the research Fellow to methodological problems and policy issues faced by a statistical agency. The program will provide Fellows with a unique opportunity to have hands-on access to Center data and firsthand experience in the application of statistical theory in all phases of data collection and analysis. For more information, contact the American Statistical Association, 806 15th Street, NW, Suite 640, Washington, DC 20005 (202/393-3253).

The Center will move in the Spring of 1986. Mail should be directed to:

Center for Statistics
Office of Educational Research and Improvement
U.S. Department of Education
555 New Jersey Avenue, NW
Washington, DC 20208-1605

[Prepared by Emerson J. Elliott, Director, Center for Statistics.]

National Center for Health Statistics

The National Center for Health Statistics (NCHS) operates a diverse survey and inventory program with legislative authority to collect statistics on:

1) the extent and nature of illness and disability in the U.S. population, including life expectancy, maternal mortality, and morbidity;

2) the impact of illness and disability of the population on the U.S. economy and other aspects of well-being;

3) environmental, social, and other health hazards;

4)   determinants of health;

5)   health resources, including health professionals by specialty and type of practice; and the supply of services by hospitals, extended care facilities, home health agencies, and other health institutions;

6)   use of health care, including ambulatory health services, hospitals, extended care facilities, home health agencies, and other institutions;

7)   health care costs and financing;

8)   family formation, growth, and dissolution, including vital statistics data on birth, death, marriage, and divorce.

At some time in their careers, nearly all demographers and health researchers will use data produced by the National Center for Health Statistics. Since NCHS has a mandate to quantify social, behavioral, environmental, and economic factors of health as well as biomedical aspects, it serves as an important source of data for the social and behavioral science research community.

Data Collection. The Center does not have a large data collection staff of its own. It collects most of its data through interagency agreements with the U.S. Bureau of the Census, contracts with nonfederal organizations, and (for vital statistics) contracts with states. Under these contracts, vital statistics data (birth, death, marriage, divorce) are collected at the state and local level and forwarded to NCHS for processing, tabulation, and publication.

Data Release. NCHS releases its data in several ways. *Health: United States,* an annual publication, includes data on health status, costs, determinants of health, use of health care, health manpower, and vital statistics. This report is an excellent way for researchers to familiarize themselves with the range of data that NCHS and some other agencies collect and publish. The *Monthly Vital Statistics Report* (MVSR) includes the latest data on births, deaths, marriages, and divorces in the United States; the MVSR Supplements contain brief reports on selected topics related to fertility, mortality, marriage, and divorce. The Annual *Vital Statistics of the United States* contains data on births (1 vol. per year), deaths (2 vols.), and marriage and divorce (1 vol.). The *Vital and Health Statistics* series contain detailed reports on the design of the various data collection systems, findings of methodological studies, and detailed findings from each of the surveys. *Advance Data* reports are brief (4 to 12 pages), timely summaries of newly available data on topics of special interest. All reports are available without charge to libraries, medical colleges, schools of public health, and other selected institutions upon request. The *Catalog of Publications of the National Center for Health Statistics* contains a cumulative list of reports which individuals may purchase from the Government Printing Office.

The Center also publishes the *Catalog of Public Use Data Tapes from the National Center for Health Statistics,* which describes the content, price, and ordering information for tapes. The majority of these data tapes are now sold by the National Technical

Information Service (NTIS). A large number of NCHS public use tapes are currently available, including:

1)   vital statistics (separate tapes for birth, death, marriage, and divorce);

2)   National Survey of Family Growth (factors affecting childbearing, such as contraception, sterilization, infertility, and breastfeeding);

3)   National Natality Survey (health factors related to childbearing);

4)   National Health and Nutrition Examination Survey (data from interviews and medical examinations);

5)   National Health Interview Survey (data on extent and impact of illness, and contact with health professionals);

6)   National Hospital Discharge Survey.

Contact NCHS for information about the specific content of the surveys and the strengths and limitations of each data set.

Requests for unpublished data are filled regularly using tabulations that have been previously compiled. When special tabulations are necessary, the requester is given a cost and time estimate. Tabulations and public use data tapes are reviewed carefully to ensure that confidentiality is maintained. NCHS also has a University Visitation Program, which consists of lectures and presentations at universities by NCHS Staff.

Questions about Center data can be addressed to:

Scientific and Technical Information
Branch Division of Data Services
National Center for Health Statistics
3700 East-West Highway
Hyattsville, MD 20782
(301/436–8500)

[Prepared with the assistance of NCHS staff.]

Chapter 7

Information Sources

Researchers in the Washington, DC metropolitan area can pick up the phone and call federal agencies for general information about research programs, deadlines, application procedures, etc. For those living in the 50 states, however, there are many government, commercial, and association publications designed to keep the research community informed of opportunities for federal funding. Most of these sources are received and reviewed by universities' sponsored research offices, and staff are prepared to respond to faculty inquiries. Thus, individual researchers may not need to spend time and money scrutinizing the multitude of information sources available.

The quality and timeliness of publications on federal funding opportunities vary greatly, particularly among commercial sources. Because federal agencies tend to change or modify their research programs frequently (whether in terms of research interests, staff, or application procedures, etc.), and because all federal programs are affected by the annual budget appropriations process, no single information source is ever totally complete or accurate. Also, it must be recognized that all organizations seeking to provide funding information to the research community, commercial or not, rely heavily on federal publications and official agency statements; and funding decisions are affected by internal interpretation, administration priorities, and individual biases. Thus, what an agency says it *can* fund is not always the same as what it *will* fund.

For those not associated with institutions that have sponsored research offices or access to on-line information networks, we have included in this chapter descriptions of a very small sample of the kinds of information sources available. In some cases, individuals or academic departments may find it useful to maintain their own library of federal funding information. The sources included here should give readers a general idea of what is available to them and provide a basic starting point for new scholars contemplating entering the federal funding arena. It should be emphasized, however, as Morrill and Duby point out in chapter 3, that it is not feasible to wait until a request for applications is published to begin formulating one's research proposal. Scientists should familiarize themselves with a variety of agencies that could have an interest in their research in anticipation of future funding competitions. Thus, there is no substitute for developing and maintaining good contacts with experienced researchers, disciplinary and other professional associations, and federal program managers.

Federal Sources

1) *Catalog of Federal Domestic Assistance,* Superintendent of Documents, U.S. Government Printing Office, Washington, DC 20402. Published annually; $36.

The complete reporting by the Office of Management and Budget of all federal assistance (including research funding); includes program information, application/review procedures, regulations, budget, examples of funded projects, and other useful information.

2) *Federal Register,* Superintendent of Documents, U.S. Government Printing Office, Washington, DC 20402. Published Monday-Friday except holidays; $300 per year.

Serves as the official public notice of federal regulations and rule-making, including announcements of agency funding priorities and invitation to comment on such, and requests for applications.

3) *Commerce Business Daily,* Superintendent of Documents, U.S. Government Printing Office, Washington, DC 20402. Published Monday-Friday except holidays; $160 per year first class mailing, $81 per year second class mailing.

The official daily listing of federal procurement invitations, contracts awarded, subcontracting leads, sales of surplus property, and foreign business opportunities. All requests for competitive contract applications and notice of sole source contract awards are published in CBD. Also included are notices of "Research and Development Sources Sought" by federal agencies.

4) *NIH Extramural Programs,* Office of Grants Inquiries, Room 449, Westwood Building, 5333 Westbard Avenue, Bethesda, MD 20892. Published biennially; single copies free.

Provides detailed descriptions of all NIH extramural research programs, areas of interest, contact persons, and funding mechanisms.

5) *NIH Guide for Grants and Contracts,* National Institutes of Health, Room B3BEO7, Building 31, Bethesda, MD 20894. Published monthly; no charge.

The *NIH Guide* contains research announcements of the National Institutes of Health and other Public Health Service agencies, requests for applications, and policy and administrative information.

6) *National Science Foundation Guide to Programs,* National Science Foundation, 1800 G Street, NW, Washington, DC 20550. Published annually; no charge.

Contains detailed descriptions of NSF programs, research interests, application procedures, targets dates, and points of contact.

7) *National Science Foundation Bulletin,* National Science Foundation, 1800 G Street, NW, Washington, DC 20550. Published monthly except July and August; no charge.

Contains news about NSF programs, deadlines, publications, meetings, and NSF staff positions open.

Nonfederal Sources

8) *APA's Guide to Research Support* (2nd ed., 1984), American Psychological Association, Order Department, 1200 17th Street, NW, Washington, DC 20036. APA members, $20; nonmembers, $25.

Published in 1984 with supplement of updated information in 1986. Includes detailed information on both federal and nonfederal sources of research support for behavioral scientists. Entries include program information, budget, application/review procedures, contacts, and funding patterns.

9) *ARIS Funding Messenger—Creative Arts and Humanities Report,* Academic Research Information Systems, Inc., 2940 16th Street, Suite 314, San Francisco, CA 94103. Eight reports annually. Individual subscriptions, $46; institutional subscriptions, $95.

Covers federal, private, state, and some foreign government funding in the fields of creative arts and humanities. Humanities coverage includes funding information for academic study of traditional humanistic disciplines. Provides information on programs, deadlines, budgets, and contacts.

10) *ARIS Funding Messenger—Social and Natural Sciences Report,* Academic Research Information Service, Inc., 2940 16th Street, Suite 314, San Francisco, CA 94103. Eight reports annually, plus supplements. Individual subscriptions, $79; institutional subscriptions, $165.

Contains information on federal grant, contract, and cooperative agreement funding as well as private foundation support for social sciences research and program development. Separate sections for social and natural sciences.

11) *The Complete Grants Sourcebook for Higher Education* (2nd ed., 1985), David G. Bauer, American Council on Education/Macmillan Series on Higher Education, 866 Third Avenue, New York, NY 10022. $85.

Contains profiles of 500 government agencies, corporations, and foundations that support higher education. Includes eligibility requirements, application procedures, contacts, interest areas, sample grants, and funding mechanisms.

12) *COSSA Washington Update,* Consortium of Social Science Associations, 1200 17th Street, NW, Suite 520, Washington, DC 20036. Published biweekly. Individual subscriptions, $40; institutional subscriptions, $90; overseas airmail, $50.

The newsletter of the Consortium of Social Science Associations contains news of federal research funding, management, and policy issues, and legislative activity regarding federal research. Also includes regular feature, "Sources of Research Support," which describes one program per issue in detail.

13) *Federal Research Report,* Business Publishers Inc., 951 Pershing Drive, Silver Spring, MD 20910. Published weekly; $117 plus $11 postage.

Contains brief descriptions of research opportunities arranged by topic, including contacts and deadlines. Includes section on social sciences.

Topical Index

In this topical index, no entries are included for the traditional major disciplinary fields (e.g, "political science," "psychology"). The index contains only research topics or topic areas. Readers will find entries for recognized subfields, such as "health economics" and "cultural anthropology," but, in the context of this index, these are defined as topical areas. They should not be taken to be of interest only to the discipline or disciplines normally associated with that subfield. (A fuller discussion of this subject is found in chapter 2.)

Index terms are not cross-referenced or hierarchically organized. For example, a researcher interested in conducting "outcome" studies will probably look under "follow-up" as well, but the index does not *instruct* users to look under such other terms. As for hierarchical structuring, the user should look for currently active research topics under the usual substantive term: "adolescent pregnancy," not "pregnancy, adolescent"; "expert systems," not "systems, expert."

Programs are indexed by those terms that naturally arose from interviews with staff, lists of previously funded projects, and print descriptions provided by the agencies. In cases where an agency's term for a topic or research area might not be generally familiar to researchers, we have used the more common equivalent term. Broad research topics specifically mentioned by an agency, e.g., "cost-effectiveness" at the Urban Mass Transportation Administration, may only be indexed to one or a few agencies. That does not imply that "cost-effectiveness" is only of interest to that one agency, but rather that it is a topic of particular interest to them.

Readers should not rely solely on this index for locating programs that may support their research. Because some agencies' missions are quite broad and research interests are loosely defined, it is impossible to list every research topic for every program. Readers are encouraged, therefore, to read through the substantive descriptions of programs in chapter 5 to locate non-obvious sources of funding.

A detailed description of the process by which the *Guide* was indexed is included in chapter 1.

Note: The numbers below refer to the page on which discussion of the relevant federal program begins—not to the page where the specific indexed term (or related term) appears. In some cases a research topic is of interest to several related programs within a division or agency; then a span of page numbers is given.

Fellowships and Other Individual Research Awards

Many government agencies support individual research and scholarship through fellowships, dissertation support, career development awards, and other mechanisms. These awards are often available in very broad areas of research where there are relatively few restrictions on disciplinary background or research experience.

Because in many cases these awards could be listed under dozens of terms in the topical index, a separate listing of them is given below.

Bureau of the Census
ASA/NSF/Census Research Program (statistics, economics, demography, sociology, and related areas), 356

Bureau of Labor Statistics
BLS Research Fellow and Associate Program (statistics, economics, and related areas), 361

Center for Statistics
ASA/CS/NSF Fellows Program (statistics, education, and related areas), 364

Fogarty International Center
Foreign Government-Supported Fellowships for U.S. Scientists (biomedical, behavioral, and health sciences), 216
Scholars-In-Residence Program (biomedical, behavioral, and health sciences), 217

Senior International Fellowships (biomedical, behavioral, and health sciences), 215

Fulbright-Hays Training Grants
Doctoral Dissertation Research Abroad Program (modern foreign languages and area studies), 135
Faculty Research Abroad Program (modern foreign languages and area studies), 136

Fulbright Scholar Program (all social and behavioral science fields, architecture and urban planning, business administration, communications and journalism, computer science, education, environmental sciences, library science, musicology, philosophy and theology, social work), 344